Choice and Control in American Education Volume 1: The Theory of Choice and Control in Education

Edited by

William H. Clune and John F. Witte

The Falmer Press
(A Member of the Taylor & Francis Group)
London · New York · Philadelphia

UK The Falmer Press, Rankine Road, Basingstoke, Hampshire RG24 0PR

USA The Falmer Press, Taylor & Francis Inc., 900 Frost Road, Suite 101, Bristol, PA 19007

First published 1990

Library of Congress Cataloging-in-Publication Data

Choice and control in American education.
p. cm. — (The Stanford series on education and public policy)
Report from a conference held May 17–19, 1989 by the Robert M. La Follette Institute of Public Affairs at the University of Wisconsin-Madison.
Contents: Vol. 1. The theory of choice and control in education / edited by William H. Clune and John F. Witte — v. 2. The practice of choice, decentralization, and school restructuring William H. Clune and John F. Witte.
ISBN 1-85000-820-5 (v. 1): — ISBN 1-85000-821-3 (v. 1: pbk.): — ISBN 1-85000-817-5 (v. 2): — ISBN 1-85000-818-3 (v. 2: pbk.):
1. School, Choice of — United States — Congresses. 2. Education — United States — Parent participation — Congresses. 3. School management and organization — United States — Congresses. 4. Schools — Decentralization — United States — Congresses. 5. Education and state — United States — Congresses. I. Witte, John F. II. Clune, William H., 1942– . III. Robert M. LaFollette Institute of Public Affairs. IV. Series.
LB1027.9.C48 1990
379.73—dc20 90-33426
CIP

British Library Cataloguing in Publication Data
Choice and control in American education.
1. United States. Education
I. Witte, John F. II. Clune, William H., 370.973
ISBN 1-85000-820-5 v. 1
ISBN 1-85000-821-3 v. 1 pbk
ISBN 1-85000-817-5 v. 2
ISBN 1-85000-818-3 v. 2 pbk

ISBN 1-85000-3
ISBN 1-85000-3 pbk.

Typeset in 10.5/12 Bembo by Best-set Typesetter Co. Ltd.

Printed in Great Britain by Burgess Science Press, Basingstoke on paper which has a specified pH value on final paper manufacture of not less than 7.5 and is therefore 'acid free'.

Contents

Acknowledgments

The two volumes on *Choice and Control in American Education* are the result of a conference convened 17–19 May 1989, by the Robert M. La Follette Institute of Public Affairs at the University of Wisconsin-Madison. The original idea for the conference came from Michael Joyce of the Bradley Foundation and Robert Haveman, Director of the La Follette Institute. Generous funding was provided by the Bradley Foundation, The Joyce Foundation, and The Spencer Foundation.

Numerous people aided in the conference and subsequent work with authors and Falmer Press to turn the manuscripts into books. Paula White has been an administrative marvel throughout this process — dealing with details, substantive ideas, complex budgets, and authors. Lisa Armstrong, Rhonda Danielson, Joyce Collins and Ramona Burton have added crucial administrative help. Alice Honeywell, Liz Uhr and Molly Rose Teuke aided in the copy editing.

Preface

Choice, Community and Future Schools

James S. Coleman

This preface explores the contradictions that arise out of two simultaneously held values that are very relevant to most Americans. The first is the autonomy and choice of parents to do all they can to raise their children to adulthood. The second is the value we place on having a society that is not fragmented by divisions imposed by segregated or exclusive upbringing. In attempting to answer how our society might choose between these two values, I argue that while a single common school made sense in the context of 1890, it does not make sense in 1990. The more appropriate answer, both within the public sector, and in a system of education including private schools, is to expand parental choice and control at the school level. This will lead to increasing diversity and innovation in education, and will enhance community, an element that we seem to have lost in our current public education system.

Educational choice is an issue that throws into opposition two values that are deeply held by most Americans. One, favoring choice, is the value we place on parents being able to do all they can do for their children as they raise them to adulthood. Given the way modern society is organized, with production outside the household, and the future occupations of children different from those of their parents, one of the things parents can do for their children is to select for them the kind of environment which is best. School is one of the most important aspects of that environment. I suspect that for many university faculty members, the choice of university is in no small part affected by choice of an environment in which to raise their children.

But my point here is not merely that each of us wants to do best for our children; it is that collectively we regard that as important. We would not want to live in a society in which parents were unconcerned about the social, moral, and intellectual development of their children. Nor would we want to live in a society in which parents, though having these concerns, were unable to do anything to implement them. For it is this concern, this deep involvement of parents with their children's development, that is the most precious asset of every society as it makes its way into the future. To lose that asset, or to impede its effectiveness, is to willfully deprive children of their birthright.

The value that we simultaneously hold which opposes choice is also strong. This is the value that we place on having a society that is not fragmented by divisions imposed by segregated or exclusive upbringing. It is this value which has always led us to look with some disfavor at the elite private boarding schools attended by children of the well-to-do. It is this value which, seeing religion as one of the potentially divisive elements in a religiously diverse society, is the basis of opposition to public support of church-affiliated schools, even to the extent of interpreting the Constitution as forbidding it. It is this value that adds strength to the forces for affirmative racial integration of the public schools to overcome the segregative effect of residence. It is this value that leads us to be suspicious of those bilingual education programs that appear intended to maintain a non-English linguistic subculture. We hold this value strongly because we do not want to live in a society that is compartmentalized, subdivided, segregated, whether by religious, racial, economic, or linguistic barriers.

There are, of course, other sources of support for or opposition to choice in education. Educational administrators prefer a compliant population of children, each of whom can be assigned to school to fit administrative convenience, and none of whose parents will object, or request a transfer. Choice upsets all this neat administrative order. But if I am correct, the major wellsprings of support for choice and of opposition to choice are the two deeply held values that I have described.

Before examining these matters further, a personal note about the earliest sources of interest in these matters on my part: I worked, one summer while still in high school, as a counselor in a summer camp. Exploring one day, I found, in the woods near a cliff which overlooked the Ohio River, a beautiful house built entirely of cedar wood. A more idyllic rustic setting would have been difficult to imagine. But the house was vacant. When I inquired about it, I learned that the owner was an artist, who had lived in the house with his wife and children. The family had left, moving to a different state, because of a conflict with state law: he and his wife had wanted to educate their children at home, but the state law required them to send their children to school, either a public school or a state-approved private school. The family, strong in its convictions, left the house and moved to a state in which home-based education in lieu of school attendance was legal.

I was unprepared for this experience. I had attended small-town public schools in rural Ohio which approximated the 'common school' that was Horace Mann's ideal. I scarcely knew of private schools, and certainly not of education at home. True, some of the farmers grumbled about having to send their able-bodied sons to high school during planting or harvest when they were needed; but even they fully accepted the principle of the public school. The public schools I attended were dictated by the exigencies of parental economic constraints, not by preferences among schools. In the 10th grade my parents moved to Louisville, Kentucky, and I attended a central-city school drawing from all parts of the city. At that move, there had been alternatives; but except for a choice between the two city public high schools, there was only the Catholic school which was not relevant for me as a non-Catholic.

This bit of personal history illustrates well the conflict of these two strongly-held values. For many of us, sent without question to the local public school, a school which in many cases was the chief source of cohesion of the community or the neighborhood, the idea of disturbing this through the potentially divisive institution of choice is a strange idea. Yet when we see a conflict between state and parent over a child's education, like the one I described, the merits of choice in education become apparent.

This experience that I have described raised questions for me, questions that are not satisfactorily answered by the institutions of school in American society. It is these questions that I want to raise now.

How might a society choose between the two values I have described, in the conflict in which they are joined? The first step toward an answer, I believe, is to carry out a mental experiment: for each of two alternative policies (or perhaps more than two), to ask: what seem to be the consequences of each of these policies for the two central opposing values, as well as for subsidiary ones? Subsequent steps toward an answer involve extending the mental experiment into an actual comparison of policies in practice. Today we cannot do that, because there are not directly comparable settings in which full choice in education in available. It is clear that there are coming to be policies involving free choice within the public sector (in Minnesota and very likely elsewhere), and I trust that there will also come to be other alternatives in some states, involving free choice across public and private sectors.

In making the mental experiment, the point of central importance is that the arguments in favor of each of the two values that are in conflict are not independent of the social context, but depend very much on that context. In fact, I will argue here that in the context in which free education began in this country, the value of non-divisiveness, opposing unrestricted choice in free education, had more arguments in its favor, while today, the value of parental choice has more arguments in its favor. I will emphasize this by stating the arguments for assignment to a single common school in the context of education a hundred years ago and the arguments for parental choice in the context of education today. Obviously some of the arguments on each side hold at both times; but stating the arguments in this fashion will focus attention on the change of context, and the effect of that on the balance between these two values.

The Arguments for the Single Common School in the Context of 1890

In 1890, about half the male labor force was employed on farms, and only a little more than half of boys between the ages of 5 and 19 were in school, as Figure 1 shows. Figure 1 shows something else: the proportion of boys of school age very closely mirrors the proportion of men employed in agriculture. Farming and public schooling as we know it have never gone well together, a fact that is brought home recurrently when there are battles between the Amish and the state over education. The farmer's complaint is 'Once he goes to school and gets a little education, he's no good on the farm any more', and the schools complaint is that 'Their fathers keep them out in the spring for planting and in the fall for harvest, and school is relegated to a few winter months'.

In 1890, the population, both rural and urban, was largely uneducated, and the public school, with a curriculum prescribed by educators, constituted a window to the outside world, and cognitive skills to make one's way in that world. Parental choice, if exercised, might be to the long-term benefit of the child, but it might instead be to the short term benefit of the parent.

There was, however, an even more important reason for a strong common school in 1890. America was a land of immigrants, with different languages, different customs, different religions, different ethnicities. The vision of a divided nation consisting of ethnic or national enclaves, each with its own schools perpetuating its language and hardening the religious divisions in society, strengthens greatly the argument against a system of state-supported independent schools, forming without the deterrence of tuition. That argument is not confined to the United States. In some

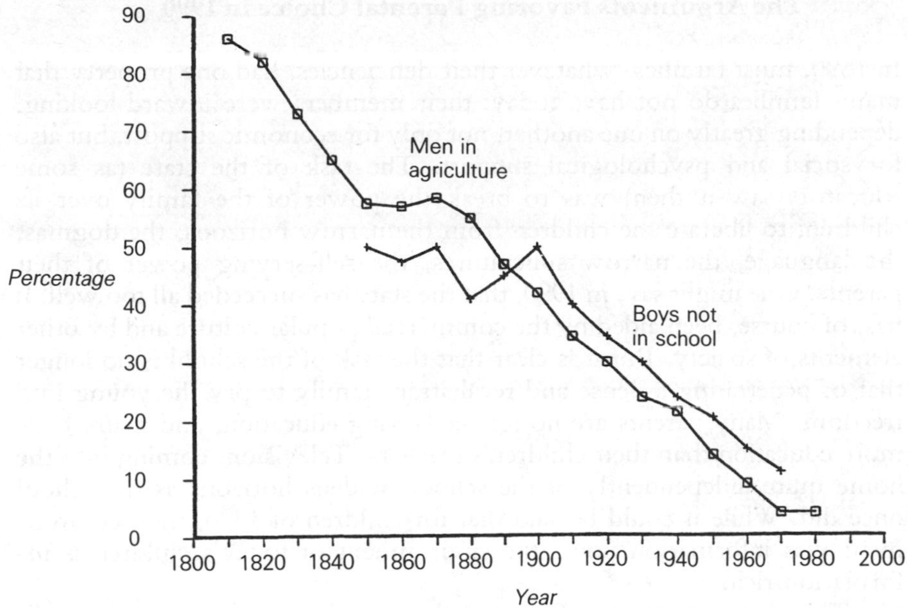

Figure 1: Farming and public schooling 1810–1982

developing nations today, as the US was then, there are even stronger proscriptions against private schools than there were and are in the US banning schools independent of the state — for very much the reasons stated here for the US in 1890: to insure that schools do not perpetuate the existing divisions in society.

The principal arguments against choice in education in the United States of 1890 (apart from the self-serving arguments of educational administrators) are the two arguments given here: that educational choice by parents, rather than by educators, is choice of ignorance, choice in pursuit of parents' interest rather than children's, choice which would restrict rather than widen children's horizons; and that educational choice by parents, in a society of linguistic, cultural, ethnic, and religious minorities, perpetuates and strengthens the division. These, I believe, are in essence the strongest arguments today against parental choice of school; but as is clearly evident, the conditions in America today are not those of America in 1890.

The Arguments Favoring Parental Choice in 1990

In 1890, most families, whatever their deficiencies, had one property that many families do not have today: their members were inward-looking, depending greatly on one another, not only for economic support, but also for social and psychological support. The task of the state (as some educators saw it then) was to break the power of the family over its children; to liberate the children from the narrow horizons, the dogmas, the language, the narrow subcultures, the self-serving power of their parents. One might say, in 1990, that the state has succeeded all too well. It has, of course, been aided by the commercial popular culture and by other elements of society. But it is clear that the task of the school is no longer that of penetrating a dense and recalcitrant family to pry the young into freedom. Many parents are no longer lacking education, and many have more education than their children's teachers. Television, coming into the home quite independently of the school, widens horizons as the school once did. While it could be said that for children of 1890, their environment was information poor, the environment of today's children is information rich.

This does not mean, of course, that in schools of today all is well. Public schools, by seeing their task as *independent* of that of the children's parents, have in some cases come close to losing for the child that most precious asset: the parents' involvement with their children's development. Little attention has been paid by schools to the effects of their policies on incentives of parents. Yet the incentives of parents — to aid, complement, reinforce, and support the school in its task — are not only an asset for children, they are the asset on which schools have always depended. It is in part the concern to maintain and strengthen this asset that is the source of current interest in educational choice.

What are the principal arguments favoring parental choice today? To answer this question requires recognizing that the full replacement of assignment by choice constitutes not merely a new freedom on the part of parents and children. Most fundamentally, it changes the relation between the consumers and the providers of education. It takes from the providers, that is, the schools, a certain set of rights, the right to a fixed allocation of students, and gives those rights to the consumers of education.

The rights, however, are separable into bundles. One way of separating them is to conceive of two levels of choice: first, choice within the public sector, as in the recently-instituted Minnesota plan; and second, choice that includes the private sector without payment of tuition, as found in many countries of Europe.

Choice within the Public Sector

For choice within the public sector, one may be misled by the imagery that the recent Minnesota legislation stimulates, that is an imagery of a set of parents and children now choosing among those institutions to which they were previously assigned. Such an imagery trivializes the potential change, just as the shift from a planned economy to a market economy in the area of housing would be trivialized by seeing that as a shift from a condition in which families that had been assigned to apartments were now given the right to choose among those same apartments.

A better imagery is that suggested by an incident of a few years ago. The incident involves the general manager of the Pontiac Division of General Motors who in 1980 raised a question for himself, about quality of the bodywork on automobiles. He asked why it was that the quality was so much higher on Hondas than it was on Pontiacs. He discovered that Honda's assembly lines were organized very differently from those of Pontiac. Pontiac employed what I will call forward policing, and Honda employed what I will call backward policing. Pontiac's assembly lines had assembly line workers, foremen, supervisors, and managers, organized in the usual hierarchical fashion. Defects were found by inspectors at the end of the sub-assembly and assembly lines, the defective cars were tagged, and repaired at the end of the line. In Honda's assembly lines, each sub-assembly line had the right to reject the incoming part, and each worker had the right to reject out-of-specification input parts — even if that rejection required stopping the assembly line. Each sub-assembly group not only had these rights of rejection; it was held accountable for those of its outputs that were rejected by the next group, for whom its outputs were inputs. The next group was in effect its customer, with the customer's right to accept or reject its inputs. Accountability to superiors was replaced by accountability to customers, that is the recipient of its products. This accountability reverberated backward through the organization from the finished product back to the initial stages of production. It constituted a backward policing that produced high quality, simply by giving each of the work groups in the organization the same rights that the final customer had — which in turn made each of the work groups accountable for its products.

How is backward policing at Honda relevant to choice in education? Taking the rights to reject inputs away from supervisors and placing them instead in the hands of the consumers of that input is analogous to taking the rights to determine school attended away from administrators and placing them in the hands of parents. But the result in automobile manfuacture is not merely a reallocation of rights: it is an improvement in quality of the product. This improvement arises because the new holders of the rights are both better motivated and better able to police the products they receive than are supervisors in a hierarchy. This in turn creates an incentive on the part of their suppliers to improve the quality of their product. The principle behind parental choice is similar: the parents are both better motivated and better able to judge the relative quality of the schooling their child receives than are administrators.

In the case of schooling, however, there are additional differences between the two allocations of rights. Because school attendance is compulsory until age 16, assignment to school imposes a requirement on the school to keep students it would otherwise dismiss on disciplinary grounds. As many public school principals who have spent long days in court well know, the law upholds the child's right to attend school, even if the child ruins the chances of other children to learn. Why do private schools not have this problem? Because as any public school administrator can quickly point out, they can expel their problem students to another school.

If, however, children are not assigned to school but can choose, then there is no reason why public school principals should have less freedom to expel students than does a private school headmaster: the child has a right to attend school at public expense, but not a particular school.[1] With a voluntary clientele, a public school can establish rules and require that students live up to them, just as can a private school. The stifling embrace in which school and student are locked would be broken, and both would benefit.

I have described only some of the arguments for choice of school within the public sector — and I have said nothing about the budgetary devolution to the school level necessary to give the school the resources and the freedom to shape its program to attract and satisfy customers. But I turn now to choice beyond the public sector.

Choice Beyond the Public Sector

The kinds of changes made possible by the second level of choice go beyond those made possible by the first level. The second level, choice including the private sector, allows a diversity of offerings less encumbered by the legal and administrative constraints that affect public schools.

Let me illustrate this by the topic of single-sex schools. American public schools are coeducational by law, though it was not always so. The presumption on which this is based is that single-sex schools, from which students of the opposite sex are excluded, do not provide equality of educational opportunity, while coeducation does so. But is that presumption valid?

Fortunately, the diversity of values among American parents is reflected in a diversity in the private sector that is missing in the public sector. There are single-sex schools among the schools affiliated with religious bodies: Catholic, Protestant, and Jewish.[2] Also fortunately, coeducation is not as highly regarded in all countries as in the United States. Because this diversity exists, and because some large-scale data-collection efforts make comparisons possible, certain questions about single-sex and coeducational schools may be studied scientifically. Research has been carried out recently comparing single-sex and coeducational Catholic high schools in the United States; and comparing single-sex and coeducational colleges, also in the United States; and research has been carried out comparing single-sex and coeducational public schools in Thailand. The Thailand analyses were carried out using the International Educational Achievement second mathematics study, the US Catholic analyses were carried out using the 1980 *High School and Beyond Study*, and the US college analyses were carried out using the 1972 National Longitudinal Survey of high school seniors, followed fourteen years beyond high school (Jiminez and Lockheed, 1988; Lee and Bryk, 1986; Riordan, 1990).

The results of these analyses are consistent: boys in coeducational schools seem to do as well as or better than comparable boys in single-sex schools, in academic achievement. Girls seem to do distinctly better in single-sex schools, an effect that is most pronounced for mathematics and science. Furthermore, they appear to show better emotional and social adjustment, and better occupational growth in the years following school and college.

Suppose these initial inferences turn out to be correct: that coeducation is beneficial to boys, but harmful to girls. This would be a cruel irony: the very institutional arrangements required by law on equal opportunity grounds are providing greater inequality of opportunity than the institutions they replaced.

The example of single-sex schools merely illustrates the possible errors that a monolithic public school system can institutionalize. The implication is not that single-sex schools are better for everyone (or even for all girls) and thus ought to replace coeducational schools. It is, rather, that choice beyond the constraints imposed on state-provided institutions can bring about institutions that function better, for particular children and youth, than do the state-provided schools. As in the earlier case of backward policing, this is in accord with the general principle that consumers of education are not only better judges of the comparative merits of different educational programs than are administrators, but also that the choices of consumers are more fully guided by the educational merit of the program than are administrators, whose choices must reflect the need to satisfy various interests in their organizations.

This example of single-sex schools illustrates the greater diversity achievable in a private sector of education as compared to the public sector. The private sector is not a *single* sector, but many: there are military schools, there are Quaker schools; there are schools with religious foundations, and schools that are aggressively secular. There are schools in which, like Eton in England, uniforms are required, and schools which, like Summerhill in England, make the absence of constraint a guiding principle. There are day schools, boarding schools, and schools that are mixed; there are coeducational schools and schools for one sex only; there are Montessori schools and there are schools like that at Telluride. Major educational innovations ordinarily begin outside the public sector, and many can survive only outside the public sector, where they need not clear the majoritarian hurdle. In a majoritarian democracy, the public schools must be creatures of the majority. If there is a single public school, it must reflect those values that the majority holds in common, a requirement that encourages blandness. If there are several, as is true where most people live, then the majority can initiate some diversity of offering. But this diversity is far less than the diversity, and the vigor in its pursuit, that arises from subcommunities in the larger society who share common values about educational environments for their children.

Altogether, the arguments for choice in schools of today are strong ones. Those very forces from which schools of 1890 were in part designed to protect children, that is parental interest and parental values, now constitute an asset to be nurtured and encouraged, lest it be lost. The way in which schools are organized can strengthen that asset or weaken it. It is clear that one of the aspects of school organization that does most to strengthen the asset of parental involvement with their child's upbringing is choice among schools which range widely in the values and principles on which they are built. This choice exists when parents are free to choose, not only within the public sector, but also among the diverse array of schools that lie outside the public sector.

The arguments for the single common school in 1890 are not entirely absent a hundred years later, and any system of school organization must deal with these arguments. But the arguments in favor of choice today are sufficiently strong that the 1890 arguments, rather than being decisive, should serve merely as constraints on the kinds of systems of choice that are created. One of those arguments concerns community, and it is to that argument that I will now turn.

Community, the Common School, and Choice

In 1890, community was built around neighborhood, and the common school was both a reflection of that community and an important element in strengthening it. Most Americans lived in small towns and rural areas (remember that about half the total male labor force was in agriculture); the common school was the focal point of the community.

Today, men do not work where they live, and increasingly, women also do not. Most persons live in relatively dense metropolitan aggregations, and the common school has given way to an array of schools, stretching from central city to distant suburb, which serve distinct and different segments of the population. The public school no longer serves to bind these distinct segments together, but because of the freedom of residence and of movement that automobiles and affluence create, it serves to keep them separate.

The conquering of space through personal transportation and electronic communication also means that the local community, though more homogeneous in economic level than ever before, is no longer a functional community of men and women who are bound together with the multiple ties of neighborhood, work, and ethnicity. Nor is it even a value community of people who share common values. The communities of adults are no longer built around ties that are neighborhood-based, but express some other common bond, and some other institutional locus. It may be a religious group, it may be a social group based on workplace, or it may be neighborhood. But neighborhood is no longer the common locus of all these ties; it is merely one among the several bases for such ties. The value communities are even less coherent; persons share values with others they do not know personally, and diverge in values from their neighbors.

In such a society, where residence, and thus the once-common school, have become economically and racially stratified, and where neighborhood no longer implies functional community nor a set of shared values, the school populations defined by geographically-defined catchment areas are no longer common schools, and the parents of these students no longer constitute communities. In this kind of society, parental choice of school cannot destroy the common school; it has already been destroyed by residential stratification. Parental choice can no longer destroy the community, which has been destroyed by ease of movement and communication. It can, under some circumstances, create or strengthen a community that reinforces parents' values. The circumstances are most fully met in the case of religiously-based schools, for the school is part of an existing functional community based on a religious institution. There are some other institutional loci that serve as the basis for a community, but in the absence of free private schooling, these have developed only in unusual settings. Many universities and colleges have 'laboratory schools' attached to them, with the university as the institutional basis for the community. A few schools, beginning with day care, nursery school, and kindergarten, have been established in workplaces, but these are rare, in the absence of free private schooling. The circumstances are least well met in the case of general-purpose independent schools, whose clientele may share a set of values about education, or may share only the aspiration that their son or daughter go to a 'good' school.

The case of religiously-based private schools illustrates another point: it is the very existence and strength of the religious community that is the basis for the fear of free religious schools, and the basis for the interpretation of the Constitution to prohibit public support for education in religiously-grounded schools. At a time when nearly everyone had an active religious affiliation, the fear that this could lead to a religiously-divided nation may have had some grounding. But what is lost by this prohibition is an opportunity to strengthen that strongest asset of the child: a parent's interest, involvement, and attention to the child's growth. The prohibition may be, in fact, highly regressive, most harmful to the least advantaged. Religious involvement is and has been stronger on average for those who are less advantaged, white and black, than for those who are more advantaged. And it is the children of the less advantaged who are most at risk of being harmed by drugs, crime, alcohol, delinquency. The possibility of having their children under the care of a church-related school offers a far greater benefit to these parents than to those whose children are less at risk. And it does so because the church constitutes a basis for community that builds upon, reinforces, and extends the most worthy of the values the parent holds and would transmit to the child.

Although the church is one basis for community that can serve as the central focus of a free private school, it is not the only one, and among the secular majority of the population, not the most important one. Anyone who scans the summer camp advertisements in the New York Times Magazine section each spring cannot help but be impressed by the diversity of goals that young people and their parents want to realize. There are camps for weight loss, swimming, sailing, horseback riding, computers, science, remedial schoolwork, baseball, basketball, tennis, and a host of other activities. The specialization that these camps provide is, of course, an overlay upon the classroom instruction in academic subjects they receive in school over the winter. It does not take too much imagination, however, to see the flourishing of schools that would combine some specialty that served as a common focus with regular classroom learning in standard subjects.

Future Schools

The visions of schools that I have encouraged in what I have just described can serve as a useful way of introducing the question of what schools of the future will be like. These visions ranged from church-related schools replacing the public school in the lives of many children who are most at risk to harmful influences, to schools focused around some special skills or goals for students from more secular families. I make no claim to be clairvoyant in predicting the nature of future schools. Thus these are only visions (and visions that could be realized only if free publicly-supported private schools were to come into being), and not predictions of the schools of the future.

I believe, however, that certain predictions can be made. Schools as currently constituted are coming close to being non-viable institutions, from junior high school upward. The school captures a declining fraction of the adolescent's time and attention, which is directed more toward part-time work for pay, participation in popular culture in the form of music, hanging out at the local shopping mall, and other out-of-school adult-oriented consumption activities. The period of 'the school', a single monolithic institutional structure within which children spend their pre-school and elementary years, and within which young people build an adolescent society, may be a period that is passing. As children and young people spend more of their time, beginning at birth, out of their parents' household, the institutions we construct to care for them and occupy their attention should probably be more diverse, more differentiated, more partial, with each possibly covering a shorter span, either in years, in months of the year, in days of the month, or in hours of the day. But the question of what form these schools of the future will optimally take is perhaps the wrong question. A different and perhaps more appropriate question is this: what way of organizing the education (and more generally the lives) of children and young people will best allow their evolution toward optimal forms? The answer I would give is that a provision of resources to parents, to free the opportunities they can provide for their children from their own level of income, will allow the growth and evolution of those institutional forms that fit optimally with the evolving structure of modern society.

The way in which this provision of resources is done cannot be careless or without design. Tuition tax credits are probably the least well designed way that has been proposed. Vouchers for education can take many forms, and these forms are important, because of the incentives they shape for parents and children. But the proper design of such a resource distribution is far more likely to lead to good environments for children and youth than is the direct attempt at institutional design on the part of educators, social scientists, politicians, or some mix of these, followed by the assignment of children to these environments on the basis of administrative convenience.

Notes

1 A reasonable principle to make that right effective would be that the student has the right to attend the chosen school for a semester, but after that time, the right is contingent on a principal's consent. This would mean that a few students would shuttle from school to school, but it would impose appropriate incentives on students to obey the rules of the school.

2 It is likely that the religious affiliation provides some insulation from legal attack. Here as in other areas, religious affiliation of schools is important to protect schools from the state, which hesitates to challenge religious values.

References

JIMINEZ, E. and LOCKHEED, M. (1988) 'The relative effectiveness of single-sex and coeducational schools in Thaliand', *Working Paper 27*, Washington: The World Bank.

LEE, V. and BRYK, A. (1986) 'Effects of single-sex secondary schools on student achievement and attitudes', *Journal of Educational Psychology*, **78**, pp. 381–95.

RIORDAN, C. (1990) *Boys and Girls in School: Together or Separate,* New York: Teachers College Press.

Introduction

John F. Witte

The state of American primary and secondary education is a critical and volatile issue. A number of controversial policy proposals emerged from the educational crisis movement, a movement stimulated by a series of national reports highly critical of America's schools. Early reform efforts emphasized tighter controls: state standards, testing, and monitoring. At the same time there was a concerted movement toward improvement within the schools, an effective schools approach. An effective school was thought to be one that had high standards and educational expectations, order, discipline, strong leadership, and a team approach. In more recent years, as these streams have continued, a movement has emerged to increase educational choice and to decentralize decision making in schools.

Although currently presented as revolutionary, the idea of choice, meaning that parents have an option to pick the school their children attend, has long been a mainstay of American education. However, to date, choice has meant essentially that parents could choose where to live, and hence the public school their children would attend; or they could opt for private schools. Current proposals consider changes in school governance and management, in order to extend choice beyond these conventional forms.

Decentralization in education, meaning that relevant educational policies and decisions affecting the organization are more heavily influenced by parents, teachers, and administrators at the school level, is also an old and a new issue. Not that long ago, the vast majority of schools were one-teacher schools, controlled exclusively by the teacher and local residents. As that system began to die out in the late nineteenth and early twentieth centuries, it was replaced for many children by a mega-school system, professionally run by large centralized administrations. Today, for example, the New York City system includes just under one million students; Los Angeles and Chicago approximately half that number. Large systems begot large bureaucracies. The current idea is that better education results from moving power and influence away from these centralized bureaucracies and back to the local school and parental level.

Although analytically choice and decentralization are separate concepts, the two current reform movements often overlap. This is the case, for example, in District 4 in New York City (see Chapter 5 in Volume 2). In that district, specialized schools, with considerable autonomy for teachers and principals, were established and parents were allowed to choose between the various schools. Additionally, as described in Chapter 4 of this volume, recent research on the difference between public and private schools has concluded that private schools are administratively much more decentralized than equivalent private school districts. Finally, there are two theoretical connections between choice and decentralization. As will be explored in several chapters in this volume, both are subsets of a large array of control mechanisms operative in American education. Second, the market analogy which is often employed to justify choice, at least in theory, is usually assumed to be a highly decentralized control mechanism. Whether or not this is true in education is one of the issues to be discussed in this volume.

Theory and practice in education policy are intertwined because practice is often driven by current theory and because theory depends on practice for clues to the adequacy of assumptions, knowledge concerning effects, and specific designs of programs that serve to test theory. Thus our division between theory and practice for the purpose of these two volumes is more a convenience than a reality. This volume, dealing with theory, examines four sets of issues: (1) the structural environment of American education; (2) the theories of control that can be applied to schools and school districts; (3) claims concerning the consequences of increasing choice and decentralizing school decision making; and (4) the normative issues surrounding choice and control options.

The Structure of American Education

It may surprise some that education experts differ in their characterization of the basic landscape and organization of American education. But they do. The differences matter because they lead to different basic assumptions that both define the current problems and suggest possible solutions. This is particularly relevant when considering analogies between the institutional system of education and economic markets, which is often raised by proponents of educational choice. Ironically, it is possible to reach similar policy conclusions from different assumed structures.

In the first chapter, I argue that in terms of both institutional arrangements and governance, American education appears to be extremely complex in its organizational structure, with wide variation in organizational forms across the country. In addition I argue that the governance structure is already quite decentralized and fragmented relative to education systems in other industrialized countries and to other US policy fields. Thus, on a continuum ranging from a uniform-monopoly model to a diversified-polyarchy, American education is much closer to the diversified-polyarchy end.

In contrast, in Chapter 2 Paul Peterson suggests that American education can best be understood as a public monopoly or quasi-monopoly. He carefully identifies monopoly as an 'exclusiveness with which a type of good or service is distributed within a particular market by a single provider'. He also clearly distinguishes this condition from a particular pattern of influence that may develop around a quasi-monopoly situation. In tracing the historical development of public education, he finds that reform movements, which had their origins in the nineteenth century but culminated in the postwar period, produced a system of education in which public schools, particularly in large cities, had an almost exclusive monopoly over education until the 1970s. In the 1970s and 1980s, that monopoly began to unravel as the poor, racial minorities, and the handicapped increased their demand on urban education systems and whites fled to the suburbs. He characterizes the present system as a quasi-monopoly in urban districts, with more competitive and successful systems existing in the suburbs. The urban systems, although under pressures from many sources, still tend to be multi-layered, highly centralized bureaucracies. Because of the political stakes and influence of key interest groups, Peterson sees little likelihood that choice plans will make major inroads in this urban-suburban pattern, even though he concludes that 'it would be difficult to concoct a politically viable system more inefficient and less equitable than one found today in most central cities of the United States'.

David Tyack, in commenting on Peterson's chapter, disagrees with his characterization of American education. He feels that despite commonalities in school districts, the monopoly metaphor is misplaced. Tyack argues that it fails to fit the legal distinction implied by the term, and that the historical sequence Peterson suggests is incorrect.

Richard Merelman is less concerned with historical consolidation and more with the recent trends Peterson highlights. Building on Peterson's exposition, Merelman points to educational quality as the key to why public school systems were able to take on monopoly characteristics, and to why the decentralization has taken place. During the period of growth in public school monopolies, educators persuaded mostly white middle-class parents that public schools provided quality education. Later as parents lost faith in this promise, decentralized choice took over. As urban systems deteriorated, parents who could, sought alternatives.

David Cohen, in Chapter 7, views the structure of American education in much the same way as Witte and Tyack. He writes: 'But if American school government has grown large, it also is remarkably diverse and disjointed: fragmentation seems at least as pronounced as centralization. Education governance more closely resembles many busy colonies of Lilliputians, working in different ways towards many different ends, than a single clumsy giant doggedly pursuing its own selfish purposes at the expense of its clients'. However, he reaches a bleak conclusion on the likely impact of choice: 'There is fragmentation and incoherence at many levels of education, which often have damaging effects. Decentralization and choice could exacerbate these problems of educational organization, even as they mobilize energy for improvement'.

In contrast to Witte, Tyack, and Cohen, commentaries by John Chubb and John Coons support Peterson's characterization of American education. Both also advocate extended choice as a policy response to failing schools with strong bureaucracies. Although in Chapter 1 I disagree with the structural characterization of American education presented by Peterson, Chubb, and Coons, unlike Cohen, when I weigh the advantages and disadvantages of choice and decentralization policies, I join Chubb and Coons in advocating experimentation. In contrast to their positions, I argue that highly fragmented and very complex systems of organization and control can benefit from market approaches.

Interestingly enough, all these authors see support for choice and decentralization as an attempt to improve the quality of education for troubled districts by offering them some of the choices already available to most middle-class families. In other words, they base their recommendations in part on the need for equality of educational opportunity. Although there is no certainty the new policies will improve educational achievement, they agree that the conditions in many large districts are so bad that risks should be taken.

Forms of Control and Choice

Just as there is controversy over the basic institutional structure of American education, there is also wide variation in what is meant by 'educational choice' and the general forms of control that describe the current and proposed changes in the decision-making structure in education. A number of authors addressed this issue, analyzing various theoretical approaches, often drawing on disciplines outside of education. What is consistently noted, and further highlighted in Volume 2, is that the forms of control in American education are diverse and complex and that in both theory and practice, terms like 'choice', 'school-based management', 'teacher empowerment', etc., cover a multitude of often ill-defined systems of control. One of the basic purposes of this volume is to illuminate this problem and clarify the nature of control in American education.

Janet Weiss, in Chapter 3, analyzes a number of different forms of control. Drawing extensively on literature from organization theory, sociology, political science and psychology, she delineates five major forms of control, which she argues coexist in education. The first form is professional control, which depends on employees trying to maintain autonomy and control through their training, credentials, and norms of professional practice. The second is administrative control, achieved through hierarchies by those who design and operate administrative systems. The third is political control, which accrues primarily to elected officials. The fourth is market control, which is based on voluntary exchange in the pursuit of self-interest. And the final form is control through values and ideas.

Weiss's position is that all forms of control are relevant and often present in the policy-making process, and that when one form seems to dominate, it is important not to overlook the others. Therefore, as market control seems to be having a major impact in recent reform efforts, Weiss advises employing interventions based on other control strategies as well.

In my overview chapter, using a somewhat different analytical framework, I also highlight the complexity of educational control systems. Distinguishing control, which implies final say over decisions, from influence, which implies an effect on decisions, I analyze control and influence in American education in terms of the multiplicity of actors and participants, the range or domain of decisions, and the basis of authority and/or strategies employed by various actors in the decision-making process. From this analysis, I conclude that the system is anything but simple and centralized and I agree with Weiss that control through choice and market exchange is only one of many ways to control educational systems.

Henry Levin, Charles Glenn, Chubb, and Coons also explore the facets of choice. Levin, in Chapter 5, carefully distinguishes and separately analyzes market choice and public choice. Market choice refers to manipulating the educational marketplace through the use of vouchers for both public and private schools; public choice refers to choice within public school systems only. His chapter describes a range of possible programs that fall in one or the other of these categories. He then evaluates them relative to private and social purposes of education. He concludes that the market approach appears to be superior in terms of private benefits and public choice systems appear better in terms of social and democratic benefits. In an unconventional argument that looks at the regulatory costs inherent in a voucher system, he concludes that theoretically neither public nor market choice has an advantage in efficiency.

Chubb, Coons, and Glenn generally defend choice plans as viable and desirable policy options. Chubb argues that there are numerous approaches to choice that can produce various results. Deploring conditions in many urban school systems, he believes choice plans offer a new and positive approach to counter the highly centralized hierarchies that run these systems. Coons defends both public and private school choice and specifically challenges Levin's contentions that the lack of a common curriculum is divisive or that choice will endanger the transmission of democratic values. His main message is that the system seems to succeed when parents of the well-off are given school options and that we must trust that those options will be exercised by parents of the poor as well. Glenn, relating the experience in Massachusetts, echoes Coons' need to trust parents and argues that choice in the public sector can be designed to enhance both quality and equity in education.

Bringing Theory in Line with Evidence

One of the central purposes of the research presented in these volumes was to ascertain what is known about the effects on students and schools of increasing parent choice and employing different forms of control in districts and schools. Is there evidence, controlling for relevant student and school characteristics, that choice leads to higher student achievement, lower dropout rates, and greater educational or employment success later in life? What are the effects on schools themselves? Does greater choice and/or decentralized decision making improve school climate, innovation, and academic expectations? What are the effects on school costs, efficiency, and effectiveness?

Several of the chapters in this theory volume deal at least in part with what is currently known about the effects of choice and decentralization on education outcomes. Richard Murnane, commenting on chapters by Henry Levin and Richard Elmore, emphasizes that it is difficult in the abstract to reach conclusions on theories of choice because, 'the consequences of any choice plan will depend on its details and on the institutional setting in which it is embedded'. Because of this problem, much research to date has focused on public and private school differences.

Levin, who covers a number of related topics, argues that the widely cited differences in achievement between public and private schools, which emerge from analyses of 'High School and Beyond' data (a survey of high school students over time), may be statistically significant, but the effects are very slight. As an example, based on longitudinal changes from the sophomore to the senior year, he states that a summary of studies indicates at most a .1 standard deviation advantage for private schools for students of similar socioeconomic background. He translates this into a mean test percentile rank of fifty-two for a private school student, compared to a rank of fifty for a public school student.

Anthony Bryk, Valerie Lee, and Julia Smith, in Chapter 4, come to somewhat different conclusions from Levin's concerning private schools, but they just as readily question proposals for choice and school autonomy as dramatic remedies for public school problems. Based on a very broad model of the high school as a community, they argue that (1) 'there is considerable statistical evidence documenting internal organizational differences between public and private schools'; (2) 'greater autonomy ... can be logically linked to ... effective organizational practices'; but (3) 'most important, there is virtually no evidence that directly links the effective organizational practices presumed to accrue through greater school autonomy to key outcomes such as students' academic learning'. Because they share the concern that educational choice may produce further social inequality, they feel that advocates must be willing to face that prospect. They end stating: 'The critical question remains "What kind of educational system do we desire?"'

Fred Newmann, in commenting on the Bryk, Lee, and Smith chapter, focuses on their critique of the national bureaucratic model of school organization and its failure to produce sustained achievement for most students, while alienating teachers, parents, and students. He attributes these problems to a decline in social consensus on educational goals and a breakdown in community and family life. These factors have added tremendously to the tasks of schools, to the detriment of the communal form of school organization.

Cora Marrett, commenting on both the Weiss and the Bryk, Lee and Smith chapters, also stresses the importance of education goals as critical organization factors. Her point, however, is that the diverse and often ambiguous goals of American education imply very different organizing mechanisms for schools and school districts. For example, she cites two forms of community, and the related education goals they emphasize. The first is community as a collection of individuals with varying and diverse interests in education; the second treats community as a 'locus of shared interests', and stresses the social goals of education. If our purpose is to promote the former, then mechanisms directed at individuals and individual diversity, such as vouchers, would be appropriate. If the latter meaning is employed, and education has a more extensive set of social goals, political and social mechanisms for 'assembling the community' are more desirable.

Richard Elmore's chapter has the intriguing slant of comparing experiments in educational choice with increasing market forces now prevalent in health care. He begins with the proposition that policy purposes and institutional structures through which policies operate must be taken into account in evaluating proposals for more or less client choice. On a number of dimensions, he finds situations of choice in education and health care to be quite different. For example, the entry requirements, management organization and style, and control over clients vary considerably in the two fields. Therefore, comparative conclusions about choice based on economic theory are questionable when the political and institutional contexts are considered.

Despite these differences, when Elmore compares choice experiments in the two services on three critical issues, he reaches the same conclusions. Choice by itself, he finds, does not adequately enhance the information required to be an intelligent consumer in either health or education, and sufficient public information will not become available unless major changes take place in the institutional structures. On this point Murnane suggests that adequately functioning markets do not require perfect information for all participants, but rather some well-informed consumers, and an exit option, based on performance, for the less well-informed.

Elmore goes on to state that there is some evidence of improved preferences and selection of services when choice options are introduced in either field. Finally, he joins Levin and Bryk, Lee, and Smith in concluding that there is ' . . . no necessary relationship in existing empirical evidence between increased client and provider choice and increased effectiveness of services'. This is particularly true in education, ' . . . where the degree of variation (in schools) and the level of information are heavily constrained'.

In David Cohen's concluding chapter he questions not only the connection between decentralization and choice on the one hand and desirable policy outcomes on the other, but also the basic assumption that any policy is necessarily connected to what happens in the learning and teaching environment of the school. In his view, it is a subject that needs considerable research and thought. Substantively he agrees that education control is highly fragmented and that the policy system consists of a multiplicity of very diverse organizations and participants. This basic assumption guides his speculation on the effects of decentralization and choice on instructional practice. He finds solace in a number of instructional practices, such as more rigorous, content-oriented instruction; unified course content from one grade to the next with coherent instructional materials; adequate national-level testing; and increasing use of the advanced placement tests for college-bound high school students. However, he questions how decentralization and choice policies might effect these practices, which have been achieved by different means in other industrialized countries.

Normative Issues

If there is one single point underscored in the chapters in the two volumes, it is that proposals to increase choice and decentralize decision making in schools generate enormous debate concerning the valued outcomes in American education. Debates on reform proposals, scattered throughout the chapters and commentary, often centered on normative criteria. The most prominent and prevalent clash was over the value placed on raising average educational achievement versus the desire to foster greater equity in achievement. This factor was crucial in the conclusions questioning choice reached by Bryk, Lee, and Smith, Elmore, and Levin. Their argument is that choice will simply accelerate the inequities between the middle class and the poor, and between suburban and urban schools. Even though the evidence on outcomes is mixed, a fundamental difference exists between those who are willing to accept higher average outcomes at the expense of equality and those who are not.

Other important criteria stress the social and democratic importance of education. The argument advanced by Levin is that reliance on private schools and/or decentralized systems of choice may affect the teaching of values essential to a democratic, free-market system. This could result from curriculum design and choices that deemphasize teaching such values, and from increasingly homogeneous student populations that could result from expanded school choice. Levin also raises the issue of efficiency, although he does not accept the narrow view of efficiency as an aggregation of individual, private benefits. Given a view of efficiency that includes a value for community and social benefits, he finds it difficult to predict whether choice in education would increase or decrease the efficient delivery of educational services.

A number of scholars argue that choice itself is an important value. In the Preface, James Coleman puts it well: 'For it is this concern, this deep involvement of parents with their children's development, that is the most precious asset of every society as it makes its way into the future'. Coleman juxtaposes this value against equality of opportunity as the central core of the debate over choice and control in education. In his historical analysis, he argues that in 1890 the quest for equality and increased educational attainment by means of a common school made sense, given the shifting demands of industrialization, an increasing emigre population, and the parochial attitudes of parents toward education. In the 1990s, however, the demands have changed, and so have the common schools. Today, a politically powerful and overly bureaucratic educational system has driven a wedge between parents and their children's education.

Choice is not an absolute, however. A number of authors raised the very real question: who currently has choice in American education? And the answer, which was not challenged, is that choice of school is greatly affected by social class. Private schools and suburban schools, which seemingly afford better educational opportunities and greater parental participation, are not randomly attended. This issue evokes two powerful and perhaps contradictory beliefs: parents in a democratic society should have a significant choice and influence over the education of their children; and, equally compelling, a democratic society should provide equal opportunity. The critical question is whether educational choice and control should be the prerogatives of the well-off?

Chapter 1

Choice and Control: An Analytical Overview

John F. Witte

This chapter describes conflicting images of the basic 'landscape' of American education. For some that landscape is conceived as a bureaucratically centralized, highly uniform, politically insulated, public monopoly. For others, including myself, the education system appears much more decentralized, widely varied, fragmented, and politically responsive (or hyper-responsive). This general description includes an analysis of the broad control structure of American education, with specific emphasis on the definitions of choice and decentralization. The theoretical framework for analyzing these control structures includes a specification of the participants in educational decisions (teachers, parents, administrators, legislatures, etc.), the domain of decisions (curriculum, fiscal, personnel, etc.), and the institutional and behavioral mechanisms of control (markets, administrative hierarchy, bargaining, protest, etc). Choice, as usually conceived, is a relatively narrow form of control (parental decision, based on school performance or specific curriculum objectives, with an 'exit', market option as the institutional control mechanism). The Chapter concludes by arguing that given a widely diversified and fragmented system, theoretically choice and decentralization could lead to more responsive and innovative schools; however, given the politics and pressure on large, urban districts, it is very unlikely that these reforms will have that lasting impact.

This chapter attempts to put into theoretical perspective current proposals to change fundamentally the power structure in American primary and secondary education. I begin by analyzing the changing 'landscape' of American education in terms of institutional organization and control. The general arguments of this section, which contradict impressions held by many (including some authors in this volume), are:

1 That the system of American education is extremely diversified rather than uniform in institutional appearance;
2 That control, including financial control, is relatively decentralized and is imbedded in a very complex system of governance rather than being overly-centralized, simple and monolithic.

The second section of the Chapter defines, discusses and describes various reforms that have been advanced under the rubrics of choice and decentralization. I then discuss the implications of the institutional organization and governance structure for the potential success of these reforms.

The Landscape of American Education

If there is any common ground among leaders of educational reform movements professing choice and decentralized control, it is that American education has become overly bureaucratized and regulated, and that policy decisions are made by centralized hierarchies that are insulated and unaccountable. Governor of Minnesota Rudy Perpich, a strong advocate of choice, puts it succinctly:

> The public school system is autonomous and answerable to virtually no one. Large, hidebound bureaucracies administer school districts of many cities, and are often too removed from the reality of the school-room to address the basic problem. (*The New York Times*, 6 March 1989)

This is echoed in scholarly articles such as the work of Chubb and Moe who stress how public school bureaucracies promote centralized control over school-based autonomy:

> The system in short is destructive of autonomy. Politicians have the authority to shape the schools through public policy, and precisely because they have this authority, they are consistently under pressure from interest groups to exercise it. It is in their own best interests to impose choices on the schools. The same is true of bureaucrats, who have occupational and professional stakes in control: a world of autonomous schools would be a world without educational bureaucrats. Thus, while principals and teachers may praise the virtues of autonomy, the 'one best system' is organized against it. Politicians, bureaucrats, and virtually the full spectrum

> of interest groups tend to see autonomy for what it is: a transfer of power and a threat to their interests. (Chubb and Moe, 1988)

In Volumes 1 and 2 of this collection, a number of authors advance the same theme. Peterson (this volume) uses the term 'quasi-monopoly' to describe the current public education system, which followed a period of straight-forward 'monopoly' (ending around 1970); Moore (Volume 2) characterizes the Chicago school system as administered in a highly centralized manner that in Chicago is sarcastically symbolized by the location of the district offices on 'Pershing Road' (Milwaukee administration is similarly symbolized by opponents as 'Vliet Street'). Chubb (this volume) makes the observation that:

> The history of school governance and organization is in part a story of growing tension between increasingly bureaucratic methods of government control of schools and ongoing efforts by teachers and principals to perform educational tasks that resist bureaucratic control ... Researchers ought to at least suspect that the tension is to a significant degree inherent in the structure of the government's control of public schools.

That highly respected scholars and practitioners carry this relatively extreme image of American education has always puzzled me because on the surface the system does not appear to be as uniform, centrally and simply controlled, or as insulated, protected, and unresponsive as this picture indicates. Part of this puzzle can be explained by the relative perspective of different authors; i.e., there may exist important differences in the comparative references against which the educational system is judged.

Theoretically we can posit a continuum ranging from decentralized, diversity to monopolistic uniformity. A highly decentralized and diverse system would consist of a wide range of school designs in terms of size, grade groupings, pedagogy, curriculum, teacher student interactions, political and social affiliations, etc. The schools themselves would be run in a very decentralized fashion, with most decisions made by school level administrators (and there would be few of them), and by teachers and parents. District, state and federal regulations would be minimized and finances would come almost exclusively from the local school attendance area, or even perhaps from fees paid directly by parents (with private funds or vouchers).

On the other end of the continuum you would have a national system where schools would be standardized in terms of size, grade structure, curriculum, teaching methods, and evaluations. Student achievement and advancement would be uniformly judged, most likely through nationally administered examinations. Political, social, and cultural affiliations would be irrelevant for purposes of education. Administration would be directed from a national center, with some form of regional or state controls to insure that national policies were being adhered to and administered properly. Financing would be based on national funds, perhaps with some regional or state matching.

The distinctions between these two models are portrayed in Figure 1.1, with the decentralized system labeled as a *diversified-polyarchy* and the centralized system depicted as a *uniform-monopoly*.[1] The characteristics depicted in Figure 1.1 will serve as a guide for the more detailed examination of the current landscape of American education which follows. I will argue that although both of these extremes are caricatures, the current system of American education leans toward the diversified-polyarchal end of the continuum.

Institutional Organization

Peterson's paper in this volume outlines historical trends, primarily in the twentieth century, that indicate a dramatic reduction in the number of school districts, ever larger schools and districts, and growth in profess-

Uniform-Monopoly	**System Characteristics**	**Diversified-Polyarchy**
	Institutional Forms:	
UNIFORM	Size Grade Organization Student Composition Curriculum Pedagogy Testing	DIVERSE
	Control System Characteristics:	
CENTRALIZED HIERARCHICAL EXCLUSIVE	A Structure of Control	DECENTRALIZED 'FLAT' PARTICIPATORY
SIMPLE MONOLITHIC	B. Complexity of Control: Number of Actors Number of Decision Points Number of Veto Points Control Strategies Forms and Concentration of Resources	COMPLEX POLYARCHAL
INSULATED UNACCOUNTABLE	C. Political Reponsiveness, Accountability	RESPONSIVE ACCOUNTABLE

Figure 1.1: Conflicting models of American education

ional, centralized bureaucracies. These trends contrast sharply with the single room schools and districts of the nineteenth century. I do not dispute those trends, but I do dispute the final picture he presents — which is a representation of the system as at best a quasi-monopoly.

Numbers and size of districts and schools

For some of the critical institutional characteristics of American education we have relevant statistical evidence. For example, there is adequate information on the size, organization, and student composition of both school districts and schools. Tables 1.1, 1.2 and 1.3 provide an historical institutional profile for the fifty-seven years from 1931 to 1987 in terms of the numbers of districts and schools, and average school and classroom sizes. During this period, the number of public school districts declined dramatically from 127,531 to 15,713. This reduction was primarily the result of district consolidations that coincided with the elimination of one-teacher schools and districts. In 1931, 143,000 of the 233,000 elementary schools were single teacher schools. By 1987, only 777 single teacher schools remained. Many of these schools were districts unto themselves, locally controlled and funded. Their passage is clearly an

Table 1.1: The number of districts and schools, public and private, 1931–1986

	Public School Districts	Public			Private	
		Elementary				
		Total	One-Teacher	Secondary	Elementary	Secondary
1931–32	127,531	232,750	143,391	26,409	9,734	3,289
1980–81	15,912	61,069	921	24,362	16,792	5,678
1986–87	15,713	60,784	777	20,000	NA	NA

Source: Digest of Educational Statistics, 1988, Table 67, p. 83.

Table 1.2: Average number of pupils per school, public and private schools, 1931–1986

	Public Schools		Private Schools	
	Elementary	Secondary	Elementary	Secondary
1931–32	91	195	245	123
1980–81	453	546	238	236
1986–87	450	531	NA	NA

Source: Digest of Educational Statistics, 1988, Tables 31 and 67; *Historical Statistics of the United States*, Series H412–432, p. 368; *Statistical Abstract of the United States*, Table 199, p. 124.

indication of an historical movement, which began much earlier with the growth of urban districts, from an extremely decentralized system toward a more unified and centralized set of educational systems.

However, the demise of the one-teacher school may mask existing institutional characteristics, which would indicate that the diversified-polyarchal model may still be very relevant in understanding current education policy. For example, over roughly the same time period, if we exclude one-teacher public schools, the consolidation movement looks considerably different. As indicated in Table 1.1, for the 50 years from 1932 through 1981, for which comparable data exist on both public and private schools, public elementary schools declined by 28,290 (31.7 per cent). However, during this same period, 7,058 additional private elementary schools came into existence. In addition, the sum total of high schools increased from 29,698 to 30,040.

Because of increasing student populations, as indicated in Table 1.2, average school size increased considerably over this period for all but private elementary schools. The five fold increase in the size of the average elementary school is affected very strongly by the demise of the one-teacher school as rural districts consolidated. Enrollment in the average public high school increased 2.8 times compared to 1.9 times for the average private secondary school.

An opposite trend has taken place in terms of classroom size. Although size is increasingly being criticized as a problem in secondary schools, and an advantage of private high schools (see Bryk *et al.* in this volume). Table 1.3 indicates that the average classroom size has decreased considerably over the last fifty or so years for elementary and secondary schools, public and private. In addition the relative advantage of small classroom sizes in private, as compared to public high schools has declined considerably over this same period.

Perhaps even more important in understanding the current diversity in the present institutional structure of education is the range in the size of school districts and schools within districts. Table 1.4 indicates the range of

Table 1.3: Average number of pupils per teacher, public and private schools, 1934–1986

	Public Schools		**Private Schools**	
	Elementary	*Secondary*	*Elementary*	*Secondary*
1934	33.8	22.3	34.0	15.3
1980	20.3	16.9	18.8	15.0
1986	19.1	16.0	17.2	13.3

Source: *Digest of Educational Statistics*, 1988, Table 51, p. 67.; *Historical Statistics of the United States*, Series H412–432, p. 368.

Table 1.4: Public school district and enrollment, by size of district, 1986–87

	School Districts		**Enrollment**	
Enrollment Size of District	*Number*	*Per cent*	*Number (in 1000s)*	*Per cent*
25,000 or more	173	1.1	10,821	27.9
10,000 to 24,999	447	2.8	6,606	17.1
5,000 to 9,999	915	5.8	6,382	16.5
2,500 to 4,999	1,823	11.6	6,363	16.4
1,000 to 2,499	3,504	22.3	5,691	14.7
600 to 999	1,754	11.2	1,371	3.5
300 to 599	2,257	14.4	987	2.5
1 to 299	4,071	25.9	522	1.3
Not Reported	769	4.9	—	—
Total	15,713	100.0	38,743	100.0

Source: Digest of Educational Statistics, 1988, Table 68, p. 83.

district sizes as of 1986–87; Table 1.5 depicts public school sizes at both the elementary and secondary levels. The general picture from both tables is extraordinary diversity. Although the mega-districts with 25,000 or more students account for 27.9 per cent of the students, they represent only 173 out of the 15,713 school districts in the country. In contrast 78 per cent of the districts are less than 2,500 students. Although we have eliminated the one-teacher school, we certainly have not eliminated the small school district. In terms of both size and dollars spent, the range goes from districts that resemble small businesses, to those that resemble medium-sized nations (with New York having close to one million students and a budget over $4 billion). At the very least one should be cautious when generalizing about 'school districts'.

The same conclusion applies to school size and organization, and, with less definitive statistics, to curriculum and pedagogical organization within and between schools. Public school size differences are noted in Table 1.5. The numbers of students in elementary schools are fairly evenly distributed between schools ranging in size from 200 to 1,000; however, this is an extraordinary range in terms of organizational structure, administration, etc. As with districts, the influence of the remaining rural systems means that the majority of schools (55 per cent) have less than 400 students; however, those larger than 400 account for 68 per cent of the students.

The story is similar for high schools — there is little concentration by size. Most students are in schools ranging from 800 to 3,000, but again this range is hardly trivial. In terms of numbers of high schools, as opposed to numbers of students, the proportions of secondary schools range fairly evenly from under 100 students to just under 2,000. Because of the

Table 1.5: Public elementary and secondary schools and enrollment by size of school, 1984–85

Enrollment Size of School	Number of Schools: Elementary	Number of Schools: Secondary	Enrollment: Elementary	Enrollment: Secondary
Per cent	100.0	100.0	100.0	100.0
Under 100	7.8	8.6	1.0	.7
100 to 199	12.2	10.3	4.6	2.1
200 to 299	15.9	8.4	9.9	2.9
300 to 399	19.1	7.8	16.5	3.8
400 to 499	15.9	7.6	17.7	4.7
500 to 599	11.5	8.0	15.7	6.1
600 to 699	7.	7.4	11.7	6.7
700 to 799	4.	6.5	8.0	6.7
800 to 999	3.9	10.3	8.5	12.7
1,000 to 1,499	1.9	14.7	5.5	24.7
1,500 to 1,999	.2	6.5	.9	15.4
2,000 to 2,999	.02	3.5	.1	11.3
3,000 or more	—	.4	.03	2.2
Total	57,231	22,320	23,018,862	15,866,964

Source: *Digest of Educational Statistics*, 1988, Table 73, p. 94.

problems associated with urban systems, and particularly urban high schools, a prevailing image of high schools is the huge, urban-mega high school. In terms of both numbers of schools and students taught this is a distorted image.

The grade organization of schools

The organization of schools by grade level presents a similarly diversified mosaic. Tyack's classic depiction of the 'one best system', drew attention to the nineteenth century emergence of common grade structures, graduation requirements, curriculum and testing patterns, along with a consistency in professional administration and teaching patterns (Tyack, 1974, especially pp. 39–59). Table 1.6, which indicates the range of public schools by grade, suggests that implementation of the one best system on this dimension (and I will get to more later) was not wholly successful across the country.

Both elementary and secondary schools are organized in a variety of ways in terms of grade structures. Although the most prevalent form of elementary school is K through 6, it represents less than 40 per cent of the schools. For secondary schools, 9 through 12 is the most common,

Table 1.6: Public elementary and secondary schools, organization by grade, 1986–87

Grade Structure	*Elementary Schools*	*Grade Structure*	*Secondary Schools*
Pre K to 3–4	5,037	7–8 or 7–9	5,142
Pre K to 5	12,164	7 to 12	3,670
Pre K to 6	22,317	8 to 12	527
Pre K to 8	5,701	9 to 12	9,771
4 to 8	7,452	10 to 12	1,682
Other	6,130	Other	614
Total	58,801	Total	21,406

Source: Digest of Educational Statistics, 1988, Table 75, p. 96.

accounting for 45.6 per cent of the schools. Because grade organization effects curriculum and curriculum coordination, advancement between schools, systematic testing and potentially pedagogical methods, this diversity is crucial to the institutional structure of American education.

Student composition

The student populations served by districts and schools add another element which suggests that our schools are more different and diversified than similar and uniform. A great deal of evidence is probably not necessary on this point because we are all aware of the dramatic differences in terms of racial composition and family income of children in urban, suburban, and rural public school districts, not to mention the compounding of these differences in private schools. Beginning with the largest unit, racial differences in state public school populations vary considerably. For example, while the 1984 average of whites in primary and secondary public schools was 71.2 per cent, the standard deviation between states was 19 per cent. Nine out of fifty states and the District of Columbia had less than 60 per cent white students, and thirteen had over 90 per cent. States such as Maine (98.7 per cent), Vermont (98.9 per cent), New Hampshire (98.3 per cent) and Iowa (96 per cent) are almost completely white; on the other hand, the District of Columbia (3.8 per cent white); Hawaii (23.1 per cent); New Mexico (44.9 per cent); and Mississippi (49.3 per cent) have less than a majority of white children, and several very large state systems such as California (52.0 per cent) and Texas (56.6 per cent) are extremely mixed racially (*Digest*, 1988, Table 37, p. 54).

The differences are even more stark at the district and (as a consequence) at school levels. As is well known, most of the largest school districts in the country are heavily minority school districts: New York (78 per cent non-white); Los Angeles (82 per cent); Chicago (86 per cent); Dade County (76 per cent); Houston (83 per cent); Philadelphia (75 per cent); Detroit (91 per cent); and Dallas (79 per cent) (Orfield and Monfort, 1988, p. 12). In addition, as varying but consistent research demonstrates, the vast majority of minority large-city schools are surrounded by mostly white suburbs. This has become considerably worse over the last twenty years as the percentage of white students in large city districts has dramatically declined.[2] In Milwaukee, for example, in 1985 the city school system was approximately 60 per cent minority while the largest percentage of minority students in the twenty-four contiguous suburban districts was 13 per cent with the average less than 5 per cent (Witte and Walsh, 1990).

This type of metropolitan segregation produces schools with very different racial compositions, and because of the relationship between race and household economic status, there are very pronounced economic class differences as well. Recent evidence from *High School and Beyond* data indicates that if we factor in private schools, we compound even further the racial and class differences in student composition (Coleman, Hoffer and Kilgore, 1982, Chapter 3).

Curriculum and pedagogy

A common, uniform system of education would not only have schools and administrative systems that look similar, but would also have relatively standard curricula that students are exposed to. Tyack's classic description of the development of the one best system emphasized the importance of curriculum, teaching practices, promotion standards and testing procedures as the foundation of the nineteenth and twentieth century reform movements (Tyack, 1974, Part V). The question is what has resulted?

It is obviously much more difficult to provide a systematic statistical picture of what is taught and tested by what method in over 100,000 schools across the country. However, there are some relevant studies that call into question any image of an overly uniform process. As we would expect, there appears to be more uniformity for elementary than high schools. However, even for elementary schools, education research has produced a wide range of often contradictory approaches to school organization, curriculum and teaching methods. In many districts, these approaches may be tried for a period and abandoned, or may live on and be added to the range of school alternatives available in districts. Thus we have seen open classroom schools; individually guided education; clinical teaching (Madeline Hunter); and now the New Curriculum Frameworks being developed in California (see Cohen in this volume).

At the high school level, a widely cited study by Powell, Farrar and Cohen (1985) argues that the hallmark of the *The Shopping Mall High School* is the diversity of courses and educational paths available in most American high schools. These authors not only highlight the range of courses and educational opportunities available, but also directly link the curriculum diversity to the diversity of the students. They write:

> [The book's] ... central theme is that [high schools] proceed by making numerous and different accommodations with students to maximize holding power, graduation percentages, and customer satisfaction. The accommodations are many because the students vary enormously. Outside observers often categorize this variation by commitment (the alienated, the passive, the motivated); by family background (blue-collar, affluent preppy, poor); or by ability (the gifted, the handicapped, the average). From inside schools, however, group labels often pale before the realities of individual differences that exist within categories. (Powell, Farrar and Cohen, 1985, pp. 1–2)

Their arguments and evidence are consistent with analyzes of *High School and Beyond* data which demonstrate not only the range of student exposure to different curricula, but also the importance of course selection and tracking practices as a predictor of achievement.[3]

Testing procedures across states and districts are even more diverse than curricula. Unlike a number of other industrialized nations, there is no national testing prior to graduate level higher education. Even college entrance testing is split between two major tests, and many public universities and colleges require no tests for in-state residents. Although increasing rapidly, few states have statewide testing of any kind, and those that do vary widely in the type of test and the purpose. They also often allow considerable local discretion in tests and procedures. Minimum competency testing is a case in point. Through 1985, forty states had some form of minimum competency testing. However, whether standards are set by states or local districts, the type of examination, the grades tested, the purposes of the test (grade promotion, high school graduation, remediation, etc.) follow every conceivable permutation (*Digest*, 1988, Table 91, p. 105). Achievement tests in many locations are no different. Different districts use different commercial or state provided tests, they test at different grade levels, and gear the tests toward fundamentally different purposes (e.g. counseling, measuring the relationship of 'ability' to 'achievement', and community or state accountability).[4]

Thus while on the surface what goes on in American school classrooms may have the appearance of common routines and methods covering similar educational subjects, there is considerable evidence for the other image — widely diverse teaching approaches, numerous methods of testing progress, and, in the upper grades, a very wide set of paths students can follow both within a single school and across schools.

Summary

The evidence presented above clearly suggests that the institutional forms of American education are numerous and widely varied. There are a large number of independent school districts and private schools. Both districts and schools vary dramatically in size and student composition. Schools are also organized in different grade patterns, and it is very difficult to point to uniform patterns of curriculum, pedagogy and testing. An analysis of the control systems governing American education reinforces the complex, diversified and fragmented pattern indicated by these basic institutional forms.

Governance: Control of American Education

The structure and complexity of control

Those who tend to view American education as a uniform monopoly, perceive the control system as a relatively simple, monolithic bureaucracy that is hierarchical and centralized. For example Chubb writes in this volume:

> The reason that the role of government [in education] is so difficult to appreciate fully is that in very basic ways the role of government does not vary from one public school to the next. All public schools are governed by democratic institutions of the same basic form at the local level and then organized into larger systems of schools governed by institutions, again of the same basic form, at the state level. All of these systems are subject to the influence and control of one set of democratic institutions at the national level. It has been said that public schools are governed by the 'one best system', and in formal respects this is nearly so: there is basically one system though it is not necessarily the best.

As indicated in Figure 1.1, the diversified-polyarchal model diverges from this view in terms of the number and arrangement of significant actors, the complexity of the decision process, and the resources and strategies that are available to participants. Because of the elusive nature of measuring 'control', it is difficult to bring direct evidence to bear on many aspects of the control system in American education, particularly quantitative evidence.[5] However, we can achieve some sense of the potential dimensions of and variation in the control systems governing American education by first looking at a mapping of potential actors, decisions, and control strategies, and second, by evaluating actual variation in school finances, geo-political designs of school districts, formal patterns of authority, and historical changes in staffing. As in the section above, the 'evidence' on the structure of control appears to favor the diversified-polyarchal end of the continuum.

For purposes of this paper, I will define 'control' and 'influence' in educational decisions as follows:

> *Control* is defined as the ability of an actor or set of actors to determine the outcomes of a specified domain of decisions.
>
> *Influence* is defined as the ability of an actor or set of actors to affect the outcomes of a specified domain of decisions in a manner consistent with their desired outcomes.

Both control and influence require specification of actors and specific decision sets. Control, thus defined, imposes definitive final say in decisions. Influence is used in a weaker sense as only affecting final outcomes, which implies other factors and actors are involved. Obviously, influence may exist for one set of actors, while on the same decisions other actors may have control. I will use the term 'power' interchangeably with control.[6]

A crude modeling of the control and influence systems governing American education is depicted in Figure 1.2. The 'actors' are arranged and approximately linked to their basic decision domains. As chapters in this volume attest, those links may be changing, particularly with the increasing role of states in the types of decisions that in the figure are linked to local districts. What is immediately apparent is that this is a very complex decision system. There are a large number of potential participants, a huge set of decisions, and a wide range of influence strategies.

Several characteristics of this control map bear on our perception of the general landscape of American education. First, although listed in a seemingly hierarchical pattern of control, the domains of decision of various actors hardly suggest a stark hierarchy of control. For example, the national role in education has been severely limited relative to the role in many other countries, and that role has only in recent decades become meaningful at all. The role has primarily been limited to protecting against various forms of discrimination and in providing limited federal assistance

Actor/Participants	Domains of Control	Authority/Strategies
Federal Legislature/Agencies	Educational Rights	
Organized Interest Groups	Discrimination	
	Aid to Disadvantaged	
	Aid to Learning Disabled	
	Aid to Handicapped	Constitutional,
		Statutory,
State Legislature/Agencies	Governance and Finance:	Regulatory Authority
Organized Interest Groups	District Organization	
	Within-district organization	Resource Control
	Collective Bargaining	Electoral Politics
	Structure	
	General Financial Aid	
	Special Financial Aids	
	Standards:	
	School/District Accreditation	
	Teacher Certification	
	School Year/hours	
	Graduation Requirements	
	Special Programs	
Local Authorities:		
City Government Officials	District/School Budgets	Administrative Rules
County Government Officials	Personnel Contracts/Policies	Bargaining
School Boards	School Organization/Location	Strikes
Superintendent	Curriculum	Legal Remedies
District Administrators	Pedagogical Approaches	
Local Teacher Associations	Grading	
Local Administrator Asso.	Reporting	
	Special Programs	
Parents		Protests
Students		Exit
Citizens		

Figure 1.2: Control and influence in American education

for programs for disadvantaged students. The basic governance of state and local schools, standards, and school building organization, procedures, teaching, are almost unaffected by national authorities.

Although state influence in education policy is considerably more than national involvement, as Fuhrman's chapter in Volume 2 indicates, in general it is only in recent years that states have begun to be active in decisions affecting actual educational practices, curricula, achievement levels, school governance, etc. In nearly all states, the geographic arrangement of districts, some aspects of district finance, and very basic accreditation and minimal educational standards are imposed by state statutes and regulations. Some states also impose the governance structure in districts (i.e. school board selection and power, powers of superintendents, etc.), and may have state-wide statutes governing collective bargaining; others leave these decisions to local levels. Only recently, and only in a few states, have state authorities attempted to manage the crucial 'production' decisions that determine what will be taught, to whom, by whom, where and how.

Thus while the actors and potential participants in educational policy are numerous, the linkages between actors are hardly hierarchical, with directions explicitly flowing from the national to the state and then to the districts. Rather the domains of control have been more or less partitioned, with most of the crucial educational choices being made at the district level. Those who argue that public education is relatively monopolistic and hierarchical might agree to this point, but insist that the relevant hierarchy is not the national-state-district chain, but rather the hierarchical organization within districts. Indeed, a district's ability to keep state and federal authorities out of key decisions may be one indication of the power of district bureaucracies. Thus the centralized bureaucrats of relevance are district administrators who control the key educational production decisions.

Although very difficult to document systematically, there is little question that in many districts administrators make an effort to control the who, what, where and how of classroom education; and this may be even more true of large urban districts that are not performing as well as their smaller rural and suburban counterparts. What is less clear are: (1) the range of control philosophies (e.g., are there, *à la* Robert Michels Iron Law of Oligarchy, inherent characteristics that lead *all* school districts to adopt a centralization philosophy?); and (2) the success of those districts that have attempted centralized, hierarchical control. Two points bear on these questions. First, in the chapters to follow, there are descriptions of major urban districts that have forsworn this type of control in favor of much more decentralized, participatory schemes. This is true of the changes over fifteen years in District 4 in New York, the revolutionary changes occurring in Chicago, the controlled choice programs described in Volume 2 by Alves and Willie in Cambridge and Boston, and the basic institutional approach being applied in Dade County, Florida.

Second, two fundamental characteristics of teaching and schools may make centralized, hierarchical control inherently difficult to achieve. First, compared to any other large organization — business, military or governmental — schools have a very flat administrative hierarchy. Essentially, at the 'production' level, we have teachers and a principal. At the high school level, there are also often assistant principals and department heads, but the former usually handle discipline, truancy, etc, and the latter vary considerably in power. Second, as a Milwaukee teacher once expressed to me: 'Once that door closes, I have control'. Although teachers may have to use agreed texts, may have to submit to external testing of students and other district or school requirements, what is done or not done in classrooms is very often up to the individual teacher. This is unlike almost any other organizational occupation, varying from assembly or manual workers to trained professionals (e.g., nurses, and, increasingly, doctors and lawyers), as well as to upper level managers in corporations, government or the military. Given teacher tenure, and the pivotal position of teachers in the educational process, this control is also difficult to overcome. Teachers who do not go along with centralized plans or are simply not successful cannot be denied promotions (because there is no place to be promoted to); it is difficult to alter pay levels (because of tenure and/or unions); and teachers cannot be released without an elaborate administrative effort. Thus while attempts to control from the center may be prevalent, they also may be futile — the hierarchies are too flat and teachers have considerable power in the educational process.

A final problem in arguing for the prevalence of district level bureaucratic control comes to light when we analyze the changing staffing of public education in the post-war years. Relevant figures are provided in Table 1.7. As is apparent, all forms of staff positions have increased both because of expanding school populations and because the staff/pupil ratios have declined. However, what is intriguing is the relative growth of different staff positions. *The least growth has occurred in district administrative staff positions.* Despite the enormous growth in special programs (disadvantaged, handicapped), reporting requirements, services (food, health, day care, etc.), curriculum expansion, etc., — all of which require some administrative attention — the district staff/student ratio has declined only

Table 1.7: Staffing in public schools, 1949 to 1986

	District Administrative Staff	*Instructional Staff*	*Principals, Assistant Principals*	*Teachers*	*Support Staff**
Totals:					
Number, 1949–50	33,642	963,110	43,137	913,671	303,280
Number, 1986–87	74,533	2,824,086	131,726	2,243,370	1,348,813
Per cent Increase	+121.5	+193.2	+205.4	+145.5	+344.7
Pupils per Staff Members:					
1949–50	746.4	26.1	582.1	27.5	82.8
1986–87	534.5	14.1	302.4	17.8	29.5
Per cent Decline	−28.4	−46.0	−48.1	−35.3	−64.4

*Includes: secretarial, clerical, transportation, kitchen, plant, health, recreation, and others.

Source: Digest of Educational Statistics, 1988, Table 61, p. 77.

28.4 per cent in the thirty-eight years from 1949 to 1987. This compares to 46 per cent for instructional staff and 64.4 per cent in support staff, the latter growing in numbers by 344.7 per cent over this period. It would appear the faceless army of district bureaucrats, who some say run our schools, are mostly secretaries, clerks, kitchen help, janitors and bus drivers. In terms of direct operating staff, the number of principals has expanded the most, again hardly an indicator of centralized, bureaucratic dominance

Although this analysis questions the assumption that education is necessarily centrally and hierarchically controlled, a final issue is the actual range and diversity of control structures that have evolved in states and districts. Figure 1.2 suggests a theoretically wide range of diversity in systems of control, and it was presented in part because hard data directly measuring control are difficult, if not impossible to come by. However, some facts again indicate that between state and between district variation is extreme on many of the relevant variables.

Several indirect measures of educational control are available. Sources of education funding is one such indicator. Federal funding is very low across the country, with an average in 1985–86 of 6.7 per cent. This ranges from 3.6 per cent in Wyoming to 13.3 per cent in Kentucky. By district the range is 0 per cent in the Richardson Integrated School District in Texas to 17 per cent in Jackson Municipal district in Mississippi (excluding the Washington DC district). Thus, to the extent money affects control of decisions, national influence over our schools, while varying somewhat, is nevertheless minimal. State funding averaged 49.4 per cent, but varies enormously between states and districts (with a low of 13.1 per cent in Montgomery County, Maryland to highs of 85.9 per cent in the unified state system in Hawaii). Local funding comprises the remainder with an average of 43.9 per cent, but again a very large range, from a low of .1 per cent in Hawaii to a high of 88.9 per cent in New Hampshire (*Digest*, 1988, Tables 71 and 108, pp. 86–93, 125).

As has been very well researched, funding per pupil also varies enormously between states and between districts in the same state. At the high end, as of 1986, Alaska spent $8,253 per student, New York $6,011, and New Jersey $5,395. This is in contrast to Utah ($2,220), Alabama ($2,325), Mississippi ($2,362) and Tennessee ($2,362) (*Digest*, 1988, Table 115, p. 133). In addition, despite court cases beginning with *Priest v. Serrano*, there remains an enormous difference in per pupil spending between districts in the same state. For example, a pivotal point in a federal judges' recent ruling that the education system in the state of Kentucky had to be completely redesigned, was a finding that district spending varied from $1,900 to $4,300 per pupil (*New York Times*, March 20, p. 1).

There also appears to be considerable variation in the organization of state education authorities and in regulatory actions of states. Both in terms of the organization of the state bureaucracies and in the arrangements for carrying out routine state administrative functions, there is again no uniform pattern of organization or control. State superintendents and state school boards exist in most states, but not in all. Some are elected by state votes, many are appointed under varying political arrangements. Statutory powers also vary considerably.

A number of recent accounts of state actions have documented the increasing attempts by states to be involved in more carefully monitoring and regulating school and district practices and student achievement. For example, a 1987 survey of states found that the majority of states (89.8 per cent) required district reporting of standardized test results, with many of these states adding this requirement in the 1980s (Accountability Reporting in the States, 1988, Table 1). In some states, such as California, where the majority of funding is coming from state coffers, local control is clearly waning on such matters as curriculum, text selection, standardized testing, etc. As Fuhrman notes in Volume 2, several states have also recently enacted legislation authorizing the state to take over 'bankrupt' districts, although to date none have actually exercised that power. What may be more telling in Fuhrman's chapter. However, is the degree to which states have remained within their traditional roles, and only very slowly are beginning to work on problems of specific school districts.

Although there does not exist a systematic comparative study of state departments of public instruction, routine functions of state authorities also appear to vary considerably. Most states certify teachers and in some cases other staff positions (e.g., counselors). It would appear that even this routine function is carried out differently across states. Teacher certification was required in forty-three states in 1986–87; however, in twenty states certification was delegated to State Certification Boards (variously selected), in twenty-one states requirements were mandated by the legislatures, and in the other two states different procedures were used (*Digest*, 1988, Table 106 p. 123). The requirements obviously varied considerably between states as well.

Another common power of states is establishing school districts. However, while the power is relatively uniform, the result is unbelievable diversity. A partial listing of the types of districts that have been established include: City, County, Municipal, Metropolitan, Integrated, Consolidated, Unified, and Special Districts. As indicated by their titles, the array of political-geographic forms is considerable, and this often dictates the governance structure of individual districts.

Variation in the type of district is mirrored by variation in formal district powers and in the relationship of districts to other local governmental authorities. Nearly all districts have professional superintendents and school boards, but after that there is little uniformity. School boards may be elected or appointed, with widely varying terms and methods of election or appointment. School boards may have dominant control over superintendents (hiring, firing, salary), but in districts following a more 'professional educator' model, the superintendent may have much more formal and informal independence. In some cases city and county executives and elected assemblies play an active role in the selection and evaluation of superintendents and/or the appointment of school board members. These bodies may or may not have control or veto over budgets. Cities vary widely in terms of political entanglements with schools. In New York, Chicago, and San Francisco mayors and controlling political parties have always been powerful actors in educational policy and administration (see, e.g., Tyack, 1974 and Peterson, 1976). In other, cities, for example county systems such as Dade and Los Angeles County, and other cities such as Milwaukee and Minneapolis, the educational system has been relatively insulated from elected officials. Again, the point is that the variation in power systems is enormous.

Political responsiveness and accountability

Much more difficult to determine is the degree to which educational systems respond and are accountable to relevant officials and to the public. The uniform-monopoly position is that the education system, by virtue of its monopoly, does not have to respond to pressures from other political authorities, parents, community groups, etc. The diversified-polyarchal model assumes a much more responsive posture. The limited and indirect evidence that can be brought to bear on this question appears somewhat mixed. For example, the increasing role of states in measuring and reporting student achievement points toward increasing accountability. However, on closer examination it was found that of the forty-four states where testing and reporting was required, only seventeen states reported results by school to parents or the public (Accountability Reporting in the States, 1988, Table 1).

At the district level, my view, from observing several large urban districts, is that on the surface they attempt to respond to a variety of pressures, going along with most new ideas and proposals thrown at them; however, the response is more often than not a superficial, public relations reaction. Thus there is reaction to pressure, which in many of these districts is intense and continuous, but hardly reactions that fulfill the demands of even modest theories of accountability (see Weick, 1976, for a similar argument).

Two interesting points may be telling on this issue. As noted by Peterson in this volume, the important shift in urban school districts that began in the late 1960s, and signaled the end of the era of monopoly (ushering in the era he terms a 'quasi-monopoly'), was the growing number of poor, minority, and handicapped students in urban districts. More importantly, as Peterson argues, programs and resources in these districts were dramatically altered to accommodate the needs of these students. Put in other words, the districts were responsive and accountable to new demands. That by most measures they have not succeeded in adequately educating these new students is in one sense unrelated to the issue of accountability as true effort, rather than result.

The example suggests an even more complicated issue, which I believe also challenges the basic idea of a uniform-monopoly model as the image of American education. It demonstrates how vulnerable school districts are to forces beyond their control. True monopolists, in the economic sense, control the crucial parameters of their environments: prices of materials and wages; firm entry; and product quality, volume and price. Do schools have parallel powers? For the most part, they cannot control the raw materials, the children who come into their districts; they cannot control firm entry because of private schools and other independent districts close by; they cannot control the volume of education delivered because states dictate how long students must be educated, and the number of students served by a district cannot be controlled. To what extent they can control 'quality' and thus the 'price' or value of education (i.e. what effect schools have on variation in achievement) is a matter of considerable debate and conjecture.

Summary

The comparison to an economic monopoly brings into focus how difficult it is to argue that American education is best perceived as a uniform, hierarchically and centrally controlled system. A simple map of the education policy system indicates large sets of relevant actors, with some, perhaps increasing, interplay between the national, state and local levels, but hardly a system that one could say is run in hierarchical fashion from the center. The majority of crucial decisions about teaching and instruction are made in the thousands of local districts and the schools themselves. Further, there are indicators that both the structure of control and the centrality of control at the district level varies considerably across states and districts. Thus, as with the mottled maze of institutional forms that define American education, the control patterns appear more like a Jackson Pollock painting than the well-ordered organizational charts we envision for a centrally structured monopoly.

Before proceeding, however, it is important to note that while the uniform-monopoly model appears to be a distortion, the model and comparison is not an unrealistic strawman. Compared either to education systems in many other industrialized countries, or to other policy arenas in the United States the model is quite realistic. On the former point, Cohen's chapter in this volume cites Japan, Germany, and New South Wales (Australia) as systems with many of the characteristics of the uniform-monopoly I have described.

Compared to other domestic polities in the United States, the centralized system described above approximates the policy making and administration of Old Age Survivors Insurance, national tax policies, many regulatory agencies, most agriculture and veterans programs, and some housing and job training programs. To be sure there are major exceptions such as welfare and health programs, and housing and unemployment subsidies. However, the point is, that even the most cursory examination of primary and secondary education in the United States, suggests a policy system quite different from the way other countries accomplish the same tasks, and quite different from the policy systems in other domestic programs in this country. Thus the uniform-monopoly model is not a strawman, it is simply incorrect as a general description of the landscape of American education.

Proposals for Choice and Decentralized Control in Education

There are numerous issues involving the institutional organization and governance of American schools. This book focuses on two recently prominent trends, which have longer histories than are usually portrayed by current-day reformers. These trends are captured by the phrases *choice* and *decentralization*. This section discusses and defines these concepts, and describes specific alternative plans that have been advanced under one or another of these banners.

Definitions and Proposals for Choice in Education

One of the confusing aspects of policy discussions in most policy arenas is that participants often employ various meanings for the same terms. Discussions of 'choice' and 'decentralization' in education are no different. Even as used in this volume, these terms have different meanings depending on the author and the plan under discussion. However, there are common features in the use of these terms that justify categorization of specific plans under a common rubric. *Choice plans* always involve parents having either influence or control over selection of the school site for their children. The difference between influence and control is of course very important. Control implies that parents have final say over the decision, which means absolute power to veto a given set of schools and acceptance in a school of choice. Influence means that they can affect a decision ultimately made by others by, for example, specifying and ranking their school options.

In both cases when the word choice is used, it is often closely aligned with an exit strategy (or the threat of exit). Thus in terms of the control structure presented in Figure 1.2, choice has a relatively narrow meaning. Nothing is directly stated about parental involvement or influence over a wide range of other decisions that will undoubtedly affect their child's education and the quality of the school in general. Although often assumed by choice advocates, just as switching cereals may or may not improve the the old brand, leaving schools may or may not improve the old school.

Choice has always existed in American education. The principal choice strategies have been: (1) selection of where one lives, which, if neighborhood attendance areas are the basis of school assignment, provides parents control over schools for their children; and (2) the option of private schools, which again provides parents with control as long as schools cannot deny their children admission. It is not unreasonable to argue, as Coons does in this volume, that this individual, unplanned choice is, and has always been very widespread.

Translated into public policy alternatives, choice 'plans' take numerous forms. The original 'choice' plan was the famous *voucher* plan proposed almost three decades ago by Milton Friedman (Friedman, 1962, Chapter 6). In such a system, the per member cost (or some portion of it) of a student's education would be provided in the form of a voucher to be used to purchase education in either public or private schools. In recent years, to offset the criticism that such plans would favor the wealthy, more elaborate voucher plans have built in progressive vouchers to offset the disadvantages of the poor, caps on auxiliary spending on education by the rich, and requirements that schools reserve certain percentages of their seats for disadvantaged students (Coons, this volume). A variant of this subsidy approach is a *tuition tax credit* plan that would allow parents an income tax deduction for tuition paid to private schools (see, for example, Coleman *et al*., 1982).

District school choice plans have also been proposed, originally as the well-known *magnet school systems*, which provide some students choices of specialty schools within the district. These plans were usually established in conjunction with desegregation orders, and were specifically intended to hold middle class whites in urban school systems. In some cities, such as Milwaukee, there were additional incentives created to allow for interdistrict transfers to specialty schools. However, most plans were confined to public schools within a single district. As Blank's chapter in Volume 2 illustrates, the original intent of magnet schools may be changing. He shows that enrollments in magnet schools and the number of schools themselves have grown significantly in the 1980s and are now being used to provide choices and educational alternatives unrelated to integration. In all of these examples, parents are limited to having influence over choice, because final assignment of students rests either with administrators or with luck (with random assignment from choice lists).

A second form of within district choice has recently emerged under the rubric of *controlled choice plans*. Alves and Willie describe this concept in Volume 2, with an extended example from Boston. The basic idea is to provide parents with as much choice between all schools in a district as possible, while at the same time maintaining racial balance in almost all schools. Parents influence selection by making ranked choices of schools. Final assignment is made by administrators following pre-arranged rules that factor in racial balance, neighborhood assignment, special student needs, siblings, etc.

A third type of plan which has been proposed, but seldom implemented, is *public school district funding of private/alternative schools*. This proposal has been limited to contractual relationships with private providers for specialized schools — alternatives for at-risk students, schools for pregnant teens, etc. Proposals to generalize these plans differ from vouchers or tuition-tax credits in that public school districts remain the contracting and regulating authority.

A final proposal that has recently been enacted in Minnesota (see Bennett's chapter in Volume 2), is a *state wide system of choice in public schools*. Under the plan enacted in Minnesota, parents can seek enrollment in any district school that is participating in the plan. Districts need not accept students, but cannot deny students exit to schools in other districts. Acceptance of students can be contingent on limits set by districts on space available in particular schools. Racial and socio-economic discrimination in choice of students admitted is not permitted. State aid follows the student, going exclusively to the district providing the education.

Definitions and Proposals for Decentralization in Education

Decentralization, along with educational choice, is consistently being touted as a central feature of the current reform movement. As with choice, in most derivations, there is a central core meaning, which is then translated into varied programs. *Decentralization* occurs either when control or influence in educational decisions is shifted closer in the chain of authority to those who teach, directly supervise teachers, or to parents and consumers. It nearly always implies shifting some decision-making authority from the district level to either sub-district offices, or to the school level.

Proposals that are incorporated under this designation vary considerably in terms of both the actors being given more influence and the domains of decisions that are affected. Three specific types of reforms have received considerable attention and are addressed in some detail in these volumes. *Decentralization to sub-district administrative units* occurred first in New York City, which created thirty-two districts, with their own school boards and administrative organizations for primary and middle schools. Fliegel, who until recently was Superintendent of District 4 in New York, describes in Volume 2 the alternative school approach that was developed under that decentralization arrangement. Chapters on Dade County, Florida and Chicago describe recent efforts in those districts to create sub-district systems that have primary administrative responsibility for schools in their geographic areas. While the powers of these units have not been fully established in Chicago and Miami, in New York, the regional districts have very comprehensive powers including personnel decisions, curriculum management, and (in some cases such as District 4) the power to reorganize and completely redefine schools.

Probably the most prevalent example of decentralization in recent years is the movement toward *school-based management*. The Malen, Ogawa and Kranz chapter in Volume 2 analyzes this movement in terms of types of programs established under this heading and the evidence to date as to their impact both on the organizational variables and on achievement outcomes. Although they find that there is little consistency in the exact design of these programs, the common thread is that some degree of current decision-making control is shifted from central districts to principals and teachers in schools. The most common domains of decision are budgets and curriculum.

Another variant of decentralization falls under the nomenclature *teacher empowerment*. Although she expresses some reservations concerning the phrase, Johnson in Volume 2 describes and analyzes that movement, which consists of a range of schemes to increase teacher decision-making influence at both the district and school levels.

A final set of proposals for decentralization involve *parental influence in schools*. This is hardly a novel idea and has long been discussed in research linking schools more directly to communities or increasing parental involvement in schools.[7] Again a variety of arrangements are possible: from parent advisory boards at both the school and district level (very common); to parents participating on curriculum committees; to the recently enacted statutory provisions in Chicago where elected parent and citizen representatives will hold eight of eleven seats on school councils that will hire and fire principals, establish school improvement plans, set standards for the school, and manage most budget decisions. Moore describes the origin and details of that plan in his chapter in Volume 2. These plans can work in concert with choice plans, but the emphasis is quite different in that parental voice and loyalty is stressed as the operative incentive and influence. Indeed, in Chicago, there was a major conflict between those stressing choice and those insisting on parental and citizen influence and control of schools (see Moore, 1990, Volume 2).

Arguments For and Against Decentralized Control and Choice

Given the range of programs and proposals that fall within these two reform movements, it is difficult to speculate on the merits of such plans or their prospects for success. However, the relationship between the general incentive mechanisms and changes in institutional and control arrangements assumed by these reforms can be analyzed in the context of the current landscape of American education. The question at this level of abstraction is not what works, with what exact results. Many of the chapters in these volumes evaluate those questions for specific programs, unfortunately often concluding that very little is known. The questions here are whether it makes sense, in the current context of American education, to experiment with reforms of this nature, and, what are the general theoretical problems that must be faced?

It was argued in the first section of this chapter that the assumption that the American education system is a uniform monopoly is very overdrawn. Rather, as a system, educational institutions and control structures are highly diverse, comprising elements of hierarchical bureaucracy, implanted within a system that contains many actors and sources of influence over a very broad agenda of issues. There is little doubt that within this system there are many school districts that have attempted highly centralized decision-making, and the most likely candidates are large urban districts. These may be offset by numerous smaller districts that operate in much less centralized fashion both in public districts (we suspect more rural and suburban) and in private schools (Chubb and Moe, 1988). And in all districts, there remains at least a suspicion that overt, coercive bureaucracy has difficulty penetrating the classroom. The questions that remain are: (1) are there general theoretical advantages that can be cited for proposals to decentralize decision making and initiate enhanced systems of choice; and (2) what cautions and fears should be highlighted if such reforms are to move forward.

The Case For Decentralization and Choice

Almost fifty years ago, Friedrich Hayek wrote the first of a series of books in which he promoted a decentralized market system and castigated a centrally planned economy and society. At the core of his argument was the premise that modern industrial societies are complex both in terms of social and economic structures and the diversity of desires and needs of the population. He argued that centralized planning, which in 1942 loomed as a very real permanent possibility in both democratic and non-democratic societies, would inevitably produce both abject tyranny and a woefully inefficient economy. The only way to avoid these outcomes was to decentralize social and economic decisions through a market mechanism. It was the diversity of desires, talents, wants, and needs, combined with a natural desire to maximize individual satisfaction of preferences, that led to this conclusion. If people are similar, want the same things, wish to work in similar jobs and organizations, and in general desire to live the same way, planning and coordination is relatively simple and innocuous. But if that is not true, a planner faces an insurmountable task of trying to know and match abilities and wants to create not only the most efficient alignment of resources, but also assignments that satisfy people. As she fails, dissatisfaction stemming from both inefficiency and coercive assignment inherently undermines the planning effort. As the system deteriorates, more resources are diverted to rationalizing decisions and coercing the population into acquiescence (Hayek, 1979)[8].

The pivotal arguments both for choice and decentralization in education, and the problems and fears they generate, are imbedded in Hayek's perceptive analysis. Although the general arguments for decentralization and choice apply to all districts, because the institutional contexts between large, centralized, urban systems and the much smaller systems that characterize rural, suburban and private systems appear to be so different, and because educational outcomes mirror these differences, the discussion focuses on urban, public school systems.

Arguments for decentralization

The absence of a monopoly does not preclude a tendency toward centralized, bureaucratic decision-making in corporations or school districts. In large school districts for example, budget decisions are usually highly centralized; questions of school structure, location, and closing are usually made by school districts and central boards; and in many districts there is centralized curriculum management, and hiring and assignment of teachers, principals and staff. Further, given the more or less continuous pressure these systems are under, if the schools fail to improve (the usual case), a natural response, both to affect further reforms and to maintain control, is to retrench even further. The question is the wisdom of this centralization.

There are several arguments favoring decentralization over centralized decision-making in the context of urban school districts. The first very general but powerful notion is negative; i.e. that efforts at centralized control may not realize the outcomes that are intended by central planners. The reasons are that these systems are large and complex, and within the formal centralized hierarchy there remain numerous points of polyarchal control and influence. Put concisely, central district administrators (or state authorities) may be unable to enforce their will on the operating units. They cannot effectively punish teachers and administrators who ignore, sabotage or get around their directives. Effective school plans, mission statements, goals, and elaborate curriculum documents can be put in drawers; teachers can adapt new pedagogical approaches to old styles to the point that the new method is unrecognizable; and teachers can always 'teach to the test' that has been mandated to insure accountability.

Likewise, parents and students are under less coercive threat than teachers — and this is without consideration of the exit option. Although some, perhaps even most parents may be constrained by time or resources or may be apathetic, considerable pressure can be applied on public policy-makers by a small, dedicated minority. Students may be more directly affected by administrative actions. However, centrally promulgated rules, punishments and procedures for insuring that students come to school, stay in classes, and behave appropriately would seem of questionable utility given the continual problems of dropping out, suspensions, and expulsions. And this speaks not at all to the larger issue of forcing students to learn. For all of these groups, the multiple points of influence that exist in education can be used to retaliate against an unpopular and overbearing bureaucracy.

A second problem is time. One appropriate parallel between American business and schools may be the time span in which actions and results are demanded. The continuous pressures that troubled districts experience mean that innovative reforms are put in place quickly. This of course may create a problem with program design, but even more importantly it means that the programs must be put in place from the center, with little, if any involvement by teachers and principals, and probably no provisions for tailor-making programs to fit individual schools.[9]

A third, and related problem is that centralized plans are inherently uniform, while the needs and effective actions for different units may be diverse. In addition to the problem of time, the knowledge and information that would allow central administrations to determine the appropriate match of different programs to the diverse units is impossible to obtain or analyze. Thus, in the absence of decentralized control, uniform directives are a school district's only option. Both because teachers and principals are only tangentially involved in program designs, and thus lack commitment to them, and because there are inevitable differences between schools, uniform plans applied to many schools face an uphill battle.

Thus, because of the local power inherent in schools, because continuous pressures create a very short time line for change, and because there are strong forces that lead to uniformity in reforms, centralized controls and reforms are likely to fail. And as they fail (or at least do not lead to major improvements in results), either central administrators are changed (what is the longevity of urban superintendents?) and/or they quickly shift to a new set of innovative proposals.

The same general arguments apply to smaller districts; however, because of the size and organizational differences, there may already be much less centralization (see Coleman and Hoffer, 1987; and Chubb and Moe, 1988, but only for public versus private schools). In addition, because performance levels are considerably higher, the time and reform pressures will be less.

Another more positive set of theoretical arguments also support experimentation with the various versions of educational decentralization as outlined above. As the chapters of this volume will demonstrate, the theoretical advantages put forward in favor of decentralization, be it school-based management, extensive parental influence, teacher empower ment, etc., are usually drawn from theories or experiences in other fields and institutions and have not been well established in education. However, the parallel logic is important and suggestive enough to support carefully monitored experiments.

One of the most pervasive arguments for greater control of educational decisions at the school level, is that it will facilitate the communal aspects of schools by: (1) increasing the legitimacy of policies; (2) motivating principals, teachers and parents because they have more say; (3) increasing morale and satisfaction; and (4) establishing and heightening collective norms that support improved academic outcomes (Coleman and Hoffer, 1987; Newmann, Rutter and Smith, 1987); see also the chapters by Bryk *et al.*, and Weiss in this volume). Although the empirical work supporting these arguments for communal school effects remains controversial (particularly on achievement outcomes, see Alexander and Pallas, 1985), there is a parallel to a vast set of research findings in corporations that show both improved morale and productivity of greater employee involvment in decisions.

A compatible set of arguments, on which unfortunately there is little empirical evidence, is that decentralization will improve educational practices through: (1) the incentive it provides for innovation; and (2) the flexibility it affords schools in implementing policies that better fit their unique situations. Curriculum, text selection, and initiation of microcomputer applications, are examples of decisions and practices that might be better made at the school site level.

Arguments for choice in education

Given the advantages of decentralization, why is choice necessary? One of the most obvious answers is that choice will facilitate and accelerate the same sort of actions that are purported to result from decentralization. This is the line of argument that follows from the public/private school controversy emanating from the *High School and Beyond* data. It is pointed out, quite correctly, that many private schools, be they secular or religious, operate either without district offices or with very small district level staffs. Studies also report greater teacher and administrator influence in a range of decisions, and higher morale (Chubb and Moe, 1988).[10] Further, private schools, most being tied to churches, rely on and are able to obtain considerably more parental involvement and interest than public schools (Coleman and Hoffer, 1987, pp. 53–6; Chubb and Moe, 1988). It is unclear whether the link in this line of evidence is caused by the different policy and organization structure of public and private schools, thus implying that if public schools would reduce bureaucracy and decentralize they would be more successful, or whether the choice situation is an independent factor.

One argument for an independent effect of choice is that shifting power to teachers and school-level administrators will by itself not be sufficient because there is no assurance that teachers and administrators will affect the changes necessary to improve educational performance. Teachers and principals already have considerable power, and with a decentralized system they will have more power. It may be true that parental power increases as decision making is decentralized, but this need not be the case, or the powers between school and parent may grow disproportionately. One answer to this problem, as exemplified in the Chicago reform described by Moore in Volume 2, is to redesign radically school-based decision making to give a prominent role to parents. Under the legislation recently enacted in Illinois, and implemented in the Fall of 1989, significant powers, including hiring principals and budget authority, will be vested in Local School Councils comprised of six elected parents, two elected community members, two elected teachers, and the school principal.

Choice systems, on the other hand, while not necessarily providing parents with direct control, provide them with a simple and certain club to use on schools. One does not have to say what exactly is wrong or what should be done to correct it; one does not have to argue, persuade, or cajole teachers or administrators; one only needs to find a suitable alternative. If there is anyone who does not believe there is power in this prospect, I would suggest they consider the general demise of urban schools as middle class parents have voted with their feet. For Hayek, and others before and after, it was this simple mechanism that drove the system to produce better and noncoercive results.

Problems and Fears

There are numerous potential problems with choice and decentralization plans. Many difficulties are discussed by authors in these volumes. For example, while the notions of decentralization and choice are often linked, it may turn out they are in conflict. It may be that parents who are most likely to have an effective role in decentralized decision-making, if given an easy option, may also be the most likely to take their children out of poor schools; i.e. they will choose exit over voice and loyalty. What would remain are very poor schools, and parents who lack the time, resources or inclination to apply pressure for change.

Another problem with decentralization, emphasized by Bryk *et al.*, in this volume and Clune in Volume 2, is that decentralization may undercut successful centralized controls. If, as they argue, the most consistent variable linked to achievement gain is the number and type of academic courses a student takes, centralized control of curriculum and mandated standards may be logical policies.

Also, as Levin argues in Chapter 5, one can question choice, particularly with private schools included, because education is essential to transmit democratic and liberal values, which can be insured in the public schools, but not in unregulated private schools. Levin also argues that in the context of American education, it is folly to believe that choice or decentralization plans will operate without excessive regulation. In fact regulatory systems could be more elaborate than under the current system.

While not slighting these arguments, I will concentrate on two issues, that seem very central and generate widespread concerns and skepticism of radical decentralization and choice proposals. As with the problems noted above, they suggest major questions that should be studied as reforms proceed.

The simplest of these, directed at radical plans to decentralize decision making, such as the experiment about to begin in the Chicago public schools (see Moore in Volume 2), is the issue of *Professional competence*. There are two strains to the argument. The first is that non-professionals lack the experience, education, and information required to make suitable policy judgments concerning detailed school practices. Unlike teachers and administrators who devote a considerable portion of their lives to education, parents and citizens do not have the time, experience, or knowledge to judge resource allocations, curriculum changes, testing procedures, etc. Putting control in their hands is likely to lead to foolish, ill-conceived decisions and is an abdication of professional responsibility. The second strain of this argument is that elected representatives will be more devoted to furthering their own ends than the collective good of the organization. Thus parents might make decisions that benefit their children, or the children of key groups that aided in their election, at the expense of other students.

These arguments challenge a central premise of market theory, not to mention central assumptions of democratic theory in general. In a pure market, individuals are the best judges of choice because they make decisions concerning only their own preferences and affecting only their own actions. But the world is different when collective organizations are involved. Decisions now affect numerous individuals; actions impinge continuously on the choices and behavior of others; and decisions are no longer the repetitive, microdecisions of say a shopper in a supermarket, but rather begin to look like general policies and rules. Thus while Hayek's advice may be appropriate if the comparative reference is very broad social planning, it may be less sanguine when we are trying to determine the appropriate governance structure of functionally constrained collective enterprises — such as schools.

Given adequate information concerning choice, the professional competence issue has less affect on arguments for choice. The nub of that argument is that parents are best able to judge what they want for their child and are able to exercise that judgment easily and decisively. That claim is unaffected by the more general notion of competence of parents and citizens as organizational decision-makers. However, as has often been argued, radical choice plans do raise major questions and fears concerning *equity*. The central premises of a market theory are that preferences and the utility derived from preferences vary between individuals, and that the quest for maximizing individual preference orderings will spur people to work and innovate, and efficiently consume resources. Equality of result has no role in this process, and, in one sense the striving to achieve individual preferences has strong, if not determinant overtones of inequality.

It may be that consumption and outcomes of education mirror this condition, but few Americans would unflinchingly admit that, and a very large legal and institutional structure has been erected to deny the premise. Thus, at a minimum, equality of educational opportunity is always listed as a primary goal of American education; and equality of opportunity often shades into equality of results (see, for example, Rae, 1980). Internally it is less clear. Grading is a sorting device; tracking also is based on inequality; and graduation(s) are milestones that produce gradations. Despite these obvious internal contradictions, few would deny that the notion of a common and universal education is an important ideological and policy factor in primary and secondary education.

The conflict between equality and choice in education is not quite as simple as has often been stated, however. On the one hand, there is the suspicion that open choice in a situation where poor, and relatively uneducated people are concentrated in one geographic area, and the educated, well-off in another, will not provide equal options for both groups. Because of geographic and transportation constraints, and because movement to the 'best' schools will mean travel to the well-off areas, choice will be unbalanced, and the result could compound existing inequality. In addition to the geographic problem, free-wheeling schools could either blatantly or subtly discriminate; the wealthy could bid up the price of quality education by supplementing public funding; and entrance requirements could be erected that would bar lateral entry into top schools from those coming from inferior schools. In theory market incentives for both schools and parents lead directly to these results.[11]

On the other hand, as is pointed out by Coons, Chubb and Peterson in this volume, and a number of other choice proponents elsewhere, the current situation is the epitome of inequality because it provides choice primarily to the middle and upper class families who can afford a home in the suburbs or the price of private schools for their children. One way of stating their position is that because choice already exists for many, government choice plans, constrained to control for discrimination, selective admission, supplemental payments, etc, must be instituted to further equity. This argument places equity alongside other theoretical advantages of choice, such as innovation, efficiency, and school autonomy.

Conclusions

The pro and con arguments for choice and decentralization are difficult to sort out. This book was conceived to help sort out both the theoretical issues and what is known empirically about the effects of such proposals both in education and in other organizational settings. As the chapters to follow will indicate, although experimentation is going on, we have as yet little conclusive evidence on results. Although this makes precise policy recommendations difficult, the logical arguments supporting decentralization and choice are compelling. Although the notion of school as a community sounds like a phrase a public relations minded principal might use, schools are very personal, labor intensive organizations. It makes sense to give those who work in them and those most directly affected by the results decision-making power in the school. In addition, given the landscape of American education, at least as I have portrayed it, centralized control seems inherently difficult and has a poor record of success where it has been most pronounced — in large, urban districts.

Finally, I find persuasive the normative argument that because many well-off families already have opportunities for real choice in education, it is equitable to extend it to those not as fortunate. The mechanisms for extending choice and the geographic barriers created by segregated housing patterns may limit what can be done without extensive changes outside of schools. However, extended choice may itself affect the other factors that have created such intolerable social and economic conditions for many urban families.

Having said this, however, it seems prudent to also caution that decentralization and choice are not panaceas for solving the complex and very serious problems that affect overall achievement and inequity of achievement in the most problematic public school districts. To trumpet these policies as the road to salvation, as the more strident reformers seem to be doing, could seriously damage the viability of both concepts. The problems in many districts extend well beyond the schools, and they have existed for a considerable period of time, outlasting numerous educational reform movements. For those districts where the problems are the most serious, undue expectations or singular adherence to these policies will have us in ten years looking backward on decentralization and choice as simply another set of failed reforms.

Notes

1 The term 'polyarchy' is associated with the work of Robert Dahl and Charles Lindblom. See Dahl and Lindblom, 1953; Dahl, 1971; Lindblom, 1977.

2 For the period from 1967 to 1986 the declines in the percentage of white students in the eight largest school districts are as follows: New York (26 per cent); Los Angeles (37 per cent); Chicago (27 per cent); Dade Co. (40 per cent); Houston (37 per cent); Philadelphia (15 per cent); Detroit (32 per cent); Dallas (42 per cent) (see Orfield and Monfort, 1988, p. 12).

3 For a review of these findings and literature see the the Bryk, Lee and Smith chapter in this volume.

4 In our study of the Milwaukee metropolitan school districts we found that twenty-five districts used eighteen different achievement tests, sometimes two or three different tests in a district. Minimum competency testing was embraced in some districts and detested in others. In districts where testing was an important means of accountability, the different tests led to different textbooks and curricula geared to the tests. Thus even at the elementary level, basic reading and mathematics skills were taught by varying methods across the metropolitan area.

5 Although the notion of control (or 'power' or 'authority') is at the center of a larger volume of political science theory, the discipline has made almost no progress in actually measuring these concepts. An excellent discussion of the empirical theory of power exists in Jack Nagel (1975) *A Descriptive Analysis of Power*, New Haven, Yale University Press. However, that theory has not been used extensively in empirical research primarily because the definition of power he employs is: 'A power relation, actual or potential, is an actual or potential causal relation between the preferences of an actor regarding an outcome and the outcome itself' (Nagel, 1975, p. 29). Because preferences and causality are very difficult to ascertain in even micro-reseach involving very limited numbers of actors and decisions, measuring power in even an indirect manner has been rarely attempted. This lack of evidence of course does not restrain us from making continuous claims concerning the power of business, labor, capitalists, presidents, administrators, etc.

6 These definitions of control, influence and power differ from the definition of Jack Nagel, or the generic precursor of that definition as advanced by Nagel's mentors, Robert Dahl and Charles Lindblom. They defined control as 'B is controlled by A to the extent that B's responses are dependent on A's acts in an immediate and functional relationship' (Dahl and Lindblom, 1953, p. 94). My intent is to limit the definition of control to relationships in a specific decision-making framework. Under my terminology, one actor could control a specific decision, even if the decision does not produce the intended behavioral outcome. For example, a district superintendent could 'control', (i.e. have final say) over decisions on math pedagogy in the third grade, but teachers could sabotage that decision once the classroom door closes. Under my terms, the superintendent would have control, but as defined by Dahl, Lindblom and Nagel, she would not.

7 Arguments for close school-community involvement and parental influence in school decisions stretch from the New Haven, Connecticut High School in the Community project in the late 1960s, to Coleman and Hoffer's recent

arguments that the close ties of Catholic schools to their communities and parents may explain their superior performance over public schools. Recent evidence by Witte and Walsh indicates that higher levels of involvement of parents in public schools are linked to higher student achievement (see Coleman and Hoffer, 1987; Witte and Walsh, 1990).

8 The lineage of this general argument extends to Adam Smith, but also includes the twentieth century work of Hayek's mentor, Von Mises, his senior colleague at the University of Chicago, Frank Knight, and his students, colleagues and those who learned and shared in his work — Milton Friedman, James Buchanan, George Stigler, and Charles Lindblom.

9 One of the most amazing incidents in a Governor's study commission of the Milwaukee metropolitan school districts that I headed several years ago, occurred immediately following the printing of the final report for the Governor and legislature. Within ten days, the Milwaukee Public School system had produced a document, considerably longer than the report, that outlined either how it was already meeting each of the thirty-five recommendations or how it would meet them in the next five years. The document was replete not only with plans and programs, but with charts, objectives, five-year goals, and precise measures. The document has long since gone to the same grave as the commission report, but my stunned reaction to this bureaucratic masterpiece remains vivid in my mind.

10 The difference reported in this article may well be exaggerated in that regression models estimating morale, influence, etc., included no controls for student or school characteristics. However, the authors report that a book-length study to follow employs extensive controls and differences remain.

11 If one doubts this, try to locate private schools that have recently begun or moved to central cities. One of the interesting findings in *High School and Beyond* data was the concentration of Catholic high schools in the suburbs. This contrasts with the origin of Catholic high schools in urban centers. It would appear, Christian motives aside, that these schools have followed the 'market'.

References

Alexander, K. A. and Pallas, A.M. (1985) 'School sector and cognitive performance', *Sociology of Education*, April, pp. 115–27.

Accountability Reporting in the States (1988) *Report of a Survey — 1987*. State Education Assessment Center, Council of Chief State School Officers.

Chubb, J.E. and Moe T. M. (1988) 'Politics, markets, and the organization of schools', *American Political Science Review*, **82**, pp. 1065–87.

Coleman, J.S., Hoffer T. and Kilgore S. (1982) *High School Achievement*, New York: Basic Books.

Coleman, J.S. and Hoffer, T. (1987) *Public and Private High Schools*, New York: Basic Books.

Dahl, R.A. (1971) *Polyarchy*, New Haven: Yale University Press.

Dahl, R.A. and Lindblom, C.E. (1953) *Politics, Economics, and Welfare*, Chicago: The University of Chicago Press.

Digest of Educational Statistics (1988) Washington: US Government Printing Office.

Friedman, M. (1962) 'The role of government in education', in *Capitalism and Freedom*, Chicago: University of Chicago Press.

Hayek, F.A. (1944) *The Road to Serfdom,* Chicago: The University of Chicago Press.

Hayek, F.A. (1960) *The Constitution of Liberty*, Chicago: The University of Chicago Press.

Hayek, F.A. (1973) *Law, Legislation and Liberty: Volume I Rules and Order*, Chicago: The University of Chicago Press.

Hayek, F.A. (1976) *Law, Legislation and Liberty: Volume II The Mirage of Social Justice*, Chicago: The University of Chicago Press.

Hayek, F.A. (1979) *Law, Legislation and Liberty: Volume III The Political Order of a Free Society*, Chicago: The University of Chicago Press.

Hirschman, A.O. (1970) *Exit, Voice, and Loyalty*, Cambridge, MA: Harvard University Press.

Lindblom, C.E. (1977) *Politics and Markets*, New York: Free Press.

Nagel, J.H. (1975) *The Descriptive Analysis of Power*, New Haven: Yale University Press.

Newmann, F.M., Rutter R.A. and Smith, M.S. (1987) 'Teachers' sense of efficacy and community as critical targets for school improvement', National Center on Effective Secondary Schools, University of Wisconsin, Madison.

Orfield, G. and Monfort, F. (1988) *Change in the Racial Composition and Segregation of Large School Districts, 1967–1986*, Preliminary report to the National School Boards Association.

Peterson, P.E. (1976) *School Politics: Chicago Style*, Chicago: The University of Chicago Press.

Peterson, P.E. (1985) *The Politics of School Reform: 1870–1940*, Chicago: The University of Chicago Press.

Powell, A.G., Farrar, E. and Cohen D.K. (1985) *The Shopping Mall High School: Winners and Losers in the Educational Market Place*, New York: Houghton Mifflin.

Rae, D.W. (1980) *Equalities*, Cambridge, MA: Harvard University Press.

Tyack, D. (1974) *The One Best System*, Cambridge: Harvard University Press.

Weick, K.E. (1976) 'Educational organizations as loosely coupled systems', *Administrative Sciences Quarterly*, **21**, pp. 1–19.

Witte, J.F. and Walsh, D. (forthcoming) 'A systematic test of the effective schools model', *Educational Evaluation and Policy Analysis*.

Chapter 2

Monopoly and Competition in American Education

Paul E. Peterson

In this chapter I shall explore the ways in which the public schools reduced choice by squeezing out potential competitors through its quasi-monopoly of education. I shall interpret the early creation of the high school as an effort by educators to secure status and influence for the organization for which they were responsible. I shall examine the ways in which the public schools defeated efforts to create a separate institution of vocational schools, crushed movements to provide public financing of religious-based education, benefited from the urbanization of the population during the early twentieth century, received increasingly centralized financing as the century wore on, and, finally, responded to pressures to incorporate disadvantaged groups into the public school system, once their monopoly position was well-established. Secondly, I shall look at the ways in which this quasi-monopoly has been qualified by more recent social and political trends, including the suburbanization of metropolitan areas and white response to racial integration. Finally, I will look at the politics that will shape the future of the public school monopoly, including the contemporary viability of the equal opportunity myth, the influence of the public school lobby, the fiscal factors limiting the growth of privately-financed elementary and secondary education, and the politics of a variety of pro-choice schemes.

It is an iron law of organizations that they seek to expand their size, their scope of operation, and their autonomy from external influence.[1] Expansion provides new resources to fulfill organizational objectives, more opportunity for promotion for organizational members, greater status in the wider society, and a capacity to diversify, lowering the risk that the failure of any particular venture will undermine the organization as a whole. If completely successful, the organization acquires a monopoly of activity within a particular domain, enabling it to impose monopoly costs on others and to enjoy privileges available only in a non-competitive environment.

Most organizations do not succeed in achieving a monopoly position. Countervailing forces and competing institutions curb monopoly ambition long before it is realized. But public schools in the United States, though also constrained by competition in many ways, have come closer than most institutions to consolidating a position of monopoly power. Yet monopolies are difficult to maintain over the long run. The recent demands for more choice in education are only the latest in a number of challenges faced by the public school monopoly over the course of its development.

The success of the public school system in fending off incursions into its monopoly position has been made possible only by capturing a powerful set of legitimating symbols: social democracy, equal opportunity, and the desirability of a common, homogenizing experience in a pluralist society. The schools also have been successful in appealing to diverse ethnic and cultural interests, reaching out first to European immigrant groups and eventually to Afro-Americans, Hispanics and Asians as well. But the group whose steadfast support was most crucial during the great expansion of the public schools in the late nineteenth and early twentieth century was the growing middle class business and professional classes, who chose public education as the vehicle for educating their children in a context where private alternatives were available.

In this chapter I shall explore the ways in which the public schools reduced choice by squeezing out potential competitors to its quasi-monopoly over the education of the next generation. I shall interpret the early creation of the high school as an effort by educators to secure status and influence for the organization for which they were responsible. I shall examine the ways in which the public schools defeated efforts to create a separate institution of vocational schools, crushed movements to provide public financing of religious-based education, benefited from the urbanization of the population during the early twentieth century, received increasingly centralized financing as the century wore on, and, finally, responded to pressures to incorporate disadvantaged groups into the public school system, once their monopoly position was well-established.

Secondly, I shall look at the ways in which this quasi-monopoly has been qualified by more recent social and political trends, including the suburbanization of metropolitan areas and white response to racial integration. Finally, I will look at the politics that will shape the future of the public school monopoly, including the contemporary viability of the equal opportunity myth, the influence of the public school lobby, the fiscal factors limiting the growth of privately-financed elementary and secondary education, and the politics of a variety of pro-choice schemes.

The Concept of Monopoly

Monopoly can be easily construed as simply a pejorative term, as a concept connoting coercive power, insensitivity to political pressures or disregard for the interests of minorities. Since we shall use the word in a more technical manner and regard the consequences of the quasi-monopoly in education as essentially ambiguous, it is worth making clear from the outset what is meant — and what is not meant — by this term.

The concept of monopoly as used in this chapter refers to the exclusiveness with which a type of good or service is distributed within a particular market by a single provider. Although in some theoretical analyses a monopoly is treated as a dichotomy — either something is or is not a monopoly — in the real world one must treat monopolies as variables — as entities that have more or less complete control of a market. Very few complete monopolies have ever been created, if only because there are almost always places where the monopolist has no control and substitutes for goods or services the monopolist provides. The 'legitimate use of violence' is perhaps the limiting case; as Max Weber pointed out, only the state has the capacity to provide this service, though even in the case of violence the state monopoly is sometimes challenged by vigilante groups or Batman-type figures whose use of force may be regarded by many as legitimate. For other goods and services monopolies, where they exist, are usually much less complete. The United States post office has a monopoly on the public mail, but alternative ways of communicating with distant others — telephone, federal express, and FAX — have severely eroded the post office's monopoly position for all but junk mail. In the field of education the monopoly position of the public school is also less than complete, and therefore I shall use the word monopoly and quasi-monopoly interchangeably to emphasize the less than perfect domination of this service sector by public schools.

The definition of a market is also problematic. Just as one can usually find a product substitute, so one can usually avoid buying from the monopolist if one is willing to travel far enough. The summer grocery store located at a remote vacation retreat can charge monopoly prices for its perishables, but the shrewd consumer can avoid paying the price by bringing his or her foodstuffs from home or periodically making long forays to a more densely populated area. Distance is also a significant factor affecting the degree of monopoly a public school enjoys. If consumers can move to a nearby place where educational services are controlled by a different authority, then public schools may find themselves competing with one another, even though each has a monopoly on the provision of service within a specific territory. If alternative educational opportunities are available only by means of long-distance moves, then the monopoly position of the local public school is more secure.

Public school monopolies can thus be made more complete in two ways. First, the more extensive the boundaries of an authority throughout a given labor market, the more complete the monopoly. A local school authority with jurisdiction over an entire metropolitan areas is more of a monopolist than a small suburban board whose writ is limited to a small geographic area. Central city school boards thus have traditionally been in a stronger monopolistic position than suburban systems. Second, more monopolistic power can be acquired by centralizing authority at higher levels of government with more inclusive territorial jurisdictions. To the extent that all school districts must follow the same policies of the state or the nation, whether by legislative fiat or judicial decree, to that extent each school authority is less constrained by competition.

The existence or extent of a monopoly is unrelated to the processes by which it came into being. Many monopolies are often established through highly competitive processes. For example, Standard Oil established its quasi-monopoly within the oil industry only after ruthlessly undercutting the prices of its competitors. In education, as we shall see, the public schools established their monopolistic position only through a complex, highly competitive process in which they drew upon the support of a wide variety of different groups and interests.[2]

Nor does the existence and extent of a monopoly tell one anything about the political relationships among those seeking to influence the monopoly. A monopoly might be held by a single individual or family, it might be held by a corporation in which competition among stockholders is intense, or it might be held by a government which is subject to a wide range of political pressures. Monopolies are generally very valuable, because a monopoly rent can be collected. One suspects, therefore, that the more complete the monopoly, the more intense is the effort to influence its policies. Should the rent go to the workers, the managers, or the stockholders? The answer may not be given until after a good deal of political struggle. In the automobile industry the union-management conflict was in fact a good deal more intense in the fifties and sixties when automobile companies still enjoyed a quasi-monopolistic position than in recent years when the industry has been subject to stronger competitive forces.[3]

Finally, one should not simply conclude that all monopolies are evil. One hardly wishes to strip from the state a monopoly of the legitimate use of violence. Many other monopolies are 'natural' or desirable, including the control of dams, major thoroughfares, sewer systems, fire-fighting companies and the like. Even monopolies that are not necessarily 'natural' such as the one enjoyed by AT&T were thought by many to be good and desirable, because the monopolist was thought to be providing higher quality and more equitable services than would have been provided by a more competitive communication industry. Informed opinion on this question is still divided, even though we have had a decade of experience with a more competitive communication industry.

Generally speaking, we expect monopolies to be less efficient but more equitable than service providers in a more competitive context. In a competitive industry each firm will try to meet market demand at the lowest cost permitted by current technology. Each firm will expect each customer to pay the marginal cost of supplying the services it receives. Any firm that does not pursue such a strategy will surrender market share, profits, and long-term viability. In the pure case of perfect competition, redistribution becomes impossible. Monopolies are less efficient because more efficient firms cannot attract business away from them by pricing goods and services at a lower cost. However, the monopolist can be more redistributive because its monopoly rent can be used for discretionary purposes, some of which may be redistributive. For example, AT&T charged residential consumers less than business consumers not because residential services cost less to provide but because the policy stabilized political support for the monopoly. We shall see that in education the closer the public school came to establishing a complete monopoly, the more vulnerable it became to redistributive demands. Only when somewhat greater levels of competition returned to the system of public education did these redistributive pressures recede.[4]

The Drive for Monopoly Control

The quasi-monopoly in public education is today so pervasive a fact of American life that its existence is pretty much taken for granted. But a century ago the place of public schools in the American educational system was not something that could simply be assumed. Nearly one-third of all high school students were being privately educated as late as 1890. Religious groups were establishing their own schools (sometimes in languages other than English as a way of maintaining the cultural life of their native land), and business groups were proposing the establishment of a vocational education system separate and apart from the public school. Public school people responded by calling for the establishment of a common school that would serve all members of society. They claimed that it could become the great instrument of democratization and homogenization that a pluralist society desperately needed. Their success in persuading Americans to accept their vision of a common school is in fact one of the great political accomplishments of the late nineteenth and early twentieth century.

The Early High School

The establishment of the public secondary school was realized only with careful political calculation. Until well into this century there had remained the potential of a two track system established along European lines, with the lower track financed publicly and the higher one financed privately or perhaps with some public support. If schools were to become 'common schools' serving all segments of the society, they had to reach more than just the children of poor immigrants. They could become genuinely common schools only if they served the needs of those groups in the population that had an educational alternative. Most important among those who had alternatives were the middle class families who might send their children to private schools but could be induced to have them attend free public schools, if those schools established respectable standards.

As a result of the need to establish respectability, the early public high schools were academically oriented institutions that served limited numbers of students with special educational talent. They were established, moreover, at a time when elementary schools were overcrowded and quite unable to serve adequately immigrant and minority populations. The most extreme examples were in the South. In Atlanta, for example, separate academically oriented high schools for white boys and white girls were established in 1870, a time when the school board insisted it had inadequate resources to provide black children with anything other than hopelessly overcrowded shacks.[5]

Similar, if less extreme examples of diverting meager resources to prestige, academically-oriented institutions, could be found in other parts of the country. In San Francisco elementary schools were also extremely crowded, children were refused access and teacher-pupil ratios were very high. Yet the school board chose to use some of its limited funds to build a boys' high school, which catered to a middle-class clientele. Working-class groups were so disturbed by this decision that the school superintendent was forced to defend his policy by claiming that the high school admitted

Table 2.1: Occupations of fathers of students at a boys' high school and composition of work force, San Francisco

Occupations	1878	1883	Work force 1890
High prestige white collar and merchants	43.8	39.0	5.0
Low white collar	27.7	40.7	25.7
Artisans and skilled workers	14.9	12.7	28.4
Semi-skilled workers	9.6	4.3	27.9
Unskilled workers	4.0	3.3	12.9
Total	100.0	100.0	100.0
(N)	(249)	(300)	

Source: Paul E. Peterson (1985) *The Politics of School Reform, 1870–1940*, Chicago: University of Chicago Press, p. 62.

children of all classes. But the data he presented to support his argument (Table 2.1) only revealed the middle-class bias of the institution. In 1878, 44 per cent of the children in the school came from white collar families, even though these families made up but 5 per cent of the work force of the city at that time.

The success that school officials had in establishing the public high school can be seen from the changes in the percentages of students attending public schools during the early decades of the twentieth century. As can be seen in Table 2.2, nearly one-third of all high school students were attending private schools in 1890; the percentage in private schools fell to 18 per cent over the next decade. The numbers in private school did not decline during this decade — in fact they increased somewhat. But

Table 2.2: Enrollment in private high schools, 1890–1985

Year	No. of students	Percentage of all high school students
1890	94,931	31.9
1900	110,797	17.6
1910	117,400	11.4
1920	213,920	8.9
1930	341,158	7.2
1940	457,768	6.5
1950	672,362	10.5
1960	1,035,247	10.9
1970	1,300,000	9.1
1980	1,300,000	8.6
1986	1,300,000	9.6

Source: US Department of Education, Office of Educational Research and Improvement. Center for Statistics (1988) *Digest of Education Statistics, 1987–88*, Table 44., p. 60.

private school enrollments were being swamped by the enormous growth in the numbers attending public school. By 1910 the percentage in private schools fell still further to 11 per cent and the steady decline continued until 1940 when but 6.5 per cent of high school students were being educated privately. A nearly complete public school monopoly had finally been achieved.

Religious Schools

Ethnic and religious interests constituted a second threat to the monopolistic development of the public schools. The populations of nineteenth century cities were swollen with European immigrants, many of whom chose to send their children to Catholic schools for various reasons, including religious training, preservation of their ethnic cultures, and a belief that the public schools were infused with a Protestant ethos symbolized by the use of the St. James version of the Bible in daily scripture reading. Catholics sought public support for the schools they had created, and in a few instances where they were concentrated in particularly large numbers they succeeded at least for a short period of time. In San Francisco, for example, the city provided funds to Catholic schools between 1852 and 1855 by means of an ordinance that stated quite frankly that schools 'formed by the enterprise of a religious society in which all the educational branches of the district schools shall be taught . . . should be eligible to receive public funds'. The policy even won the endorsement of the state school superintendent on the grounds that denominational schools eased the state's cost of providing education to its children.

Public support for educational and religious diversity was a short-lived experiment, however. The California legislature prohibited the practice in 1855. In so doing, they were only following a powerful national trend that was mainly motivated by the prejudice and suspicion of Protestant America toward the large numbers of immigrant Irish and southern European Catholics that had prompted the formation of the Know-Nothing Party, the American Party and other ethnically and religiously self-conscious political groups. The most intense effort to win public assistance for Catholic schools took place in New York City during the 1840s. The conflict was intensified by the fact that tax dollars were already being used to sustain a school system operated by a private, religiously-based organization, misnamed the Public School Society, which was openly Protestant in orientation.

New York Catholics criticized the Public School monopoly of education more for its religious than its educational consequences:

> Should the professors of some weak or unpopular religions be oppressed today, the experiment may be repeated tomorrow on some other. Every successful attempt in that way will embolden the spirit of encroachment . . . and . . . the monopolizers of education, after having discharged the office of public tutor, may find it convenient to assume that of public preacher.[6]

Catholics managed to dismantle the Public School Society and replace it with a state-run school system, but they were unable to win public grants for their own schools.

The opposition to public support for Catholic education became a nationwide political movement after the Civil War. Even the great war hero, Ulysses S. Grant, as president urged 'that every child in the land may get a common school education unmixed with atheistic, pagan, or sectarian teaching'.[7] Grant made these comments in the midst of a campaign by Republican Presidential hopeful James G. Blaine to pass a constitutional amendment prohibiting the use of state funds for sectarian schools. The campaign was extraordinarily successful, and the bill won the necessary two-thirds vote in the House of Representatives. Although the constitutional amendment failed in the Senate, the issue remained lively in state politics. Eventually, the argument would be made, more or less successfully, that the Constitution already prohibited aid to denominational schools, thereby achieving by court interpretation that which could not be passed even in the hey-day of anti-Catholic sentiment. And in the course of this controversy public school educators led the fight against aid to parochial schools. As early as 1869 the National Teachers Association, forerunner of the National Education Association (NEA), declared that 'the appropriation of public funds for the support of sectarian schools is a violation of the fundamental principles of our American system of education'.[8] Twenty years later John Jay, speaking at a NEA convention, accused the Roman Catholic church of a 'conspiracy to defraud the common school', aided in its dirty work by "the foreign element, uninstructed in American civilization".[9] When the Catholic archbishop John Ireland, founder of the prestigious College of St. Thomas, was finally invited to address the NEA the following year, he 'felt he had to preface his remarks by saying that he was not and never had been un-American or an enemy of public education'.[10]

Unable to win public support for aid to parochial schools, Catholics consequently objected to paying taxes for schools they did not use. They also consistently opposed the 'extravagances' of special subjects in public schools, claiming that '. . . the rudiments of a sound English education — reading, writing and arithmetic, with perhaps a little history and geography — are all the State should be called upon to provide for by taxation'.[11]

Over time Catholic opposition to public schools retreated to a simple reluctance to pay high taxes for public schools their children did not attend and an attempt to maintain parish schools in the face of an increasingly well-endowed competitor. Once it was decided that parochial schools could not receive public funds, the public schools pretty much ignored the parish schools. Although they represented a competitive element in the public school environment, Catholic schools lacked prestige, educated an immigrant, working-class population, and constituted neither a symbolic nor material threat to public school dominance. But gradually, almost imperceptibly, Catholic education acquired an enhanced standing and distinction that came with the integration of Catholic immigrants into the mainstream of the American economy and society. The significance of this development would become apparent only in the 1980s when the first national study of public and private education discovered that Catholic parochial schools provided a better learning environment for both white and black Americans.[12]

Vocational Education

The struggle for monopoly position by the public school advocates did not end with the containment of the influence of the private, academically-oriented day and boarding schools, or the check of the threat posed by parochial education.[13] In fact the major problem for the public school came not from private education, whose role had been fairly well circumscribed by the end of the nineteenth century, but by the rising interest in vocational education. This new threat to the public school had to be taken seriously, for it had the vigorous backing of some of the most powerful business groups in America. Although the battleground for this struggle would eventually be nationwide, the seriousness of the contest can best be understood by looking at the way in which the issue developed in Chicago, a city where class conflict during the early twentieth century was particularly intense.

Beginning in the late nineteenth century many educators, business groups and trade unions had been advocating some form of occupationally-related training for young adults upon the completion of their elementary school education. One of the earliest, most vigorous advocates of vocational education was the Chicago Commercial Club, a group of the city's leading businessmen. In their view the appropriate structure for vocational education was an institution separate and apart from the public schools, headed by a board consisting of two businessmen, two skilled employees and the superintendent of schools.

The Commercial Club's proposal was backed by Edwin Cooley, Chicago's school superintendent from 1900 to 1909, who was strongly committed to vocational education, and who, in fact, established a commercial high school near the downtown business district during his term of office. Upon his resignation as superintendent, he devoted many years to the active promotion of vocational education, and the major bill to provide vocational training in Illinois became known as the Cooley bill.

Cooley had not been popular with educators, reformers or labor officials during his tenure as school superintendent, and their view of him did not improve with time. Labor was afraid a separate vocational education system would be used to indoctrinate workers against trade unionism.[14] School people were more concerned that a separate vocational educational system would divide public education into competing sets of institutions, weakening the monopoly position of each. As Ella Flagg Young, Cooley's successor as superintendent, declared:

> Under one head and one authority all great projects have been brought to successful results. To divide the responsibility is to weaken the result. Not from any personal idea, but from an idea for the community's best good, I oppose the . . . (Cooley) bill.[15]

The stance of public educators was dressed up in fine pedagogical terms, of course. Business leaders were looking for training in specific skills that could lead to immediate employment. They thus favored an administrative structure devoted solely to vocational education. Many educators insisted, however, that vocational education be thoroughly integrated with a child's general education. By providing children with a direct encounter with specific occupational experiences in a context where broader educational purposes were also embedded, a child's curiosity could be awakened and turned toward larger questions that could be satisfied through the study of science, the fine arts, and languages.

The debate in Chicago was repeated throughout the country and in fact became a national political issue in the years just prior to World War I. The National Association of Manufacturers advocated 'independent boards of vocational education, composed mainly of employers and employees'.[16] The American Federation of Labor agreed that trade instruction should be supported with public funds and also felt an advisory committee consisting of representatives from business and labor was appropriate, but 'it was adamant in its insistence that vocational education . . . not be separated from the public school system'.[17] School officials could not have said it better.

The issue was more or less resolved when a Commission on National Aid to Vocational Education was appointed by President Woodrow Wilson in 1914. It recommended that money be granted to three types of public schools: 'all-day secondary schools in which about half of the time was spent in vocational education, part-time schools for young workers, and to evening schools'. As implemented by the Smith-Hughes legislation in 1917, the money in fact went solely to public schools.

Educator commitment to the ideal of an integrated educational experience seems to have been more deeply held in theory than in practice. In Chicago, as in other American cities, the kind of vocational education that emerged within the public schools was twofold. The least successful was the vocational wing of the comprehensive high school; when visitors looked at these programs as they were operating in the 1980s, they seemed little more than '"dumping grounds" for students deemed unlikely candidates for college preparatory courses'.[18] Vocational instruction was rudimentary because neither staff nor equipment was available for more advanced courses. As one school administrator explained 'Our shops are not truly vocational'. The most successful courses were those in secretarial training, but even in this area equipment was badly outdated. 'The wisest investment we could make, if the money was available', one administrator said, 'would be to update all our typewriter labs so that they were entirely electric'.[19]

Full-time vocational schools established within the public school system were much more successful. Popular among students, well-supported by unions and industry, endowed with fairly up-to-date equipment, these vocational schools provided sophisticated training in specialized vocational activities as well as basic educational instruction. Apparently, Chicago educators had nothing against vocational schools as long as they were under the direct control of the school system.

The Big Big City School System

Even in the absence of competing educational systems, the public school monopoly was not complete. Quite apart from private schools, religious schools, and vocational education, public schools were potential competitors with each other. Even within one city, each neighborhood school competed with other public schools in other parts of the city. This competition was usually contained, however, by school board policies requiring that parents send their children to the school serving their particular neighborhood.

Some parents were still able to exercise choice by selecting as a place of residence the catchment area for a desired school. Because the best schools usually were located in residential areas where property was particularly valuable — the quality of the school itself helping to drive up the value of that property — this option was, of course, more readily available to the relatively affluent. School boards usually attempted to contain as best they could this kind of competition as well. The most popular method of controlling interschool competition within a school district was by establishing citywide policies that insured that all schools had the same resources. Even Chicago, a city better known for its machine-style politics and particularistic adaptation to specific political pressures, had rigid formulae allocating resources, such as the following one that addressed the question of class size:

> In the elementary school the class size from room to room should not deviate any more than is absolutely essential. As a 'rule of thumb', the class size . . . should not deviate by more than 10 per cent — 15 per cent as a maximum. In a large school this deviation should be far less than 10 to 15 per cent. (Peterson, 1976, p. 124)[20]

Rules designed to distribute resources evenly were applied not only to programs within a school but also to the allocation of resources among schools. A study of Chicago and Atlanta found that in both cities, expenditures per pupil, teacher/pupil ratios, expenditures for supplies, and most other resources were equally distributed to schools attended by groups of all income categories.[21] These findings were confirmed by a second study of these cities, which included a third city, Boston, as well. According to the analyst, 'The three cities are strikingly similar in the relatively equal distribution of expenditures per student'.[22]

Such rules were not of modern vintage. As early as 1897 similarity of treatment of diverse ethnic groups was evident in both Chicago and San Francisco. Schools in Chicago attended by Italians, Anglos, the Irish, Swedes, and Germans varied in average class size by only between forty-seven and forty-nine pupils per teacher. The variation in San Francisco in the late nineteenth and early twentieth century was similarly small — different ethnic groups attended schools that varied in class size by no more than two or three students.[23]

Uniform school board policies minimized the competition among schools within large central cities. And it was in the big central city that American education was growing most rapidly during the early decades of the twentieth century. Between 1900 and 1940 the percentage of the US population living in cities over 250,000 in size increased from 14 to 23 per cent; the percentage living in cities over 50,000 increased from 22 to 34 per cent (Table 2.3). For the next three decades — until 1970 — the percentage

Table 2.3: Distribution of US population among political jurisdictions of various sizes, 1900–1986

Year	Percentage living in cities		
	Above 250,000	*Above 50,000*	*Less than 50,000*
1900	14.3	22.1	68.5
1920	19.6	30.7	57.9
1940	22.8	34.2	52.6
1970	20.7	35.9	45.0
1986	17.9	33.5	50.0

Sources: US Bureau of the Census, *Historical Statistics,* Series, A 57–72; US Bureau of the Census, *Statistical Abstract of the United States*, Table 37, p. 32.

of Americans living in these large aggregations remained fairly constant (though there is a slight drop in those living in the largest cities after 1970). Americans had learned to live and work in big, industrial cities governed by political entities that had control over hundreds of thousands of their neighbors. In this context public education became a matter over which individual families had very little say. Choosing among neighborhoods was to choose within the limits established by the big city school board. Choosing outside the boundaries of the big city was not a realistic choice for most urban dwellers. Public educators realized as monopolistic a position as they would ever enjoy.

This trend to bigger, more centrally controlled schools can be seen in school statistics as well. As late as 1930 the average sized public school was under a hundred pupils (Table 2.4). Over the next two decades it would nearly double in size; between 1950 and 1970 its size would more than double again to nearly five hundred pupils. Much of this transformation was simply the elimination of the one-room schoolhouse in rural America. But the trend toward bigness was broader than that. Quite apart from the decline in the one-room school, average school size would increase from around 200 in 1930 to nearly 350 in 1950 and then to over 500 in 1970 (Table 2.4). The size of the school attended by the average child was, of course, much larger, because many more students were taught in schools above the average than below it. The only available estimate of the size of the school attended by the average student is for 1980. In that year the average student attended a school of about 1250 students, almost twice the number of students in the average schools.[24] If the same ratio applies for earlier periods, the school attended by the average child increased in size from around 200 in 1930 to nearly 1300 in 1970.

The trend toward bigger schools was not accidental. On the contrary,

Table 2.4: Average size of public schools and public school districts, 1930–1980

Year	Pupils/School	Pupils/School (Non-Rural)	Pupils/District
1930	97.9	187.7	201.0
1940	122.1	232.7	217.2
1950	164.3	347.8	300.0
1960	299.1	331.1	868.3
1970	503.6	513.0	2,558.3
1980	479.8	479.0	2,575.9

Source: Calculated from US Department of Education, Office of Educational Research and Improvement, Center for Statistics, *Digest of Education Statistics, 1985–86.*

educators, who at this time enjoyed more credibility and influence than ever before or since, were extolling the virtues of the comprehensive high school and the sophisticated elementary schools that could provide diverse educational experiences within a single building. School superintendents were building big new schools to house the baby boomers entering the educational system, and state departments of education were hounding small, rural school districts out of existence. Even James Conant, more thoughtful than many of the efficiency-minded educators of the day, concluded that a good high school needed a graduating class of one hundred to operate effectively.[25]

It was not only schools that were becoming bigger. School districts, too, were growing in size, in part because the United States was becoming a more urban country, but also in part because it was believed that big systems could operate more efficient, more effective schools. While the average school district in 1930 served only two hundred students and the average district in 1950 served just three hundred, by 1970 the average district served over 2500 (Table 2.4). The American educational system was growing bigger and, presumably, better. At the very least, it seems that educators worried very little about the virtues of choice and decentralization. At most, they saw quite clearly the advantages of a monopoly position.

Centralizing the Financing of Public Education

Rural, small-school, small-district education had been locally financed. As late as 1930 over 85 per cent of the cost of public education was paid for out of local government funds. But during the depression local school districts went bankrupt, teachers could not be paid, and the limits of the property tax as a source of revenue became painfully obvious. Schools turned to the

Table 2.5: Revenue sources of public elementary and secondary schools, 1920–1988, in percentages

Year	Federal	State	Local
1920	0.3	16	83
1930	0.4	17	83
1940	2	30	68
1950	3	40	57
1960	4	39	56
1970	8	40	52
1980	10	46	45
1988	6	50	44

Source: US Department of Education, Office of Educational Research and Improvement, Center for Statistics (1986) *Digest of Education Statistics 1985–86*, Washington, DC: GPO, Tables 26, 69; National Education Association (1988) *Data Search: Rankings of the States, 1988*, West Haven, Ct: NEA, p. 43.

state for help, and over the next two decades state aid to public education increased from 17 per cent of the total in 1930 to 40 per cent in 1950 (Table 2.5).

The move toward state aid had several advantages to those responsible for public education. Not only did it secure for the schools more stable financing, but it also helped protect educators from intense local scrutiny. As schools and school districts were growing in size, and as parental choice was diminishing, the power of the purse was also shifting from the local community to a more amorphous, statewide jurisdiction in which the organized power of educational professionals would have greater weight.

The shift toward more centralized financing would continue after 1950 but at a significantly slower pace. The local percentage of support would fall from 57 to 44 per cent between 1950 and 1988 (Table 2.5). Although this continued shift away from local financing was not inconsiderable, it is probably significant that whereas the shift away from the local community was occurring at a rate of 1.3 per cent a year between 1930 and 1950, it slowed to a rate of less than .4 per cent after 1950. After 1980 the shift away from the locality is barely perceptible; the increase in state aid was merely replacing the diminishing number of federal dollars.

The Incorporation of Minorities

In the years after World War II the triumph of the public school seemed complete. A stable, near complete monopoly had been established in spite of competition from private preparatory schools, Catholic demands for state funding, and business promotion of separate vocational schools. More children were being educated in larger schools located within larger school districts funded increasingly by state monies. Ironically, it was this very success of the public school educators in establishing their monopoly position that made them vulnerable to forces that would eventually erode their position of nearly uncontested power. As monopolists, they would be held hostage to the egalitarian symbols they had long espoused. They could no longer deny the equal access to public education that minorities had fruitlessly demanded during the many years that public schools had been struggling to win acceptance from dominant social groups. Once the monopoly had been institutionalized, the demand for equal access to the institution became overpowering. But once the demand for equal access was conceded, dominant social groups began to doubt the desirability of a public school monopoly after all.

The process by which the public school became more vulnerable to demands from minorities has been well-told in other places.[26] Needless to say, the incorporation of blacks, Asians, the handicapped and other needy groups did not come at the insistence of most public school officials. Although some educators called for school desegregation and other reforms, most school boards became the stubborn target of civil rights demonstrations, court suits, and federal regulations. But as these pressures mounted, public schools *had* to respond in large part because they *could* respond. As monopolists, they did not need to worry about what would happen to their other consumers if they opened their doors to previously excluded groups.

The response of the public schools to minority demands in the Nineteenth Century shows how little concerned public educators had been about providing equal educational opportunity at the time they were creating what they called the 'common school'. Asians in California were first denied access to public education in the late nineteenth century, and then segregated into separate, inferior schools. Blacks in the South were even more systematically excluded from public educational services. The first public high school in the South was not constructed until 1924, and that was accomplished in Atlanta only because blacks defeated school bond referenda until this concession could be wrung from the school board.[27] In the United States as a whole only 6 per cent of blacks between the ages of 25 and 29 had received a high school education in 1920 and nearly 45 per cent had not received as much as five years of elementary schooling (Table 2.6). After World War II these figures improved dramatically. The percentage of blacks completing high school increased from 12 to 39 per cent between 1940 and 1960, and the percentage with less than five years of school fell to as little as 7 per cent. But it was in the 1960s and early

Table 2.6: Number of school years completed by persons ages 25–29, by race, 1920–1985

Year	Percentage completed			
	Less than 5 yrs		4 years of high school or more	
	Black	*White*	*Black*	*White*
1920	44.6	12.9	6.3	22.0
1940	26.7	3.4	12.1	41.2
1950	15.4	3.2	23.4	55.2
1960	7.2	0.2	38.6	63.7
1970	2.2	0.9	58.4	77.8
1985	0.5	0.8	82.4	86.8

Source: US Department of Education, Office of Educational Research and Improvement, Center for Statistics, *Digest of Education Statistics, 1985–86*, Table 10.

Table 2.7: Percentage of black students in desegregated schools, 1968–1986

	Percentage in predominantly minority schools		Percentage in 90–100% minority schools	
Year	*United States*	*South only*	*United States*	*South only*
1968	76.6	80.9	64.3	77.8
1972	63.6	55.3	38.7	24.7
1980	62.9	57.1	33.2	23.0
1984	63.5	56.9	33.2	24.2
1986	63.3	N.A.	32.5	N.A.

Source: Gary Orfield (1988) 'Race and the liberal agenda', in Wier, M. Orloff, A. and Skocpol, T. (Eds.) *The Politics of Social Policy in the United States*, Princeton, N.J.: Princeton University Press, p. 349; and Gary Orfield, 'Separate and unequal in the metropolis: The changing shape of the school desegregation battle', unpublished manuscript, p. II–5.

seventies that the greatest strides towards racial incorporation took place. Not only did the percentage of blacks completing high school increase from 39 per cent to 58 per cent between 1960 and 1970, but this was the only time that the degree of racial segregation in the public schools declined markedly (see Table 2.7). In the five years from 1968 to 1972 the percentage of blacks in predominantly minority schools fell by 13 percentage points nationwide and by 25 percentage points in the South. Since then racial segregation has remained quite constant and segregation among Hispanics has actually increased in the past twenty years (Table 2.8).

School boards were initially no more anxious to serve the handicapped than they were to admit minorities. In fact, until the end of World War II and the entry of baby boom children into the public schools, middle class

Table 2.8: Hispanic segregation by region, 1968–1986

Region	**Percentage of students in predominantly minority schools**		**Percentage of students in 90–100 % minority schools**	
	1968	*1986*	*1968*	*1986*
West	42	70	12	25
South	70	75	34	39
Northeast	75	78	44	46
Midwest	32	54	7	24
Total US	55	71	23	32

Source: Office for Civil Rights Data Tapes, from Gary Orfield 'Separate and unequal in the metropolis: The changing shape of the school desegregation battle', unpublished manuscript, p. II–7.

handicapped children were usually considered the responsibility of their parents and were routinely excluded from the public schools. At the end of World War II, the numbers of handicapped children needing special education increased dramatically, as did the school age population as a whole, causing an enormous strain on an already totally inadequate system. Some analysts estimate that as many as one million or more handicapped children received no formal schooling at all as late as the early 1960s [28]

By the late 1960s, however, things began to change. In addition to the pressure created by sheer numbers of school-aged handicapped individuals, the civil rights movement, activism within the handicapped community itself, and the evolving profession of special education all forced a new understanding of the rights to which the handicapped were legally entitled. The most effective weapon used by the handicapped coalition was litigation. Basing their claims on the equal protection clause of the Fourteenth Amendment, advocates for the handicapped won major law suits.[29]

School boards, faced with expensive litigation and court-ordered programs, saw the writing on the wall and grudgingly accepted the reality of reform and concentrated on obtaining state and federal funds to help finance the newly created special education programs.

In the late 1960s and early 1970s, Congress passed fifty pieces of legislation on issues of interest to the handicapped, including the 1975 Education for All Handicapped Children Act (PL94-142) which required, among other things, individualized education programs, due process procedures established to give parents a direct say in their child's educational placement, and least restrictive placements. Under the provisions of the law, parents or guardians have the power to challenge unfavorable

Table 2.9: Enrollment in public school special education programs for exceptional children, United States, 1963–1985

Year	**Special education enrollment**	
	Number	*Percentage of total enrollment*
1963	1,570,370	3.9
1971	3,025,000	6.7
1980	4,142,000	10.1
1985	4,374,000	11.0

Source: Digest of Education Statistics, Washington, DC: US Government Printing Office, 1987–1988, p. 57; 1983–1984, p. 40; 1975–1976, p. 42.

school decisions concerning their children's school placement. As a result of these legal innovations, the number of children identified as in need of special education more than quadrupled as a percentage of total school enrollment between 1963 and 1985 (see Table 2.9).

Had it not been for the schools' monopolistic position, it would have been much more difficult for them to have responded to the demands of minorities and the handicapped. A century earlier the public schools concentrated on winning a middle-class clientele; had they focused their energies on the needs of a foreign-born, religious minority or the well-being of ex-slaves, their success as political institutions would have been much more problematic. But in the 1960s their middle class constituency could be taken for granted, and the front door could be opened to newcomers without fear that those already inside would walk out the back. That is at least what those calling for social reform expected. The reality turned out to be somewhat more complicated.

As monopolistic as the big city public school system had become, it was not entirely without competition. In addition to a variety of parochial and other private schools, big city school districts were surrounded by a growing suburban hinterland that provided educational alternatives under separate political control. The significance of this competition was first demonstrated in a controversial, early study of white flight that seemed to indicate that the rate of decline in the proportion of whites attending central-city schools increased significantly following the implementation of desegregation plans.[30] Subsequent studies seemed to show that changes in the proportion of white attendance in central-city schools were much less than this original study seemed to show.[31] But even though the initial debate provoked a good deal of acrimony, a scholarly consensus now seems to have emerged: whether or not white flight occurs depends very much on the context in which the desegregation takes place. If desegregation occurs within a system in which a metropolitan-wide monopoly desegregation plan exists, white flight is relatively small, simply because whites have no place other than expensive private schools or another metropolitan area to which to flee. But where desegregation plans are limited to the central city, then white flight regularly occurs, frequently undermining the desegregation objectives of the original plan.[32]

Most central-city school systems now find themselves in a competitive context where they are unable to construct metropolitan-wide desegregation plans. Although court decisions affecting metropolitan-wide desegregation are mixed and inconsistent, relatively few cases compel desegregation beyond the lines of the school district in which segregated policies were found to exist. As a result, central-city schools, with their large minority populations, are expected to desegregate their schools. But surrounding suburban districts, with very few black students, are under much less pressure to desegregate.

One consequence of the uneven pressure on school districts to desegregate is the increasing segregation of the metropolitan area into central cities that are predominantly minority in their composition and a suburban ring that is overwhelmingly white. The trends toward minority concentration within the central city predate the implementation of school desegregation in the late 1960s. Between 1950 and 1970 the percentage minority of central cities in the United States increased from 13 per cent to 22.5 per cent (Table 2.10). But after 1970 the racial differentiation of the metropolitan area continued to accelerate rapidly. According to census data, by 1980, 30.8 per cent of the central city population was comprised of minority groups.[33] It is expected that the percentage minority in the nation's central cities in 1990 will be 45 per cent.

The demographic trends in public schools were even more dramatic.

Table 2.10: White and minority central city and suburban populations, 1950–1980

Year	**Central city**		**Suburban**		**Percentage suburban of SMSA**
	White	*Minority*	*White*	*Minority*	*All races*
1950	87.0	13.0	94.8	5.2	41.5
1960	82.2	17.8	94.8	5.2	48.6
1970	77.5	22.5	94.1	5.9	54.2
1980	73.2	26.8	91.6	8.4	62.3

Sources: US Bureau of the Census, *Historical Statistics*, Series A 276–287; *1980 Census of Population, General Social and Economic Characteristics*, Washington, DC: US Department of Commerce, Bureau of the Census, Table 74, p. 1–12.

Between 1970 and 1982 the proportion of minority enrollment doubled in the public schools of Seattle, Portland, and San Diego. In Boston minority enrollment shot up from 36 per cent to 70 per cent after a thorough-going and heatedly contested desegregation plan was implemented. By 1982 four cities — Atlanta, the District of Columbia, Newark and San Antonio — had minority enrollment of over 90 per cent.[34]

As the twentieth century was nearing its end, metropolitan America seemed to be evolving two quite different educational systems. The first system, still found in the central city, was the system of quasi-monopolistic public education that had been slowly constructed by public school officials during the first half of the twentieth century. It is to the character of the second system, to be found in the suburban belt surrounding the central city, that we now turn.

Emergence of Decentralization and Opportunities for Choice

As big city school systems were taking further steps toward the homogenization of educational choice by beginning to racially integrate their student populations, a system providing much greater educational choice was developing around them. After more than a century of movement toward centralized, monopolistic educational power and control, educational choice began to increase willy nilly, almost accidentally, without the sponsorship of any well-defined political movement. But if central city containment within a ring of suburbs began without any definite purpose, it soon acquired one. The autonomy of the small suburb against the encroaching power of the big city was vigorously defended against those who pressed for metropolitan reform or central-city annexation of the suburban hinterland. Middle-class Americans who had given up choice to get free public schools discovered that they could have both free schools and educational choice in a decentralized suburbia where each community had its own school board, its own tax base, and its own educational ethos.

It is quite clear that parents choose schools when selecting a suburban residence. In two separate studies, one of New Jersey suburbs, the other in the Los Angeles area, analysts discovered that as performance of high school students on verbal ability tests in a community improves, so do the property values of the community.[35] Both studies can be criticized for not taking into account the endogenous relationship between property values and student test scores. But in both studies many other factors affecting property values, such as the size and age of the home, the accessibility of the community to centers of employment, the community tax rate, and median family income were controlled. It seems especially significant that the effect of test scores on property values obtained even after the effects of family income had been taken into account.

Test scores are not the only school variables that affect suburban property values. According to several studies carried out in New Jersey, Illinois, Massachusetts, and California, where expenditures on education are higher, property values are enhanced.[36] Once again, the question of an endogenous relationship arises. But in all the studies the positive effects of education held even after controls for median family income, tax rates, size of home, and age of home had been introduced. Apparently, homeowners are willing to pay more for houses located in communities where educational expenditures are higher.

To the extent that choice of residence is influenced by public perceptions of the quality of local schools, to that extent local school boards and the superintendents they direct have strong incentives to provide services that parents want. If school services deviate too much from parental wishes, some families will leave and it will become more difficult to attract newcomers to the community. Property values will fall, and other homeowners will have a stake in pressuring the school board to keep the community from declining. Intelligent, rational managers of local public schools in such a competitive situation have every incentive to keep such a trend from developing in the first place.

It is this kind of decentralized, choice-creating educational system that has been on the increase in the United States in recent decades. Even by 1950 41 per cent of the metropolitan area population was living outside the central city (Table 2.10). By this time city boundaries in most parts of the United States were fixed, and efforts to create metropolitan-wide political jurisdictions that would effectively extend the boundaries of the central city were singularly unsuccessful. Suburbanites regularly voted against metropolitan-wide plans both in referenda and through their representatives in the state legislature. In most parts of the country opposition to metropolitan wide plans was so entrenched that they were never proposed in the first place.

Suburbia expanded rapidly in the next decades after 1950. By 1970, 54 per cent of the metropolitan population lived outside the central city, and by 1986 the percentages had escalated to 62 per cent. By their choice of residence and their opposition to metropolitan-wide reforms Americans were expressing a desire for decentralization, local control, and choice in the provision of public services.

The turning point in education seems to have come around 1970. After that year both central-city decline and suburban growth accelerated.

The average size school, after having steadily increased for at least a half a century, now became smaller once again (Table 2.4). Another way of looking at the same phenomenon is to examine the percentage of students in school districts of various sizes. This data is only available from the early 1960s, but it, too, shows continued movement toward bigness until the early seventies, when the numbers begin to shift in the opposite direction (Table 2.11). The percentage of pupils in districts of 25,000 and more slips a percentage point, as does the percentage in districts 6,000 to 25,000. The smaller school districts, after having been steady losers in the sixties, begin to regain slightly higher percentages of the pupil population. The trends in school finance show a similar trend. Although the percentage of educational costs paid locally continued to decline in the seventies, by the 1980s this, too, came to a virtual halt (Table 2.5).

Private education also rebounded in the late seventies. The position of private education had actually become quite problematic in the late sixties. In the immediate post-war era the Catholic church had made a strong commitment to elementary education, and the percentages of students in nonpublic schools had increased from 9.3 per cent in 1940 to 13.9 per cent in 1960 (Table 2.12). But after 1960 the cost of education was increasing so rapidly both for public and private schools that the private schools found it increasingly difficult to maintain their enrollment. By 1975 private school enrollments had fallen to 10 per cent of total enrollment. The prognosis for private education had in fact become so problematic that in 1972 the President's Commission on Non-public Education recommended federal intervention to save the private system from what was feared

Table 2.11: Percentage of students enrolled in schools in districts by size of district, 1962–1987

Year	**Size of school district**			
	25,000 or more	6,000–25,000	1,200–6,000	Less than 1,200
1962	26.3	26.1	33.1	14.5
1967	28.7	29.7	31.6	10.1
1972	29.3	31.6	31.2	7.9
1975*	28.3	32.4	31.5	7.8
1983*	26.1	30.9	34.4	8.7
1987*	27.9	30.3	33.2	8.5

*In these years information was available for slightly different categories; estimates were made by assuming that the number of students enrolled in a given distribution of districts was homogeneous across size of district within category.
Sources: Digest of Education Statistics, various years.

Table 2.12: Percentage of elementary and secondary students enrolled in private schools, 1900–1990

Year	Percentage
1900	8.0
1920	7.3
1940	9.3
1960	13.9
1970	10.6
1975	10.0
1980	11.5
1985	12.6
1990	12.7

Source: Calculated from US Department of Education, Office of Educational Research and Improvement, Center for Statistics, *Digest of Education Statistics, 1985–86*, Tables 3, 4.

would be near total collapse.[37] Since 1975 the trends have been in the opposite direction and by 1990 private schools will have come close to restoring the percentage of pupils they were educating in 1960.

The seventies were also the years when blacks were succeeding in becoming full-fledged participants within the public schools. As racial integration was becoming an increasingly pronounced feature of big, central-city schools, Americans began to discover anew the virtues of the small community, the smaller school, the private school, and the ability to make choices in education. Decentralization, grass-roots democracy and individual choice had always been popular themes in American political discourse. But in practice Americans had, for more than a century, been willing to cede increasing responsibility for the education of their children to a quasi-monopoly. But when that monopoly began attending to the needs and interests of minority and disadvantaged citizens, the position of the monopoly began to erode.

The Future of Choice and Decentralization

The current dual system of quasi-monopoly control of education within central cities and quasi-competitive systems of education in the suburban ring around these cities is likely to be quite stable for the foreseeable future. Those who have a stake in the dual system comprise a formidable coalition. They consist of what has come to be known as the public school lobby — the organized groups of school boards, school superintendents, teacher organizations, and parent-teacher associations who have a stake in preserving and extending the quasi-monopoly that has been created. They also consist of the upper middle class business and professional suburbanites, who have the benefits of a free, publicly supported educational system along with a fair degree of educational choice. The coalition also includes many in rural America, for whom the community school has long constituted a primary community resource, functioning as a center of community activity. In addition, the public school enjoys the steadfast support of the civil rights movement which has long regarded public education as the primary mechanism by which blacks are to be integrated into the mainstream of American society. The coalition is large enough to be strongly represented within both political parties and in all regions of the country.

These groups are not allied on all education issues. But until now they have pretty much agreed on issues having to do with public support for nonpublic schools either through tax credits, tuition vouchers, or some other mechanism that would put public and private schools on a more similar financial footing.

These diverse interests agree on support for the dual system, even though the suburban component of the system is more competitive, more efficient and provides higher quality educational services than does the central-city component. It would seem that minority interests have been among the losers in a dual system divided between a monopolistic central-city system and a more competitive suburban system. Minorities have neither the efficient schools that come with competition nor the genuinely equal access to public education that monopolies theoretically should be able to provide. They have been unable to achieve a more thorough-going monopoly, because court decisions have exempted suburban areas from most desegregation plans. And defeat of tuition voucher schemes even as part of any compensatory education program has sharply restricted their choice. Minorities do have the symbols of equal access, and so far this has been enough to sustain the support of civil rights groups (many of whose middle-class members are employed by the public school system).

Those favoring greater choice are a motley collection of diverse interests whose views of the appropriate alternative to the existing system are hardly congruent. Those favoring greater choice include neoconservatives interested in using market economies to improve public services, leftists suspicious of centralized bureaucracies, some Evangelical Protestants who would like government support that would help them establish schools less infused with secular doctrines, Roman Catholics who would like public aid to help finance their increasingly pressed alternative to the public schools, and a limited number of academics interested in discovering whether choice-mechanisms could be designed in such a way as to improve both the quality of education and the equality of educational opportunity. The combination reminds one of a small band of Jedi attackers, using their intellectual powers to fight the unified might of Death Star forces led by Darth Vadar, whose intellectual capacity has been corrupted by the urge for complete hegemony.

This Jedi-like band was in its strongest political position during the Reagan Administration. The President had campaigned for greater choice in education and had explicitly endorsed tax credits against some portion of the tuition parents paid for their children's private education. When re-elected President in 1984, he appointed William Bennett, an outspoken conservative, as Secretary of Education. The Secretary deplored the power and self-centeredness of teacher organizations in public schools, praised private education, and proposed a revision of the compensatory education program so that vouchers would be given to low-income families, who could then select compensatory services from either a public or private provider.

The Secretary's proposal seemed a particularly promising way of introducing greater choice into the educational system. It addressed the problem created by a 1984 Supreme Court decision, *Aguila v. Felton*, which had ruled unconstitutional direct assistance for compensatory education purposes to schools that provided religious instruction.[38] Since this court decision undermined the broad political coalition of both public and parochial school educators that had helped pass the original compensatory education program in 1965,[39] a revised proposal that did not have the same constitutional defects but still provided aid to nonpublic schools had its political advantages. Also, the new proposal, unlike tax credits, did not favor upper income families; on the contrary, it was designed with the most educationally and economically disadvantaged groups in the society in mind. The taint of elitism that hung about most choice proposals was totally missing from this one. Finally, the bill, unlike tax credits, placed no new fiscal burdens on the US Treasury at a time when high fiscal deficits were ruling out many other policy initiatives.

The Secretary's proposal was nonetheless treated as dead on arrival when it reached Capitol Hill. The public school lobby formed a unified front immediately. Mary Futrell of the National Education Association condemned the idea without reservation:

> The intent of the Administration's proposal is not to improve but to impoverish public schools, to weaken the very institutions that have most helped the most needy. Vouchers are a hoax, a guise for funneling public monies to private schools. When this strategy is

> defended on the grounds that it will unleash the potential of 11 million disadvantaged children, the hoax becomes hypocritical, odious, and cruel.[40]

Civil rights groups and black Congressmen were equally opposed to the legislation, though it seemed to provide black families, ostensibly among the main beneficiaries of this program, with greater choice in selecting compensatory services for their children. Faced with such unrelenting opposition, members of Congress were unwilling even to hold hearings on the legislation. Congressional Republicans were as unwilling as Democrats to touch this political hot potato.

In light of these defeats in national politics and similar setbacks at state and local levels it is difficult to be optimistic about the possibility of creating significant, new alternatives to publicly-controlled education. Modest efforts made in the past to introduce voucher plans or establish alternative schools have met with significant opposition, even during the Reagan administration when the power of the pro-choice forces was at its zenith. In spite of the idea that choosing one's own school would be the ideal, creating competition among public schools and forcing them to improve to survive has proven too threatening to the powerful public school monopoly.

Although alternatives to public education are likely to remain limited, choice within the public sector could well increase, if only to forestall the call for fundamental reform. In many central cities magnet schools have been developed, which offer parents a choice among schools offering somewhat different educational programs. In some places, most notably, Minnesota, students are even allowed to choose schools across district boundaries. The choice is usually limited, however. Sometimes magnet schools have formal educational standards — grade averages, teacher recommendations and the like. In other cases, they are rationed on a first-come, first-serve basis, thereby giving the more committed parents and/or students a chance to attend the school of choice. In many cases racial balance requirements also limit the degree of choice for one or another racial group. These and other choice mechanisms can be expected to proliferate because they create some increase in educational quality. But these changes either singly or together are unlikely to undermine the dual system of American education in which public schools enjoy a virtual monopoly over central-city education while they are forced to compete with one another, at least to some extent, in the surrounding suburban hinterland. Except in the unlikely event of strong legislative or judicial action, we will see little major change for some time to come in the modus vivendi public schools have worked out with other societal interests.

Some may applaud this dual system, because its monopolistic component permits a small element of redistribution. Others may criticize it, because the gross inefficiencies of a monopolistic form of organization are everywhere evident and most especially in the nation's central cities. Some may feel that reforms that would give meaningful choice among many different kinds of schools — both public and private — would increase inequality. Others may feel that a planned, centralized choice mechanism could increase efficiency and equity simultaneously. Of only one point am I myself quite certain: it would be difficult to concoct a politically viable system more inefficient and less equitable than the one found today in most central cities of the United States.

Notes

1 With apologies to Robert Michels (1962), who made an equally unequivocal statement about organizations. The author wishes to thank Carol Peterson, who provided research assistance for this chapter.
2 David Tyack thus errs in his comments on this chapter when he concludes public schools do not enjoy a quasi-monopolistic position because a century ago they were shaped by pluralist prcoesses.
3 Tyack errs again when he draws the conclusion that a public school monopoly does not exist from the mere fact that many groups compete with one another for control over school policies. One would expect competition for control of a monopoly, because the winner is able to collect a monopoly rent — in the form of, say, high administrative salaries, high teachers' salaries, special programs for the gifted, or the handicapped, or whatever. There are many ways in which monopoly rent can be collected.
4 Tyack errs also when he concludes that schools are not monopolies because they serve minorities and the handicapped. The fact that the schools could respond to these demands is, on the contrary, evidence that they had achieved a monopolistic position. Tyack wants to equate monopoly with inequity, coercion, and evil. If one avoids a value-laden for a technical definition of monopoly, then the more ambiguous consequences of monopoly become apparent.
5 Paul E. Peterson (1985) *The Politics of School Reform, 1870–1940*, Chicago: University of Chicago Press, Chapter 6.
6 Diane Ravitch (1974) *The Great School Wars: New York City, 1805–1973*, New York: Basic Books, p. 49.
7 David Tyack and Elizabeth Hansot (1982) *Managers of Virtue: Public School Leadership in America, 1820–1980*, New York: Basic Books, p. 77.
8 Tyack and Hansot (1982) p. 75.
9 *Ibid.*, p. 75.
10 *Ibid.* David Tyack presumably read the preceding section before making the

following comment on this chapter. 'Most of Peterson's examples of aggrandizement and monopoly control concern 20th century developments, yet causality cannot run backwards.' One can only conclude that the final degree program of educational historians should include examinations in reading comprehension.

11 Peterson (1985) p. 56.

12 J.S. Coleman, T. Hoffer, and S. Kilgore (1982) *High School Achievement*, New York: Basic Books; T. Hoffer, A.M. Greeley, and J.S. Coleman (1985) 'Achievement growth in public and Catholic schools', *Sociology of Education*, **58** pp. 74–97; John E. Chubb (1988) 'Effective schools and the problems of the poor', in Dennis P. Doyle and Bruce S. Cooper (Eds.) *Federal Aid to the Disadvantaged: What Future for Chapter 1?*, Philadelphia: Falmer Press. pp. 244–70.

13 Tyack notes in his comments that the proportion of children in public schools was in fact somewhat higher in 1900 than in the 1980s, concluding from this statistic that public education must have gained its monopolistic position by 1900.

Certainly, the public schools were very successful in the last few decades of the 19th century in precluding private secondary schools from expanding to serve an increasing proportion of the age cohort. But the battle for monopoly control did not end in 1900. Public school people had yet to secure their position as the provider of education to people ages 13 to 18, most of whom were as yet unschooled in 1900. They also had to fend off the movement to establish separate vocational schools.

14 As one typographical union leader observed at the time, 'Many union men, . . . fear that the schools may be turned into what has been bluntly termed "scab factories".' *Chicago Tribune*, 1913, p. 4.

15 *Chicago Tribune* (no date) 1912, p. 4.

16 Lawrence A. Cremin (1961) *The Transformation of the School*, New York: Random House, p. 53.

17 *Ibid.*

18 Paul E. Peterson and Barry G. Rabe (1984) 'Career training or education for life: Dilemmas in the development of Chicago vocational education'. Paper prepared for the National Commission on Vocational Education, pp. 49–51.

19 *Ibid.*, pp. 49–51.

20 Paul E. Peterson (1976) *School Politics Chicago Style*, Chicago: University of Chicago Press, p. 124.

21 Jesse Burkhead *et al.*, (1967) *Input and Output in Large City High Schools*, Syracuse, New York: Syracuse University Press.

22 M.T. Katzman (1971) *The Political Economy of Urban Schools*, Cambridge, Mass.: Harvard University Press, pp. 135–6. The results of a study of Oakland differed somewhat: There was a tendency to allocate extra resources to schools in both the poorest and richest neighborhoods; see Frank Levy, Arnold J. Meltsner and Aaron Wildavsky (1974) *Urban Outcomes: Schools, Streets, and Libraries*, Berkeley, CA: University of California Press.

23 Peterson (1985) *The Politics of School Reform.*
24 This estimate was provided in personal conversation by John Chubb, who based it on information available in the *High School and Beyond* sample of American schools for 1980. For a further discussion of the size of schools, see John Chubb and Terry Moe, *America's Politics, Markets and Schools* (Brookings, 1990).
25 James Conant (1963) *The Education of American Teachers*, New York: McGraw-Hill Book Co.
26 Gary Orfield (1978) *Must We Bus*? Washington, DC: Brookings; Jennifer Houchshild (1984) *The New American Dilemma*, New Haven: Yale University Press.
27 Peterson (1985) Chapter 6.
28 Marvin Lazerson (1983) 'The origins of special education', in J.G. Chambers and William T. Hartman (Eds.) *Special Education Policies: Their History, Implementation, and Finance*, Philadelphia: Temple University Press, p. 38.
29 Jack Tweedie, (1983) 'The politics of legalization in special education reform', in J.G. Chambers and W.T. Hartman (Eds.) *Special Education Politics: Their History, Implementation, and Finance*, Philadelphia: Temple University Press, p. 53.
30 J.S. Coleman, S.D. Kelley and J.A. Moore (1975) *Trends in School Segregation, 1968–1973*, Washington, DC: Urban Institute.
31 C.H. Rossell, D. Ravitch and D.J. Armor (1978) 'Busing and "White Flight"', *Public Interest*, **53** pp. 109–15.
32 Gary Orfield (1978) *Must We Bus?*; Gary Orfield (1975) 'Symposium desegregation and white flight', Washington, DC: Center for National Policy Review; Jennifer Hochshild (1984) *The New American Dilemma.*
33 Donald J. Bogue (1985) *The Population of the United States, Historical Trends and Future Projections*, New York: The Free Press, p. 135.
34 *Ibid.* p. 146.
35 H.S. Rosen and D.J. Fullerton (1977), 'A note on local tax rates, public benefit levels and property values', *Journal of Political Economy*, **85** pp. 433–40; G.S. McDougall (1976) 'Local public goods and residential property values: Some insights and extensions', *National Tax Journal*, **20**, pp. 436–47.
36 Wallace E. Oates (1969) 'The effects of property taxes and local public spending on property values: An empirical study of tax capitalization and the Tiebout hypothesis', *Journal of Political Economy*, **77**, pp. 957–71; Rosen and Fullerton (1977) pp. 433–40; G.R. Meadows (1976), 'Taxes, spending and property values: A comment and further results', *Journal of Political Economy*, **84**, pp. 869–77; M. Edel and E. Sklar (1984) 'Taxes, spending and property values; Supply adjustment in a Tiebout-Oates model', *Journal of Political Economy*, **82**, pp. 941–54.
37 President's Panel on Nonpublic Education (1972) *Nonpublic Education and the Public Good*, Washington, DC: US Government Printing Office.
38 Bruce S. Cooper (1988) 'The uncertain future of national education policy: Private schools and the federal role', in William Lowe Boyd and Charles

Taylor Kerchner (Eds.) *The Politics of Excellence and Choice in Education*, Philadelphia: Falmer Press, pp. 168–70.

39 Paul E. Peterson (1983) 'Background Paper' in TWENTIETH CENTURY FUND, *Report of the Twentieth Century Fund Task Force on Federal Elementary and Secondary Education Policy*, New York: Twentieth Century Fund, Chapter 3.

40 Cooper (1988) p. 172.

Commentary

Knowledge, Educational Organization and Choice

Richard M. Merelman

Paul Peterson ably describes the evolution of American public schools to a position he describes variously as a 'monopoly' or a 'quasi-monopoly' (p. 49). He then portrays the current movement towards greater choice in public education, a movement epitomized not so much by voucher systems (which are mostly abortive), but by decentralization of public schools through suburbanization. The strength of his analysis lies in its recognition that the drive towards monopoly or quasi-monopoly is mainly *endogenous* to schools — deriving from the desire of educational professionals to expand their power. This Weberian explanation avoids both the Scylla of naive pluralism, which portrays a (partly fictional) public demand pushing school expansion, and the Charybdis of neo-marxism, which ascribes educational expansion to the 'needs' of capitalist elites, most of whom, unfortunately for the hypothesis, maintained little direct connection to public schools. Peterson puts the responsibility where it rightly belongs: namely, with the professional educators who, after all, had more immediately to gain from the expansion and consolidation of the public school than did any other group.

The crucial question which Peterson does not adequately address, I think, is one which deeply engaged the conference: Why, after a full century's sustained consolidation and growth towards monopoly, has the tide seemingly been reversed? Why is there now more choice, decentralization, and even fragmentation in American public schools, and why are there demands for still further anti-monopoly reforms? Peterson ascribes the reversal mainly to two forces: demographic drift towards suburbanization and white flight initiated by desegregation. As he acknowledges but does not emphasize, the two phenomena are intimately linked. Although suburbanization predated school desegregation in most urban areas, Peterson shows that parents today choose their suburban residences for educational reasons, one of which, no doubt, is the racial mix (or non-mix) on offer. The sad fact is that white parents translate this mix into a judgment of educational quality. Thus, despite their quite separate origins, today suburbanization and school desegregation are a single driving force decentralizing American public schools.

The puzzle, of course, is why the educational professionals who nimbly absorbed earlier challenges from religious, class, and vocational competitors cannot now forestall 'the current dual system of quasi-monopoly control of education within central cities and quasi-competitive systems of education in the suburban ring' (p. 71). It is no good responding that the current situation satisfies the public education establishment. While the more extreme forms of choice in the forms of voucher systems or tuition credits may fail, the current situation is hardly ideal from the point of view of the educational establishment. The recent growth of private schools, for example, is a significant departure from the past experience of uninterrupted passage towards quasi-monopoly. More ominous yet is public anxiety about the schools' failure to meet the demands of a high-tech world economy in which American competitiveness is suddenly very much in doubt. No. The current reversal is a significant challenge to public schools, and demands an explanation which Peterson does not offer.

My intention is to proceed some little way towards such an explanation, one which both builds upon and modifies Peterson's effort. I believe the key to the puzzle is the connection between the expansion of public schools as *organizations* and the nature of the *knowledge* schools dispense. Simply put, schools expand and school professionals flourish only when schools can offer an acceptable educational product to their diverse constituencies. Schools contract, fragment, and decline when their constituents lose faith in the sorts of knowledge schools provide — or at least conclude that they themselves no longer benefit significantly from such knowledge.

Ignoring the connection between organizations and knowledge causes Peterson to overdo the opposition historically between monopoly and choice in American public education. My dictionary defines monopoly as 'exclusive control of a commodity or service in a particular market'. This definition does not describe public schools exactly (as Peterson's vacillation between 'monopoly' and 'quasi-monopoly' implicitly concedes). The 'commodity' in question — 'educational knowledge' — has changed shape and meaning over time as it has adapted to different school constituencies. As a result, the public school *combined* educational choice with organizational monopoly, so that the diverse constituencies initially forced under the school's tutelage found their educational choices eventually *enhanced* by their submission. Although theirs was not a 'sweet' surrender, it had about it at least some elements of seduction.

For example, the ambitious middle class which educators first lured into the mainly yeoman public schools gained for their children quality schooling at reduced prices. As Peterson notes, educators established academic high schools to court the middle class. While this diversion of funds temporarily embittered the existing yeoman clientele, the policy could be sold as a way of providing worthy children from *all* classes an opportunity to rise in society. Academic education thus lured both the powerful middle class and, eventually, segments of an aspirant yeomanry.

Similarly, the Protestant clientele of late nineteenth century public schools gained much from the decline of Catholic parochial schools. Since the ambience of public schools was implicitly Protestant and explicitly 'American', Catholic public school children would fall under the necessary — and undeniably wholesome — tutelage of middle class Protestants. Meanwhile, Catholics — though losers in this particular struggle — could at least console themselves in the knowledge that religious education as such — and the Church — did not actually *demand* a state-supported parochial school system, but could survive apart from such support. Moreover, Catholic children who received a public school education would gain credentials and knowledge which would make them more competitive and socially acceptable in a society still run mainly by Protestants. Finally, a separate system of Catholic universities serviced those of the faithful who were unwilling to accept these compromises with the American mainstream. Thus, for Catholics, expanded choices on new fronts helped to compensate for diminished opportunities on old.

The same story, with variations, can be told about vocationalism. Existing public school clienteles had little to fear from accepting vocational education. After all, educators consigned vocational students either to separate, inferior academic tracks or to separate schools. Indeed, academically-oriented children derived bogus status superiority by distinguishing themselves from vocational students and avoiding vocational courses. Nor did the new vocational clientele entirely suffer from this arrangement. As Peterson points out, public vocational schools provided 'sophisticated training in specialized vocational activities as well as basic educational instruction' (p. 58). More important, until the mid-twentieth century entry into most manual and lower-white collar occupations did not require any uniform set of educational credentials at all, vocational or otherwise. Finally, with the advent of university credentialism, much vocational education and specialization does not really begin until college anyway. Therefore, vocational education in public schools has become something of an anomaly.

As the clienteles brought under the school umbrella broadened and diversified, so also did what the school certifies as its product — 'education'. A pluralistic school constituency requires pluralistic forms of knowledge. So a wide range of 'electives' supplanted the classical curriculum of the past; and a plethora of extra-curricular activities provided at least some means of interesting many less gifted students. By the early 1970s the high school curriculum embraced everything from driver training to 'values clarification', from trigonometry to sex education. Within disciplines equally diverse curricula appeared. English courses offered everything from Shakespeare to Vonnegut to Spiderman; in my own discipline — political science — schools could choose between old-fashioned institutional civics courses or the thoroughly modern 'Comparing Political Experiences' program the American Political Science Association endorsed. Small wonder the contemporary American high school curriculum has been described as a 'shopping mall'.

It is well to re-emphasize that educators themselves — acting as political entrepreneurs — drove this process of monopolization forward, seeing in the defeat of religious, class, and vocational competitors an opportunity to enhance their own power. This fact is important, because it, above everything else, signifies the difference between the now-concluded period of sustained growth and the recent impulse toward choice and fragmentation. As contrasted with the earlier period, it has not been educators, but parents, courts, interest groups, and elected political leaders who have promoted school desegregation and the integration of the handicapped into public schools. What has changed? The answer, I think, is that — *pace* Peterson — educators do not believe it possible to combine a quasi-monopoly organizationally with educational choice and quality so far as the absorption of racial minorities and the handicapped is concerned. Educators have lost the initiative because they believe that — whatever the morality of the matter — their own best political interests are not served by incorporating these two new claimant groups. And here, I think, is where the core of an answer lies to the question 'Why have things changed from a quasi-monopoly in one "big, big system" to a system of quasi-monopoly and quasi-competition in many smaller systems?'

Of course, the diminished initiative of educators is something of a response to the school's principal clienteles. Whereas in the period of growth, public school clients accepted new claimant groups, they no longer do so gladly. Instead, they do not believe their own children well-served by the integration of minorities and the handicapped. One may denounce this reaction as racism and ignorance, but whatever its motivation, it is expressed in terms of 'quality education' and 'efficiency'. The suburban white middle class and the urban white working class feel their children's futures may be harmed by attending schools in which the definition of 'knowledge' must adjust to serve the interests of minorities and the handicapped. Instead, they view such a definition as a recipe for throwing good money after bad, and for 'reverse discrimination'.

The question this formulation begs, of course, is why educators have loosened their control over the definition of 'knowledge', a control which heretofore they have used effectively to promote the public school monopoly. The answer, I think, is that in order to promote the integration of minorities and the handicapped against reluctant educators, the courts, the responsible federal officials, and the claimants' interest groups have also found it necessary to contest educators' control of 'cultural capital'. Such control has not actually *passed* from the one group to the other, of course; however, in concert, calls for affirmative action, for a curriculum responsive to the needs and particular experience of minorities, for greater minority access to higher education, and for a major effort to redress the wrongs of the past dispute the power of educators over their own standards of educational quality.

A further comparison with the past helps us understand the present dilemma — and the claims I have made. When Catholics entered the public schools they came without having their own culture legitimized. Instead, they were forced to accept the forms and content of knowledge existing public school elites controlled. Indeed, their entry into public schools actually reinforced the cultural hegemony of the establishment, for their confinement initially to lower tracks confirmed the educational superiority of the established WASP clientele. By accepting this hegemony (albeit grudgingly) Catholics ultimately won reluctant admiration from the Establishment and assured that at least some Catholic children would meet standards WASPs themselves had put in place. For these successful Catholic children there could be no legitimate denial of success.

By contrast, many handicapped children cannot succeed in the public school system according to traditional educational standards. In addition, and more significantly, application of traditional public school curricula and practices — such as tracking — resegregate minority children within ostensibly integrated schools. Minority parents can hardly be expected to enjoy having their children judged as 'inferior' according to 'legitimate', 'fair' educational standards. After all, their case has been built upon the opposite theory that the educational deficits of minorities are consequences of inferior schooling in a racially segregated school system.

Thus, minority claimants in integrated public schools have but two real choices: (1) to attempt to alter standards and practices of schooling in order to allow their children to compete in integrated settings; or (2) to return to segregated schools where, by definition, many of their children will do well, at least in terms of class rankings. A third possibility — though widely prevalent in integrated schools — is the least attractive, namely, to accept the *status quo*. But to do so relegates minority children to positions of educational inferiority in integrated settings, and thus 'proves' to many that minority students generally cannot do 'well'.

The first strategy — that of altering standards and practices — creates conflict with educators and encourages white parents to withdraw their support from public schools. The second strategy resegregates public schools and, in so doing, generates heavy fiscal demands for an essentially minority city school system. In neither case does the established white clientele of public education have reason for enthusiastic support. Moreover, the third alternative — accepting the *status quo* — diminishes the quality of education for both whites and minorities, as Coleman has shown.

I concur with Peterson that the current uneasy balance between choice and monopoly in public schools will endure for the foreseeable future. Nevertheless, I am perhaps less sanguine about the situation than is he. After all, the real contributions of a public school system to democracy do not inhere in any particular organizational pattern for education. Rather, these contributions lie in the image of American politics and national identity schools impart. It is worth wondering whether this image suffers as we slip into a system where choice is increasingly expressed in private schools and white flight, and in which central city schools dispense noncompetitive education to a frustrated, resentful urban constituency which feels, rightly enough, that its hopes for equal educational opportunity have been blighted.

As myth, the 'American dream' promised people that individual choice might actually contribute to common bonds of nationality. By providing large numbers of parents and children an education which combined choice and broad community, the public school contributed markedly to that dream. It follows that the partial decoupling of choice from the American public school detracts from the creation of cultural unity among Americans. Put simply, as things are we may have to remove the public school from the shrinking roster of institutions in which Americans come together as equals to confront and collaborate with each other, rather than retreat into their separate, private worlds.

Observers usually argue the chief losers in this struggle are the poor, the minorities, and the handicapped, who lack the resources to gain effective choice. Without in any way disputing this analysis, let me in conclusion offer another. When the public schools succeeded in luring the middle classes into the high school, they insured that many future American political leaders — drawn overwhelmingly from this class — would have at least some early experience and emotional identification with members of other social classes. I suspect that recruiting political leaders from public school backgrounds contributes ever so slightly to the sympathetic understanding leaders ought to feel for their fellow citizens in a democracy. Should the middle class now abandon the heterogeneous common school for homogeneous suburban enclaves and exclusive private schools, they will deny their children previous experience with and sympathy for the diverse people whom almost certainly they will be called upon to govern. It is no use protesting that the poor need more of their own leaders, and that they should not rely on the largesse of others. Of course, this is true. But the plain fact is that political mechanisms for recruiting a representative cross-section of leaders are noticeably weak in the United States. For the foreseeable future the needy will continue to rely on many leaders who are very much unlike themselves in origin. Given this fact, it would be well for those leaders and the needy at least to know each other as youths in school. If they do not, then we may all be poorer culturally for the fact.

Commentary

The Public Schools: A Monopoly or a Contested Public Domain?

David B. Tyack

Paul Peterson's chapter is provocative. I agree with him that a central historical question is why have public schools so expanded in size, scope, and political and fiscal power that they have become the standard form of education for almost nine out of ten young Americans. This issue bears heavily on policy today. I also agree with his political assessment that private market solutions to educational problems do not have a strong constituency or a promising future (although I am more optimistic than he about increasing choices within public schooling).

I believe, however, that characterizing public education as a monopoly or 'quasi-monopoly' confounds more than clarifies the issues, in part, as Witte observes, because 'the system does not appear to be as uniform, centrally and simply controlled, or as insulated, protected, and unresponsive as this picture indicates'. Since he and Merelman deal more with Peterson's analysis of the current educational scene, I shall focus more on Peterson's historical argument.

The OED defines monopoly as 'exclusive possession of the trade in some commodity'. Since the *Pierce* decision explicitly protected the right of parents to send children to private schools, and since more than one tenth of students do not attend public schools, public education does not fit that strict definition. But do not be so literal-minded, Peterson could say, and recognize that public schools 'impose monopoly costs on others and ... enjoy privileges available only in a non-competitive environment'. In that broader sense (and not disregarding the traditionally pejorative associations of the term), is not public education a monopoly?

I do not think so, for these reasons:

1 If judged by its market share of students, public schools were more 'monopolistic' in 1900, when they had 92 per cent of pupils, than today when they have about 87.1 per cent. One has to ask, then, how did public education gain such a monopolistic position by 1900? Peterson does not help much here. Although he does mention the establishment of the public high school and religious contention as parts of the 'drive toward monopoly control' in the nineteenth century, most of his analysis of monopolistic aggrandizement deals with the twentieth century. Surely he does not believe that causality runs backwards. What were the public schools like at the turn of the century when they were most 'monopolistic' by the OED definition? Outside the cities they were small, highly decentralized in control, diverse in curriculum, and responsive to the pluralistic communities that supported them. There were more school board members than teachers in rural areas. The US Office of Education was minuscule in staff and weak in its powers, as were almost all state departments of education. What happened at the grassroots during the nineteenth century was that citizens chose to build public schools and parents to send their children to them. Who and where were the 'monopolists' who created such a system of public schools?

2 Monopolies must have monopolists, a limited set of persons who benefit from exclusive control. Peterson is initially vague about who these are — 'the schools' or 'educators' — until later when he defines them as a public school lobby of organized school boards, superintendents, teachers, and PTAs. But then he extends the coalition to include prosperous suburbanites, rural Americans, and civil rights organizations. The circle grows. Is it not possible that most Americans have a stake in this 'monopoly' but in fact many disagree about what schools should do? And has not this competition produced public schools that have been and are quite diverse as a result of widespread public participation in their shaping?

3 Public education from its origins to the present has been contested political ground. Peterson's own prior work on the pluralistic character of school politics has richly documented that different status groups have ardently competed to influence public schooling and that no one of them won definitive control. Indeed, 'control' may be a misnomer for so diverse a political arena as the schools, for different groups wanted quite different kinds and degrees of influence, sometimes instrumental (like jobs and contracts or what Peterson calls 'monopoly rent') and sometimes symbolic (like the teaching of 'temperance' or the inclusion of the

German language or black history). Does it not oversimplify the political story to suggest that all this conflict took place within a monopolistic framework? Did these many actors simply become coopted by the monopolists or seek to become monopolists themselves? Or is it more reasonable to think that the concept of monopoly is inappropriate when applied to so multiform a set of aims and outcomes?

4 Like Merelman, I find the discussion of the incorporation of minorities confusing. Peterson first suggests that 'public schools *had* to respond [to minority demands] in large part because they *could* respond. As monopolists, they did not need to worry about what would happen to their other consumers, if they opened their doors to previously excluded groups'. But later he notes that when desegregation reaches inner city schools — the most 'monopolistic' part of the public system — 'white flight regularly occurs'. Is not a quite different interpretation of civil rights in education closer to the mark, one which stresses not monopoly but the ways in which protest movements and the legal system pressured different kinds of communities in different ways to change their schools?

In short, I find the public school monopoly to be a good slogan but a murky concept for analyzing school politics. In the rest of my remarks I would like to suggest historical perspectives on two related matters:

What is the relation of choice to power?

What decisions are best made in a decentralized fashion or in a centralized way?

About choice: in this individualistic society, we tend to glorify the ability to choose and forget that choice is often a luxury conferred by privilege or an opportunity barred by discrimination. Blacks in the South, for example, had no choice but had to attend segregated, vastly inferior schools. Catholics had no chance to express their religious values in public schools that were dominated by Protestants. Those who were born female had a radically restricted range of vocational training. Choice has often been a badge of privilege. Social movements thus can be understood in part as campaigns to extend choices and participation in educational decision-making not just to individuals but also to collectivities.

American public schools do provide such a wide array of electives and programs that the shopping mall has become a familiar metaphor for high schools. It is a *public* system for *public* purposes but allows many individual choices within that system. There are many points of entry and reentry compared with educational systems in most other nations. Because of the collective importance of education, however, few policy makers in past or present have been entirely laissez-faire about what the next generation should learn. Conservatives, liberals, and radicals have all wished at one time or another to constrain the educational choices that parents and students made. Note that a conservative like William Bennett, who extols the advantages of choice and competition in schooling, wants to limit electives and has proposed a definite set of required courses. He wants a free market in schooling but prescriptions within the academic curriculum. Thus does a command economy enter even a free market solution.

Today many people speak about education as a consumer good, a matter for individual choice. This departs from a long American tradition of regarding education as a common good, a benefit like the air in which all participate and from which all may potentially benefit. The way in which the next generation is educated affects everyone ultimately. The recent debates about the role of schooling in assuring national economic competitiveness is just one chapter in a long history of claims that education was necessary for the prosperity and even the survival of the republic, for individual morality, and for many other social and civic goals. During most of our history Americans have wished to limit the power of government and have been niggardly in offering public services, but education has been an exception. Because they have seen education as a common good, they have been willing to provide it more lavishly and universally than has any other nation.

In the past, only rarely have Americans framed educational issues primarily in terms of the classical liberal values of free markets and private autonomy. In the nineteenth century, one such debate concerned whether secondary education should be provided only by private schools, but that was settled in a series of court decisions and by growing public support for high schools. Even the court case in *Pierce* preserving the right of parents to send their children to private schools asserted the public interest in the civic education of all children.

Choice in education, then, is in part a function or power and not something that most people want to be totally unconstrained. But at what institutional level should decisions be made? On the question of centralized v. decentralized decision-making Americans have engaged in fierce debates for over a century. While the secular trend has been toward greater centralization, the movement has not been linear but jagged. The history of state centralization in California in the nineteenth century, for example, illustrates a zig-zag course between more and less state control over curriculum, a strong superintendency, and state certification of teachers.

Both conservatives and radicals have advocated both local and central control, though for different reasons. Business and professional elites at the turn of the twentieth century wanted more centralized control of urban schools at a time when they believed that decentralized ward control was inefficient and corrupt. Today, by contrast, many businessmen exalt decentralization and choice. Following *Brown* many blacks wanted the federal and state governments and the courts to promote desegregation, while others pushed for community control and decentralization in city schools. The distribution of power at any one time at different levels of governance — who was in control and who was out — has shaped the strategies of contending groups.

In a society so diverse as America's and with governmental structures so multilayered, we face the task of balancing parochial and universal values, local discretion and mandates from central agencies. It is easy to romanticize local control; it has in fact produced schools that have been highly unequal in resources and discriminatory toward low-power groups. Centralized checks are necessary to prevent abuse of civil rights and liberties. Some degree of centralized funding is necessary to correct fiscal inequities between and within states.

But to claim that professional experts know best or that federal and state governments have the wisdom to decree a 'one best system' of schooling is not only arrogant — it also disregards the checkered recent history of instructional reforms imposed from without. Policy makers need to examine which decisions are best made at local and which at higher levels, not to advocate either centralization or decentralization as an omnibus solution. Because Americans have conceived of education as a public good but defined that good in different ways, the great mass of citizens has seen the matter of centralization *versus* decentralization as one of uneasy balance. And this is as it should be.

Chapter 3

Control in School Organizations: Theoretical Perspectives[1]

Janet A. Weiss

Control is a concept that demands disaggregation. In this chapter I look at five kinds of control that are important ingredients of education policy: professional norms and styles of work, political processes and institutions, administrative direction and control, market forces and pressures, and the articulation of values and ideas. I review the theoretical claims about each type of control, including distinctive strengths and difficulties. The analysis suggests that all five are important forces that policy makers must reckon with in the search for improved educational outcomes. This multilayered portrait of control provides one possible frame for the debate about proposals to decentralize authority.

To those who theorize about organizations, policy proposals to decentralize school districts seem sensible but raise many questions. What should be decentralized and what should remain centralized? What is likely to be different once control is lodged at a different level in the organization? All complex organizations struggle to balance the need for predictability and coordination with the need for flexibility and autonomy by members of the organization. Striking the right balance contributes mightily to the organization's success. But finding the right balance is a perennial challenge.

Policy proposals to strengthen market pressures on schools by increasing parental choice also raise fascinating questions about school organizations. How does choice translate into control? How will existing patterns of control in schools be altered by the advent of parental choice? How will those currently in control adapt to enhanced influence of parents? All complex organizations struggle to balance the need for internal efficiency, equity, and stability with the need to respond to external constituencies. Strengthening the hand of one of the external constituencies changes the balancing act required of school administrators in complex, not altogether predictable ways.

Both decentralization and choice selectively alter the allocation of control in school organizations in the hope of producing desirable change in their performance. How realistic is that hope? In this chapter I review some of the major theoretical perspectives on control to address that question.

The various social science disciplines have devoted substantial attention to the subject of control. Although the resulting literature is huge, it is sprawling and spotty. Still a review may be useful in understanding the exercise of control in elementary and secondary schools and school districts. In my review I cover single organizations and interdependent networks of organizatons. I focus on those theories pertinent to organizations that do professional work and are either operated or regulated by the state. Hence I omit literatures dealing with technical control of work, fiscal control in non-professional business organizations, military models of control, and control in untrammeled markets — perspectives that do not readily apply to educational organizations.

By control I mean the ability of one actor (whether individual or institutional) to limit the range of acceptable behavior by another actor (again, individual or institutional) in order to achieve some policy objective. This definition focuses on control as a relationship. People or institutions do not have control in general; they have control only with respect to identifiable targets (Weiss and Gruber, 1984b). Typically people also have control over their targets only with respect to specific domains of work-related behavior. My definition excludes control for personal or interpersonal purposes, as my intent is to discuss the allocation of control as a policy tool. If control granted for policy purposes is turned to personal ends, that constitutes a distortion of the control relationship.

There are strong family resemblances among the terms control, power, and influence. I use 'control' because it carries connotations useful for my analysis. Control may be exercised intentionally or as an incidental by-product of action taken on other grounds. Those on the receiving end of control may or may not feel manipulated or coerced. Control may lead actors to choose among an array of desirable options, or may make it easier for actors to do what they prefer. So long as the targets' behavior has been successfully constrained, they have been controlled, by my definition. One of my major themes is that the resources that enable actors to exercise control may be quite varied, including legal authority, rank, imagination, position, expertise, charm, money, or physical force.

I discuss control of five sorts: professional norms and styles of work, administrative direction and control, political processes and institutions, market forces and pressures, and the articulation of values and ideas. In the following section, I review the theoretical perspectives that deal with the five kinds of control, sketching their central themes and assumptions. I consider which actors are most likely to exercise control of this type. I also review the characteristic disadvantages associated with control of each type, focusing on the difficulties in using control to achieve desirable educational outcomes.

This analysis strongly suggests that all of these kinds of control always coexist in schools. They are present in varying degrees under different circumstances. They may work together or at cross-purposes, tightly coupled to one another or quite independent. As scholars, politicians, parents, or administrators talk about policy prescriptions for improving schools, we often focus on one or another kind of control, without remembering the multiple kinds of control and the interactions among controls in organizations. When one kind of control is exercised by one actor (for example, when federal bureaucrats seek to promote new curricula), other actors may respond with other kinds of control (for example, parents complain to the school board or teachers seek more control over classroom use of the curricula). Sensitivity to these interdependencies prepares us for the likely results of any given intervention.

I return at the end of the chapter to the challenges of translating theory about control into policy proposals dealing with decentralization or choice. Some of these theoretical perspectives tell a story of control that is deeply entrenched or hopelessly fragmented — in either case requiring very substantial long run commitments to channel in new directions. Others point to affordable levers of change in the short run. For policy makers who seek major change in educational outcomes, it is tempting but misguided to ignore the former and focus on the latter. Because of the many different kinds of control circulating in districts and schools and the interactions among them, proposals for policy change must address both intended changes in the allocation of control and the unintended but crucial adaptations to those changes. Thinking about control as I have proposed provides a conceptual map of the territory of control that encourages a wide-angled perspective on reform.

Five Kinds of Control

Professional Control

The fundamental activity of a school is teaching, and teaching is professional work. The work teachers do is like that of other professionals: it is predominantly intellectual, requires the consistent application of judgment, cannot be standardized or routinized, and calls for prolonged preparation through specialized education. Professionals typically seek control by using their training, credentials, and the norms of professional practice to obtain autonomy and support that enable them to work effectively.

In Freidson's (1987) analysis, 'the minimal characteristic of the professional employee, then, is technical autonomy, the freedom to employ discretion in performing work in the light of personal, presumably schooled judgment that is not available to those without the same qualifications' (p. 141). Teaching requires discretion to meet the variable needs of students, subject matter, and circumstances. When efforts are made to standardize or routinize the process of instruction, teachers resist. When efforts are made to standardize or routinize the outcomes of instruction, teachers protest that too, pointing to the variability of the students they serve. Teachers typically work in isolation from one another, each practicing her craft on her own students. Like other professionals, teachers defer to one another's professional judgment and prefer not to interfere or evaluate one another's work.

These distinctive qualities of professional work have complex consequences for control in schools (Freidson, 1987). First, teachers expect control over many of their own daily tasks in the classroom. Several crucial domains of educational decisions are designated as professional in content, and left virtually undisturbed by other control mechanisms in the schools. The day to day practices of instruction, evaluation of student performance, and maintenance of order are usually left in the hands of individual teachers. Through these practices, teachers have a great deal to say about what and how students learn (Powell *et al.*, 1985). More subtly, their work establishes the effective policy of the school as a whole toward individual students (Lipsky, 1980). This occurs through the teacher's contributions to the students' permanent records, decisions to refer students to various specialists by attaching labels to student behavior, and use of formal disciplinary procedures. Finally teachers often face the job of integrating state and federal policy initiatives with the existing school program. Administrators and specialists at state and district levels communicate these initiatives downward, but where the rubber meets the road, teachers decide how to manage student time and attention across the multiple demands of the administration.

Second, professionals resist supervision or control by non-professionals. In those domains where administrative supervision is possible and legitimate — hiring, assignments, resource allocation, discipline, coordination, rewards — other professionals with the training and credentials of teachers are called upon to fill these roles. Because they share the training and perspective of the professional employees, they are expected to appreciate, support and perpetuate the professionals' needs for autonomy.

Third, teachers are embedded within an active professional group that is larger than any school, district, or state. The profession of teaching has several influential components, including unions, professional associations, and university schools of education. These professional groups shape the training of new teachers, standards for both occupational and institutional certification, legislation and regulation affecting schools, conditions of work for teachers, and the status of the profession. They also influence teachers' attachment to their professional status and provide new ideas and models of high quality teaching through professional journals and meetings.

This constellation of control resources derives from the professional technology of work. The basic assumptions that support this source of control are:

- Good teaching cannot occur without a close and indispensable personal relationship between the professional employee/teacher and the client/student.
- The successful management of relationships with students of diverse ability, background, and need demands considerable discretion and autonomy for practitioners.
- Professional training means that professional workers require little or no external supervision; their behavior is controlled by their training and norms of practice.
- Only peer professionals are qualified to supervise and evaluate professional workers.
- The intrusion of control by nonprofessionals disrupts and impedes the exercise of good judgment in relationships between professional and client, thus tending to lower the quality of service.
- By training and inclination, professionals work in the interests of the clients (students and, indirectly, parents) and thus should have considerable influence over the goals and directions of the organization.

Although these assumptions are imperfectly reflected in real life, they nevertheless permeate the behavior of teachers and teachers' organizations in their relationships with other actors in schools.

Disadvantages of professional control

The characteristic difficulties associated with professional control are well known. Teachers, through training and selection, are committed to their work. They think they have learned how it should be done, what work is interesting, and which activities are worthy of their training (Freidson, 1987). They tend to treat with suspicion any pressure from administrators, teachers or school boards to reduce costs or improve productivity. In their commitment to a narrow conception of autonomy, they may resist new ways of working, new kinds of students, or new ways of allocating resources that may improve the operation of the school as a whole. Moreover, teachers, like other professionals, purport to serve the clients' interests, but may substitute their own conceptions of need or problem for those of the client. They may categorize or standardize individual problems, depersonalizing the students they teach. They treat students and parents of lower social status than their own with elitism, intimidation, and arrogance. They may place more emphasis on maintaining order than on learning, on mastery of tests than on thinking. These tendencies (which are by no means unique to teachers) become serious problems for a school when professional norms prevent administrators from noticing such unacceptable behavior or from doing anything about the behavior that does come to their attention.

When teachers are given the autonomy they need to teach, they are perforce given the autonomy to fail. Not all teachers are equally competent, motivated, or well trained. Resistance to evaluation and supervision in the name of autonomy permits mediocre teachers to escape notice, permits poor teachers to escape disciplinary action or dismissal, and permits all teachers to escape the possibility of improvement through feedback or coaching. As a group, teachers, like other professionals, seek to preserve their control over the training and supply of teachers, whether to safeguard quality or to enhance the economic value of a teaching credential. Efforts to control official credentialing produce possibly artificial restrictions on supply of able teachers. Efforts to regulate the accreditation of schools and universities produce possibly artificial expansions in demand for credentialed teachers. Although teachers have been historically less successful than some other professional groups (like lawyers and doctors) in controlling supply and demand, the incentive to do so remains in place.

I mentioned earlier that I would not consider the use of control for personal ends. But when people have access to control to achieve substantive purposes, they are unavoidably tempted to satisfy substantive goals in a way that simultaneously promotes personal interests. Professionals distort their use of control to ease their own situations in subtle ways that are nearly indistinguishable from legitimate demands for professional autonomy and support.[2]

Administrative Control

Perhaps the largest body of the control literature is devoted to the administrative hierarchy. The administrative hierarchy allocates authority over certain domains of activity in schools. Those who design administrative structures and systems, and those who operate the structure and systems achieve control over the work of others. My coverage here is even more sketchy than for the other four kinds of control, for this literature is so broad and diverse that volumes can be, and have been, devoted to it. I focus on the activities of administrators at school, district, and state levels, and their contributions to the performance of the educational system. The assumption in this section is that management of employees and internal allocation of resources exert control over what goes on in schools and, hence, over educational preformance.

Administrative control can be examined from three levels of analysis: the individual, the organization, and the interorganizational network.[3] In each case, theorists have considered a variety of relationships between administrative control and organizational outcomes.

Individual administrators

At the individual level of analysis, most theorists assume that the manager or leader has the task of goal attainment. Rational, goal-directed theories of the individual assign to the manager the task of designing an incentive and control system to induce everyone else in the organization to work efficiently and effectively toward the organization's goals (Merchant, 1985). From the days of Taylor's scientific management to contemporary theories of behavior modification, goal setting (Locke *et al.*, 1981), path-goal leadership (House, 1971), and corporate strategy (Porter, 1980), a significant point of leverage in the organization is assumed to be the manager who can set goals and provide the stimulus for others to achieve them. These managers may not be perfectly rational in pursuit of the organization's goals; bounded rationality is sufficient to fulfill the spirit of these theories (Simon, 1976).

Other theorists focus on the leadership qualities of administrators. From Weber's (1947) charismatic leader to Burns' (1978) transformational leader, many analyses assert that energetic, forceful, and skillful leadership by senior managers can have dramatic results on organizational performance. The foundation of this control may be the admiration and affection that employees feel toward the leader, or it may be the vision or authority that the leader conveys. In either case, people accept the leader's control over a wide range of behavior. Some of the work on the role of superintendents or school principals falls in this category.

A third perspective on the individual administrator considers the manager's role in interpretation, providing a language and framework for people to understand their work and the organization. Weick (1979), for example, suggests that the manager's role is to facilitate and enrich the causal reasoning of others in the organization. Creating shared language and vocabulary, gaining acceptance of shared meaning, offering plausible interpretation of puzzling situations, promoting activities with symbolic impact, and constructing social order are keys to effective management (Pfeffer, 1977).

Organizational factors

Theory at the organizational level of analysis treats administrative control as residing in organizational structure and processes. Control is exercised in the way work is divided up among employees and the way individual jobs are specified (Edwards, 1979; Hackman and Oldham, 1980). Some modes of work restrict the autonomy of employees; others enhance it. Some modes of work make performance visible and measurable; others make it difficult to measure. Managers are constrained by the technology employed in their organization. But within these constraints they enjoy significant choice of ways to structure and coordinate the organization's tasks. For example, different schools make different choices about using teachers for various non-instructional tasks, like supervising the cafeteria or hallways. Different schools assign different responsibilities to subject matter departments. Different schools make different opportunities available for joint projects, trips, or team teaching.

Allocation of resources is another managerial process that offers control over employees. Budgets, space, supplies, personnel slots, and such are typically controlled by administrators, who dole them out to further the interests of the organization as they see them. The choices of books or computers, teacher aides or librarians, a new roof or playground equipment provide scope for administrators to bolster some activities and starve others. Gamoran and Dreeben (1986) show how such administrative choices influenced the arrangement of students in courses, allotment of time, and the content of instruction. Allocation of resources permits managers to structure patterns of incentives to employees to perform well on their designated tasks. These incentives do not always work, and are not always administered fairly, but they afford administrators opportunities for control that operate through the administrative hierarchy.

Rules, procedures, and routines of work are highly visible forms of managerial control. They are mechanisms of coordination and accountability that managers use to ensure that work is done and done appropriately (Weber, 1947; March and Simon, 1958). They also provide predictability and protection to employees because they order and structure the relationships among employees and between employees and administrators (Perrow, 1986). Because the typical design of work in schools provides considerable autonomy to teachers and principals and low visibility of performance, school administrators tend to rely heavily on rules and procedures to substitute for direct supervision (Peterson, 1984; Miles, 1981).

Behavioral economists (Williamson, 1981; Moe, 1984; Pratt and Zeckhauser, 1985) see organizations as devices for structuring exchange relations between employees and management. The administrative task is to craft contracts, implicit or explicit, that induce employees to do the work that management wants at the lowest cost. Williamson (1981) writes 'use of a complex structure to govern simple transactions is to incur unneeded costs, while to use a simple structure to govern a complex transaction invites strain'. If the contracts are not well designed, employees who pursue their own self-interest, which is to say everyone, will engage in opportunism and shirking. If the contracts are well designed, management can discourage opportunism and shirking, and employees will perform at desired levels. Unfortunately, these contracts cannot be written out fully and explicitly. Administrators are uncertain about what future contingencies may arise, and how employees should respond to them when they do. The more contingencies are unknown, the more the organization is forced to provide general guidance rather than explicit instructions to employees. This makes careful design of organizational structure all the more important. Design must be well matched to the features of the exchange relationship, and in particular to the relative market power of the employees *vis-a-vis* the organization.

Applying this perspective to schools involves a logical stretch, for the behavioral economists see competitive pressures for efficiency as the driving force in organizational structure. As public institutions, schools and districts are not shaped by efficiency pressures in the same ways. However, some concern for efficiency surely guides educational administrators, and they seek to reduce opportunism and shirking by school employees. This can be done in two ways. One is to introduce better output measures of performance, so that managers can monitor the output of each employee. This is the most straightforward way to detect and deter shirking. If that proves infeasible, as it so often does in education, the second option is to rely on process measures of performance. Making the educational process more visible (perhaps by teaching in groups or more frequent surveillance of classrooms by administrators) allows employees to demonstrate their good faith efforts to perform as management wishes. Other strategies to reduce shirking include reducing the size of organizational units and moving some instructional activities outside the boundaries of the school organization by contracting with independent vendors for instructional services. The smaller the unit, the easier it is to detect shirking. The use of vendors permits the drafting of contracts between managers and instructional staff that are more specific and limited in scope and duration than the broad, open-ended contracts that must be given to permanent staff members.

Contingency theorists explore the relationship between organizational structure and outcomes by emphasizing the mediating role of context. They argue that there is no straightforward effect of structure on outcomes (Thompson, 1967; Child, 1972). But given the technology employed by the organization and the characteristics of its environment (for example, uncertainty, resource munificence or scarcity, or degree of competition), then some structural features produce better results than others under the specified circumstances. Thus technology shapes the skills and autonomy required by the work force, and hence the kinds of administrative controls that must be employed. Routine technologies permit more centralized and formalized structures to be successful; uncertain technologies require substantial discretion to be left to employees. Similarly environmental uncertainty and complexity require organizations or units to be structured in ways that match the uncertainty and complexity they face (Lawrence and Lorsch, 1967). This line of work assumes that the structural arrangement used by organizations must be congruent with the environment for the organizations to perform well.

The special technological and environmental challenges faced by educational organizations have spawned a literature on the organizational structures best suited to schools. By reasoning along lines characteristic of contingency theory, Weick (1976) suggested that an organizational structure in which internal elements were loosely coupled was well suited to the indeterminate technology and complex environment of schools. 'By loose coupling', Weick wrote, 'the author intends to convey the image that coupled events are responsive, but that each event also preserves its own identity and some evidence of its physical or logical separateness'. The administrative structure of the school or district might include levels and units that respond to one another, but that operate with considerable independence. Other theorists have expanded on this theme. Meyer and Rowan(1977) highlighted the gap between the school's technical core — that is, instruction — and the complex demands placed on the school by the environment. They argued that school administrators absorbed the external demands, buffering the technical core from disruption. Firestone (1985) argued that principals may enhance the performance of their schools by loosening the bonds between the school and the district, thereby allowing teachers more discretion to react to their students. Mills *et al.*, (1983) concluded that the direct contributions of students to the 'production process' of schools, like other professional service organizations, generates high levels of task uncertainty that can only be managed through loose coupling and professional discretion.

Networks of organizations

At the interorganizational level of analysis, theorists have looked at the relationship between one organization and the other organizations in its environment. Administrative control provides the vehicle for managing the relationships that permit the focal organization to thrive or wither. The two major schools of work in this area are resource dependence and institutional theory.

The resource dependence perspective (Pfeffer and Salancik, 1978) notes that organizations require resources from outside their boundaries in order to function. An organization depends on those that provide those resources, and this dependence makes the organization responsive to the demands and needs of organizations or groups in the environment who control critical resources. Managers focus on these external dependencies, both to ensure the survival of the organization through the continued flow of resources and to acquire, if possible, more autonomy and freedom from external constraint (Pfeffer, 1982). In this perspective, administrative control is important in two ways. First, administrators must be sufficiently responsive to external groups to keep resources flowing into the organization, without diverting resources to complying with other external demands that are not crucial to the organization's success. One common strategy for doing this is structural differentiation, establishing subunits to cope with the most urgent external demands. Second, administrators seek to reduce their organization's dependence on others, through becoming more self-sufficient, diversifying, forming alliances and coalitions, restricting access to information about their activities, seeking legal protection from influence, or attempting to co-opt external actors. In short 'the environment' is not altogether given. It can be nudged, shaped, even recreated to the organization's advantage, if administrators are skillful.

Institutional theories also look at the interorganizational level of analysis. Scott (1987), Zald (1970), Zucker (1988), Meyer and Scott (1983),

Selznick (1957) and other theorists of this stripe see organizations embedded in social and political contexts, serving social and political functions in addition to economic and technical ones. These complex contexts are inevitably incorporated into the organization's structure, which reflects some combination of efficiency imperatives and social and political values. The incorporation may be planned and designed by administrators using a selfconscious and strategic vision of the organization (Selznick, 1957). Or it may occur willy-nilly, when administrators are distracted with their technical tasks.

Meyer and Scott (1983) describe the emergence of institutional societal sectors, clusters of organizations that provide a given type of service and the suppliers, clients, funders, regulators, and support agencies that interact with them. Organizations receive support and legitimacy from other members of the sector, and must in turn conform to the rules and expectations of the sector. According to Meyer and Scott, the structure of authority within sectors has implications for control at the level of the individual organization. Fragmented authority leads to cumbersome and complex control systems requiring complex administrative arrangements for four reasons: attempts to use fiscal controls require extensive auditing, reporting and record-keeping; the independent influence attempts of many external controllers aggregates to a confusing barrage of control at the lowest level; when scattered procedural controls are not effective, would-be controllers ratchet up their efforts; fragmented authorities find it difficult to achieve coordination among themselves or among the organizations they seek to influence. (Hill (1979) shows what this phenomenon looks like in school districts.) DiMaggio and Powell (1983) suggest that organizations within institutional sectors become increasingly alike over time, as managers try to bolster their organization's legitimacy and make it easy to attract resources from external sources.

In all these ways administrators have a central role to play and distinctive kinds of control to use. Their actions, whether calculated or inadvertent, the systems they design and guide, and their decisions are theorized to have major implications for the performance of educational organizations.

Disadvantages of administrative control

The weaknesses of administrative control are legion. Each kind of administrative control is associated with characteristic problems and undesirable side-effects. I highlight a few of the weaknesses that seem especially glaring to observers of educational organizations.

In organizations that do professional work, administrative control is in persistent tension with professional values. By valuing predictability and order, administrative control reduces flexibility, diversity, and discretion that professionals need to do their work. Even though in schools, as in most professional organizations, administrators are themselves professionals, the controls they use exert constant pressure on teachers to conform to school-wide or district-wide or even state-wide categories of input and output. McNeil (1986) argues that 'when the school's organization becomes centered on managing and controlling, teachers and students take school less seriously'. In her study of four high schoools, administrators who focused on minimum standards and social order achieved minimum standards and social order, but little learning or thinking. Only administrators who provided autonomy and support to teachers, at the expense of routine mass-processing of students, were rewarded with high quality teaching.

Administrative control, like all the other types I have considered, may be used in self-serving ways. In the extreme case, the administrators' control over organizational resources is turned to personal ends. But more common and more insidious is the use of control to protect the administrators and the organization from embarrassment or criticism. A prominent example is restricting access to information about the organization's performance or budget. When administrative control is used to perpetuate the interests of the existing group of administrators, schools and districts become unresponsive to the preferences of the other participants in the educational process — teachers, students, parents, school boards, etc. In the interorganizational realm, self-serving behavior leads to individual schools or districts behaving in ways that maximize advantage or discretion for their administrators but lead to unfortunate results for the system as a whole. For example, failure to share resources or coordinate programs, diversion of funds away from politically powerless groups toward politically influential groups, or pushing unsuccessful or unruly students out of school may make the day for one group of administrators, while making trouble for others.

Administrative control tends to focus on what can be demonstrated, rather than on what is important. As Wildavsky (1979) writes, 'because organizations wish to be regarded as successful, they try to replace objectives whose achievement depends on variables either unknown or outside their control with objectives that can be attained by manipulating the instruments that those groups do control' (p.49). The original goals of education are displaced by goals that are more easily attainable, dealing with internal operations rather than improvement in student outcomes. Raising the standards for certification of teachers, increasing numbers of credit hours in academic subjects, lengthening the school year, equalizing resources across schools in a district, and buying computers for each classroom are expensive, but easier and more measurable than producing better educated students. Administrative effort tends to focus on the former, measurable, attainable goals at the expense of the important but unmeasurable, perhaps unattainable latter goal.

Administrative control is supposed to be exercised by rational managers who pursue efficient goal attainment on behalf of the organization. Although administrators do try to be purposive, reasonable, and efficient, they succeed only intermittently. The job is simply too complex for any administrator, no matter how talented and energetic, to attend to all organizational problems and opportunities at once (Cyert and March, 1963). Depending on the composition of the dominant coalition of interests within the school or district, some issues attract attention and others languish in the shadows. Because administrators are forced by goal complexity, causal indeterminacy, and bounded rationality into a pattern of sequential attention to issues, their movement from issue to issue communicates a lack of focus and strategy. The frequent charge of slavish adherence to fashion among educators probably stems from this difficulty in setting administrative priorities and implementing them consistently over time.

The administrative controls that proliferate in sectors with fragmented authority are cumbersome, inefficient, and expensive. The federal government, states, intermediate districts, and local districts attempt to influence schools. In these influence attempts, they all rely nearly all the time on control over procedures, not outcomes. Thus teacher certification substitutes for assessing teacher competence. Graduation rates substitute for measuring student learning. Audits substitute for measuring competent resource allocation. Attendance substitutes for student engagement. If good outcome measures were available, they would facilitate the efficient exercise of control, by allowing schools to achieve given levels of outcome with any combination of resources that worked best for their circumstances. Because we as a society cannot agree how to measure educational outcomes (Weiss and Gruber, 1987), administrators at one level of the system cannot control others through outcomes. We are stuck with some variety of process controls. Not all process measures are equally inefficient. But all tend to produce at least some of the problems described here.

Political Control

Public schools are political institutions, funded with tax dollars and governed by layers of democratically elected officials.[4] After all, children are our collective future. Their education is central to the skills of the nation's work force, the resources for the nation's politics, and the quality of life in our communities. As an economy, a nation, as states and communities, we all have a stake in how well schools work. To protect that stake, government has been intimately involved in funding and policy making in education.

Political control is derived from the legitimacy of election results and the corresponding accountability to the public of political institutions. Such accountability to the community is widely regarded as desirable (Chubb and Moe, 1988; Tyack, 1974), if cumbersome (Cohen, 1982). The most direct sort of political control is exercised by elected local boards, but other elected officials (federal, state, and sometimes local) and their designates (federal and state education agencies) also have control by virtue of their mandate from the voters. Voters intermittently speak directly in elections on school bonds and tax rates. And courts (federal and state) interpret the laws passed by elected officials.

Even private schools are influenced by political control, although they are not public themselves. Private schools must meet legal obligations decided upon by state and federal legislators and enforced by state and federal courts. For example, they must meet various criteria in order to maintain tax-exempt status. In various states they may need to hire teachers with specified qualifications, have a school year of a certain length, teach courses that satisfy graduation requirements, provide a safe physical plant. Their clientele is enlarged by laws requiring school attendance. They are indirectly but profoundly affected by the policies and financing of the public schools, which are their competitors. Thus public policies that promise to improve (or harm) public education in various ways have considerable impact on private schools.

Local school boards typically assume responsibility for the broad policies of the local district including such matters as curriculum, ancillary services, budget, funding, capital improvements, negotiating with organized employees, hiring and evaluating the superintendent. The local board members are usually elected by the community served by the district (although sometimes they are appointed by elected officials) and constitute the heart of local control over the schools. In some states, the school board raises its own revenue, usually from property taxes; in others, cities and towns raise property tax revenue that is then turned over to the board. In the latter case, the schools have another set of local elected officials to deal with. Mayors, city councils, aldermen, and the like must wrestle with the claims of the schools along with competing claims for police, fire, trash collection, roads, parks, economic development, and the rest of the agenda of local government. Although schools are frequently insulated from direct conflict with other spending priorities, their budgets alone make them unavoidably prominent in local politics.

State and national governments also direct authority over some functions of the schools. State taxes now pay the single largest share of the school budget, and these taxes are enacted and allocated by state legislators. Educational finance is an enduring topic of political conflict in most state capitols. State and national legislators have established a host of specialized educational programs, often to force local schools to do things that many districts historically preferred not to do. Programs like those for civil rights, vocational education, disadvantaged children, handicapped children, children whose first language is not English, nutrition, and driver education illustrate the willingness of legislators to mandate activities to be carried out in schools.

Because of the public and political status of decisions by and about schools, the courts have also become centrally involved in school decisions. Through the courts, political authority is asserted over a range of school decisions (Wise, 1979). This authority is political because the legitimacy of legal intervention in school policy comes not from the need to enforce private contractual agreements but from policy, that is from the interest of the polity in fair and reasonable educational practice that complies with the laws adopted by political actors. In a handful of educational arenas, legal intervention has been framed as a matter of rights of individual participants: the right to equitable access to state resources, the right to attend desegregated schools, the right to due process in disciplinary proceedings. Under these circumstances the courts evaluate the claims of those who have come to see their individual complaints as matters of legal or constitutional principle. However, the connections between individual complaints and moral or political principles are social constructions; in different times and societies people reach different conclusions about the kinds of problems for which they can legitimately feel aggrieved and expect a legal remedy (Stone, 1988). Both the construction and enforcement of legal rights ultimately depend on political dynamics.

Political control operates in several streams: budgeting, policy making, and procedural requirements. Budgeting is straightforward. Both the total amount of resources directed to education and the allocation of resources among states, districts, and schools are decided upon by political actors. Policy making produces mandates, inducements, regulation, and support that directly concern education and that affect schools indirectly (for example, through policies regulating the employment of minors or compulsory military service). Procedural requirements govern the relationships between schools and their various constituencies, by requiring, for example, parent involvement, public meetings of the board of education, or competitive bidding for school construction contracts.

Political control, like professional and administrative control, has two faces. Its strengths are the responsiveness of school organizations to the goals and preferences of the citizenry, the need for public accountability in the expenditure of public funds, and the energy and vitality injected into the system by the political arena (Aberbach and Rockman, 1988). Political control counteracts the tendency of bureaucratic agencies to serve narrow or self-regarding purposes. It creates vehicles for the oversight of school activities by people who are not educators, who represent the varied clients of educators — parents, employers, taxpayers, and neighbors. It enhances the legitimacy of the educational enterprise: elected officials have blessed the enterprise with their participation, if not exactly their approval. Because elections are held regularly, citizens have regular opportunities to express their satisfaction or dissatisfaction with the way things are going.

The actors who exercise political control behave in accordance with the structure and rules of political institutions. Elected officials serve at the pleasure of their constituents, and they are guided by a mix of concerns for reelection, effective representation of their jurisdiction, and the public well-being. Interest groups form to articulate and promote the views of school constituents before these actors. These constituents range from school employees to parents of students who feel ill-used by the schools to boosters of school athletic teams to suppliers of school lunch programs. Battles that cannot be won in-house escalate to larger arenas as interest groups appeal to the multiple layers of political actors who assert some jurisdiction over school activities. This arrangement permits and legitimizes the participation of a wide array of actors in educational decisions.

Disadvantages of political control

The very qualities of responsiveness and participation that make political control desirable have a darker side. Political control is, by definition, external control, in which schools are governed by groups at some distance from the daily work of teaching children. This creates distinctive problems. It virtually guarantees that schools will be held responsible for multiple, not altogether compatible goals. Because several levels of governance are involved and because these different levels represent constituencies of differing size and heterogeneity, the preferences of these constituencies are seldom identical. As a result, local, state, and national governments will each impose legitimate goals for schools to achieve. This creates dilemmas at the school level, as each school wrestles with the appropriate balance among the multiple goals (Goodlad, 1984; Kirst, 1984).

External control sets up a severe principal/agent problem in which elected officials (the 'principals') face the challenge of getting school staff (the 'agents') to comply with their decisions (e.g., McCubbins, Noll and Weingast, 1987). As I discussed in the previous section in the case of administrative control, there is inevitably leakage between the principals' demands and the agents' response. In the case of political officials as principals, the leakage becomes a flood in the face of the differing incentives facing political actors and school staff. Politicians can try to monitor performance more closely to reduce shirking. But this is costly, especially for part timers like school board members or state legislators. Given the use of unclear technologies to achieve multiple, conflicting outcomes (as in teaching and administration), even very costly supervision cannot be expected to reduce shirking significantly. Note that the problem of shirking looks very different when seen through the theoretical perspective of professionalism. What economists call shirking is what professionals see as the reconciliation of the general guidance and intervention of lay politicians with their own judgment and expertise about quality education.

Political actors must rely on policy instructions to those who actually carry out the practice. Frequently these instructions take the form of law or legally enforceable procedures. The procedures that schools develop to comply with external requirements are therefore subject to legal scrutiny. Litigation or the threat of litigation have come to influence many relationships within schools (Wise, 1979). Distinctively legal styles of reasoning and intervention often lead to remedies that address legal concerns but create educational ones. For example, Horowitz (1977) describes the distortion of teacher assignment policies forced on an urban school district by a court order to equalize spending across schools. Elaborate rules and procedural mechanisms protect the school from legal intervention, but constrain administrative and professional discretion and judgment.

Political control creates the potential for paralysis or capture of the decision making apparatus by groups pursuing narrow interests. The strategy of giving everyone a voice in school decisions can create the sense that no one has a voice (Murphy, 1981). More troubling and more frequently, the interest groups that are most likely to organize effectively to exert political pressure are those whose lives are touched most directly by school decisions: school employees, book publishers, accrediting and testing organizations, and others with broad financial or occupational interests in educational choices. Mechanisms of political participation tend to produce distorted effects, as when the voices of relatively narrow but well organized interests (like the advocates of school lunch programs, for example) are treated with more seriousness than the voices of diffuse but broader interests (like parent advocates for the academic curriculum; see Kirst, 1984). Although in principle political control is available to all, the reality is that organized and/or middle class clienteles have more clout than diffuse and/or poor clienteles. This general tendency reflects the reliance of political institutions on elections as the means to recruit members and legislation as the means to conduct work (Chubb and Moe, 1988; Schattschneider, 1960).

Political control creates the potential for political patronage in hiring, promotion, and assignment decisions, which undermines merit criteria in staffing schools. At the turn of the century, decentralized school boards treated jobs in schools as spoils of office. Especially in large cities, political connections were essential for securing employment in schools (Tyack, 1974). Modern reincarnations of this practice appeared following the decentralization of the New York City school board (Rogers and Chung, 1983). Although patronage need not be destructive, many school administrators strongly prefer to keep control over personnel matters in their own hands. This is another example of the tension between political control and administrative control.

In addition to these generic weaknesses of political control, a particular concern in education is the weakness of local school boards as political institutions. Although in theory school boards reflect and focus the priorities of the community, elections for school board typically attract a small fraction of the electorate. The views of the majority do not receive voice. In most places elections are nonpartisan. As a result, it is difficult for voters to know the political stands of the candidates and candidates do not have access to the organizational capabilities of the political parties to identify and mobilize potential supporters. With low levels of participation and poor information on the part of many of those who do vote, the mechanisms of representative democracy are not exemplified by these institutions.

Market Control

Under market control, patterns of social behavior are determined by the interaction of many autonomous parties who exchange resources in pursuit of self-interest. Schools exist in their current form only so long as someone is willing to enter into exchanges that provide the necessary resources. In the case of education, the resulting market controls determine the flow of resources into schools. When these 'paying customers' become unwilling to exchange resources for the benefits they receive, the educational system faces a threat to survival. The crucial market factors are (1) the willingness of states and local communities to provide funding to public schools within their jurisdictions; (2) the willingness of people with talent to work as school teachers; (3) the willingness of parents to live (and pay taxes) in given jurisdictions populated with the current mix of other parents and children and to send their children to particular schools in those communities; and (4) the willingness of children to attend school. In the case of private schools, the first market force is replaced by the willingness of parents to pay tuition.

Market control fits my definition of control less comfortably than the other four kinds. Market forces are the result of collective patterns of behavior that are not deliberately designed to influence the discretion of any particular actor. The power of market controls is in the collective pattern, but collective patterns are made up of individual acts. Individuals and institutions choose to allocate their resources in ways that contribute to market effects. If much market control is not calculated to constrain specific individuals or schools, it has the effect of constraint on identifiable targets. Although this kind of control differs in important ways from the other four, it does involve individuals and institutions systematically behaving in ways that constrain the discretion of other individuals and institutions, and hence exercising control over their activities.

In all cases, the resources (whether financial or behavioral) available to the interested actors are scarce, and the demands of education compete with many other demands for the same resources. The resources available to education depend heavily on the size of the resource pool, the opportunity costs of investing resources in education, and the price of achieving desired levels of educational outcomes. Changes in any of these factors may lead to significant shifts in access to resources. Hence, these market forces may have considerable impact on the choices and structures of schools and school districts.

It is obvious that state and local decisions about how much education to consume are not subject to the identical market forces that govern household consumption. For one thing states are constitutionally required to provide at least some education, and states historically have spent substantial fractions of their budgets on education. But there are real market-based pressures on state budgets that influence the resources allocated to elementary and secondary education. Administrators of public schools must justify their expenditures to those who pay the bills. The resources come from diverse sources: members of the local community who vote on local tax and bonding questions, state legislators who appropriate funds for education that are usually distributed according to a formula, and state education bureaucrats who divvy up discretionary grants. Such decisions to spend are made through a political process rather than by a unitary consumer, but they are, nonetheless, decisions to spend guided by the state's or community's pursuit of value.

State and local funding is influenced by the wealth of the state or local community, the level of taxation the state or community is willing to impose on itself, and the competition of other needs for tax dollars. Although wealth tends to be moderately stable over time, the other two factors may change with economic and political conditions. For example, changing demographics have left parents of school-aged children as a rather small block of voters, compared to the larger blocks of older and younger citizens, and the growing group of non-parents. In some jurisdictions, voters without children in school have become increasingly resistant to proposals to increase school taxes or school spending. This trend appears most serious in large urban districts.

The price of education also varies considerably from place to place. Differences in the cost of living across jurisdictions mean that equal expenditures do not purchase equal services. In expensive regions of the country, teacher salaries, building and maintenance costs, utilities, books and supplies are all more expensive. In large urban areas, school districts must pay extra to induce teachers to work in high crime neighborhoods, to protect schools from vandalism, to provide for higher proportions of children with learning difficulties, to respond to the availability of illegal drugs, and to accommodate other special challenges of contemporary urban life. This trend, coupled with the resistance of city dwellers to school taxes, has placed many large urban districts in severely straitened fiscal circumstances.

In private schools tuition dollars and subsidies from religious organizations replace the funding available to public schools. While the budgets of states and communities are always large enough to accommodate significant educational expenditures, the budgets of parents often are not. The opportunity costs of tuition for parents often loom larger than the opportunity costs of educational finance for state and local governments. Because parents of private school students always have a cheaper option available to them, private schools have strong incentives to keep perceived quality high enough to justify the expenditure.

The second market dynamic that affects schools is the labor market for teachers. Education is a labor-intensive service, and its cost is directly tied to professional salaries. Although these salaries have increased in the last few years, the decline of the 1970s has left them lower than those in many occupations that draw from the same pool of college students. The vast majority of school districts base pay on experience and training, rather than on performance. Flat and mechanical salary schedules, combined with challenging work conditions, tend to discourage prospective teachers from making a career in education. Women who used to go into teaching because other professions excluded them now have more options. Thus the pool of prospective teachers has contracted, raising concern about the quality of those who do pursue teaching as a career. In short schools must compete for limited numbers of high quality teachers, without having the resources to raise salaries enough to deepen the pool of applicants (Murnane, 1985).

The third market dynamic is the willingness of parents to live and send their children to school in given jurisdictions. Parental choice is frequently constrained by public school practices that limit that choice. However, we do see evidence of parental choice at work in a variety of circumstances: the flight of white middle-class parents from urban districts, higher real estate prices in desirable school districts, use of transfer policies and magnet schools within districts, and exit to private schools.

These examples demonstrate that parents are sensitive to at least some properties of the schools their children attend. This sensitivity has been most thoroughly researched in the case of urban desegregation, where white parents appear to have left city schools in large numbers in response to changes in student assignment policies or changes in the proportion of minority students in their local school (Orfield, 1978). Although decisions about where to live are based on many factors, schools seem to be one of them, at least for some parents.

Recent innovations that expand opportunities for parents to opt for schools other than the one to which their children are assigned, such as those in Minnesota and Milwaukee, will provide further clues about patterns of parental choice. The hope of the advocates is that breaking the monopoly of the local public school will lead schools to be more responsive to parental concerns and preferences. What those concerns will be (whether, for example, racism will continue to play a significant role in school choice) and how responsive schools can be are yet to be seen.

Even without giving parents the option to select another public school, most schools seem to make serious efforts to respond to those parents who try to influence them. For example, half of the suburban school principals surveyed by Peterson (1984) reported that the central district office used reactions from parents as the most important source of information in evaluating the performance of the principals. Hill *et al.*, (1989) report on a handful of large districts that are attempting to involve parents and other community representatives more frequently and more deeply in school activities. Because superintendents and principals need community support to keep local resources flowing, they do have incentives to respond to parent pressure. Lacking trustworthy measures of administrators' performance, school boards and superintendents rely on parent evaluations and complaints. Of course many parents do not exercise pressure, because they do not understand the subtle mechanisms that would allow them to have influence.

The final market mechanism to consider is the willingness of students to attend school. Although students are required to attend school at least until the age of 16, schools experience variable attendance throughout a student's career and variable drop-out rates after 16. Any high school must be attuned to student preferences so as to encourage attendance and to discourage dropping out. As attendance drives state aid formulas and drop-outs are a visible sign of failure in the community, administrators are motivated to respond to student preferences.

Student willingness to attend school can be affected by school practice. Powell, Farrar and Cohen (1985) discuss the curricular and teaching adaptations that high schools make to keep students coming to school. Two prominent features of these adaptations are the agreement not to demand much beyond attendance and the provision of a wide range of curricular choices. Goodlad (1984), too, emphasizes the conflict between students' expectations and aspirations and the academic functions of high schools. More students in his survey said they valued high schools for the opportunities they provide for social life, personal growth and vocational training, than for the opportunity to learn. To keep students attending school, the social, personal and vocational functions must receive sufficient emphasis to attract adolescents in large numbers.

Of course schools do not bear the full burden of keeping students in school. Other social and economic institutions push in the same direction. High school graduation is a ticket that must be punched for college entrance and for most high paying jobs. Even recruiters for the armed services give preference to high school graduates. Employers do not expect 17 year olds to know Elizabethan poetry or calculus, but a growing number demand literacy, numeracy, and discipline at least at the level of high school graduates.[5] These realities of the labor market help to keep students in attendance, by limiting the range of alternatives to school.

These four market flows — of funding, teachers, parents, and students — create the environment in which schools attract resources and provide services. None of these market dynamics operates independently of social and political institutions. They are all embedded in social practices that guide and constrain exchanges. All markets show distortions from efficiency criteria attributable to networks of personal relationships (Granovetter, 1985). Moreover, as people decide how to spend, where to live, and how to invest their energies, they define self-interest through social lenses, guided by socially constructed visions of what is possible and desirable. Market controls are imperfectly predictable and efficient, but they are nevertheless real and important in the world of schools.

Disadvantages of market control

The weaknesses of market controls in education are also real. All participants' decisions to invest in schooling are handicapped by difficulty in making informed decisions about quality of the services delivered by a school. In ideal markets consumers have perfect information about alternative uses for their resources. In the case of professional services, people may know the result they want to attain, but neither funders (public or private) nor students can easily evaluate the quality of education they receive. Standardized test results, graduation rates, student evaluations — all have severe limitations as indicators of success. Even other professionals have trouble assessing quality reliably, as witnessed by the squabbles over merit pay.

Spending more does not necessarily buy better education (Hanushek, 1981). When markets work well, with multiple buyers and sellers engaged in frequent interaction, the price of a service tends to reflect its quality. In education consumers (be they parents or state legislators or employers) cannot trust price as a signal of quality. This difficulty is compounded by the limited choices confronting parents in search of better quality education. When choosing among the local public school, private school, or moving the family into a better school district, parents are hard put to know whether their willingness to spend will be reflected in the quality of services received by their children.

School district administrators may want to respond to market signals from legislators, teachers, or parents, but may not be able to. Part of the difficulty is that the customers do not speak with one voice. The challenge is to satisfy as many as possible, but their demands are often incompatible. Heterogeneous coalitions of consumers can be brought together to rationalize their demands, as when broad community consensus unites behind a school reform package. But this does not happen often. A second problem is that administrators working with an uncertain technology cannot necessarily steer their ship where they will. Agreeing to improve writing skills or reduce drug abuse is one thing; accomplishing it is another. Finally, market controls fail consumers when school officials choose not to respond to the inducements offered.

Variation in schools responsive to student and parent preferences may not satisfy aggregate social and economic needs for educational output. When decisions are highly decentralized, businesses tend to underinvest in capital needs (Stieglitz, 1974). Left to their own devices, states, communities, or households may invest less in human capital than the society and the economy need to grow and compete.

The wealthy are advantaged in the market compared to the poor, not only in direct transactions where extra resources are an advantage, but also in their mastery of skills in negotiating market transactions. Reliance on market forces tends to amplify initial inequality in the distribution of resources. This pattern may be observed at the level of the state, community, school, household, or individual.

Control Through Values and Ideas

Actors exert control over the organization and activities of schools by articulating and promoting values and ideas about what schools should do and can be. The control of values and ideas is grounded in the assumption that the behavior of individuals and institutions depends on how people think about their work and circumstances. Control is achieved when people come to think differently about their situation — believing that more desirable means exist to achieve their ends, or coming to value different ends. This kind of control overlaps the domain of professional control, but extends beyond it by considering actors other than professionals and other kinds of values and ideas than those transmitted through professional training and norms. Unlike the other four types of control, control through values and ideas is not the special province of any identifiable subset of actors. All kinds of actors have access to this kind of control, and all kinds of actors use it.

V.O. Key wrote, 'one of the great functions of the bureaucratic organization is as a conservator of the values of a culture. In the purposes, procedures, ceremonies, outlook, and habits of the bureaucracy are formalized the traditional cultural values' (*cited* in Lipsky, 1980, p. 180). Many of the values reflected in schooling are affirmative. In the US, for example, we exalt individualism, creativity and choice, as the Japanese exalt cooperation, hard work and mastery of detail (Leetsma *et al.*, 1987). Other values reflected in the organization of schools are socially divisive. Ethnocentrism, racism, sexism, class distinctions — each society incorporates its own version of these values in the structure and practices of schools (Bowles and Gintis, 1976). I am not referring here to the content of the curriculum. I mean that social values, good and bad, control the organization of schooling. Thus racist values in the community may lead to a systematic bias in which schools in white neighborhoods enjoy richer resources than schools in minority neighborhoods, or programs for handicapped students receive more emphasis than programs for disadvantaged students. In this sense, advocates of given values exert control over how schools work.

Values and ideas also constrain schools from venturing outside the mainstream conventional wisdom. Meyer and Rowan (1978) describe elaborate social agreements about appropriate behavior in schools for teachers, students, and administrators. So long as all participants play their designated parts, the adequacy of schooling is taken for granted. No one looks closely at how much education actually occurs. Only when teachers or students refuse to honor the mainstream script does trouble ensue. These scripts or rituals call for clear distinctions between, for example, certified teachers and other adults, between classrooms and everywhere else. Education occurs when certified teachers work with students in classrooms, and not when children are with other adults in other settings. Schools are forbidden by these social agreements to experiment with staffing or less traditional settings. The agreements are enforced by the expectations of teachers and administrators, but also by the same expectations held by students, parents, school boards, and the community about what 'real' schools are like.

Other analysts have focused on the control of values and ideas over organizational choices and behavior. In classic works of organization theory Simon (1976) and Kaufman (1960) have outlined the influence of premises on organizational behavior. Managers attempt to control the behavior of their subordinates and peers by controlling what they think about their work, by 'preforming their decisions' in Kaufman's phrase, or by setting the premises of decision in Simon's terms. Through training, socialization, and communication, organizational members learn about the organization's goals, strategies, and priorities, and apply that learning to their work. The more closely that employees identify with organizational goals, the more those goals control their behavior. The efficacy of premise control can be remarkable. In Kaufman's (1960) study of forest rangers, rangers who were geographically dispersed and coping with a wide array of unpredictable factors and pressures nevertheless behaved in accord with the basic goals of the Forest Service and successfully resisted the incursions of mining and timber interests. Kaufman credits this success to their assimilation of the values and priorities of the parent agency.

Ideas and values also shape individual behavior by controlling what people pay attention to and what they ignore. Because social environments are intricate and ambiguous, and because the human capacity to process information is limited, people attend to only some of the information available to them. Because of the multiple goals of schools and the complexity of the social relationships developed to promote those goals, teachers and administrators attend to only some of the demands on them at any one time (March and Olsen, 1976). From this feast of possibilities, what do they attend to and what do they ignore? The stream of attention and focus come partly from what they think is important, partly from a mix of constraints and signals about what other people expect them to attend to. 'Does a [person] live for months or years in a particular position in an organization, exposed to some streams of communication, shielded from others, without the most profound effects upon what he knows, believes, attends to, hopes, wishes, emphasizes, fears, and proposes?' (Simon, 1976, p. xv). Obviously not.

Some gurus of strategic decision making in business emphasize the overriding importance of clear and specific direction from the top to guide the attention of the rest of the organization (especially Peters, 1988; also Porter, 1980). Once senior administrators have clarified their goals and priorities, other employees can understand their own jobs and choices in terms of the larger organization's interests. This is one of the most efficient ways to supervise the work of others, requiring much less follow-up and monitoring than bureaucratic and coercive modes of management (Perrow, 1986). The catch, of course, is that senior administrators must be able to articulate a clear policy, by reconciling the multiple and conflicting demands placed on them. Many business enterprises have great difficulty in doing so, and public enterprises seem to have even more difficulty (Lynn, 1987). But when those at the top can be clear about strategic policy, that direction can be a powerful tool in moving the organization along the desired path.

In schools, top management is divided between administrative and political control. Many people and groups attempt to claim the attention of school employees. One illustration of how this can be done is found in Weiss and Gruber's (1984a) study of civil rights data in schools. The federal Office for Civil Rights periodically surveys a sample of school districts about their behavior with respect to civil rights. Weiss and Gruber found that the survey promoted a theory about what is important in schools, a theory that emphasizes the race, sex, and handicap of students. The survey led school and district officials to see their worlds through this lens, alerting them to the differential consequences of their behavior for different groups of students. Through this lens, they saw things that they had not noticed before. Over time, they became used to noticing them in this way. Although noticing did not automatically produce changed behavior, it sometimes did. In these and other ways school administrators compete for control over the attention of their staff on the assumption that such attention is a useful lever on performance.

Another example in education is the movement between 1983 and 1986 or so to emphasize excellence (Gross and Gross, 1985). A clear message emerged from many sources that excellence should receive higher priority than before. As a result, a wide variety of choices at the local level came to be seen as possible vehicles for the enhancement of excellence, although they may have been decided on altogether different grounds in the past. By directing the attention of teachers and administrators to excellence as a priority, the reformers succeeded in introducing new ways of thinking about educational practice, ways that downgraded the importance of other priorities. Given the realities of educational policy, it has been difficult to sustain heightened attention to excellence. Other priorities have simply proved too pressing to stay long in the shadows. Nevertheless the example shows that even temporary consensus that systematic attention should be devoted to given priorities can exert real control over school practice on a wide scale.

Finally values and ideas exercise control by persuading people to do what they otherwise would not (Lindblom, 1976). Both individuals and institutions can be influenced by offering them information about new alternatives, or about the costs or benefits of existing alternatives, by making some of their preferences more salient than others, or by persuading people to accept different values and preferences. Individuals' preferences about policy goals are not fixed and immutable. People can learn to value previously neglected ends. When people who work in organizations and agencies change their preferences or reorder their priorities, those organizations and agencies can also adopt new goals and priorities. People can also learn new tricks. As they become willing and competent to carry out new roles, institutions become capable of taking on new responsibilities and activities. In short, people and institutions can learn. As the instruments of learning, values and ideas change behavior, or in the terminology of control, constrain behavior, in the direction desired by those who convey the values and ideas.

Disadvantages of control through values and ideas

The weaknesses of control through values and ideas are the possibility of totalitarian control over ideas, difficulty in fine-tuning control to rapidly changing circumstances, the lack of tangible sanctions to force resistant constituencies to accept control, the inability to produce uniform results using this kind of control, and the difficulties posed by conflicting priorities and ideas about schooling.

The power of ideas is profoundly disturbing to those who are reminded of the massive, centralized, unilateral political indoctrination of fascist regimes. As Lindblom (1976) notes, ideas can be 'a principal instrument of totalitarianism . . . employing indoctrination to capture men's minds so that they would "willingly" do what harsher controls did not therefore need to compel'. Ideas and values have great potential for oppression, it is true, but so do all sources of control.

Control through ideas and values tends to be a slow process, and is characterized by considerable inertia. Socialization to cultural values, extensive social agreements about schooling, inculcating premises and values in organizations — these take time, sometimes generations, to establish. Once in place, they are not easily changed, even when changing circumstances render them obsolete.

Although some people worry about the overwhelming power of ideas, to others values and ideas have the reputation of being weak instruments of control. This is because they are not associated with tangible sanctions for failure to obey. In the other realms of control, the controller can withhold valuable resources (professional, political, administrative, or market) if the target of control resists. Disapproval, lack of synchrony with other's expectations, and doubt are the penalties associated with resistance to the control of values and ideas. These can be powerful. But they do not carry the weight and aura of formal authority or legal redress or financial sanction.

Depending on their previous preferences and beliefs, policy actors differ in their receptivity to given ideas and values. They translate those ideas and values into action in ways that differ from place to place contingent on local interpretation. Of course the same is true for other kinds of control, but some of the others include explicit provisions for correcting misinterpretations. In the case of ideas and values, controllers typically must be content with variable results.

Societal disagreements about the purpose and practice of schooling send off an unremitting stream of conflicting signals about what and how to teach. Schools are bombarded with hopes, dreams, and expectations that cannot be simultaneously satisfied. In this context it is extremely difficult for anyone to act on the lessons learned from the private sector about the paramount importance of clarity of vision and purpose.

Tapestries of Control

I assert, rather than demonstrate, that these five kinds of control coexist in schools, because I hope that this has become self-evident. Certainly all are not equally important all the time, but all are important some of the time. See Table 3.1 for a brief summary of the comparisons among the five.

Various participants in the educational enterprise have differential access to the five kinds of control. Each actor has a stake in preserving those kinds of control that it finds easiest to exercise. Professionals claim exclusive possession of professional control. Individual teachers, teachers' organizations, universities (especially schools of education), and other participants (administrators, bureaucrats, consultants) who happen to have strong professional credentials find it easy to assert the expertise and the need for autonomy that is associated with professional control. Political control comes naturally to elected officials at all levels of government, bureaucrats who enforce laws and policies adopted by elected officials, lawyers and judges who hold schools accountable to legal requirements, and voters, both organized and disorganized. Administrative control is most readily exercised by administrators at school, district, state, and occasionally federal levels. Each group also has access to the other kinds of control; none has a monopoly. But each is the most prominent agent of its own kind of control.

The last two types of control are less concentrated in the hands of identifiable subgroups. Market control is exercised by those who control and compete for the supply of necessary resources: parents and prospective parents, students and former students, teachers and prospective teachers, legislators at state and local levels who regulate the flow of funding into schools and legislators who prefer to spend tax dollars on prisons or road repair. Control through values and ideas can be exercised by nearly anyone who can articulate a vision and persuade people to move toward it. Those in and out of formal roles exert influence over the educational enterprise through ideas about what can be done and why.

Table 3.1: Comparing five kinds of control

Kind of Control	**Control Resources**	**Primary Agents**
Professional	Professional training and credentials Norms of professional practice	Professionals and organizations that support the profession
Administrative	Authority attached to position in administrative hierarchy Control over design of administrative systems and structures	Administrators at all levels
Political	Legitimacy conferred by election results (may be direct or indirect) Accountability to public	Voters Elected officials Government bureaucrats Courts
Market	Access to scarce resources	Legislators Teachers Parents Students
Values and Ideas	Information, expertise, beliefs, aspirations	Any of above

Because they tend to be associated with different participants, the five kinds of control tend to be connected to somewhat different goals and values. Professional control typically focuses on either working conditions for teachers or student outcomes. Political control orients toward demonstrable accountability to public concerns or to giving voice to constituencies that have been neglected by administrators. Administrative control works on efficient allocation of resources, order and predictability, or showing good performance on measurable outcomes. Market controls promote flexibility by advancing responsiveness to funders, students, and parents (in private schools, these are the same customers; in public schools, these are different customers) who may seek diverse outcomes. Value and idea controls promote alignment with beliefs, norms, and values about education and its role in society. Depending on which goals one hopes to achieve, some kinds of control will probably come to mind ahead of others. These crude generalizations by no means account for all uses of control. They represent tendencies in which groups of people have relatively easy access to certain kinds of control and have incentives to use that kind of control to the specified ends.

More interesting questions arise as different kinds of control interact with one another. These questions strenuously resist crude generalization. Let me instead sketch some examples of how these interactions occur.

The interaction that has received the most attention in the literature is that between professional and administrative control. Some of this has already been discussed. Those who value professional discretion argue that administrative control disrupts and impedes the crucial personal relationship between the professional and the client. A top-down, hierarchical style of supervision is inherently inappropriate for an organization delivering professional services (Schon, 1983). Those who place more faith in administrative control acknowledge the costs of constraining professional employees, but believe that, left to their own devices, professionals are profligate with the organization's resources. Only through conventional administration can the organization allocate resources fairly and efficiently across large numbers of professionals serving diverse clients (Lipsky, 1980).

Some organization theorists have discussed the relationship between administrative control and value control. Selznick (1957) and Simon (1976) describe how value control reduces the need for administrative control. When the premises and values of the organization are clear and communicated effectively to members, then they substitute for bureaucratic mechanisms and structures in controlling work and performance. Peters (1988) goes even further, arguing that value controls are much more effective than administrative control when the organization faces an uncertain and demanding environment, and they are most effective when administrative controls are sharply pruned.

Another interesting line of work has emerged around the interaction between political and administrative control. Meyer and Scott (1983) conclude that political control has increased the complexity of administrative control. As more political actors seek to influence school activities, central district offices become more elaborate to establish relationships with those actors. Cohen (1982) argues along the same lines, that the expansion of federal and state education policy has stimulated growth in the administrative capacities of schools and school districts. The growth and complexity identified by these authors is not an unmixed blessing. The proliferation of administrators and specializations has increased interdependence across levels of government, stimulated conflict, confused lines of decision making, introduced expertise and fresh perspective, diversified the talent pool, blurred accountability, and made the educational enterprise more responsive to more public concerns. When administrative and political control are intimately linked, changes in one tend to have repercussions, often unexpected, for the other.

Chubb and Moe (1988) have explored the interaction between political and market controls. Current arrangements for political control over public schools, they argue, compete with pressures from parents and students, and hence reduce the efficacy of market pressures for performance. Parents and students constitute only one small constituency for the public schools, which alone diminishes the importance of market forces in public schools compared to private schools. Furthermore, parental control over participation is constrained by political rules that raise the price of exit. Chubb and Moe (1988) believe that schools can be improved by strengthening the market pressures on school administrators. Other work in this line takes a dimmer view of market pressures. Some researchers who have examined white flight to avoid desegregation have suggested that policies in support of racial equality must further restrict the choices of individual parents in the service of broader social goals (Orfield, 1978).

Some of the theorists who have taken seriously multiple sources of control in schools have approached control as a zero-sum proposition. The more control administrators have, the less control is available for parents or professionals, for example. But many theorists argue compellingly that control is not zero-sum at all. Under some circumstances many participants have considerable control; under others hardly anyone does.

Tannenbaum (1968) summarizes some of the mechanisms by which the total amount of control in an organization may expand or contract. Extending the organization's reach over a larger number of issues may expand total control by allowing more opportunities for decision and influence. Increased opportunities to exercise control internally (for example, through increased delegation or reorganization) may increase members' involvement in the organization and hence increase their interest in exercising control. By including members more fully through participation in decision making or promoting identification with the goals of the organization, the organization acquires control over a wider range of members' behavior and energies, hence increasing the total amount of control available. Whether we think of this as co-operation (Selznick, 1949) or democratic participation (Likert, 1961), participative systems of management imply more active involvement of members and more control over heretofore untapped capabilities of those members.

Kanter (1983) describes this phenomenon in the corporate realm. Having proposed that innovation is essential to competitive success, she shows how pushing power downward in the organization stimulates people to create new possibilities for corporate action. The more power seeps down to the bottom, the more power the senior executives have to choose among the initiatives and opportunities that are pushed upward by the innovators. Perrow (1977) makes a similar argument, describing what he calls the 'bureaucratic paradox'. By delegating more control to subordinates, managers acquire more control over performance of their subordinates. This occurs because, free of the need for detailed supervision, managers are able to devote more of their energy to problem solving, negotiations with outside units, and shaping of premises. These more strategic controls are often more effective than constant monitoring and rule enforcement.

There is good reason to expect to see the same dynamic in schools. In the effective schools literature, strong principals seem to empower teachers, leading to an overall rise in total control experienced in the schools (Purkey and Smith, 1983). Chubb and Moe's (1988) analyses of survey responses from private school teachers and principals suggest that both teachers and principals think they have more influence and autonomy than their public school counterparts, raising the possibility of non-zero-sum dynamics of control. Along similar lines, control by the district office may not be reduced by school site management. Freed from day-to-day operational control, central office administrators may devote more energy to problem solving, relationships with outside groups, and intellectual leadership. Hill *et al.*'s (1989) description of effective urban superintendents accords with this model of increased outward orientation and intellectual agenda-building. Contrary to many fears, activist school boards may unleash energy and enthusiasm in the district, rather than suck all control up to the board level.

The dynamic also works in reverse. McNeil (1986) suggests that administrative efforts at detailed supervision of teachers tend to reduce the total amount of control in the school. Teachers' resistance to intrusive supervision not only subverts administrators' control, but also reduces their own capacity for professional control over their work. Efforts by the state education agency or the district office to collect more information from schools may leave the state or district office worse informed, rather than better (Kaufman, 1973; Hanf and Sharpf, 1983).

If different kinds of control interact with one another, and the total amount of control fluctuates, then researchers face a more complex agenda than is typically appreciated. Research and theory will be most useful when it can accommodate the flexible, multicolor, interwoven character of control. The work I have discussed in this section suggests how promising this conception can be. Sophisticated practitioners have already mastered the notion that schools are tapestries of control. The patterns are often well-defined and intricate. Although they are relatively stable, shifting breezes and perspectives reveal new facets and patterns. Pulling one thread at a time does violence to the relationship between each part and the whole.

Translating Theory into Policy

This conception of control can inform the analysis of proposals for policy reform and the evaluation of policies that have tried to improve school performance. It does not offer a recipe for successful schools. It does highlight important considerations for those embarked upon school improvement.

Control and Decentralization

Policy in education frequently consists of changes in political control intended to influence behavior in schools. For example, policies that sought to desegregate school districts required districts to meet externally imposed targets for the distribution of students across schools, and made external support contingent on meeting those targets. Such interventions run into various kinds of trouble, as described earlier in the section on the disadvantages of political control. Such interventions also can be frustrated by the mobilization of other sorts of control in response to new policy initiatives. For example, teachers are often offended by the efforts of elected officials to substitute their judgment for that of trained professionals; outrage leads to resistance and failure to implement the policy initiative.

Thus some policy initiatives reach beyond political control. For example, policies promoting decentralization within states and local districts are primarily addressed to administrative control. Through political control, policy makers hope to induce administrators to use administrative control differently.

Informed by theory about control, a policy maker might ask three questions about proposals for decentralization: (1) Which controls are to be decentralized and which are not?; (2) How will other controls be affected by the proposed decentralization?; (3) What difference might it make for control to be exercised at one level rather than another?

Decentralization of which controls?

Decentralization of control can occur in many different ways, depending on which kind of control is at stake and which actors are involved. Control may be divided in a host of ways among the superintendent (the strategic apex, in Mintzberg's (1984) language), central office staff (the technostructure), principals (managers of units), and teachers (operators). When we include actors other than administrators — parents, students, school boards, state legislators, voters, courts, etc., — the possibilities increase geometrically. General statements about the advantages or disadvantages of decentralization are far too simple to offer any guidance for policy.

Most proponents of decentralization focus on administrative control. Contingency theory suggests that the degree of administrative centralization should depend on the nature of the technology and the complexity and uncertainty in the environment (Thompson, 1967). All schools operate with a causally indeterminate technology and a complex, uncertain environment. Under these circumstances, a highly decentralized organizational structure is deemed most appropriate. Although persuasive arguments can be made on behalf of more centralized structures that create economies of scale and increased efficiency in resource allocation, most educators agree that smaller, decentralized units are best adapted to the task of instruction.

Some theorists of federalism promote decentralization of political control, from federal to state to local levels. Decentralization locates control in the hands of local elected officials who are close to problems and have the best information about the immediate situation (Conlan, 1988). This permits policies to be adapted to local exigencies and needs. Wildavsky (1979) makes a somewhat different argument on behalf of decentralization, calling it a bias toward federalism. Spreading authority among large numbers of smaller units will produce better results than concentrating it at the federal or state level, he argues, because there are no economies of scale attributable to the larger units and because the conflicts that arise among smaller units are healthy expressions of diverse goals and approaches that would otherwise be submerged. Other students of politics argue the advantages of more centralized political control. Political units with larger, more diverse constituencies are more likely than local communities or neighborhoods to respond to the needs of minorities, the disadvantaged, and unpopular causes (Peterson, 1981). Local communities are more likely to be dominated by an elite power structure that makes policy in its own interest, ignoring other conceptions of the public good.

Among those who write about professional power, there is more agreement. The sociologists of the professions (e.g., Freidson, 1987; Lipsky, 1980) propose that decentralization of discretion and authority to the operating professional (the classroom teacher) is essential to high quality service. Administration must be arranged in the service of professional autonomy (Mills *et al.*, 1983). But a few dissenting voices peep up. In larger units, professionals may receive access to better training, aspire to more improvement in their skills, and connect more readily to the broader professional community.

Market controls almost by definition argue the merits of decentralization. Only a decentralized market with many buyers and sellers in frequent interaction produces the desirable effects of better services at lower prices. One prime source of market failure is excessive centralization in the hands of a few buyers (as when the state funds the public schools) or a few sellers (as when parents can only look to their neighborhood public school for services).

Control through ideas and values also may be more effective when decentralized. When such control is unilateral, it smacks of totalitarianism. Free interchange in the marketplace of ideas can help to correct for the repressive effect of any one ideology or value. Others suggest that centralized control exercised through values and ideas can provide a guiding vision that energizes and directs the efforts of administratively decentralized units (Peters, 1988). This seems to have been Secretary of Education William Bennett's conception of a useful federal role in education (Reich, 1988).

Many theorists who see advantages in decentralization also assume, implicitly or explicitly, that not everything will be decentralized at once. Finding the right mix is a theoretical challenge that has not yet been met.

Interactions across types of control

When one stream of control is rearranged, other kinds adapt to the new circumstances. In interdependent systems of purposive actors, control, I have said, is not zero-sum. People will continue to pursue their habits, goals, and interests, even under a new set of political or administrative arrangements. Any efforts to decentralize will be greeted with a range of responses, some of which may further the goals of the decentralization, others of which may frustrate them. Attention to these potential responses is important for predicting the net effect of the change.

For example, providing more choice to parents may trigger a chain of moves and counter-moves that produces less choice in the end. This happened in the public school district I attended. A voluntary transfer program was introduced to allow parents to send their children to any elementary school in the district. After the first September, the one school with a majority black enrollment became exclusively black. Because racial segregation had worsened, black parents sued the district. The district ended up with a federally mandated desegregation plan, eliminating not only choice for parents but also choice for administrators and the school board.

For example, decentralizing authority over textbook selection may result in choices less adapted to local needs. Overworked classroom teachers may have no choice but to rely on publishers' aggressive marketing propaganda rather than on careful evaluation of the hundreds of books published each year. State wide or district wide committees have more resources and expertise to devote to the task, and may (not necessarily, but possibly) make choices better suited to local needs.

For example, the growing share of educational funding paid by states may permit more diversity at the local level, rather than less. As California has assumed a large share of educational finance, the state has made resources available for school-based improvements, through the School Improvement Plan. This focuses local energy at the level of the school, not just the district, and builds a direct link between state administrators and principals.

These illustrations are intended only to suggest the variety of secondary effects that may be set in motion by decentralization. My main point is that there will always be some such effects. Decentralization is a process, rather than a discrete intervention, which has a strand of deliberate, planned change and another strand of adjustments and adaptations to the planned change.

The consequences of decentralization

If control is decentralized from state to local levels or from district to school levels, what difference will it make? Decisions in a decentralized regime will be made by different individuals than was previously the case

(Simon, 1979). Action will be taken by different institutions than was previously the case (Clune, 1987). These individuals and institutions may have access to differing amounts and kinds of control resources than their centralized counterparts. Are these differences meaningful enough to transform current conditions into improved behavior and outcomes? The value of decentralization rests on the answer.

If the new decision makers have access to better, richer, more recent information than the old, then they may make better decisions. If the new decision makers have more incentive to take the decision seriously, to use a vigilant style of information processing (Janis, 1989), they may make better decisions. If the new decision makers have a different disciplinary or professional perspective that frames the decision and available alternatives in fresh and creative ways, then they may make better decisions. If the new decision makers bring a more coherent or deeply felt set of goals and values to the decision, they may make better decisions. If, on the other hand, the new decision makers must work with the same information, come from the same background, value the same ends, and cope with the same barrage of concerns as their predecessors, there is little reason to expect better results under a decentralized system. It is altogether plausible that new decision makers will be *less* qualified and informed, and decentralization will reduce the quality of decisions made.

More diversity of goals, competencies, and access to information is in many ways a great strength. It equips schools to notice and respond to local variation in students, parents, and employers. In this sense variation in school practices and outcomes is a constructive adaptation to environmental pressures and stakeholder aspirations. Schools or districts may get much better on those dimensions that are now under the control of more talented, decent, energetic, and motivated people than was previously the case. However, they will get much worse on those features of institutional life that are now under the control of less talented, decent, energetic, or motivated people. Some will improve across the board. Others will decline. Decentralization creates variation, for better and for worse.

Many proposals for decentralization aim to supplant administrative control with professional control. What consequences may ensue from relying more heavily on professional control? Perhaps decentralization promotes local rather than cosmopolitan perspectives on teaching, more concern with school events and less with broader professional norms, subtly undermining the commitment to professional control. Perhaps decentralization empowers principals, making them less likely to become petty tyrants, making them more likely to support teacher professionalism. Perhaps decentralization reduces the access of teachers to their colleagues in other schools or districts, reducing the social supports for professional improvement. If policy makers have thought about the relationship between administrative and professional control, they may see that professional control will not automatically flourish because administrative controls have been pruned. When control is not zero-sum, less administration does not translate into more professionalism. To improve the quality of professional service in the classroom, policy makers need to cut back on administrative controls *and* find ways to enhance the professional capabilities of the instructional staff.

Using Theories of Control

March and Olsen (1987, p. 365) wrote: 'Students of organization have often dampened enthusiasm for institutional reform, preferring to note the numerous complications in sustaining a sense of efficacy . . .'. In the same vein, Wildavsky (1979, p. 404) noted: 'knowing what (which is hard) is different from knowing why (which is harder) [and] differs from knowing how (which is hardest)'. The theoretical analyses in this chapter help to know why. But in the tangle of many whys, they tend to squelch enthusiasm, to urge caution, to bewail complexity, even to encourage cynicism about the prospects for improvement. The example of decentralization suggests that policy makers contemplating reform need detailed knowledge of ways that control is exercised by the institutions and individuals involved before they can design strategies to reallocate control with any hope of improving outcomes. Even so they will be unable to anticipate all the repercussions of their intervention. In this case, as so often in the social sciences, theory sows doubt.

Doubt has its uses. We are often well-advised to consider more thoughtfully the advantages and disadvantages of the course we are about to embark upon. But doubt cannot lead the charge for successful institutional change. Knowing *how* requires knowing why and then some, knowing how to overcome doubt and build commitment.

Unhappily, the analysis of control advanced in this chapter offers less guidance for knowing how. But it suggests a few places to look to discover how. Look first at whether the proposed change in control arrangements has a direct, logical connection to the desired behavioral outcomes. Giving some people more control resources and others less does not necessarily mean that the controllers who have been advantaged can exert sufficient leverage over specific targets to produce significant, lasting change in specified domains of behavior. If the goal is for students to take more demanding academic courses, do not seek to control the requirements for teacher certification; use controls closely tied to course-taking and course content.

Look second at whether the proposed change in control arrangements is likely to trigger counter-mobilization in other control arrangements. This means understanding the interactions among kinds of control and the interests and resources available to actors who seek to exercise control. If the goal is to increase market control available to parents by giving them choice about school assignment, consider how administrators may use their resources to shape and filter parental access to information, thus guiding and constraining parents' choices. It means anticipating the unintended consequences of implementing change, and making sensible adjustments to neutralize the worst effects of unplanned control efforts.

Look third at introducing multiple interventions that work on several kinds of control at once. The most sophisticated policy makers understand the futility of expecting one intervention to produce major institutional change. A coordinated attack that simultaneously rearranges several kinds of control to exert pressure toward the same goal (and to remove pressure toward conflicting goals) is much more likely to succeed.

These instructions are seldom easy to follow in the policymaking arena. Although simplicity and clarity help to attract political support and facilitate implementation, the multiple layers of policy that tend to follow from my analysis seem confusing and off-putting. Nevertheless sustained attention to the realities of control can, in the end, produce more satisfying results than the optimistic hope that these realities can be finessed or ignored.

Notes

1 I acknowledge with gratitude the suggestions and comments of the organizers and participants of the May 1989 conference on Choice and Control in American Education.

2 As we shall see in subsequent sections, this occurs with other kinds of control as well.

3 These are not the only three levels of analysis that might be fruitfully explored. Two others that have sparked some fascinating work are group and intergroup relations and policy sector. In the interests of brevity, I have omitted them from this analysis.

4 My focus here is schools in the United States. Although some of the argument in this section applies in countries with different political arrangements, much does not.

5 A shortfall between employers' expectations and the skills of even those students who have completed high school has been a spark to the increasing involvement of business in education reform.

References

Aberbach, J.D. and Rockman, B. (1988) 'Mandates or mandarins: Control and discretion in the modern administrative state', *Public Administration Review*, **48**, pp. 606–12.

Bowles, S. and Gintis, H. (1976) *Schooling in Capitalist America: Educational Reform and the Contradictions of Economic Life*, New York: Basic.

Burns, J.M., (1978) *Leadership*, New York: Harper and Row.

Child, J. (1972) 'Organizational structure, environment, and performance'. *Sociology*, **6**, pp. 1–22.

Chubb, J.E. and Moe, T.M. (1988) 'Politics, markets and the organization of schools', *American Political Science Review*, **82**, pp. 1065–87.

Clune, W.H. (1987) 'Institutional choice as a theoretical framework for research on educational policy', *Educational Evaluation and Policy Analysis*, **9**, pp. 117–32.

Cohen, D.K. (1982) 'Policy and organization: The impact of state and federal educational policy on school governance', *Harvard Educational Review*, **52**, pp. 474–99.

Conlan, T. (1988) *The New Federalism: Intergovernmental Reform from Nixon to Reagan*, Washington: Brookings.

Cyert, R. and March, J. (1963) *The Behavioral Theory of the Firm*, Englewood Cliffs: Prentice-Hall.

DiMaggio, P. and Powell, W.W. (1983) 'The iron cage revisited: Institutional isomorphism and collective rationality in organizational fields', *American Sociological Review*, **35**, pp. 147–60.

Edwards, R. (1979) *Contested Terrain*, New York: Basic Books.

Firestone, W. (1985) 'The study of loose coupling: Problems, progress, and prospects', *Research in Sociology of Education and Socialization*, **5**, Greenwich, CT: JAI Press.

Freidson, E. (1987) *Professional Powers*, Chicago: University of Chicago Press.

Gamoran, A. and Dreeben, R. (1986) 'Coupling and control in educational organizations', *Administrative Science Quarterly*, **31**, pp. 612–32.

Goodlad, J. (1984) *A Place Called School*, New York: McGraw-Hill.

Granovetter, M. (1985) 'Economic action and social structure: The problem of embeddedness', *American Journal of Sociology*, **91**, pp. 481–510.

Gross, B. and Gross, R. (Eds.) (1985) *The Great School Debate*, New York: Simon and Schuster.

Hackman, J.R. and Oldham, G. (1980) *Work Redesign*, Reading, MA: Addison-Wesley.

Hanf, K. and Scharpf, F. (Eds.) (1983) *Interorganizational Policymaking*, Beverly Hills: Sage.

Hanushek, E.A. (1981) 'Throwing money at schools', *Journal of Policy Analysis and Management*, **1**, pp. 19–42.

Hill, P.T. (1979) *Do Federal Programs Interfere with One Another?* Santa Monica, CA: Rand Corporation.

Hill, P.T., Wise, A.E. and Shapiro, L. (1989) *Educational Progress: Cities Mobilize to Improve their Schools*, Santa Monica, CA: Rand Corporation, R-3711-JSM/CSTP.

HOROWITZ, D.L., (1977) *The Courts and Social Policy*, Washington, DC: Brookings Institution.

HOUSE, R.J. (1971) 'A path-goal theory of leadership effectiveness', *Administrative Science Quarterly*, **16**, pp. 321–38.

JANIS, I.L., (1989) *Crucial Decisions: Leadership in Policymaking and Crisis Management*, New York: Free Press.

KANTER, R. (1983) *The Change Masters*, New York: Simon and Schuster.

KAUFMAN, H. (1960) *The Forest Ranger*, Baltimore: Johns Hopkins University Press.

KAUFMAN, H. (1973) *Administrative Feedback*, Washington: Brookings.

KIRST, M.W., (1984) *Who Controls our Schools?* New York: Freeman.

LAWRENCE, P.R. and LORSCH, J.W. (1967) *Organization and Environment: Managing Differentiation and Integration.* Boston: Harvard Graduate School of Business Administration.

LEETSMA, R., AUGUST, R.L., GEORGE, B. and PEAK, L. (1987) *Japanese Education Today: A Report from the US Study of Education in Japan*, Washington, DC: US Government Printing Office.

LIKERT, R. (1961) *New Patterns of Management*, New York: McGraw-Hill.

LINDBLOM, C.E. (1976) *Politics and Markets*, New York: Basic Books.

LIPSKY, M. (1980) *Street Level Bureaucracy*, New York: Russell Sage Foundation.

LOCKE, E.A., SHAW, K., SAARI, L. and LATHAM, G. (1981) 'Goal-setting and task performance, 1969–1980', *Psychology Bulletin*, **90**, pp. 125–52.

LYNN, L.E. (1987) *Managing Public Policy*, Boston: Little, Brown.

MARCH, J.G. and OLSEN, J. (1976) *Ambiguity and Choice in Organizations*, Bergen, Norway: Universitatsforlaget.

MARCH, J.G. and OLSEN, J. (1987) 'Popular sovereignty and the search for appropriate institutions', *Journal of Public Policy*, **6**, pp. 341–70.

MARCH, J.G. and SIMON, H.A. (1958) *Organizations*, New York: Wiley.

MCCUBBINS, M., NOLL, R. and WEINGAST, B. (1987) 'Administrative procedures as instruments of political control', *Journal of Law, Economics, and Organization*, **3**, pp. 243–77.

MCNEIL, L. (1986) *Contradictions of Control*, New York: Routledge.

MERCHANT, K.A. (1985) *Control in Business Organizations*, Boston: Pitman.

MEYER, J.W. and ROWAN, B. (1977) 'Institutionalized organizations: Formal structure as myth and ceremony', *American Journal of Sociology*, **83**, pp. 340–63.

MEYER, J.W. and ROWAN, B. (1978) 'The structure of educational organizations', in MEYER M. (Ed.) *Environments and Organizations*, San Francisco: Jossey-Bass.

MEYER, J. and SCOTT, W. R. (1983) *Organizational Environments*, Beverly Hills: Sage.

MILES, M. (1981) 'Mapping the common properties of schools', in LEHMING R. and KANE M. (Eds.) *Improving Schools.* Beverly Hills: Sage.

MILLS, P., HALL, J.L., LEIDECKER, J.K. and MARGULIES, N. (1983) 'Flexiform: A model for professional service organizations', *Academy of Management Review*, **8**, pp. 118–31.

Mintzberg, H. (1984) 'A typology of organizational structure', in Miller D. and Friesen P. (Eds.) *Organizations: A Quantum View*, Englewood Cliffs, NJ: Prentice-Hall.

Moe, T. (1984) 'The new economics of organization', *American Journal of Political Science*, **28**, pp. 739–77.

Murnane, R.J. (1985) 'An economist's look at federal and state education policies', in Quigley, J. and Rubinfeld, D. (Eds.) *American Domestic Priorities*, Berkeley: University of California Press.

Murphy, J.T. (1981) 'The paradox of state government reform', *The Public Interest*, **64**, pp. 124–39.

Orfield, G. (1978) *Must We Bus? Segregated Schools and National Policy*, Washington, DC: Brookings Institution.

Perrow, C. (1977) 'The bureaucratic paradox: The efficient organization centralizes in order to decentralize', *Organizational Dynamics*.

Perrow, C. (1986) *Complex Organizations*, 3rd edition, New York: Random House.

Peters, T. (1988) 'Restoring American competitiveness: Looking for new models of organization', *Academy of Management Executive*.

Peterson, K. (1984) 'Mechanisms of administrative control over managers in educational organizations', *Administrative Science Quarterly*, pp. 573–97.

Peterson, P.E. (1981) *City Limits*, Chicago: University of Chicago Press.

Pfeffer, J. (1977) 'The ambiguity of leadership', *Academy of Management Review*, **2**, pp. 104–12.

Pfeffer, J. (1982) *Organizations and Organization Theory*, Boston: Pitman.

Pfeffer, J. and Salancik, G. (1978) *The External Control of Organizations*, New York: Harper and Row.

Porter, M. (1980) *Competitive Strategy*, New York: Free Press.

Powell, A.G., Farrar, E. and Cohen, D. (1985) *The Shopping Mall High School*, New York: Houghton Mifflin.

Pratt, J. and Zeckhauser, R. (1985) *Principals and Agents: The Structure of Business*, Boston: Harvard Business School Press.

Purkey, S.C. and Smith, M.S. (1983) 'Effective schools: A review', *Elementary School Journal*, **83**, pp. 353–89.

Reich, R.B. (1988) 'Policymaking in a democracy', in Reich R. (Ed.) *The Power of Public Ideas*, Cambridge, MA: Ballinger.

Rogers, D. and Chung, N. (1983) *110 Livingston Street Revisited*, New York: New York University Press.

Schattschneider, E.E., (1960) *The Semisovereign People*, New York: Holt, Rinehart and Winston.

Schon, D.A. (1983) *The Reflective Practitioner: How Professionals Think in Action*, New York: Basic Books.

Scott, W.R. (1987) 'The adolescence of institutional theory', *Administrative Science Quarterly*, **32**, pp. 493–511.

Selznick, P. (1949) *TVA and the Grass Roots*, Berkeley: University of California Press.

SELZNICK, P. (1957) *Leadership in Administration*, Berkeley: University of California Press.
SIMON, H. (1976) *Administrative Behavior*, New York: Free Press, 3rd edition.
SIMON, H. (1979) 'The consequences of computers for centralization and decentralization', in DERTOUZOS M. and MOSES J. (Eds.) *The Computer Age*, Cambridge: MIT Press
STIEGLITZ, H. (1974) 'On concepts of corporate structure: Economic determinants of organization', *Conference Board Record*, February, pp. 318–29.
STONE, D.A. (1988) *Policy Paradox and Political Reason*, Glenview, IL: Scott, Foresman.
TANNENBAUM, A.S. (1968) *Control in Organizations*, New York: McGraw-Hill.
THOMPSON, J. (1967) *Organizations in Action*, New York: McGraw-Hill.
TYACK, D. (1974) *The One Best System*, Cambridge: Harvard University Press.
WEBER, M. (1947) *The Theory of Social and Economic Organization*, New York: Free Press.
WEICK, K.E. (1976) 'Educational organizations as loosely coupled systems', *Administrative Science Quarterly*, **21**, pp. 1–19.
WEICK, K.E. (1979) 'Cognitive processes in organizations', in STAW B. (Ed.) *Research in Organizational Behavior*, **1**, Greenwich, CT: JAI Press.
WEISS, J.A. and GRUBER, J. (1984a) 'Deterring discrimination with data', *Policy Sciences*, **17**, pp. 49–66.
WEISS, J.A. and GRUBER, J. (1984b) 'Using knowledge for control in fragmented policy arenas', *Journal of Policy Analysis and Management*, **3**, pp. 225–47.
WEISS, J.A. and GRUBER, J. (1987) 'The managed irrelevance of education statistics', in ALONSO, W. and STARR, P. (Eds.) *The Politics of Numbers*, New York: Russell Sage Foundation.
WILDAVSKY, A. (1979) *Speaking Truth to Power*, Boston: Little, Brown.
WILLIAMSON, O.E. (1981) 'The economics of organization: The transaction costs approach', *American Journal of Sociology*, **87**, pp. 548–77.
WISE, A. (1979) *Legislated Learning: The Bureaucratization of the American Classroom*, Berkeley: University of California Press.
ZALD, M.N. (1970) 'Political economy: A framework for comparative analysis', in ZALD, M. (Ed.) *Power in Organizations*, Nashville: Vanderbilt University Press.
ZUCKER, L.G. (Ed.) (1988) *Institutional Patterns and Organizations*, Cambridge, MA: Ballinger.

Chapter 4

High School Organization and Its Effects on Teachers and Students: An Interpretive Summary of the Research

Anthony S. Bryk, Valerie E. Lee and Julia B. Smith

This chapter summarizes diverse literatures concerning the structure of high school organizations. It focuses on both the influence of external characteristics on internal operations of schools, and the effects of these internal organizational components on teachers and students. The review draws from analytic essays, recent qualitative and quantitative studies which provide empirical evidence on relationships of interest, and syntheses of previously published literature. The conceptual framework, employed in the review, sees schools as organizations which are both shaped by external factors and mediate the influence of these externalities on both teachers and students. We focus on four external factors: school size, governance structure, parental and community involvement in the school, and student body composition. Important relations between these features and internal organizational characteristics typify how a school's organization is either responsive to external influences or is buffered from such influences. The primary focus of the chapter is on four components of the internal organization of schools which impact both teachers and students: the cultural system of the school, administration, the formal organization of the school as a workplace for both teachers and students, and the social relations among the adult and student members of the organization. We identify two distinct streams of research related to successful school organization. The first focuses on curricular functions, policies and practices affecting assignment of students and teachers to schools and classes within schools. The research here clearly indicates that curricular organization has powerful effects on academic achievement and how it is distributed with regard to race/ethnicity and class. The second stream focuses on the nature of the social relations within a school, and has identified such cultural elements of community as social cooperation and shared beliefs as having positive effects on teacher commitment and student engagement in schooling. This contrasts with portraits of modern comprehensive high schools marked by distrust, misunderstanding, social conflict, and a lack of personal regard for the individuals who staff the institutions.

Introduction

Background

The publication of the *Equality of Educational Opportunity Report* by James Coleman and others in 1966 initiated the large-scale quantitative investigation of school effects. Two different conceptual frameworks were employed in this early research. Economists offered us input-output analyses of school effectiveness. They sought to estimate the production functions linking fiscal resources such as numbers of books in the library, average teacher salaries, and student/teacher ratios to student achievement. Human capital theory strongly influenced the basic conceptualization of this research, where a key concern was how best to deploy new federal resources in advancing educational equity. Other social scientists, mainly sociologists, pursued issues of social stratification, particularly the role of education in status attainment. With years of schooling as the key independent variable, the primary focus was on the consequences of schooling for occupational and social mobility.[1]

These two streams of work, however, shared a common viewpoint: the organizational structure of the school was conceived as a 'black box' whose internal workings were not central to the inquiry. Neither program of research offered much insight into how the process of schooling actually produces the desired outcomes or how the institutional structures of schools shape the overall distribution of these outcomes.[2]

These two frameworks dominated research on school effects throughout the 1970s. It was not until the end of the decade, with the emergence of the 'effective schools' literature, that research attention was directed to the organizational properties of schools and the larger institutional structures in which schools are embedded.[3] Although this new work represented a major shift in focus, strictly speaking it was not a new development. Rather, as Dreeben (1988) points out, it represented a renewed connection with the seminal studies on schools as institutions offered earlier in this century by Waller (1932) and Sorokin (1928).

Moving in parallel with these new empirical studies of schools was a significant effort at reconceptualizing basic ideas about schools as organizations, the schooling process, and the complex linkages between these two.[4] Central to these arguments was the observation that student learning is a process which occurs over time and is embedded in a multilevel structure. The distinctive activities, policies and practices at different levels (such as federal, state or district) both provide incentives and create constraints on action at subsequent levels (such as schools and classrooms). Further, the allocation of resources (people, time, and materials) is a major focus of work at each level. In these processes, a key property of American schools as differentiating institutions is revealed. One result of the numerous decisions made at each level is a substantial variability in teachers' conditions of work and students' opportunities to learn, even within the same school.

These theoretical reconceptualizations of schooling and the new empiricism on effective practices have now merged with a rush of ethnographic work on schools to generate a rapidly growing literature on school organization and its effects on teachers and students. It is primarily to this literature of the 1980s that we looked in developing this review. Recent historical accounts of schooling in this century further enriched the perspective.[5]

Conceptual Overview of the Review

In a major paper, Bidwell (1965) described two different ways in which research on schools has been pursued. Drawing on a fundamental sociological distinction set out by Weber and applied to schools by Waller, Bidwell articulated a rational-bureaucratic and personal-communal conceptualization of the school. From a bureaucratic perspective, a school is a 'formal organization' characterized in terms of: a functional division of adult labor into specialized tasks; defined teaching roles by subject matter and types of students; an emphasis on social interactions that are rule-governed, affectively neutral, and with limited individual discretion; and a form of authority that is attached to the role within the organization rather than to the person. In contrast, from a communitarian perspective, a school is conceived as a 'small society', where emphasis is given to informal and enduring social relationships and a strong attachment to a common ethos. An operational consequence of this view is a diffuse adult role and a minimal division of labor.

The vision of the 'good school' from a bureaucratic perspective is captured in the ideals of progressive urban reformers who sought to create comprehensive high schools. Such institutions would be efficiently organized to serve large numbers of students of varied backgrounds and interests by offering specialized services and a diverse array of courses.

Managing this multiplicity of organizational goals would require a large and specialized administrative staff. Social relations within the school would be formalized in accord with rational-legalistic norms.

The communitarian ideal, on the other hand, has a nostalgic flavor reminiscent of an earlier, simpler society where schools were small and organizational goals less complex. The curricular offerings were fewer in number, and a common experience for all students was emphasized rather than specialized services. Social relations were personal, and there was a natural deference to adult authority.

The bureaucratic perspective has dominated both research activities and reform efforts over the last two decades. It has provided a powerful framework for an expansion of schooling that sought to efficiently deliver new educational opportunities in a non-discriminatory fashion. But in viewing schools as a production process, this perspective has tended to undervalue the personal and communal aspects of school life. It ignored, for example, the observation that for teachers to be effective, they must interact informally with students and engage them in very personal relations. It also underestimated the important educative role played by normative features in the small society of the school.

Increasingly over the last decade, these weaknesses in the bureaucratization of schooling have been exposed, and a renewed emphasis has emerged on strengthening the social ties between students and adults around the place of the school and its educational activities. These communitarian critiques have also initiated more fundamental discussions about school aims, the values that underlie these aims, and the nature and meaning of the work of students and adults in such places.

In this regard, recent writings on schools connect with a broader re-examination of the basic organizing features of contemporary society. As the structure of community and family life has changed radically in the last twenty years, the traditional supports available for socializing children into adult roles have diminished. The school, increasingly, is being forced to consider how it should reorganize itself in ways that draw in and support both students and parents around the educative tasks of schooling.

Model Overview

We have structured our review around a conceptual model of the internal organization of schools and its effect on teacher and student outcomes (see Figure 4.1). The basic categories considered under internal organizations include: the underlying beliefs, values, as well as explicit goals of the

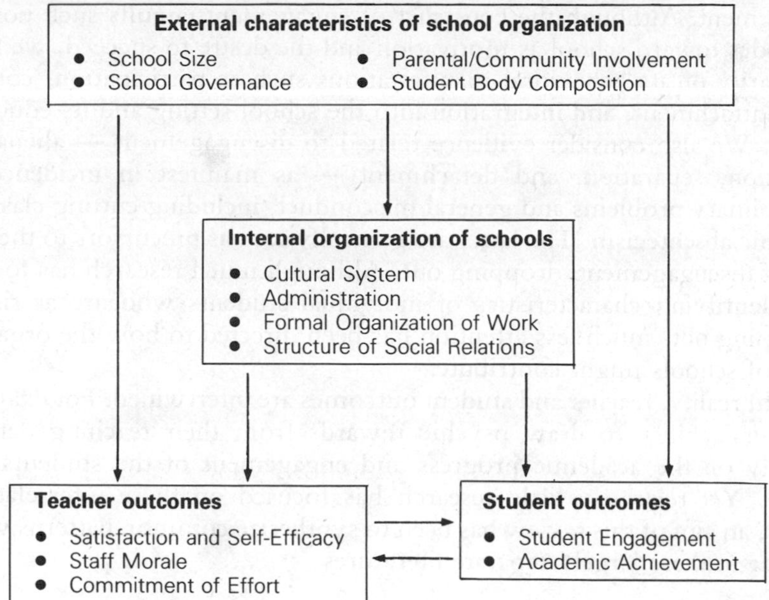

Figure 4.1: Heuristic model of a school's organization and its effects

school (labeled 'cultural system'); the nature of school administrative activity; the formal organization of teachers' and students' work, and the structure of social relations. While the internal organization of a school directly affects teachers and students, each school is also embedded in a larger environment which shapes the internal organization in significant ways. Consequently, we also consider in this review selected aspects of the external environment of schools, including school size, student body composition, nature of parental involvement, and school governance, all of which are strongly linked to a school's internal operations.

In defining the outcome variables of interest, we have looked to the research on both student learning and teacher professionalism. Teacher outcomes discussed here include: satisfaction with teaching, teachers' sense of efficacy in accomplishing instructional goals with their students, staff morale as a collective property of adult work within a school, and teachers' commitment of effort. This latter concept is indicated by measures such as time spent in school-related activities, intensity of professional development efforts, and the amount of absences from school.

In terms of student outcomes, academic achievement — as measured by student performance on standardized achievement tests — is obviously a principal concern. In addition to achievement, we also consider student engagment. Although the construct of engagement engulfs such positive attitudes toward school as motivation and the desire to succeed, we focus primarily on its behavioral manifestations such as participation, connection, attachment, and integration into the school setting and its educative tasks. We also consider evidence related to disengagement — alienation, isolation, separation, and detachment — as manifest in incidences of disciplinary problems and general misconduct, including cutting class and chronic absenteeism. The latter are generally seen as precursors to the final act of disengagement: dropping out. Although much research has focused on identifying characteristics of individual students who are at risk of dropping out, much less attention has been directed to how the organization of schools might contribute.

In reality, teacher and student outcomes are intertwined. For example, teachers' ability to draw psychic rewards from their teaching depends largely on the academic progress and engagement of the students they teach. Yet relatively little research has focused on these interrelations. Thus, an aim of this review has been to synthesize common patterns which appear in these largely separate literatures.

Methodological Considerations

The review which follows draws on four distinct categories of scholarship. The first is analytic, consisting of theoretical expositions from sociology, social psychology, and historical accounts of American schooling. Although such writings often make reference to a wide range of extant empirical evidence, they nonetheless have the character of logical arguments whose validity depends largely on their internal structure. Proper judgments about such matters are invariably somewhat subjective.

The second category of research encompasses field studies as well as more intensive ethnographic investigations of individual school sites. A large amount of recent empirical-descriptive evidence has been presented in this genre. The difficulties here lie in the largely private character of the research process.[6] Interpretative problems also arise in including such studies in a literature review, since we are forced to confront the generalizability issue. Even assuming that we are willing to accept the authors' inferences as they apply in the particular instances studied, the proper range for further generalization remains unspecified. Thus, much like the analytic scholarship described above, we must exercise a fair degree of personal judgment in the review.

The third category consists of quantitative research which, in the case of this particular review, encompasses everything from small-scale formal experiments to causal modeling of large-scale survey data. In principle, such studies represent our strongest evidence base. Unfortunately, they typically lack the depth of understanding possible in analytic and case study work, with the latter constituting the price extracted for specificity in measurement and potential gain in generalizability. Much more problematic are the fundamental methodological difficulties encountered in past quantitative research on school effects. As Lee Cronbach (1976) has stated:

> The majority of studies of educational effects — whether classroom experiments or evaluation of programs or surveys — have collected and analyzed data in ways that conceal more than they reveal. The established methods have generated false conclusions in many studies.[7]

Two basic features of research on school effects — that children's learning is typically the object of inquiry and that such learning occurs in formal organizational settings — have caused many of these problems. First, children's learning is a process occurring over time. This logically implies a need for multi-time point data, yet most inferences about school effects are based on a single cross-section of information.

Second, as Bidwell and Kasarda (1980) have noted, most studies of school effects fail to make a crucial distinction between the school as an organization and the instructional processes of schooling. By typically using aggregate measures from individuals as proxies for organizational characteristics in analyses of student outcomes, school effects research has systematically underestimated organizational effects. Substantive conclusions from such research that 'schools don't matter much' are flawed by a misconception of *how* schools actually affect student learning.

More specifically, since the work of both students and teachers occurs within settings that deliberately differentiate the experiences of these individuals, school effects may be manifest not only in mean differences among schools, but also in dispersion and distributional effects captured in the idea of 'slopes-as-outcomes'.[8] Although there are a few notable examples where research design and analysis have been deliberately organized to study distributive effects, school research continues to be dominated by analyses searching for mean differences.[9]

Space does not permit a full discussion of the methodological issues raised here, nor of the new statistical methods which provide more appropriate techniques for the analysis of school effects.[10] A major concern, however, is that the extant empirical literature is potentially limited in some serious and unknown ways. Thus, in the review which follows, we have chosen to highlight broad findings and to focus on areas where agreement appears with case study research. We have not attempted to reconcile conflicts, evaluate differences among individual studies, or to be exhaustive. In short, we have focused on major findings which we believe are also sturdy.

The last category of literature considered is synthetic, consisting of previously published literature reviews. Although to the best of our knowledge, there is nothing in the literature that has the same scope as the present effort, we rely on the general findings from other major reviews on particular topics. This decision also required some judgment on our part, as the vast majority of these reviews are not formal research syntheses.

Finally, our main focus is on the organization of secondary schools, although we also consider some relevant literature from elementary schools. In general, the internal organization of elementary and secondary schools is quite different, and these distinctions merit more careful consideration than we are capable of here. Although much of the early research on effective schools focused on elementary schools, much of the recent case study and quantitative research considers high schools. This shift occurred because of important policy concerns raised in reports such as *A Nation at Risk*, and the availability of the *High School and Beyond* (*HS&B*) survey data.

External Characteristics of School Organization

The array of external characteristics which can influence the internal organization of schools is vast. We focus in this section on a small number of key factors, closely linked to the school site, which the literature suggests are important for school operations. The first topic we consider is school size. High schools range from small facilities with less than 300 students to very large institutions with enrollments of several thousand. Such differences in size have important consequences for the array of programs that a school may offer and the nature of social interactions which occur there.

Second, the organization of a school is responsive to the kinds of students to be educated. The characteristics of students, particularly in terms of academic and social background, play an important role. From a production function perspective, student background constitutes one of the major inputs into the educational process.

Third, the ways in which parents and the larger community are involved with a school also shape internal operations. This is a central concern in some recent school improvement plans in urban districts such as Chicago. A fourth consideration is how schools are governed, i.e., whether they are subject to political control, as in the public sector, or respond to market forces, as in the private sector. Closely coupled with this are several specific school features — selectivity of students, control over faculty entry and exit, and decision making autonomy which combine to shape the degree to which a school is open or closed to its external environment.

While most research has focused on the linkage between these external factors (i.e., size, student body composition, parental involvement, or school sector) and student outcomes, the actual mechanism by which such effects occur is largely mediated through the impact of these externalities on internal school organization. That is, external characteristics influence the internal organization of schools, which in turn affects student and teacher outcomes.

School Size[11]

There are two important streams of research on school size. The first reflects an economies of scale argument about schooling, including concerns about the available resource strength of the school and the possibilities for specialization of instructional programs. The second line of work directs attention to the influences of size on the bureaucratic formalization of social interactions within the school, and the consequences which flow from this. These two perspectives on school size lead in opposite directions. The economies of scale argument implies that benefits for academic learning should occur as a result of the consolidation of effort in larger schools. In contrast, the social interactional focus suggests that 'small is beautiful', with greater informality and higher levels of social engagement more likely in such settings.

Economies of scale

Much research examining school size focuses on the assumption that larger schools are more cost-efficient operations.[12] It is argued that financial savings accrue as core costs are spread over a larger pupil base. In principle, these savings create marginal resources which can then be applied to strengthening a school's academic offerings. It is not clear, however, that the cost benefits projected by proponents of school consolidation have ever materialized.

In a major review, Chambers (1981) describes two proposed sources of savings from consolidation: decreased administrative and support staff and greater efficiency in procuring materials. His evidence indicates, however, that large schools (as well as large districts) actually increase support and administrative staff to handle the greater bureaucratic demands accompanying their larger size. Further, in rural areas, the greater costs of distributing materials and transporting students to school tend to offset savings from consolidation. Thus, Chambers finds little evidence supporting actual economies of scale in schooling.

It has also been argued that greater resource strength accompanies increased size.[13] Studies indicate that the number of students served either by a school or a district is associated with availability of fiscal resources for teachers' salaries, instructional materials, and support for professional development.[14] More students can also mean more financial support from the state and greater political strength within the local community.[15] Specifically, numerical strength of the school system can be used to build a stronger political base with which to procure resources by increasing direct community ties to the school (i.e., when more students mean a higher proportion of families with children in school).[16]

The actual academic consequences of economies of scale and greater resource strength are far less clear.[17] Bidwell and Kasarda (1975) offer some evidence of an indirect relationship between resource availability for a high school and positive student achievement, mediated through the hiring of better-trained teachers and greater numbers of support staff for students' needs. More recent research suggests that the relationship between school system size and resource availability does not operate equally across communities, but rather is contingent upon the socioeconomic background of the community itself.[18] While larger districts in lower income areas may access greater resources than do small districts, the higher incidence of 'exceptional problems' (for example, delinquency, drug abuse, learning disabilities) in such contexts introduces constraints and contributes to reduced organizational performance.

Further, while school resources are generally measured in terms of average per pupil expenditure, some researchers have suggested that, in larger systems, the actual distribution of resources among schools and students within schools must also be considered.[19] Although the average level of resources may be high in larger districts, greater stratification among schools in access to resources may also occur. A similar argument applies within schools. While a larger school may have more aggregate resources to support instruction, the resultant educational opportunities may be distributed to students in highly differentiated ways.

Another dimension of the economies of scale argument focuses on the relationship between organizational size and program specialization. In principle, larger schools have larger numbers of students with similar needs and are thus better able to create specialized services to address those needs.[20] In contrast, smaller schools must focus their resources on core programs, with the consequence that marginal students are either excluded or absorbed into more general programs which may not meet their needs.[21]

The actual consequences of program specialization, however, are more complex than the scenario just described. Specifically, recent research indicates that the greater curriculum specialization in larger schools amplifies initial background differences among students. Lee and Bryk (1989) found that both school size and curriculum differentiation were positively associated with achievement stratification in terms of student's social class and academic background, but were unrelated to average achievement.[22] These findings build on more general empirical studies linking differences in students' academic experiences to social stratification in academic outcomes.[23] Thus, while economies of scale afford more diversity in academic offerings to meet specialized student needs, it is far from clear that the aggregate consequences are actually beneficial.

Bureaucratic formalization of social interactions

Weber forecast the rise of bureaucratic structures resulting from organizational growth and noted that such structures are predicated on objective relations where there is little place for the personal ties that characterize a community. In Weber's view, the rationalization process which accompanies expanding organizational size is, in many ways, the antithesis of community.[24]

These observations are particularly salient for schooling where teachers' work requires considerable human judgment and individual commitment, both of which are ill-suited to a rigid bureaucratic environment.[25] Educational theorists have argued that the bureaucratization prevalent in large schools produces negative social consequences for both students and faculty. Recent *HS&B* analyses support these contentions.[26]

Closely related findings emerge in the research on school climate, where size is viewed as an 'ecological' variable, part of the physical or material environment which helps to determine the structure and nature of social interactions. Components of social interaction which appear particularly related to size include frequency of communication between members of the organization, group cohesion, role specialization and group management.[27] As the number of individuals in the school increases, several consequences occur. First, more communication links are involved in transmitting information, increasing the distance between any one person and a source of information, and making necessary more formalized systems of communication.[28] Second, large organizations are more likely to formalize cultural beliefs in order to counteract the effects of large numbers of people holding conflicting goals. This formalization, however, can negatively influence group cohesion, as tacit beliefs of individual members are not officially engaged and, therefore, never integrated in the organizational life. Rather, these disagreements reside beneath the surface as a potential oppositional force.[29] Third, the formal division of labor which accompanies large size creates a static set of roles for individuals at every level in an organization. The resulting role specialization and role exclusion turns individuals away from an overall organizational focus to loyalty to some sub-unit, often fostering alienation in the organization.[30]

Ultimately, the social consequences of school size on students and teachers depend on the link between the structure of social relationships within a school and educational outcomes. Not surprisingly, the outcomes most strongly influenced are social or affective in nature, such as 'isolation', 'alienation', or 'social engagement'.[31] Further, while size clearly influences the structure of interactions within a school, attempts on the margin of the organization to mitigate the effect of size on communication, cohesion, roles, and management organization (such as establishing schools within schools or house systems) have been only partially successful.[32]

In sum, the bureaucratic perspective has led to the development of large schools, based on assumptions about greater efficiency, greater resource strength, and the ability to offer more specialized programs. Little research evidence, however, supports claims about economies of scale. Greater resource strength and specialized programs are more common in larger contexts, but it is far from clear that the aggregate consequences have been desirable. In general, the negative effects associated with large schools, as predicted by a communitarian perspective, have dominated both recent case study reports and survey analyses. Large schools are characterized by social stratification in learning opportunities and actual academic outcomes, as well as a heightened alienation and detachment of students and teachers from the school and its aims.

In our view, school size requires a careful balancing: neither too large to inhibit a strong sense of community nor too small to offer a full curriculum and adequate instructional facilities. At least as compared to the current state of affairs in major urban centers, small is clearly better. The evidence we have reviewed is consistent with the advice offered by Goodlad (1984), who suggested that the ideal size of a high school is between 500 and 600 students.

Student Body Composition

A basic organizational problem for schools is how to respond to the diversity in students' background, abilities, and interests. Athough there is substantial research on the relationship between individual characteristics of students and academic outcomes, much less is known about the consequences of student body composition on school organization. We focus our discussion below on three specific features: racial composition, social class composition, and the distribution of student ability.

Why does school composition matter? Although empirical research on how student body composition affects the internal organization of schools is rather sparse, this topic has been a prominent concern in the theoretical literature on schooling.[33] These arguments have mostly focused on elementary schools, and in particular, on the consequences of classroom composition for how teachers organize instruction. Barr and Dreeben (1983) provide an excellent empirical example of this in their research on reading in first grade. A key aspect of their study focused on how the ability distribution of students within elementary classrooms influences teachers' formation of reading groups and the pacing of instruction. Their research, and subsequent investigations, have demonstrated that the characteristics of a student group significantly influence teachers' work.

A related argument draws on the observation that classroom composition (in terms of students' background, abilities, and interests) represents a direct resource for student learning. This feature of composition is particularly important for instructional techniques such as cooperative learning and peer tutoring.[34]

As we extrapolate these ideas to the secondary level, the focus shifts from classroom grouping to the effects of school composition on institutional structure and functioning. The overall distribution of student characteristics shapes the curricular offerings of a school and the policies which map students into courses.[35] There are also important implications in the social domain. High concentrations of disadvantaged students can make the maintenance of social order in the school difficult and can foment peer cultures which act in opposition to the academic aims of the school.[36]

A major problem in past research on this topic has been the weak measurement of these key organizational properties (Bidwell and Kasarda, 1980). In principle, the entire distribution of student attributes may be of interest, including dispersion and skewness, and not just mean level. For example, Barr and Dreeben (1983) found that classrooms with high numbers of low-ability students (low mean combined with positive skewness) were the most problematic environments for organizing reading instruction. Unforunately, few investigations have such conceptual clarity and empirical specificity. Much of the research referenced below focuses on the direct link between composition and outcomes without any explicit consideration of the organizational mechanisms involved. Nonetheless, there is sufficient evidence to conclude that aspects of student composition influence organizational operations and these features, in turn, impact both teachers and students.

Racial composition

The trumpeted finding offered by Coleman *et al.* (1966) in the *Equality of Educational Opportunity Report* — that minority achievement was higher in racially integrated schools — focused attention on the effects of a school's racial composition on student achievement. The extant research on this topic has been primarily within the milieu of school desegregation efforts. We summarize below the basic findings from two major reviews. Most of this research, however, has not examined possible organizational differences in schools resulting from changes in racial composition. Fortunately, some recent case studies offer evidence on this account.

Mahard and Crain (1983) summarized the research on the effect of desegregation on student achievement. Some of the studies were methodologically rigorous, including a few with randomized designs. In those with the strongest design, desegregation was shown to raise first and second grade minority students' IQ by as much as four points in a single year. While these positive effects were sustained thereafter, student gains did not increase with time spent in a desegregated environment. Larger positive effects were found for desegregation plans which included entire metropolitan areas as compared to those restricted to smaller areas. In general, minority achievement was greatest in schools with the largest proportions of whites. The authors speculated that high expectations and an internalized locus of control, where students are made to feel responsible for their own behavior and progress, were crucial factors that explained the positive effects of desegregation on minority student achievement. No direct investigation of school organizational arrangements was considered in this review.

The review by Schofield and Sagar (1983) focused on the dynamics of human relations within desegregated schools. In contrast to the findings from Mahard and Crain where minority achievement was greatest in schools with the smallest concentration of minorities, this review concluded that intergroup relations were better in schools with a higher proportions of minorities (20–60 per cent). In mostly white schools, minority students felt isolated and therefore tended to withdraw into a protective clique. Taken together, these two reviews suggest that the academic and social effects of school racial composition may be somewhat different.

This desegregation research must be viewed in the light of several case studies which have described the deterioration of the learning environment in large public secondary schools in the late 1960s and early 1970s. As Cusick (1983) noted, 'biracialism' (i.e., forced integration) was a strong contributor to conflicts among students, and it impeded the formation of any consensual basis for resolving these conflicts. In a related vein, Metz (1978) pointed out that keeping order in these biracial schools — at any price — became paramount for school authorities. Schools increasingly used specific 'professional activities' such as teacher workshops, multi-ethnic materials, and sensitivity training to compensate for the breakdown of community in these contexts.

Further, as Eyler, Cook and Ward (1983) noted, desegregating schools did not ensure that students of different races would actually experience schooling together. In fact, case studies document that the bureaucratic response to the increased student diversity accompanying integration efforts resulted in resegregating students within schools through specialized programming.[37] As both Grant (1988) and Cusick (1983) chronicled, schools expanded the number of non-demanding curricular offerings which allowed students to engage in the academic life of the school in very different ways. Thus, while students of different races actually attended the same school, rode the same bus, and ate in the same lunchroom, their schooling experiences — both social and academic — were nonetheless highly differentiated.

From an institutional perspective, the consequences of desegregation on school organization were quite profound. These case studies argue that significant changes occurred in organizational structure (such as the curricular expansion noted above), internal functioning (such as the rise of a laissez-faire attitude on advising students about course taking), and a general demise in adult moral authority.

Thus, the positive effects reported by Coleman *et al.* (1966), which occurred in schools that were naturally integrated, proved hard to attain through direct policy intervention. The communitarian ethos of the public high schools of the 1950s, albeit often discriminatory and intolerant, was clearly broken by formal desegregation efforts. Schools attempted to cope with the problems arising from increased student diversity through a variety of bureaucratic mechanisms. The restructuring of curriculum and related efforts to repair social relations within the school, however, failed to create strong institutional norms promoting academic achievement for all students.

Social class composition

The social class composition of schools varies considerably. In the late 1970s, this topic was considered in several studies of educational and occupational aspirations based on a status attainment model.[38] Alexander *et al.*, (1979) and Alwin and Otto (1977) found the average social class level of the school to be weakly related to average school achievement, in comparison to individual measures of students' social class. In contrast, Lee and Bryk (1989) found, using *HS&B* data, that the school social class is strongly associated with average student achievement in mathematics, and also mediates the relationship between student social class and achievement. Further, the structure of these relationships is quite different in public and Catholic schools. In general, school social class plays a much more powerful role in the public than in the Catholic sector. Affluent public schools are much more socially differentiating environments than comparable Catholic schools.

Recent research on the characteristics of effective schools has also indicated important influences of social class. Hallinger and Murphy (1983; 1986) reported that the distinctive characteristics of school effectiveness (e.g., opportunity to learn, instructional leadership, clear school mission, high expectations) are not identical in low and high social class schools. They also found that effective principals in low social class schools exercised more direct control and authority over school operations, particularly with respect to expectations and achievement, than did effective principals in high social class schools.

In general, the simplest perspective on social class composition views it as a proxy for fiscal and human resources. This is implicit, for example, in production-function analyses of schooling. In contrast, a communitarian view of the school directs our attention to the differences in beliefs, values, and expectations that students, parents and staff bring to the school, and how such cultural features influence organizational behavior. In this regard, we note that the survey research on schooling has tended to ignore the role which teachers' background may play in shaping institutional norms. Further, if there is a correlation between the social class composition of students and the social class background of the school staff (which seems likely), then at least some of what is typically ascribed to student background may actually be staff composition effects.

Ability composition

It is argued that schools need a nucleus of motivated and academically able students to provide a stable institutional base. This idea is advanced, for example, by Rutter and his colleagues in a study of twelve lower-class London secondary schools. Rutter *et al.* (1979) found that a particular ethos characterized schools with high levels of academic achievement and other student behaviors positively related to academic progress. They noted that an 'academic balance in the intakes to the schools' played an important role in achieving these effects. Schools which had a substantial nucleus of children of at least average intellectual ability showed better examination success and lower deliquency rates.[39] Closely related here is the work cited earlier from Barr and Dreeben (1983), who documented that teachers of classes with large numbers of low-ability children have special problems and are constrained in ways that teachers with more favorable class compositions are not.

Sorenson (1987) offers a theoretical exposition of the relationship between the ability composition of a school and a student's opportunity to learn. According to vacancy theory, access to an active educational environment is determined to some extent by the students with whom an individual must compete. The number of instructional groups in a school is limited by the available resources (i.e., teachers, materials, and time), and is largely independent of the characteristics of the pool of students who might be assigned to them. The number of places in each of these instructional groups is similarly limited. For these reasons, the structure of ability groups does not necessarily match the distribution of student ability. Supporting this view, Hallinan and Sorenson (1983) found that the size and number of ability groups in elementary school classes were quite stable, regardless of the actual ability distribution within a class.

A similar phenomenon exists in high schools where prerequisites and course sequencing constrain students' academic opportunities. Garet and Delaney (1988) found that the probability of enrolling in advanced science and mathematics courses varied systematically among the four California high schools they studied. The basic structure of the curriculum in these schools — the number of levels of vertical differentiation and the number of course sections at each level — directly influenced the subject matter to which high school students were exposed. In related research, Lee and Bryk (1988) argued that the greater academic coursetaking in the Catholic sector results from the constrained curricular offerings in these schools coupled with a proactive stance by adults encouraging students' academic pursuits.

In general, the research demonstrates that different high schools respond differently to students with similar entry characteristics. The academic structure of the organization and its underlying belief system shape student academic experiences and subsequent outcomes. A central tenet of the bureaucratic perspective is that the differences in students' academic background and interests are a major constraint on the work of schools. Within this perspective, a psychology of individual differences is offered as a theoretical justification for specialization of instruction for different groups.[40]

From a communitarian view, however, only the most gross differences among students merit an institutional response. Greater emphasis is placed on fostering a common experience for all students, and the rationalizing function of a psychology of individual differences is less salient. Clearly, the curricular offerings of a high school must be differentiated and aligned, to some degree, with the interests and academic abilities that students bring to the school. But the degree of differentiation required to effectively educate remains an open question. The extant research, both from field studies and survey analyses, suggests that high schools are probably more internally differentiated now than can be justified on scientific grounds.

Parent Involvement

We have organized this section around the three broad aspects of parent involvement with schooling. The first consists of political reform movements to incorporate parents in school decision-making, sometimes referred to as 'parent empowerment'. The second emphasizes the role of the parents in the home-learning of their children. This perspective leads naturally to a focus on 'parent education'. The third focuses on efforts among school staff and parents to form a functional community around the school where concerns of both educators and parents are addressed. This directs our attention to the socialization functions of schooling and a cultural view of the school.

Political action and community control of schools

Local control of schooling is a fundamental tenet in American education. Recent moves toward school-site management, community control, and parent-school partnerships involve, in varying ways, a reaffirmation of this concept.[41] Although there are different versions of site-based governance schemes, these plans generally share an aim of fostering greater collaborative decision-making between parents and school-based professionals.[42] By altering the basic decision-making relationships, it is claimed that schools will become more responsive to their clients and, ultimately, that learning will improve. Some combination of factors external to the individual school site — bloated and non-responsive central office bureaucracies, entrenched professional interests, and external policymaking bodies at the state and federal level that are insensitive to local needs — are generally seen as 'the problem' to be solved by greater parental involvement.[43]

Most of the research in this area consists of detailed case studies of efforts to introduce greater community control in schools.[44] Because of the highly contextual nature of these efforts, such research is not easily generalized. We summarize the main findings from two significant studies and consider the implications that these efforts might hold for the larger question of community control.

Although discussions of community control are particularly salient at the moment, such efforts have been active for several decades.[45] The most extensively studied case is the decentralization of New York City schools which began in the late 1960s.[46] Reform in New York was spawned out of longstanding frustrations with a nonresponsive public school system. Specifically, the system had failed to affect significant racial desegregation and positive educational outcomes for minority students, especially blacks.

Set in the context of an emerging black power movement, the idea of 'community control' received strained support in New York City. Because it represented a direct attack on the control of professionals over public schooling, their opposition was not surprising. At a more basic level, community control raised fundamental questions about the goals of public schooling. The impersonal universalistic norms held by the professionals conflicted with the particularism of community consciousness advanced by at least some proponents of local control.[47] Thus, it was not solely a clash over administrative strategies to affect more positive academic outcomes. It was also in part a confrontation over aims.

Rogers and Chung (1983) provide a ten-year follow-up assessment on the New York City school decentralization. *110 Livingston Street Revisited* is an important book because an organizational reform as expansive as school system decentralization can be adequately judged only on the basis of a long-term study. Rogers and Chung report there were several positive consequences of decentralization. Many schools and districts, particularly in minority areas, now have a legitimacy among their clientele that they lacked in the 1960s. Principals tend to be more sensitive to local needs than prior to decentralization, when they 'took orders from above'. Many new educational programs emerged, culturally relevant curricula have become commonplace, and linkages with outside agencies were established.

In terms of student academic outcomes, however, the evidence is less clear. Although there is some indication that reading test scores may have improved over the decade, there are many alternative explanations for the limited data presented, and Rogers and Chung are cautious in their interpretation of these results. More generally, they concluded that 'Despite the many positive developments under decentralization, there remain many unresolved problems [relating to district governance, program administration, and district-school system relations] . . . [These problems] will have to be addressed more systematically in the future if the New York City school system is to realize the potential that the best of the decentralized districts have demonstrated' (p. 216). Thus, while community control succeeded in changing some aspects of some schools; decentralization did not result in broad-based improvement in student learning.

In tone, the conclusions of Rogers and Chung are similar to those offered by Gittell *et al.* (1972) in their evaluation of the demonstration school districts which preceded the system-wide reform in New York City. According to Gittell *et al.*, while decentralization held much promise, the task was considerably more complex than most imagined at the outset, and the full potential had not been realized in the demonstration sites.

Similar conclusions are offered by Malen and Ogawa (1988) in a critical test of school-based governance in Salt Lake City. The plan at Salt Lake incorporated a number of features deemed essential to school-site governance. Parent-professional councils located at each school were charged with broad policy-making responsibilities. Protections were introduced to assure real power to parents in these activities, and training was provided to help parents exercise power. In addition, the Salt Lake community was much more homogeneous than other urban contexts, such as New York, where the cultural gap between professional staff and minority homes was exceptionally wide. Nonetheless, the results of this fifteen year effort at collaborative decision making were disappointing: 'Despite the presence of these highly favorable conditions, teachers and parents did not wield significant influence on significant issues in site-council arenas' (p. 266). The authors caution against over-generalization from this one case and suggest a number of adjustments in the design of future school-site governance plans that might yield more positive results.

In sum, while researchers remain optimistic, it is also quite clear that the desired ends are not easily attained. In the cases examined so far, at least, professional authority has held sway, and the promise of parent involvement which is more than symbolic has not materialized. At the other extreme, if we look back to the turn of the century, we find ample evidence of the excesses created through ward-based political control of schools which is hardly a model for a better way.

Parental involvement and home-learning

Substantial psychological research documents the central role of parents in children's development, and identifies specific types of parental behavior and attitudes that have positive effects on children.[48] Some research has also examined how social and cultural attributes of families influence parental engagement in such activities.[49] In general, these studies have found important relationships between social class, and in particular parents' level of education, and children's home experiences. These findings, in turn, have contributed to prescriptive activities for parents to provide a more stimulating home learning environment.[50]

In general, parents influence their child's learning through the enforcement of normative standards concerning education, and by the specific behaviors which contribute directly to learning.[51] The more active parents are in determining the educational experiences of their children, the more children gain from those experiences.[52] Specifically, it has been shown that parental expectations for their children's achievement and the importance that parents place on education are positively related to academic outcomes.[53] Even in high school, adolescents are strongly influenced by their parents' beliefs, goals, and values concerning education and achievement, and they tend to incorporate these standards into their own. This influence can also operate negatively, when parents do not value education or do not regularly enforce standards.[54]

Specific parental behaviors — monitoring student homework, engaging in tutoring (or hiring a tutor), minimizing distractions from school work, and engaging in active choices concerning children's educational programs — have also been shown to have strong positive effects on students' educational outcomes.[55] A relatively large body of empirical research on this topic has been conducted particularly on pre-school and elementary school children.[56] A number of general findings have emerged: (1) parental participation in their children's home learning is positively related to parental social class, with the parents' level of education being the prime consideration; (2) the amount of involvement appears directly related to the extent to which the parent feels informed and able to contribute to the child's learning; (3) parental participation appears to decrease as the child progresses through school, although parents continue to express interest in being involved in their child's school work through the secondary level; (4) the amount of parental involvement in homework and curriculum decision making is positively related to student achievement and to students' pursuit of academic coursework, even after taking social class into account; and (5) parents desire more involvement in their children's education.[57]

Over the last fifteen years, a major use of these research findings has been to train parents to become better home educators. Most of this attention has been focused on young children. Elementary school teachers and pre-school coordinators have been encouraged to actively engage parents in activities which will increase their children's learning.[58] In general, studies of these intervention programs report positive consequences for both parents and children. Mowry (1972) and McKey *et al*., (1985) document that parent education efforts in Head Start programs have significant and long-lasting effects. Similarly, Becher (1984) reports significant improvement in elementary student learning when parents were trained by the school to engage in supportive academic activities.

In general, much less effort has focused on developing parent education programs at the high school level. Correlational studies support the contention that parental involvement continues to be an important consideration in secondary schools.[59] However, such interactions are not seen as part of the formal responsibilities of high school teachers. Either additional support staff (whose function would be to provide such parental training) or a restructuring of the teacher's role would seem to be required, were this to be seriously pursued in high schools.[60]

Strengthening school-family ties

A very different line of scholarship addresses the need to strengthen the school as a communal institution. James Coleman's recent theories about the effects of functional and value communities on the work of schools are germane in this regard.[61] In an argument offered to explain the particular effectiveness of Catholic schools, Coleman and Hoffer (1987) hypothesized that functional communities organized around churches bring parents and students together. Such functional communities promote greater face-to-face social interactions across generations and, as a result, constitute a form of 'social capital' that facilitates the work of the school.[62] While this idea is appealing, Coleman and Hoffer provide no direct empirical evidence that such social relations among schools and families actually characterize modern Catholic high schools.

At a narrower and more instrumental level, substantial research indicates positive consequences for both students and teachers when parents volunteer in their children's schools and classrooms. In a comprehensive synthesis of research on Head Start, McKey *et al*., (1985) concluded that the extent to which parents operate as volunteers or as staff members in Head Start was positively associated with cognitive gains for disadvantaged preschoolers. Similarly, in a review of research on home and elementary school relationships, Epstein (1985) found that parental activity in the school was positively related to efforts by teachers to use more home-learning activities. The positive association of parental involvement with student achievement is further supported in a research synthesis by Henderson (1987). This review includes several empirical studies which link involvement of parents in school to their children's academic success, for all levels of schooling. Moles (1987), however, notes that such parental involvement depends on a variety of social attributes, with women, whites and higher social class parents more likely to engage in such behavior. Moles also argues that too much of the impetus for seeking involvement is left to parents. Secondary school parents (especially those in the inner city) report being contacted only when there is bad news.

At least one recent study claims that positive parent-school relations have important organizational influences in secondary schools. Chubb (1988) states that, 'All other things being equal, schools in which parents are highly involved, cooperative, and well-informed are more likely to develop effective organizations than schools in which parents do not possess these qualities' (p. 40). In these 'organizationally effective' schools, parents visited classrooms, had regular consultations with teachers, and were involved in parent-school activities. These results are consistent with Coleman's theories that good schools benefit from positive social relations between the school and its families.

There is actually a long history of concern about strengthening school-family ties under the rubric of 'community schools'. Wayland (1958) describes efforts starting at the turn of the century which attempted to use schools to build social ties within (predominantly urban) communities as part of a larger concern for assimilating immigrants into American values. These community schools provided social service programs both for students and parents in school facilities.[63] Efforts by the C.S. Mott Foundation marked a revitalization of this approach during the Depression.[64] Activity here was directed towards poor and working-class Americans who had suffered both a loss of income and social support networks.

In considering these efforts, many historians have focused on how 'community schools' attempted to shape the attitudes of the working class towards obedient citizenship and docility to group norms.[65] They have expressed particular concern over how professional values and aims took precedence in such efforts over the concerns and needs of the communities being served. This scholarship also notes how community education was used, in some instances, to reinforce segregated schools and racist values.[66] In general, it is unclear whether these earlier efforts succeeded in providing 'functional communities' which reflect the democratic values that are now espoused for American schooling.

Currently, attention focuses on the deinstitutionalization of urban neighborhoods and their declining capacity to support family life.[67] Churches have diminished in membership and number, good child care is increasingly problematic, and practical finances have increased the necessity of parents spending much of their time outside the home.[68] Many urban families are moving frequently in a search for adequate housing, and this high level of transience weakens the social ties necessary to bind neighborhoods together. To counteract this loss of 'social capital', it is argued that schools must take on increased responsibility to strengthen the social connections among parents around the school itself.

The work by Comer (1980) in two New Haven elementary schools is the best example of the approach.[69] Comer's efforts were based in part on the observation that many minority and low-income parents transmit conflicting signals to their children about education and learning. Actual parental behavior often contradicts a spoken emphasis on going to school and getting an education. Specifically, he argues that low-income and minority parents feel a sense of exclusion, low self-esteem and hopelessness concerning formal education, and they are likely to convey these attitudes to their children. Similar concerns are raised by Ogbu in his research examining minority parents' and teachers' perceptions of one another.[70] Ogbu suggests that an atmosphere of mutual distrust and suspicion permeates the values and goals of each group. Teachers described parents' goals and values as destructive to students' academic accomplishments. Parents in turn believe that teachers are antagonistic towards the home culture of the child, discounting the experiences and knowledge to be gained from it.

This concern, characterized by Comer as a social misalignment of values between home and school, directs attention to reshaping the relationship between schools and parents around the best interests of children. Comer's school-based efforts sought to build an alliance between the family and the school staff, in order to provide a consistent set of social experiences which would promote children's sense of personal well-being and a constructive environment for learning. These reformers directly attacked the bureaucratic ethos of social services organizations which segments authority over children.[71] Instead, they sought to strengthen the social ties among all of the adults who are responsible for children. The participating schools in New Haven worked to develop a functional community among children, staff, parents and other caretakers around the education of children.

In looking across the various efforts to promote parental involvement in schools discussed above, we are reminded that the forging of a vital collaboration between community, parents and school staff is illusive and by its nature inherently problematic. Parents and children have both rights and responsibilities in the educational process. Schooling is a public good, essential to a vital democratic society, as well as a private benefit increasingly essential to individual economic well-being. As a result, both broad societal concerns and individual interests must be recognized. In terms of actual school operations, the professional knowledge, pedagogic skill, and personal commitment of teachers are critical and must also be assured. Identifying the specific contributions which each group can bring to the enterprise and structuring a process which secures these strengths while protecting against an arbitrary use of power are the difficult tasks which must be engaged in forging a true community-school collaboration.

In different ways, each of the three strategies for promoting parental involvement attempts to respond to the problematic socialization function which schools, particularly those in poor communities, must play. If the children of poor families are to have access to the opportunities of mainstream American life, then socialization toward that end must occur. How this function of schooling becomes negotiated between parents and school staff remains a critical question. Community control advocates see the solution as parents taking control of schools. In its most exteme form, this represents a pure communitarian response that 'only we can educate our children'. How educational expertise (and with it middle class socialization) appropriately enters such contexts, however, remains unclear.

Under the second approach, parent education is viewed as a necessary effort in order to facilitate the real work of schools. This approach is firmly rooted in a bureaucratic view of the school which sees the home environment as the problem to be solved through an appropriate training of parents. By adding this extra service, students will come to school better able to respond to existing classroom demands. The control of education remains with the professionals, and concerns about possible social misalignment of values between home and school may never be directly addressed.

The third option, developing functional communities around the school, represents a hybrid of bureaucratic and communitarian views. It stresses the importance of productive social relations among all connected with the school, and thus provides a legitimacy to all school members — children, children's caretakers, and professional staff. Furthermore, the basis of these relationships is fiducial rather than contractarian. On balance, this approach also recognizes that while each group has something important and necessary to contribute, these are not relationships among equals. The school is a limited community focused on educational aims. As such, professional expertise of school staff continues to be accorded a special role, and structuring schools to promote student learning remains the central consideration.

School Governance

The operation of an individual school is subject to a wide range of controls which operate through its governance structure. Much of the current interest in school governance and its effects can be traced to the 1982 report by Coleman, Hoffer and Kilgore on *Public and Private Schools*. This widely publicized and controversial study concluded that private schools produce superior academic achievement compared to their public counterparts. These advantages, moreover, were greatest for disadvantaged youth. Based on this statistical evidence, Coleman and colleagues advanced an argument supporting tuition tax credits for private schools. Although the original research was criticized extensively on methodological grounds, the basic findings withstood a spate of reanalyses, including subsequent investigations with longitudinal data.[72] Most importantly, Coleman and colleagues had again catalyzed a major policy debate — this time on parental choice and schooling — that would endure through the decade of the 1980s and perhaps beyond.

Subsequently, researchers sought to explain why private schools were especially effective in promoting student achievement. The earliest responses to the Coleman *et al.* work were apologies for public schools, pointing out a variety of conditions affecting public schools with which private schools did not have to contend. These arguments rapidly evolved, however, from a spirited defense of public schools into a discourse on how aspects of the external environment of schools shape their internal operations. Some writings have focused on the effects of specific policy differences between public and private schools, such as control over the entry and exit of faculty and students and decision-making autonomy at the local school-site. Other arguments have been broader in scope, emphasizing how differences in control mechanisms can have pervasive effects on schools' internal organization.

Control over student entry and exit

One of the major objections to the work of Coleman, Hoffer and Kilgore was based on the proposition that student selection is an integral feature of private schooling which statistical adjustments for differences in student background are incapable of parceling out.[73] These critics claim that the processes enabled through a school's selection of students and through the choice exercised by parents and students in seeking admission fundamentally alter subsequent organizational life. In particular, selectivity helps to assure a value consensus between parents and school, to legitimate the moral authority of teachers, and to secure a high level of commitment among the school's clients. At a more instrumental level, having a student body composed primarily of individuals who want to be there can affect students' commitment to the school and engagement with academic work. Since such students are likely to be easier to teach, teachers' sense of efficacy and satisfaction should be greater because students' progress will be more readily manifest.

Although these arguments have considerable face validity, they have not been subjected to extensive empirical examination. Bryk and Driscoll (1988), as part of their investigation of communal school organization, constructed a composite measure of school selectivity.[74] After controlling for other aspects of student background, they found significant relationships between selectivity and student absenteeism, academic interest, and achievement gains. Teacher absenteeism was also lower in more selective schools, but there was no indication of selectivity effects on teacher efficacy and satisfaction, enjoyment of work, or staff morale.

Since selectivity was not the principal focus of the Bryk and Driscoll study, the evidence here is somewhat limited. Nevertheless, it appears that, as an organizational property, selectivity has an effect on student academic outcomes distinct from the effects of individual student background. In terms of the hypothesized impact on teachers, however, the evidence is less conclusive.

It was also argued in the original responses to Coleman *et al.* that private schools have more flexibility in removing troublesome students. This has not been (and cannot be) systematically explored with *HS&B*, since the data do not provide detailed information about the alternatives available to school principals to remove disruptive students and the difficulties involved in exercising these options. Although we know that the actual number of expulsions in private schools is quite low, we have no basis for directly assessing the organizational consequences of any differences in expulsion policies and procedures among schools.[75]

Grant's account of Hamilton High (1988) provides the most direct field study evidence in this regard. Grant describes the overly-legalistic environments which developed in public high schools in the 1970s, where concerns about due process produced complex procedures for collecting evidence, assembling witnesses, and conducting formal hearings before an expulsion (or in some cases even a suspension) could be undertaken. This environment made teachers hesitant to institute proceedings and thereby further emboldened disruptive behavior on the part of students. While the confrontational environment of the late 1960s and 1970s has abated somewhat, Grant argues that the legalism surrounding adult responses to student misbehavior remain part of the negotiated 'peace' in today's public high schools. Futhermore, student expulsion is limited almost entirely to disciplinary problems. The idea of 'flunking out' is almost unheard of in public schools today.

Control over faculty entry and exit

Chubb and Moe (1988) provide detailed descriptive comparisons of public and private schools in terms of prinicipals' authority to control faculty membership.[76] While over 80 per cent of public high schools are unionized and over 80 per cent of the teachers have tenure, both practices are rare in private schools. Public school principals are much more likely to report problems attracting good staff because of excessive central office control, including forced transfers. Similarly, complex administrative procedures and union rules have resulted in a time-consuming process to remove an incompetent teacher from a public school.

Bridges (1986) offers a detailed account of the slow and cumbersome process which public schools confront when dealing with incompetent teachers. It is often a frightening picture of incompetence tolerated far too long. Teacher problems typically emerge around issues of maintaining discipline. The first steps by school administrators are aimed at reforming the incompetent teacher. By the time administrators resign themselves to the failure of these salvage efforts and begin administrative dismissal, the teacher is usually in a state of 'performance collapse'. Several cohorts of students may have been adversely affected over this time frame. In contrast, private schools typically offer teachers one-year contracts, and the primary constraint on teacher removal is the principal's conscience.[77] Intuitively, these organizational differences seem likely to have significant consequences both on a school's staff and on student outcomes. This link, however, has not been explored in quantitative investigations of school organization.

Control mechanisms: Politics and markets

We limit our remarks here to a brief summary of the arguments and a commentary about the state of extant evidence as it pertains to these arguments. One argument about the relative effects of government control of schools in the public sector versus the consequences of voluntarism in the private sector can be traced to a paper by Salganik and Karweit (1982).[78] In brief, they note that public schools are based on a rational-legal authority within a bureaucratic mode of organization, whereas private schools continue to rely on more traditional forms of hierarchical authority. Over the past twenty years, an increasing rationalization of public schooling has narrowed the authority of teachers, demeaned their personal role, and diminished the autonomy of school staff relative to external forces.[79] It has also made public schools more complex organizations with less internal integration. Such complexity, it is argued, reduces the coherence of a school's programs and is thereby detrimental to school operations. Considerable evidence supports this characterization of organizational life in public schools and clearly differentiates them from schools in the private sector.[80]

A second argument is offered by Chubb and Moe,[81] who claim 'the influence on learning does not depend on any particular educational practice, on how [schools] test or assign homework or evaluate teaching, but rather on their organization as a whole, on their goals, leadership, fellowship, and climate. What is more, their institutional structure and character is shaped by their environments . . .'[82] They further state that positive parental relations and decision-making autonomy at the individual school site are critical for an 'effectively organized high school'.

These claims, however, pose a fundamental dilemma for public schools. Greater authority to individual school sites can seemingly be achieved only in exchange for extensive monitoring systems to assure accountability. The latter, however, threaten to be overly prescriptive and ultimately counterproductive. According to Chubb and Moe, the mechanism of the market offers a greater potential for promoting schools which are responsive to their clients than do the bureaucratic controls typically employed by modern democratic institutions.

It is not possible at this point to make a full, detailed, and balanced assessment of this policy argument, since the statistical analyses on which it is apparently based have yet to appear. We can comment, however, on the relationship of other available evidence to the general propositions advanced by Chubb and Moe. First, syntheses of the effective schools literature have found little systematic evidence supporting the efficacy of particular instructional features such as curriculum articulation, maximizing student learning time, and monitoring instructional impact on student outcomes, although the conclusions are suspect, for methodological reasons.[83] Second, considerable descriptive evidence exists documenting important differences between public and private schools across a range of organizational characteristics.[84] These data are consistent with the claim that the internal operations of a school are influenced by the nature of its governance arrangements.

Much less clear, however, is the evidence connecting the specific organizational features, considered by Chubb and Moe, to teacher behavior and attitudes. In a recent study, Newmann, Rutter and Smith (1989) found no evidence supporting the hypothesis that principal leadership or teacher influence in decision making had direct effects on teacher efficacy or sense of community. Similarly, Rutter (1986) reports very weak effects for principal leadership and teacher collaboration on teacher engagement.

Some supporting evidence is offered, however, by Lee, Dedrick and Smith (in press) who report that teachers' sense of school community and perceptions of strong principal leadership are positively related to teacher satisfaction and self-efficacy.[85]

In terms of the link to student outcomes, we must rely on Chubb's (1988) description of analyses yet unpublished. The evidence here appears to be of two sorts. First, there are bivariate descriptive comparisons of high- and low-performance schools, in which no controls were introduced for differences in the characteristics of students enrolled. High- and low-performance schools differed dramatically in student body characteristics and informal organization, but were relatively similar in terms of school resources and classroom practices. In multivariate analyses which directly examine the effects of school organization on student achievement, he reports that a composite school organization factor (including measures of school academic emphasis, quality of staff relations, amount of homework, graduation requirements, and percentage of students in the academic track) had the second largest impact on test score gains, trailing only a proxy for student aptitude.

While the latter is an important empirical finding, its proper interpretation is not straightforward. Chubb acknowledges that a key component of the 'school organization index' — percentage of students in the academic track — has a powerful independent effect on students' academic achievement. What remains unclear is whether any of the other components of the school organization index beyond tracking would have any direct effects on student achievement once a fully specified model of tracking and coursetaking were introduced.

In fact, the substantial research on high school curricular organization raises serious doubts in this regard. These studies consistently document powerful effects of students' academic experiences on achievement and the significant role of curricular organization in determining the opportunities to learn afforded different kinds of students. As we conclude from our review in the next section, when academic achievement is the primary concern, interest must focus on core features of instruction, such as coursetaking, curricular materials, teaching efficiency, and homework, and how the organization of schools influences these. Global school characteristics are likely to have only a modest, and primarily indirect effect on academic outcomes, by fostering some increase in teacher and student effort. On the other hand, if attention shifts to social outcomes, such as teachers' satisfaction, morale, and efficacy, or student engagement behavior such as class cutting, absenteeism, and dropping out, the influence of organizational arrangements may be much greater.[86]

Internal Characteristics of School Organization

We now turn our attention to those features which comprise the internal organization of a school and directly influence outcomes for both teachers and students. We have organized this section around four broad considerations. First, we focus on the school as a cultural entity. We examine the belief systems in schools (including their climate or ethos), the goals which schools set for themselves, and the distribution of these cultural beliefs and goals among staff and students.

A second lens for examining the internal organization of schools is administration. While one aspect of school administration emphasizes the outward reach into the school's external environment, our primary focus is on the major functions of administration inside the school — mediation, management, and leadership.

A third focus centers on the formal organization of the school. Specifically, we consider how schools are organized as workplaces for teachers and students. Are teachers seen as subject matter specialists? Do they have opportunities to interact with students through a varied set of organizational roles? From the student perspective, how is the curriculum structured and how are individuals mapped into it? Above and beyond the question of 'who takes what?' and how this is influenced by the overall structure of the curriculum, we also consider the process by which students and teachers are assigned to (or choose) curricular tracks and courses within those tracks.

The last organizing lens considers the nature of social relations among the various participants in secondary schools. The relationships among teachers, among students, and between teachers and students affect how schools work and how teachers and students work within them. Such relations include peer group formation and functioning, extra-curricular activities, personal counseling, and social and academic collegiality among faculty.

Cultural System

Some of earliest empirical work on school culture appears in psychological studies of climate.[87] The basic topics considered in this research include: teacher commitment; peer norms; academic expectations and emphasis; goal consistency, clarity and consensus; and teachers' use of rewards and praise. In addition to these 'cultural aspects' of climate, this research has also considered ecological characteristics of schools (such as building size), milieu descriptors (such as teacher and student morale), and social system variables (such as administrative organization and ability grouping).

In general, climate research has a strong empirical bent, but a weak theoretical base.[88] The typical study measures a variety of climate variables and seeks to relate them to some outcome such as students' academic achievement. The complex relationships among the sociological, social-psychological, and psychological phenomena included within climate research are rarely addressed. Further, as Anderson (1982) notes in a thorough review of this literature, a variety of (sometimes inconsistent) causal models are used, research designs and statistical analyses are often inadequate, and statistical results are frequently misinterpreted.

More recently, the idea of a school culture has been advanced by educational anthropologists. This research is concerned with the values of members of the organization and the practices and activities derived from these beliefs, including their symbolic representation in traditions and rituals.[89] In general, the term 'culture' does not imply a particular configuration of beliefs, but rather may comprise any collection of values and related activities. In fact, research on school cultures tends to emphasize the unique aspects of each school.[90]

The presence of shared values among a school staff is an aspect of school culture that has received particular attention in effective schools research. Such values include norms for instruction, which affect the way teachers' work is conducted and student learning takes place, and norms for civility, which affect the relations among individuals in the institution.[91] Norms for instruction include beliefs about students' abilities to learn, about appropriate classroom conduct on the part of teachers and students, and the futures toward which students' education are directed. Such norms easily arise when a school has a specific purpose or charter, such as in military academies and elite private schools. They can also accrue out of a cohesive faculty culture.[92] In contrast, norms for civility involve the routine expression of feelings about the welfare of others as part of the round of daily life. Lesko (1988) provides a good example of this in her ethnographic account of St. Anne's Catholic High School, which she describes as a caring community. In general, norms for civility can have positive affective consequences for both teachers and students, enhance the academic efforts of the school,[93] and promote psychic rewards for teachers.[94]

Within a bureaucratic perspective, related ideas appear in the literature on organizational goals.[95] Three types of goals are described for schools: official, operative, and operational. Official goals are formal statements of purpose concerning the mission of the school. These are generally abstract, and function primarily to secure legitimacy and support from the constituency. Operative goals, in contrast, represent the actual intentions of individuals within the organization. Operative goals may or may not reflect official goals, and may not even be articulated. Operative goals may be internally inconsistent and not directly connected to the technical core of instruction. In contrast operational goals are the specific criteria and procedures used for evaluation. In principle, operational goals are closely linked to official goals, in that they reflect specific evaluations conducted for public consumption.

Studies of effective schools often use a goal model as a framework for examining administrative activity.[96] Hoy and Ferguson (1985) describe such a model where 'rational decision makers in the organization are guided by a specific set of goals, and these goals are both few enough in number and defined clearly enough to be understood and taken on by participants' (p. 118). One difficulty with a goal model of this type is that while it may characterize some elementary schools, it is less appropriate for secondary schools which are more complex institutions with multiple and sometimes conflicting goals.[97]

In addition, a focus on official school goals tends to underemphasize the influences of the more tacit operative goals which can significantly shape the contour of social relations within a school. Further, if the operative goals of individuals conflict with expressed official goals, social cleavages within the institution may result. Rather than a school being characterized by a single effective ethos,[98] there may be distinct subgroups, each with its own ethos.

Another difficulty with past research using a goal framework is the lack of attention paid to the actual content of organizational beliefs. Here again, a communitarian perspective is helpful. As Bryk and Driscoll (1988) point out, not any set of beliefs is necessarily consistent with common descriptions of good schools. For example, in a study of medical education, Becker *et al.* (1961) found that, although students shared many common activities, an institutional emphasis on individual competition discouraged cooperation. Since the staff did not see personal ties and cooperative behavior as central to organizational life, supportive personal relations did not occur. While it is true that a set of shared values impelled organizational life, the lack of community and the degree of cut-throat competition which resulted in this case is inconsistent with the social aims typically espoused for public schooling. The intolerance of alternative life views promoted in fundamentalist academies provides another example of clear and consistent institutional goals which conflict with core democratic values.[99]

Administration

The literature on the role of administration in school organization is substantial. Murphy's (1988) review covered 202 articles, reports, and other reviews, all written since 1970. Bridges (1982) reviewed 322 research reports drawn from dissertation abstracts and published journals between 1976 and 1980. In fact, only a modest portion of this literature is actual research reports, and an even smaller amount is published in scholarly journals.[100]

The research reviewed by Bridges (1982) involved predominantly descriptive surveys using questionnaires, and suffers from significant methodological problems including lack of generalizability, lack of causal design, and the need for multilevel analysis.[101] Another limitation of this research is its singular focus on the administration of public schools (especially 'effective' public schools) and the relative absence of detailed ethnographic investigations.[102] Any synthesis of results from existing research must be understood within this context.[103]

School administration involves diverse functions.[104] We summarize the research in terms of three roles: the management role — allocating resources, developing and enforcing rules, and supervising staff development and evaluation; the mediator role — facilitating communication within the school and its external constituencies, buffering the technical core from disruptive influences, and communicating policy decisions and problems across the organization; and the leadership role — shaping and defining the official and operative goals of the school, and providing guidance and supervision in instruction.

The management role of school administration

This role consists of a number of related functions: (1) coordinating activities and allocating resources; (2) establishing and enforcing rules; and (3) supervising staff development and evaluation programs.[105] Each is described briefly below.

(1) Communication of information and resource allocation
Case studies of high school administrators indicate that the primary management role involves communication of information and resource allocation.[106] The principal is typically responsible for coordinating resources and information as they are needed by teachers for school operations. How this function is carried out, however, is usually context-specific. In particular, school size can affect the

amount of contact teachers have with the principal, and influence the degree to which procedures for obtaining resources, communicating problems, or accessing information are formalized.[107] This in turn is important because both the efficiency and informality of managerial action positively influence teacher satisfaction.[108]

(2) Rule administration

Management strategies which decrease school disruption and increase the safety of students are associated with a range of positive outcomes for both teachers and students.[109] Clear and consistent school rules and policies tend to improve the general disciplinary climate of the school and contribute to improved staff and student morale.[110]

The principal's role in maintaining the social order is complex. Clear and consistent enforcement of rules engenders a positive disciplinary climate, which is in turn related to academic achievement.[111] But this process involves more than just systematic rule enforcement. Basic human understandings about issues of justice and responsibility are also central. For example, students' perception that the handling of disciplinary matters is unfair and ineffective has been linked to students' dropping out of school.[112] The subtle aspects of rule administration are poignantly reflected in Grant's account of Hamilton High, where the moral authority of adults collapsed during the 1960s and early 1970s. Doing the 'procedurally correct thing' became more important than 'doing the right thing'. The explicit formulation of rules and their impersonal and neutral enforcement took precedence over concerns about students' social learning about issues of fairness, justice, and personal responsibility. In this regard, the managerial role has an important instructional function, as social teaching occurs in adult responses to student misbehavior.

Rule administration is also related to teacher outcomes. Caldwell and Lutz (1978) found that clear establishment and consistent enforcement of rules were more important for teacher satisfaction than was the actual personal involvement of teachers in rule enforcement.[113] Similarly, Rosenholtz (1985), in her synthesis of the effective school literature, concluded that formal rules contribute to a reduction in teacher role ambiguity and uncertainty, which in turn is related to teacher satisfaction.

Some care is required, however, in interpreting this evidence. When teachers' efforts are subject to external accountability, teachers prefer an explicit systematic statement of rules against which their behaviors will be judged. That is, when school life has become highly bureaucratized, expressions of 'Just tell me what you want me to do' are not surprising. Ironically, such teacher behavior can be counterproductive to advancing quality teaching and good schooling.[114] This argument is nicely detailed by Cohen (1988), who notes that the inherent ambiguity and uncertainty in teaching induces a high degree of dependence upon students' effort in order for teachers to achieve success. To take risks in such an environment requires social support from both colleagues (internal) and parent communities (external). In the absence of such trust, teachers become risk-averse and fall back on clear, explicit standards (by which they will be judged) as safeguards against capricious administrative action. This is another instance when a communitarian perspective on the school, as reflected in ideas about social collegiality and parental trust, offers a distinctly different interpretation of the educational context.

(3) Staff development and monitoring

Research on school improvement places heavy emphasis on administrative responsibility to implement staff development programs, to encourage ongoing training and retraining of teachers, and to supervise monitoring programs.[115] Some research suggests a significant increase in teachers' knowledge about teaching and subject matter as a consequence of such programs.[116] Other research on the same topic is a bit more sanguine, concluding that unless teachers are involved in the planning of thoughtfully executed programs, teacher dissatisfaction and alienation may result.[117] According Rosenholtz (1987), the critical factors predicting success include the amount of intrusive administrative operations (e.g., filling out forms, interrupting classrooms), the extent to which the goals of the development programs coincide with existing operative goals of teachers, and the collegial atmosphere already in operation in the school.

The mediator role of school administration

In his discussion of the school as a formal organization, Bidwell (1965) described 'buffering' as a critical role performed by school administration. As a mediator, the principal has three essential functions: (1) to represent the needs and concerns of the external constituency to the internal organization of the school; (2) to protect the technical core from disruptions which could hinder teachers' productivity; and (3) to facilitate interpersonal interactions, mediating problems as they occur within the hierarchy of the organization.

(1) Relation to external constituencies

Because of the governance structure of public schooling, most of the research on this topic focuses on the activities of school superintendents. This literature suggests that a primary function involves communicating about the school to its constituency, and bringing the concerns of that external constituency back to the internal organization of the school.[118] A school which does not communicate its successes to the community may lose support for its operations. The nature of this communication function depends on parental and community involvement in the school, which in turn is influenced by the school governance structure.[119] If parents are in regular communication with the school, interactions are less formal and greater consensus between school and community is the likely result. In this regard, the governance structure strongly shapes the amount and type of interactions of external individuals and groups with the school and the recourse available if the school is unresponsive.[120]

(2) Protecting the technical core

A somewhat different perspective is reflected in the effective schools research, where buffering the technical core is viewed as an important function of the principal.[121] The presumption here is that much of the external efforts to intervene in schools are actually dysfunctional. From this perspective the loose-coupling characteristics of schools — where central administrators have little direct authority over classroom operations — is a good to be preserved.[122]

(3) Facilitating informal social interactions

Another function of the administrator as mediator is the extensive amount of time prinicpals spend in informal social interactions.[123] Principals, according to Firestone and Wilson (1985), increasingly use cultural mechanisms, in addition to standard bureaucratic procedures, to influence school operations. They argue that bureaucratic procedures alone (the roles, rules, and authority relations which formally regulate the behavior of organization members) are insufficient to control the organization, and must be supplemented with cultural strategies (drawing on the subjective personal relations among school members). Cultural linkages can be especially influential in mediating disputes, contributing to collegiality, and promoting a cooperative working environment.

The leadership role of school administration[124]

The research on leadership notes that school life is shaped by prevailing ideology, tradition, and the rituals embedded in the daily routine.[125] Working through such symbolic expressions, the school 'leader' can shape the central mission of the school. The role of the school leader, then, is to articulate and 'stand for' the school's purpose, both within the organization and to the external constituency of parents and community.

Perhaps the key bureaucratic expression of school leadership is the formulation of clear, educational goals.[126] It is argued in the effective schools literature that such goals are fostered by strong leadership in the school,[127] although the causal direction of this relationship is uncertain. Some claim that effective leadership may actually be an outcome rather than a contributing feature of effective schools. That is, a strong central purpose may ease the job of a school administrator by clearly identifying his or her functions within the organization. Such clear definition is likely to facilitate the principal's role and make him/her appear 'effective'. The best available evidence on this issue comes from case studies that describe significant institutional changes occurring as a result of educational leadership.[128] The latter supports the contention that individual school leaders can significantly affect their institutions.

Much research focuses on the 'personality' of school leaders, and in particular on how leaders use charismatic qualities as a source of authority.[129] The latter is particularly salient in schools which are loosely coupled, i.e., where administrators exercise little direct authority to influence instructional operations.[130] On the other hand, it has also been noted that at least some school-site administrators use forms of rational-technical authority to develop a shared sense of purpose for the school.[131] Over time, principals can shape organizational goals by hiring teachers with similar beliefs about education, by monitoring instruction, and by encouraging both formal and informal communication within the school about its educational mission.

In general, research on administration from a communitarian perspective tends to emphasize the cultural dimensions of administration, the importance of personal actions of the school head, and how these influence the relations within the institution. Under this framework, leadership is encapsulated in very context-specific terms. In contrast, the bureaucratic perspective generally focuses on more managerial aspects of administration, concentrating on rules, policies and procedures, rather than situations, personalities, and an historically accrued set of norms and understandings.

Formal Organization of Work

The function of departments

As noted in the introduction, much of the theoretical argument and empirical research on school organization has focused on elementary schools, and in particular on the organization of classroom instruction in different subjects.[132] At the secondary level, a new organizational subunit — the academic department — emerges. The existing field research, while limited, suggests that departments play an important role in the diurnal life of secondary school teachers. Teachers see their social ties primarily to their departments, rather than to the school, and often describe themselves as subject matter specialists. Important curricular decisions occur here, and significant consequences may accrue in terms of teachers' efficacy and staff morale.[133] Specifically, case studies suggest that it is in the departments where key decisions are made about the courses to be offered, the assignment of students to classes, and who will teach them. Further, much of teachers' sense of efficacy and satisfaction is closely connected to the consequences of these decisions (i.e., the courses offered and the types of students taught), since teachers depend largely on their students' success for their psychic rewards.[134]

Although the salience of high school departments is firmly established in the case study literature, the actual functioning of departments and how this may be shaped by larger institutional forces has not been systematically investigated. From a bureaucratic perspective, the department is a device to efficiently organize teachers' work within the larger context of a modern high school. In principle, it can enhance the academic collegiality among faculty, focusing attention on teachers' development of pedagogical skills and strengthening their commitment to teaching. Thus, under bureaucratic theory, departmentalization is a deliberate organizational device to enhance academic learning.

However, we know very little about the possible social consequences which may also follow from this aspect of school organization. It seems plausible, however, to expect significant differences among departments within a school in terms of teachers' beliefs, work commitments and social relations. Further, this differentiation both within and between departments may be amplified by stratification with regard to such teacher attributes as race, gender, and seniority. When such stratification occurs, both goal consensus and program coherence may be difficult to achieve. It is easy to envision, for example, large comprehensive high schools with highly differentiated social structures consisting of a number of relatively closed social networks which combine to form an overall work environment characterized by distrust, detachment, and, perhaps, anomie.

The latter is important, because research is beginning to link teacher alienation and lack of engagement to the absence of a sense of community among teachers.[135] Along a related line, Bryk and Driscoll (1988) have unpacked this idea of a 'sense of community' to detail specific features of high school organization that act to create such climates. Using *HS&B*

data, they found teachers in communally organized schools[136] more likely to report satisfaction with their work, to be seen by students as enjoying their teaching, and to share a high level of staff morale than are teachers in schools not so organized. In terms of consequences for students, various forms of social misbehavior (class cutting, absenteeism, and classroom disorder) were all less prevalent, and school dropout rates were lower.

Bryk and Driscoll did not investigate the social structure and functioning of departments, as *HS&B* did not collect such data. They did consider school size, however, and found that a communal organization is much less common in large schools. Since the case studies mentioned above indicate that departmentalization is a characteristic of middle size and larger high schools, it seems plausible that departmentalization may be a contributing feature to a lack of community. Specifically, if departmentalization acts to foment subgroup closure, the research on communal organization suggests that negative social consequences may occur across the whole school for both teachers and students.

Teacher role

The functional division of labor is a central component of bureaucratic organization.[137] In this regard, departmentalization, as discussed above, is certainly a key element. Faculty role, and in particular work specialization, is another. The organization of instruction by age and grade level represents the earliest form of teacher specialization. The movement toward specialization accelerated in the late 1960s, fueled by federal and state categorical programs. The latter brought attention to a wide range of special needs, and resulted in an expansion of school activities including the introduction of health and social services.[138] The contemporary high school has considerable differentiation among staff who have specialized responsibilities according to students' special needs (for example, compensatory education, bilingual education, special education), special programming areas (for example, drug and alcohol abuse, teenage pregnancy, and suicide prevention), and special functions (for example, college counseling, job placement). The vertical curriculum, with multiple distinctions among nominally equivalent courses tailored to student ability and interest levels, offers further opportunities for teacher specialization.

Under bureaucratic organizational theory, staff specialization enhances the capacity of the school to deliver its educational services in an efficient manner.[139] Whether benefits actually accrue to students from such specialization is a complex and largely unaddressed question. A proper investigation would require a careful assessment of the direct effects of each specialized program or activity, as well as possible indirect effects on the overall school organization that may result from the more complex structure required to maintain this enterprise.

Newmann (1981) takes up the topic of specialization as part of a larger essay on how high schools contribute to student alienation.[140] He reminds us that adolescence and youth are critical developmental periods during which individuality must be balanced by integration within community. Yet questions about how school structure, activities, policies, and procedures might foster social integration for students has received little direct attention. Similarly, concerns about youth disorder, including dropping out, suicide, teenage pregnancy, and substance abuse are routinely defined as problems of the individual with the possible contribution of school organization seldom considered here.[141] From a communitarian perspective, staff specialization becomes problematic when it fosters transient interactions between teachers and students and creates barriers to more generalized affiliative adult-student relationships.

In response to concerns about student detachment and fragmentation of experiences, Newmann articulates an alternative teacher role where staff have broad responsibilities that extend beyond specific classroom duties and a delimited focus on a particular subject area.[142] A similar concept of a diffuse teacher role has been described by Parsons (1960). This extended or diffuse adult role recognizes that schools seek to influence students' social and personal development and that such influence requires a pervasive ethic of caring throughout the school. Furthermore, this role concept is based on the premise that to attain these ends requires continuous and sustained contact of students with a few adults who respond to the students as whole persons, rather than as clients in need of a particular service.[143]

In addition, there is some ethnographic evidence that a diffuse teacher role can also facilitate classroom instruction.[144] Teachers can use the understandings they acquire through informal student interactions as they address academic tasks. It can help them link current subject matter to experiences meaningful in students' lives. Further, the personal relationships that teachers establish with students outside of class can provide the human connections needed to catalyze students' engagement in class. Such personal relations also benefit teachers, as they are a common source of the intrinsic rewards that teachers find important in their work.[145]

Thus, both departmentalization and staff specialization reflect the tension present between bureaucratic and communitarian conceptions of a school. In intent, these organizational instruments promote academic efficiency, but they may also have negative social consequences. Further, these negative consequences may be inequitably distributed, with the alienating effects of high school environments especially salient for disadvantaged youth.[146]

Curricular organization and students' academic work

The central features of schooling that influence students' academic learning are the processes of instruction and the school structures, policies, and routines which influence how this instruction occurs.[147] The recent research on instruction at the secondary level is limited mostly to field investigations and ethnographic accounts.[148] In general, these describe students as passive recipients of teaching that is often characterized as routinized and deadening. Equally important, these field accounts indicate that the nature of classroom instruction is highly stratified. Top track students are much more likely to be found in small classes where teaching is stimulating and engaging. However, exceptions to this general pattern of social and intellectual stratification have been reported, particularly in field accounts of Catholic high schools.[149]

A much larger volume of theoretical and empirical research has focused on the mechanisms by which students are mapped to course content, how students' social background relates to such decisions, the effects of these processes on student outcomes, and how these effects are distributed with regard to characteristics such as race/ethnicity and class.[150] This overall pattern may be termed the social distribution of student outcomes.[151]

A substantial portion of this research has focused on a particular organizational feature of high schools, tracking, and how schools control students' 'opportunities to learn' through it.[152] The traditional characterization of curricular organization as consisting of a small number of well-defined programs, or tracks, for students of different abilities and interests, however, does not adequately capture the processes at work in today's high schools. The enormous expansion of high school curriculum over the last two decades means that the typical student now confronts extensive curricular options. These options have, in turn, produced great diversity in students' programs of study even in the same high school.[153] As a result, empirical research has begun to focus on actual course enrollments rather than nominal track designations. While the latter represents an important clarification for research purposes, we summarize together the results of research on tracking and coursetaking since both investigate the same basic concern — the differential exposure to academic subject matter and the consequences which derive from this exposure.

Regardless of these conceptual issues, one finding clearly emerges from the recent spate of *HS&B* analyses. Student course-taking and tracking are the most powerful predictors of academic achievement, far outdistancing the effects of personal background and a wide range of student attitudes and behaviors.[154] The strength of this finding is especially remarkable, in that the measure of course-taking typically employed is based on student self-reports, and no account is taken of the differential content and instructional quality that may occur in courses with similar titles. The policy implications flowing from this research seem quite clear — any effort that seeks to affect academic achievement must target the policies and practices which determine students' exposure to subject matter.[155]

In this regard, recent research has focused particularly on the differential learning opportunities provided to students within schools and on the role that these opportunities play in structuring the social distribution of achievement. As noted in the introduction, this research builds on an important distinction between the school as a context for learning and the instructional processes of schooling through which learning actually occurs. From this theoretical perspective, the explicit function of a school organization is to create differential learning opportunities. This is the 'student side' of the arguments on specialization of labor in teaching discussed above.

Several recent studies are particularly relevant in this regard. Lee and Bryk (1988) presented an interrelated set of analyses examining differences in the academic experiences of students in public and Catholic high schools. After adjusting for social background and academic achievement at sophomore year, they found that in the Catholic sector a much larger proportion of students was in an academic track, and that students' background was less strongly related to track placement. In terms of academic course enrollments, they reported that the largest public-Catholic differences were in the non-academic tracks. In general, they found less internal differentiation in course-taking and track placements in Catholic schools. While a portion of this difference is related to variations in the types of students enrolled in public and Catholic schools, the assembled evidence strongly indicates independent effects of school organization.

In the same issue of the *Sociology of Education*, Garet and Delaney (1988) reported on a detailed investigation of mathematics and science course-taking using transcript data from an entire cohort of students from four high schools. After controlling for student background characteristics, they found substantial school-by-school differences in the probability of taking advanced courses. While the latter can be partially explained as a function of student compositional differences among the schools, differences in curricular organization among the four schools also played an important role. Garet and Delaney concluded that stratification in students' opportunities to learn resulted, at least partially, from school decisions about course and section offerings.

Closely related is research on the role of guidance counseling in channeling high school students into tracks and courses. Although it has been advocated that guidance counselors should take a more proactive stance in being 'attentive to the process by which students make educational choices [about courses] to eliminate the impact of sex, race, and class socialization on such choices',[156] the reverse appears to operate. Lee and Ekstrom (1987), in a study examining social differences in access to counseling about curricular programs and courses, found that social class, ethnicity, and educational aspirations were all associated with such access. The students most likely to need counseling because they were least likely to have access to good advice at home (i.e., low-SES, minority, and students with lower aspirations) were least likely actually to see counselors. These empirical findings are consistent with field accounts that describe a process in which students are allowed extensive choice over their programs of study, with the social consequences of such choice not deemed a school matter.[157]

Lee and Bryk (1989) provide the most direct empirical investigation of the role of curricular organization in affecting the social distribution of academic achievement. They found that the 'common school' effect, originally reported by Coleman *et al.* (1982), can be explained largely as a result of differences in curricular organization between Catholic and public schools.[158] The constrained academic structure in Catholic schools acts to minimize the normal differentiation effects that accompany wide latitude in course choices. Further, the smaller school size in the Catholic sector acts as an organizational 'accomplice'. Quite simply, it is easier to create a more internally differentiated academic structure in a larger school.

In principle, initial differences among students can be either amplified or constrained as a result of subsequent school experiences. While the amplification effect is more common in the public sector, Lee and Bryk's analyses suggest that the same mechanism is at work in both contexts.[159] That is, there is no indication that the governance properties of schools (i.e., public versus private) have an independent effect on social distribution of academic achievement, once differences in academic organization are taken into account.

Lee and Bryk (1989) also provide some evidence that normative elements influence academic outcomes. Staff problems, as indicated by principal reports about teacher absenteeism and lack of commitment, were related to the social distribution of achievement. Achievement, particularly for minorities, was higher in schools with orderly, safe environments (i.e., even after adjusting for student background and academic organization). Students' perceptions that adults handled disciplinary problems fairly and effectively were also linked to less differentiated student outcomes.

It is important to note that this recent research has significant methodological implications. Increasingly, attention is focusing on the processes through which aspects of school governance, external environments, and school-based policies effect differential opportunities to learn within schools. From a statistical modeling point of view, these concerns represent hypotheses about the effects of school and context variables on within-school structural relationships or regression slopes. Simply adding school variables to a student or school-level linear model implies that the school variables influence mean differences across schools, rather than differentiating effects within them. Such analyses inherently assume that school variables affect all students within the school equally. In short, the assumptions embedded in the statistical models routinely employed in research on school effects conflict in fundamental ways with the basic phenomena under study. Such research requires a multilevel formulation for proper estimation and inference.[160]

The Structure of Social Relations

Recent accounts of the influence of normative aspects of school life connect with observations offered by Waller (1932) that the school is not only a formal organization, but also a small society where the contour of social relations significantly influences the overall operations of the 'society'. Waller particularly focused on fundamental conflicts embedded in teachers' roles. To engage students and to motivate them to learn requires affective bonds between teachers and students. Developing such bonds, however, clashes with basic bureaucratic notions about professional behavior, such as an emphasis on standard procedures administered in an affectively neutral fashion.[161]

Waller's observations echo a strong theme in the writings of John Dewey, who saw education as a social process and the school as a form of communal life deliberately designed to promote it:

> . . . the school must itself be a community life in all which that implies. Social perceptions and interests can be developed only in a genuinely social medium — one where there is give and take in the building up of common experience. (Dewey, 1966, p.358)

And elsewhere:

> Much of present education fails because it neglects this fundamental principle of the school as a form of community life. It conceives of the school as a place where certain infomation is to be given, where certain lessons are to be learned, and where certain habits are to be formed. (Dewey, 1966, p.238)[162]

Thus, the 'modern dilemma of school organization' — where the intensely personal nature of education co-exists with expectations that it be conducted within formal structures that sharply constrain such action — actually has a significant history. The current predicament can be viewed as a logical, albeit extreme, manifestation of this tension.[163]

As Bidwell (1965) noted, the small society of the school involves two distinct social groupings — collegial ties among staff and peer relations among students — and a set of human connections across these groupings. These human connections can have important consequences for the engagement of students and teachers in school life, and may either support or inhibit the academic efforts of the school. The research on this topic consists primarily of theoretical arguments and field accounts, with few relevant quantitative studies.

Faculty colleagueship

Collegial relations among faculty is a major theme in both the effective schools literature[164] and the literature on innovations and school change.[165] From a bureaucratic perspective, collegiality is a vehicle for promoting horizontal communication within an organization, where the aim of such communication is to focus the collective technical expertise of a faculty on specific school problems.[166] This view directs attention towards formal strategies that promote professional relationships within a school in order to enhance directly the academic work of the school. From this perspective, effective schools are described as having a cooperative work ethic, and engaging in collaborative organizational processes.[167]

But collegiality also has an informal social component. Teachers who spend time with colleagues in academic and non-academic activities are more likely to perceive the school as having a friendly atmsophere and to derive satisfaction from working there. In fact, academic and social purposes are routinely intertwined. Even when formal control structures and hierarchies are present in effective schools, these coexist with more informal social networks that provide both professional assistance and personal support. Such personal connections can reduce teachers' sense of isolation and vulnerability and provide encouragement.[168]

In short, the research on collegiality documents its centrality to an effective school operation. Cooperative relations among faculty are seen as critical to accomplishing the academic work of the school. But, faculty relations also have an important personal dimension. The sense of isolation and vulnerability built into the basic structure of teaching can be ameliorated through genuine face-to-face relationships with colleagues. This suggests that schools must also attend to the personal relations which affectively tie individuals to one another. Further, the salience of these personal connections may be greater now than ever for two reasons. First, the demise in teachers' social status as afforded by the larger public has undermined the moral authority necessary for teaching.[169] As a result, social support by colleagues becomes even more critical in the context of an unfriendly external world. Second, such needs are further amplified by general features of modern life where the influences of traditional sources of personal support — community, church, and extended family — have been weakened, and individuals look toward work-based relations to fill the void.

Peer influences[170]

The research on peer influences suggests important effects on a range of educational outcomes. The direction of such effect is not necessarily uniform, however. Coleman (1961) argued that peer interactions within and outside the school create a student culture that is non-academic or even anti-academic in character. More recently, negative consequences of peer interactions on student achievement have also been reported in research by Csikszentmihalyi and Larson (1984), who found that the amount of time spent with peers had negative consequences on academic achievement.

Increasingly, research is focusing on how compositional and contextual features of peer groups influence academic and social outcomes. Epstein (1983) found that students who had low-achieving friends had significantly lower achievement scores one year later than students who had high achieving friends, regardless of students' own ability. This finding suggests that peer influence on academic outcomes is mitigated by the types of peer groups involved (high- or low-achieving). Similarly, results from studies involving peer influence on misconduct suggest that, while perceived pressures toward misconduct tend to increase with age, the degree of pressure varies by type of group examined ('toughs', jocks', 'populars').[171]

In general, it appears that peers may operate either to promote or to inhibit positive educational outcomes, depending on the student's position in the peer group, whether the group approves or disapproves of academic effort, and the amount of time devoted to activities which might detract from academic outcomes.[172] In addition, the social structure of student interaction may operate either in synchronization with or in opposition to the orientation of the school, based on features within the school such as curriculum organization, general cultural environment, and the types of interactions students have with teachers.[173]

Common activities which promote adult-student relations

Occasions for shared activity can play an important role in sustaining positive social relations. Through school rituals, for example, students and teachers are initiated into the organization and are bound symbolically to it. In this way, rituals contribute to the overall coherence of organizational life. When such activities are vital, they manifest the shared values of the school, bring members of the school together, and are logically connected to expressed institutional norms. These rituals may center on athletic, religious, or other communal activities, and may also involve the school's academic programs.

The symbolic value of common activity has been underscored by many social theorists including Durkheim (1956, 1961). More recently, Meyer and Rowan (1983) have remarked about the 'ritualistic significance' of activities and how this 'maintains appearance and validates an organization'. They note that, no matter how symbolic the events, such occasions can have powerful effects encouraging participants to make their best efforts in situations where reasons for such commitments might be doubtful.

Rituals that unite students and teachers can take many forms. School athletics can be a major unifying force (see, for example, Coleman, 1961). Wilkinson's (1964) work on British public schools documents the unifying function of chapel ceremonies in these institutions. Weinberg (1967) also notes that these ceremonies communicate a school's message to student and faculty alike.

While some shared activities physically assemble participants in a single place at a given time, a round of activities in which all students participate at some time can also exercise a unifying effect. Take, for example, the experience shared by different cohorts of students who attend the classes of a particularly memorable teacher. In some cases, the personality of the individual teacher may take on mythic proportions, and participation in special classroom activities organized by such individuals can become a major event in students' academic lives.[174]

In a school where students have little choice in their educational program and electives are consequently restricted, the academic life of the institution can become a special kind of ritual. One individual's course of study does not differ substantially from the 'average' academic experience. And if this curriculum remains essentially unchanged from year to year, students share the bulk of their academic experiences with students from previous years. Such a curriculum not only provides opportunities for students to get to know one another, but also has symbolic value, in that it links each student to a school's tradition.

While the actual research on the role and function of rituals in school life is unfortunately sparse, the theoretical and ethnographic accounts summarized above are, nonetheless, quite compelling. Certainly, there is much in this literature which is likely to align with personal reflections about education, and with basic notions about the small society of the school. At the very least, this suggests that a closer scrutiny of such matters is warranted in future studies.

Alienation and disengagement: The consequences of overly-bureaucratic social relations

Attention to the social relations within schools has come to the fore particularly in the context of current problems in urban education. Poor attendance, high dropout rates, and student-teacher conflicts indicate high levels of student alienation from schooling.[175] Complaints about teacher absenteeism, lack of commitment, and problems of 'burnout' also abound.[176] In a recent multi-site case study, Firestone and Rosenblum (1988) argued that these diverse problems are indicative of a more general issue — the alienating quality of contemporary school life which fails to promote an affective attachment of both students and teachers to school work.

Building on basic ideas about the small society of the school, Firestone and Rosenblum noted that teachers and students form two distinct social groups that are mutually dependent. Teachers' expectations, for example, can influence student academic achievement,[177] and an absence of teacher caring is a routine report from high school dropouts.[178] Conversely, teachers derive few rewards from teaching apathetic students, and student academic ability is a powerful predictor of teachers' sense of efficacy.[179] Problems with student misconduct are also influential in this regard. Further, in some urban schools, these inter-relations form a vicious cycle, whereby teacher alienation contributes to student alienation and vice versa. Firestone and Rosenblum suggest that several factors can break this cycle, including: students' perceptions of the relevance of what they are learning; students' and teachers' sense that they are respected by each other and by school administration; high expectations for student achievement; and faculty influence over school decision-making which affects their lives.

Surprisingly, there is little empirical research linking the specific school features considered by Firestone and Rosenblum to students' experiences. For example, the studies on dropping out have only recently considered the possible effects of schools on students' subjective experiences within these contexts and the decisions which may flow from these.[180] Similarly, the inter-relationships between teacher and student commitment and the factors which might jointly affect the engagement of both teachers and students have been little investigated.[181] One exception is the study by Bryk and Driscoll (1988), discussed earlier, which found strong effects of communal school organization on a range of teacher outcomes (including satisfaction, staff morale, and absenteeism) and student misbehavior (including class cutting, absenteeism, and dropping out).

In concluding this section we note that the bureaucratic and communitarian perspective reflects two different orientations toward the structure of social relations within schools. The bureaucratic focus is instrumental. Social relations should be efficiently organized in order to attain formally stated, primarily, academic ends. The social interactions involved in schooling are simply another organizational feature to be managed. In contrast, the communitarian perspective reflects an ongoing concern for the quality of human relationships as a central feature of education, no matter what procedures might exist to manage other aspects of schooling.

Interpretive Summary and Conclusions

We have attempted to locate the voluminous literature on school organization and its effects within two broad perspectives on schools — as formal organizations and as small societies. As a shorthand, we have termed these views as bureaucratic and communitarian respectively. As we noted in the introduction, the bureaucratic perspective has dominated research and policy efforts for several decades. As perceptions have spread, however, that 'there is something fundamentally wrong with our schools', a renewed interest has emerged in the communitarian alternative. We conclude our review with a few synthetic remarks about these two perspectives and offer an assessment of their implications for current efforts at school reform.

Consequences of the Bureaucratization of Schooling

Many of the current difficulties in school organization may be traced to ideas espoused by Conant (1959) in his influential book, *The American High School Today*. Concerned about enhancing the academic offerings of secondary schools, Conant advocated school consolidation. While his arguments about the efficiency necessary to achieve universal secondary schooling have a long history, they achieved new vitality in the 1960s, as part of a larger societal embrace of the modern public bureaucracy. Rapid gains in education were predicted through increased technological and human resources coupled with modern management techniques. It was also thought that a modern school bureaucracy could assure equal educational opportunities to the poor, minorities, and other disadvantaged groups. Through specialization of teachers' work and a broadening of curricular offerings, the high school would become a universal institution.

These aims, however, have not been achieved. The incidence of dropping out actually increased through the 1970s and remains depressingly high, with rates in excess of fifty per cent not uncommon in urban schools.[182] There is no indication of broad improvements in academic achievement, although some relative gains for minorities may have been registered.[183] Further, as summarized in the section on 'Formal organization of work', the high school has become a highly differentiated intellectual environment, with educational opportunities and academic outcomes stratified along race and class lines. Recent field accounts of high schools tell us that, whatever its intended aims, the expansion of school bureaucracy over the last two decades has instead contributed to student passivity and teacher alienation, both of which are now pervasive.[184] A system of mass education relying on processes of specialization and centralization has promoted a breakdown in human commitment. These organizational mechanisms have contributed to the creation of transient relationships, a disintegration of common bonds, and a retreat from shared responsibility. The work ethic of the modern school has become 'that's not my job!'

Increased school size, greater curriculum complexity and a dense external policy network with conflicting accountability demands have resulted in organizational environments marked by distrust, social conflict and a lack of personal regard for the individuals who staff the institutions. These forces appear especially disruptive in large urban districts, where everything tends to be more extreme: more programs, larger school size, greater density of conflicting political demands, and more severe resource constraints.

The Communitarian Critique

For some at least, the current situation is not a surprise. In a 1967 essay on 'Education and community', Newmann and Oliver noted that even during the initial hopefulness of the 'Great Society', large numbers of individuals were feeling a sense of loss. Missing were life experiences where people know and are concerned about each other, depend on one another, and share responsibility for problem solving.[185]

Today, Newmann and Oliver's comments seem prescient. In an ironic turn of events, the cornerstones of the modern public bureaucracy (and the 'Great Society') — rationality, technology, and legalism — are now seemingly major problems. As we redefine basic notions about 'good' institutions, places 'with a sense of community' are now seen as lighthouses for the future.

In the current search for 'nonbureaucratic' possibilities,[186] elements of community — such as cooperative work, effective communication, and shared goals — have been identified as key to successful organizations of all types, not only schools. Yet, there is something a bit troublesome about this too. As Newmann and Oliver pointed out, the social elements of community are not instruments but rather ends in themselves. We are social beings whose life meaning is defined through the interactions which occur in the communities of which we are a part.[187] From this point of view, enlisting features of community as instruments for social control has an Orwellian feel. It adds a need for social connectedness to individual avarice and a desire to avoid pain as basic incentives available to the modern manager. It fails, however, to recognize that human meaning is not intrinsic in social behavior. Rather, meaning is an interpretive phenomenon arising out of participation in affairs of perceived value. Thus, we remain skeptical about attempts to extract the social elements which naturally give rise to human meaning in some contexts, and then use these as means of control in other contexts which routinely strip social interaction of any meaning.

This perspective resonates strongly with the comments from John Dewey quoted earlier in the chapter. The social interactions of schooling are not simply a mechanism for accomplishing some other aim, but rather are education itself.[188] The school is a distinctive workplace where the social relations among adults and students are not just another factor to be manipulated in facilitating academic production.

This point is recognized in the idea of a communal school which emphasizes the engagement of adults and students in a coherent school life. Membership within the organization literally 'makes sense to its members'. School activities provide ample opportunities for informal, sincere face-to-face interactions among adults and students. The social bonding among these individuals is nurtured when an ethic of caring is conveyed through such interactions. School symbols and active rituals, in turn, locate the current social group within a larger heritage which can be an important source of human meaning. Lastly, the underlying values of the institution, shared by its members, provide the animating force for the entire enterprise.[189]

Academic Organization and the Technical Core of Instruction

While much in this review reinforces this communitarian perspective, it is also clear that such views must be coupled with an appreciation for the structural and functional aspects of schools that instrumentally affect instruction and academic learning. The research on tracking and academic course-taking is especially relevant in this regard. Both field studies and quantitative investigations provide solid empirical verification that key components of curricular organization have powerful effects on student achievement. For example, after controlling for the types of students enrolled, most of the differences in achievement between public and private schools can be explained through the different academic opportunities afforded by schools in the two sectors.

The extant research strongly supports the conclusion that the curricular organization of high schools (including course-taking requirements, guidance functions, and policies affecting the assignment of students and teachers to schools and classes within schools) is the primary mechanism influencing both the average level of student achievement and how that achievement is distributed with regard to background characteristics such as race and class. The statistical relations here are by far the strongest links between any aspect of school organization, either internal or external, and student achievement. Quite simply, the principal determinant of academic achievement is course-taking. The structural effects of schools on students' academic outcomes accrue through the influence of curricular organization on these critical schooling behaviors.

Likewise, although the literature on classroom instructional practices at the secondary level is spare, it would be a mistake to assume that such features are not central to academic achievement. Available survey data such as *High School and Beyond* were not designed to assess classroom effects, and the basic methodology of effective schools research is similarly flawed. Where carefully designed studies of classroom practice have occurred, however, powerful statistical relations have also been detected.[190]

In this regard, it is important to point out that many current school reform efforts do not take curricular organization as their principal focus. To be sure, the emphasis in these reforms on the nature of social relations within the school and how these are influenced by externalities is justified in terms of the consequences on student engagement and teacher commitment, as discussed above. However, improvements in academic achievement are unlikely to occur if reform of the technical core of instruction is not also directly addressed.

More generally, any embrace of the vision of a school as a community must be integrated with a view of the school as a formal organization that seeks to rationally, effectively and efficiently promote student learning. Although each perspective illuminates distinctive features of good schools and would lead us toward different reform emphases, neither alone is sufficient. Rather, it is only by giving serious attention to both perspectives that the true depth of good schooling can be discerned.

Implications for Reform Efforts Based on Parental Choice

Much of the impetus for increased parental choice draws at least implicitly on claims about the superiority of private schools and the distinctive organizational features of these schools which contribute to their effectiveness. It is important to keep in mind what has actually been demonstrated in the research comparing public and private schooling. First, there is considerable statistical evidence documenting internal organizational differences between public and private schools. Second, one can logically link the greater prevalence of 'effective organizational practices' in the private sector to the individual autonomy of these schools, although the empirical evidence supporting this proposition is not definitive. Third, but most important, there is virtually no evidence that directly links the 'effective organizational practices' thought to accrue through greater school autonomy to key outcomes such as students' academic learning. While this does not necessarily imply that efforts to improve schooling through greater parental choice are conceptually flawed, it does suggest that we take a closer look at their underlying logic.

The simplest argument is based on the premise that a market system of control will promote greater responsiveness on the part of school staff to client needs. At close scrutiny, however, this micro-economic argument bears little relation to ideas about schools as communities discussed above. The 'market' view of schools as efficient service providers to individual clients, where teachers respond out of entrepreneurial motives, employs a language and basic conceptualization quite antithetical to the social foundations of schooling. Although individual entrepreneurship may fuel economic development, it rings less true as a basic motivation for processes of human betterment. There is no evidence that such motives currently play much of a role for teachers in either public or private schools. Further, should such a system of schooling eventually emerge, there is little reason to assume that it would produce anything like the positive consequences typically associated with private schools.

As we have noted at several junctures, there are longstanding arguments — from Aristotle to Dewey to contemporarists such as Philip Jackson and Nel Noddings — that caring and individual commitment are the basic ground of the teaching act.[191] In our view, market incentives, much like externally imposed policy sanctions, are not likely to be a compelling force toward caring. A better justification seems needed.

A more promising argument focuses on how the selection of a school by both parents and staff can fundamentally alter the human dynamics within schools, create a social base of adult authority, and locate parent-teacher relations on a foundaton of trust. This perspective is based on the observation that much of what happens in schools involves discretionary human action. Within the current bureaucratic structure of schooling, great effort may be required to secure basic agreement on issues which are intrinsically judgmental.[192] It is argued that, under a choice system, the social capital expended on fostering such agreements can be redirected toward the actual work of schooling.

Much in this review supports this argument. It is certainly consistent with critiques of the hyper-bureaucratization of schooling and communitarian arguments about the intrinsic social features of teaching and learning. Nonetheless, we remain troubled about parental choice as a panacea for public schooling. Specifically, it remains unclear how the social equity issues surrounding schools, which have played such a large role in creating the complex state of current affairs, will suddenly become 'non-problems'.[193] In fact, the experiences with curriculum reform during the 1970s provides reason to raise such concerns.

It was argued, beginning in the late 1960s, that high schools were deadening institutions and that more relevant curricula, responsive to individual students' interests and abilities, were needed. Coincident with a rapid expansion of course options within high schools, students were afforded much greater choice to construct their own programs of study. This too was seen as promoting students' interest in learning. While high schools developed some new programs that were apparently quite good, the overall consequences for students have not been uniformly positive. On average, there is little evidence that the system got better. In fact, many critics believe it got worse. Most important, the field accounts and quantitative studies reviewed above strongly suggest that curriculum reform actually promoted greater social inequities, both in access to quality academic instruction and in actual academic achievement.

Whether efforts to introduce more choice among schools would produce similar inequities is unclear, but the experience with increased curricular choice within schools certainly counsels caution. Greater autonomy may produce some very good schools, but such developments may demand a price of increased variation in outcomes among schools, with these consequences inequitably distributed along ethnic and racial lines.

Clearly, the actual consequences of any school choice plan will depend on the specific conditions and rules imposed in implementing the plan. In principle, we can envision a regulated choice system which assures that disadvantaged children can attend good schools and that disadvantaged communities can have strong neighborhood institutions. Whether the public will and resources necessary for such developments can be assembled, however, is far less obvious.

The Significance of Educational Values and Normative Understandings

We close with a final observation about the autonomous character of good schools. Many of the descriptors of effective schools as places where faculty have a 'sense of ownership' and adults and students share an 'organizational saga' have a strong particularist bent to them. That is, the conditions which are now described as breeding organizational excellence in an earlier time were seen as promoting intolerance and exclusivity. In our view, much more attention is required to the actual content of the shared values that are operative in effective schools and the consequences which derive from them.

Here again a brief consideration of the research on private schools is instructive. Many of the positive effects associated with Catholic schools are not characteristics of non-Catholic private schools. For example, the more equitable social distribution of achievement, the so called 'common school' effect, is unique to Catholic schools and not found in other private schools. Similarly, the reduced dropout rates and unusual effectiveness of Catholic high schools for at-risk youth is not characteristic of private schools in general.[194] Emerging evidence also suggests that the special effectiveness of Catholic girls' schools may not generalize across the private sector as a whole.[195]

This pattern of differential outcomes among private schools is significant because many 'effective organizational practices' linked to school autonomy are actually more prevalent among non-Catholic private schools, yet the positive student outcomes described above do not occur there. These results challenge notions that a move toward greater privatization of schooling will assure a better aggregate set of student outcomes. In our view, it is not simply a matter of private versus public, political-bureaucratic versus market mechanisms, or school-based accountability versus centralized control. Rather, we must also consider the actual values operative in each school context, how these are manifest in organizational structure and function, and the consequences that emerge as a result.

In the case of Catholic schools, field research describes strong institutional norms directly linked to basic religious beliefs about the dignity of each person and a shared responsibility for advancing a just, caring society.[196] Not surprisingly, the educational philosophy that derives from these ideals is well aligned with social equity aims. When such understandings meld to a coherent organizational structure, desirable academic and social consequences appear to result.

In a real sense, the most significant feature in the communitarian critique of contemporary schooling is that it draws our attention to the importance of individual commitment and how specific beliefs, values and normative understandings ground such commitments. Educational reform efforts — whether 'community control', 'school choice', 'school site autonomy' or any other such proposals which might emerge in the future — will continue to disappoint us until we seriously engage these concerns.

Notes

1 Dreeben (1988) provides an excellent historical account of American efforts in sociology of education in this century. We are indebted to him for the arguments presented in this section. Related material can also be found in Bidwell and Friedkin (1988).

2 The concept of a 'social distribution in achievement' is discussed in Lee and Bryk (1988; 1989). It refers to how students' social background (for example, social class, race/ethnicity) is related to individual achievement.

3 See for example Rutter *et al.* (1979); Brookover *et al.* (1979); and Edmonds (1979). This was followed by a descriptive case study literature on the internal workings of good (Lightfoot, 1983) and not-so-good schools (see, for example, Cusick, 1983; Grant, 1988; Powell *et al.*, 1985).

4 Major contributions here include Bidwell and Dasarda (1980), Brown and Saks (1975; 1981), and Barr and Dreeben (1983). Sorenson and Hallinan (1977) is also relevant.

5 Useful references here include Ravitch (1983), Hampel (1986), and the 'Origins' chapter in Powell *et al.*, (1985). For an historical account of the changing character of an individual high school from 1953 to present see Grant (1988). For a more general treatment of the intellectual and social

forces that have shaped American schools in this century see Cremin (1988).

6 By this we refer to the fact that enormous amounts of textual information are gathered in such studies. The choice of what will be considered as evidence in the data collection process, and the subset of which will be presented to the reader is exclusively determined by the individual researcher and it not open to public scrutiny to the same degree as in quantitative research. Similarly, to the extent that the author suggests conclusions/implications, proper methods for validity assessment are usually unspecified.

7 See Cronbach (1976, p. 1). Rousseau (1985) offers a similar pessimistic assessment in a more recent review of organizational research.

8 Burstein (1980) provides both a good review of the methodological issues raised in research on school effects, and a full discussion of the relevance of 'slopes-as-outcomes' to school effects research.

9 In the context of classroom research, the work by Barr and Dreeben (1983) on the effects of ability grouping stands out as exemplary. In research on the effects of high school curriculum, see Garet and Delaney (1988) and Lee and Bryk (1989).

10 For a further discussion of the methodological issues raised here and why the new developments in hierarchical linear models provide a promising response see Raudenbush and Bryk (1986) and Bryk and Raudenbush (1988). For a detailed statistical treatment see Raudenbush (1988). The recently edited text by Bock (1989) is also a useful reference.

11 Strictly speaking, size is a structural feature of a school and not a true externality. We have included it in this section of our review, however, because the effects of size on teacher and student outcomes are indirect. Size both facilitates and constrains the internal operations of schools in ways that have important impacts on teachers and students. In this sense, it shares a common feature with the other topics considered in this section — their effects occur through influencing the internal structure and functioning of the school.

12 Guthrie (1979) reviews the efficiency arguments which have been used to justify efforts at school consolidation since the end of World War II. These developments are detailed in Callahan (1962) and Tyack (1974). Guthrie also discusses current movements towards consolidation to increase the volume of school 'production' in the face of decreasing or stable enrollments.

13 Guthrie's (1979) distinction between the roles played by district, schooi, and class size becomes important in this regard. The size of a school district, which functions primarily as a financial and political unit, is not likely to influence instructional outcomes within specific schools. School size can influence instruction, but as Guthrie notes, this variable is less associated with either financial or political conditions. Finally, class size would presumably have the strongest influence on instruction, but is only distantly related to the district-level finance and politics at issue.

14 Bidwell and Kasarda (1975), for example, observed this result as an indirect effect of structural characteristics of a school on student outcomes. Chambers (1981), suggests that by increasing the size of a school, one gains quality

in terms of 'specialization of personnel and more effective use of particular kinds of capital equipment (not only school buildings but also audiovisual equipment, tape recorders, and other such instructional equipment) (p 31)'. For similar discussion, see also Daft and Becker (1980) and Fox (1981).

15 This perspective was reflected in an historical movement away from small schools which took place in the mid-twentieth century. For reviews see Tyack (1974) and Cremin (1988). The argument for consolidation as it specifically relates to high schools, however, was probably best articulated by Conant (1959).

16 See Michelson (1972) for a further discussion of the sources of school resources, as well as their distribution within and across districts.

17 Coleman *et al.* (1966) originally looked for strong effects of resource availability, as measured by items such as the number of books in the library, on student outcomes as part of the tide of concern over segregation of public schools. That they did not find these effects generated a flood of research examining the effects of schools on student outcomes. The same argument was articulated by Jencks *et al.* (1972) and in the reanalyses of the data used by Coleman *et al.* (1966) which appeared in Mosteller and Moynihan (1972).

18 This result is suggested in the work of Friedkin and Necochea (1988) on the size and socio-economic level of school districts. To our knowledge, the relationship between community SES and actual school size has not been rigorously and empirically examined. Such an examination may prove problematic, as it becomes necessary to examine and compare both funding structures of districts and allocation procedures within districts across communities.

19 Jencks *et al.* (1972) allude to this problem in their discussion of inequality. In claiming that the effects of 'schooling' may not be the same for all students, Bidwell and Kasarda (1980) offer a theoretical position on this question. However, empirical examinations have been weak because of data limitations and other methodological reasons suggested by Bidwell and Kasarda (1980).

29 Both Oakes (1985) and Powell *et al.* (1985) describe the response of schools, in perceiving diverse student needs, towards greater specialization and diversification of course offerings. Both offer historical overviews of this development.

21 This was the argument employed by Conant (1959) advocating school consolidation. His arguments, as well as others, in favor of school consolidation, are reviewed by Tyack (1974).

22 Along a related line, research on special education suggests that mentally impaired as well as physically impaired students are served better in 'mainstream' general academic programs, rather than through placements in specialized programs (see, for example, Hart, 1981). For a further elaboration of this argument for the general student population, see subsequent section on 'Formal organization of work'.

23 This is the general conclusion of recent research on tracking (c.f. Alexander, Cook and McDill, 1978; Garet and Delaney, 1988; Heyns, 1974; Lee and

Bryk, 1988), as well as more general treatments of course-taking and social stratification of learning opportunities. Sorenson (1987) supplies a useful theoretical argument. Empirical validation of these ideas can be found in the case study work by Powell *et al*. (1985) as well as more quantitative investigations such as that by Lee and Bryk (1989).

24 For a further theoretical elaboration of this argument see Driscoll (1989).

25 Bidwell (1965) suggests the need for a 'small society' character in the human interactions between teachers and students to support the academic endeavors of teaching. More recently, examinations of teachers' satisfaction and efficacy in teaching (Ashton and Webb, 1986; Lee, Dedrick and Smith, in press; Lortie, 1975; Newmann, Rutter and Smith, 1989) suggest that frequent informal social interaction with students is related to teachers' feeling of success in their teaching.

26 Bryk and Driscoll (1988) found that school size had a strong negative effect on social attitudes and behavior of both teachers and students.

27 The role of social systems in the organization of work within a school are reviewed in Anderson (1982) as part of studies on 'school climate'. Other research related to these results can be found in Bryk and Driscoll (1988) and in Newmann (1981).

28 The research done by Bridges and Hallinan (1978) points specifically to a central role played by the communication of information in the formalization of social organization in schools. Related research is reviewed by Anderson (1982).

29 Much research suggests that group size acts as a significant constraint on achieving goal consensus within the organization. See for example, Fuller, Wood, Rapoport and Dornbusch, (1982); Forsyth and Hoy, (1978); March and Olsen, (1976); Rutter *et al*. (1979).

30 Newmann (1981) discusses the social consequence for students of teachers' role specialization. Barker and Gump (1964) describe the relatively static number of roles available for student and teacher participation, which suggests that as enrollment size increases, the relative representation of students or teachers in those roles diminishes. Additional research concerning the operation of specialization in school social organization can be found in research by Gottfredson and Daiger (1979); and Neufeld (1984).

31 Chambers (1981) reviews the evidence that suggests that larger size may be associated with a decrease in affective and behavioral outcomes. Most of this evidence echoes Newmann's (1981) description of lowered frequency of interaction, more bureaucracy, and consequent alienation in larger, more bureaucratic schools. Chambers supports the relationship posed by Barker and Gump (1964), arguing that the increase in diversity in educational offerings tends to be offset by a decrease in student engagement and involvement.

32 This evidence is reviewed by Goodlad (1984) and by Newmann (1981). Both suggest that the bureaucratic processes introduced by large schools to counteract the problems encountered therein do not address the central problems involved in loss of community within the school.

33 See, for example, Bidwell (1972); Haller and Woelfel (1972); Bidwell and Kasarda (1980).
34 Slavin (1983) provides a good example of this line of work.
35 See, for example, the subsequent discussion on vacancy theory (Sorenson, 1987).
36 There is a long history of research and scholarship on this topic beginning with Waller (1932) and revived in Gordon (1957) and Coleman (1961).
37 We know, for example, that minority students are more likely to be found in low-ability groups and non-academic tracks. See, for example, Barr and Dreeben (1983); Coleman, Hoffer and Kilgore (1982); Heyns (1974); Lee and Bryk (1988); Oakes (1985); Rock, Ekstrom, Goertz, Hilton and Pollack (1985).
38 See Buell and Brisbin (1982); Cusick (1983); and Metz (1978).
39 Rutter *et al.*, 1979, p. 178.
40 This perspective is nicely described by Oakes (1985) in summarizing the basic argument from G. Stanley Hall (1905).
41 The most recent of these efforts is the newly enacted school reform legislation for the city of Chicago, SB 1840, The Urban Education Reform Act of 1988. This act creates a local council at each school site composed of a parent majority. They have a range of powers, including principal selection, evaluation, determination of contract renewal/termination, and approval authority over both the school budget and an annual school improvement plan.
42 The introduction to Malen and Ogawa (1988) provides a succinct discussion of such plans and an extensive set of references on this topic. See also Williams (1989).
43 Such descriptions can be found, for example, in Rogers' (1968) discussion of the situation in New York City, in Weinberg's (1983) description of the problems in Crystal City, Texas, and in Malen and Ogawa's (1988) description of the issues in Salt Lake City.
44 An historical model for community control of public schools is found in what Michael Katz (1987) calls 'democratic localism'. This movement, quite popular in New York City and Massachusetts in the 1830s and 1840s, was developed in opposition to paternalistic voluntarism on the one hand, and bureaucracy or centralization on the other. Advocates of democratic localism encouraged control of schools by 'families interested in it', and stressed responsiveness, close public control, and local involvement. See Katz (p. 32) for an exposition of this educational model.
45 These issues, of course, have a much longer history. The current system of centralized professional control of schools was introduced early in this century as a progressive reform of patronage-ridden local schools, which had been operating on a decentralized ward basis. For a further discussion see Cronin (1973) and Cremin (1988).
46 See Gittell *et al.*, (1972) for an evaluation of three demonstration projects in local school control which began in 1966. The politics leading up to the system decentralization in 1970 is chronicled in Rogers (1968) and evaluated

in Rogers and Chung (1983). Levin (1970) is a major reference work on the general topic of community control of schools.

47 This argument is further detailed in Fein (1970). On the development of the secular paideia and its relationship to progressivism, see Cremin (1988).

48 See Henderson (1987) for a review of these studies.

49 See, for examples, Grant and Sleeter (1988); Epstein (1985); or Keith *et al.*, (1986).

50 See Henderson (1987) or McKey *et al.* (1985).

51 Berger (1981, p. 95) suggests that parents operate in essentially six main roles with respect to their children's learning: that of spectator, teacher, 'accessory volunteer', educational volunteer, employee of the school, and policy maker. Baker and Stevenson (1986) specifically investigated parents' use of both expectations and modeling in contributing to academic achievement in their children. However, because this study was correlational, the causal directionality remains uncertain. For an ethnographic description of these relationships see Johnson and Ransom (1983).

52 See Keith *et al.*, (1986) and Grant and Sleeter (1988).

53 These outcomes include such dependent measures as achievement, educational aspirations, and participation in more challenging coursework on the part of the child. For relevant studies, see Baker and Stevenson (1986); Biddle, Bank and Marlin (1980); and Epstein (1985).

54 This relationship may not be strictly linear. There is some evidence to suggest that extremely high parental expectations may actually inhibit student performance. See, for example, Biddle, Bank and Marlin (1980); and Keith *et al.*, (1986).

55 See, for example, Biddle, Bank and Marlin (1980); Keith *et al.*, (1986) and Raywid (1985).

56 See Epstein (1985; 1987). However, Keith *et al.*, (1986) provide some evidence to suggest that continued parental participation and involvement is important for positive student outcomes through high school.

57 For reviews concerning parental involvement for elementary school students, see Epstein (1985; 1987). For specific discussion of the role of parental supervision for high school students, see studies done by Baker and Stevenson (1986); Grant and Sleeter (1988); Johnson and Ransom, (1983); Keith *et al.*, (1986); and Lee and Ekstrom (1987).

58 Epstein (1985; 1987) provides a set of analyses which explore the effects of this type of teacher encouragement on parents, and the relationships which develop between parents and teachers as such programs are implemented.

59 See, for example, Keith *et al.*, (1986); Wagenaar (1977); or Phillips, Smith and Witte (1985).

60 The argument made by Wilson, Herriot and Firestone (1988) suggests that institutional beliefs about students at the secondary level support a division of authority between parents and teachers, reinforcing a distance between these two groups.

61 For an overview of this argument see Coleman (1987; 1989). He argues that schools which operate around the shared values of both parents and a broader

community are quite effective.

62 Variants on this theme are advanced by both Coleman and Hoffer (1987); and Cohen (1988).

63 For reviews of these programs see Fisher (1984); and Hatton (1979).

64 The first of these experiments took place in Flint, Michigan, under the supervision of Frank J. Manley. Additional attempts took place in Brockton, Massachusetts, Springfield, Ohio, St. Louis, Missouri, and the Comal Independent School District in New Braunfels, Texas. For a review as well as problems encountered in these efforts, see Minzey (1981).

65 For further discussion of class issues embedded in community reform efforts, see Katz (1973); Spring (1972); and Violas (1978).

66 See, for example, Meier and Rudwick's (1973) discussion of community organization in Springfield, Ohio, which was dominated by the Klan. Williams (1989) offers an overview of this issue.

67 For a full development of these ideas see Wilson (1987).

68 See introduction to Comer (1980) for a more thorough articulation of this argument. It should be noted, however, that theorists remain divided about this conceptualization of community in urban neighborhoods. For a discussion of two conflicting views — 'community lost' and 'community saved' — see Miller (1981) and Williams (1989).

69 Newmann and Oliver (1967) describe the loss of social capital in American society as part of the rise of the industrial society and a consequence of wide-spread urbanization. Parts of this theory harken back to Durkheim's concern over social dislocation and the disruption of controls by traditional standards. This topic has received little empirical attention in educational studies.

70 These ideas were initially articulated in Ogbu (1974) and have been thoroughly developed in Ogbu (1986; 1988).

71 The problem of service coordination in urban communities has been extensively discussed. For an elaboration of these ideas in the particular context of schools see Heath and McLaughlin (1987).

72 Whole issues of journals, such as the *Harvard Educational Review* (November, 1981) and *Sociology of Education* (Spring, 1982), were dedicated to the debate. Most of the scientific arguments concerned a number of methodological limitations associated with the *High School and Beyond* (*HS&B*) data set employed by both Coleman *et al.* (1982) and in related research by Greeley (1982). In particular, the initial data from *HS&B* consisted of a single cross-section of sophomores and seniors. Without longitudinal data that tracks experiences and progress over time, it is very difficult to draw clear inferences about school effects on learning. Even in the absence of a controversial political debate over tuition tax credits (the policy issues raised by Coleman *et al.*), scientific arguments about the findings were inevitable.

After a brief hiatus, the debate resumed with the release of the first longitudinal information from *HS&B*. (See *Sociology of Education*, Spring, 1985.) While all participants agreed that this was a far better source of information for examining questions comparing Catholic and public school effects, beyond this the consensus quickly broke down. Even when the researchers agreed about the likely size of the Catholic school effects, they disagreed about their significance. In our judgment, Jencks (1985) offers the most balanced summary. The accumulated evidence indicates that the average achievement is somewhat higher in Catholic high schools than in public high schools, and suggests that Catholic high schools may be especially helpful for initially disadvantaged students.

73 See, for example, Murnane (1981); McPartland and McDill (1982); and Salgnik and Karweit (1982).

74 The composite measure assessed the degree to which a school exercises some control over its student membership. It is based on principal reports from *HS&B* about the percentage of students who apply and are admitted, whether the school has a waiting list, whether students must meet any special or academic requirements for admission, and whether any other criteria are applied for determining student admission to high school.

75 Catholic high school principals report expelling an average of less than two students per school per year (NCEA, 1984). Moreover, substantial proportions of these principals also reported admitting students who had been forced out of public schools for either disciplinary or academic reasons.

76 Additional supporting evidence on this account can be found in Driscoll (1989).

77 See Chubb and Moe (1987).

78 Talbert (1988) further details this argument. It is also extended in a related paper by Scott and Meyer in the same volume.

79 The basic argument here is laid out in Wise (1979) and further detailed in Scott and Meyer (1988).

80 See references in the two previous notes as well as Chubb and Moe (1987; 1988).

81 The basic descriptive comparison of public and private school organization can be found in Chubb and Moe (1987; 1988). Chubb (1988) presents the policy argument summarized here. The actual empirical evidence, as mentioned earlier, has yet to be published (Chubb and Moe, forthcoming).

82 Chubb (1988), p. 29.

83 Reviews of this literature include Purkey and Smith (1983); Corcoran (1985); Rosenholtz (1987); and Stevenson (1987a). We note that interpreting the evidence on effective instructional practices is particularly problematic because such practices may be quite varied within a school and even within a classroom. In this regard, the effective schools paradigm, because it takes the school as the primary unit of analysis, may be badly biased against detecting the effects of instructional practices. That is, there is a critical dysjuncture between the locus of effects (classroom) and the primary unit of research (the school). Firestone and Heriott (1982) also raise serious doubts about the relevance of much of the effective schools literature in discussions about secondary schools.

84 See Chubb and Moe (1987) and Talbert (1988).

85 The difference between the Lee *et al.*, study and the other two studies is primarily methodological. The study by Newmann *et al.*, and by Rutter

both used aggregate measures to predict individual outcomes, which can underestimate their impact. The study by Lee, Dedrick and Smith (in press) used hierarchical linear modeling which considers effects at both the teacher and school level. In general, the survey research of the topic is troubled by issues of reciprocal causation. Both the organizational properties and teacher behaviors tend to be measured through teacher perceptions and self-reports. As a result, questions arise about the validity of any structural relations estimated with such data.

86 For a further elaboration of this argument, including a rationale for connecting the social organization of schools to academic outcomes, see Bryk and Driscoll (1988). The statistical evidence assembled on the effects of a communal school organization provides strong support for the hypothesis of extensive social consequences from internal features of such organization.

87 For a comprehensive review of this research see Anderson (1982).

88 For a discussion of this research paradigm see Shulman's chapter (1986) in the *Handbook of Research on Teaching*.

89 This idea is delineated in a number of places, including Rossman *et al.*, (1988); Schein (1985); Deal and Kennedy (1982); Corbett, Dawson and Firestone (1984); Kottkamp (1984); and Sarason (1971).

90 See, for example, the discussion in Rossman *et al.*, (1988).

91 For a full discussion of norms for instruction and civility see Bird and Little (1986).

92 For a further discussion of these ideas, including supporting literature on these various points, see Bryk and Driscoll (1988) and Driscoll (1989).

93 Such results have been reported in the school effectiveness syntheisis by Murphy *et al.* (1985). See also Griffen (1985). On the value of informal teacher-student contact, see Cszikzentmihalyi and McCormick (1986). For a more general discussion of the ethic of caring and its function in contemporary schools, see Noddings (1988).

94 For studies specifically concerning effects of such norms on teachers see Devaney (1987); and McLaughlin *et al.*, (1986).

95 This discussion draws on ideas elaborated in Hoy and Ferguson (1985), who articulate a theoretical framework for organizational effectiveness of schools from a goal model perspective. Closely related ideas also appear in Herriott and Firestone (1984).

96 A review of these studies is provided by Purkey and Smith (1983), and also by Anderson (1982). In general, one aspect of an effective school which emerged from the studies such as Edmonds (1979) was a 'consensus of school purpose', and has been since measured by a non-parametric ordering coefficient called 'Kendal's Coefficient of Concordance'. While it is true that this measure has been significantly correlated with other measures of effectiveness in schools (see, for example, Herriott & Firestone, 1984), it remains unclear exactly what this measure tells us about school organizations.

97 This point is argued by Firestone and Herriott (1982). See also Herriott and Firestone (1984), and empirical evidence given by Wilson, Herriott and Firestone (1988).

98 See, for example, the research by Rutter *et al.*, (1979) and, more recently, by

Mortimore *et al.* (1988).

99 See Peshkin (1986) for further elaboration of this argument.

100 Both Ralph and Fennessey (1983) and Murphy (1988) note that a large portion of the literature on this topic consists of 'prescriptive advice'.

101 For a more complete analysis of the existing problems in this literature, see Murphy (1988).

102 Only very recently, in contrasting differences in governance structures, has administration in the private sector been considered (Chubb, 1988; Chubb and Moe, 1987). These studies focus on cross-sector comparisons rather than on a careful investigation of administration in each sector. An alternative approach to studying school administration is ethnographic in nature (Barth, 1980; McPhee, 1966; Pitner and Ogawa, 1981; Wolcott, 1973). Studies such as McPhee's portrait of Frank Boydon, the headmaster of Deerfield Academy for almost forty years, highlight the power of a charismatic personality in defining and unifying a particular school.

103 The present analysis relies primarily on material from three sources: (1) reviews of research on school administration; (2) reviews of material concerning the role of leadership in the literature on effective schools and on school improvement; and (3) selected formal quantitative and case studies which have been considered critical in these reviews. As such, it is representative, but far from exhaustive, of the material on school administration currently available.

104 For example, in a review of the correlational studies, Glasman (1984) identified two main roles a principal performs: educational and administrative. Within the educational role, activities were categorized as instructional, political, buffering, and change agent. Within the administrative role, the subcategories included institutional authority, planning and evaluation, and management. Such distinctions, however, are not uniformly held. For example, in his review of 'instructional leadership', Murphy (1988) includes articles which other reviewers characterize as management functions rather than instruction, such as the study by Bossert, Dwyer, Rowan and Lee (1982). Among other things, the focus of the research tends to influence the way researchers define administrative roles. For example, effective schools research tends to describe school administration in terms of 'instructional leadership'. (See descriptions of administration provided by Rosenholtz, 1985; and Brookover *et al.*, 1979). On the other hand, the school improvement literature tends to focus more on the role of school administration as a change agent for innovation (see descriptions of administration provided by Stallings and Mohlman, 1981 and by Pitner, 1986).

105 These three functions are consistently identified by researchers as central to the basic task of administration in schools. See, for example, Gersten, Carnine and Green (1982); Herriott and Firestone (1984); Murphy (1988); and Purkey and Smith (1983).

106 Methodological concerns must be raised, however. Such case studies tend to focus attention almost exclusively on perceived daily behaviors, ignoring more subtle aspects of these relationships. For examples of research on this area, see Hannaway (1988); Martin and Willover (1981); and Pitner and

Ogawa (1981).

107 The role of organizational context in the operation of this function is suggested by the work of Bridges and Hallinan (1978); Fuller and Izu (1986); and Godding and Wagner (1985).

108 For quantitative evidence relating the character of social relations to aspects of organizational community see Bryk and Driscoll (1988). For evidence on specific consequences for teachers see Newmann, Rutter and Smith (1989) and Lee, Dedrick and Smith (in press).

109 The case study provided by Metz (1978) is particularly compelling in this regard. See also Bossert, Dwyer, Rowan, and Lee (1982) and Edmonds (1979).

110 The study by Caldwell and Lutz (1978) makes explicit a link between rule administration and teacher morale. See also Stallings and Mohlman (1981).

111 See, for example, Coleman *et al.* (1982) and Di Prete (1981). The most extensive *HS&B* analysis and literature review can be found in Myers *et al.* (1987).

112 See Wehlage and Rutter (1986). Bryk and Thum (1989) provide some corroborating evidence in terms of effects on student absenteeism.

113 This argument is also made by Firestone and Rosenblum (1988) in their multi-site case studies on building commitment in urban high schools.

114 This is certainly antithetical to a diffuse teacher role, which is linked to student engagement (Newmann, 1981; Bryk and Driscoll, 1988; Grant, 1988; and Lightfoot, 1983). See also related agreements about classroom effects in NcNeil (1988b).

115 For a more general discussion of the operation of staff development in school improvement programs, see McLaughlin and Marsh (1978) and Miller and Wolf (1978).

116 See previous note. This issue is also discussed in Clark, Lotto and Astuto (1984).

117 This argument is supported by evidence provided by Rosenholtz (1987) and Stark and Lowther (1984).

118 See, for example, discussion in Chubb (1988); McGuire (1984); and Pitner and Ogawa (1981).

119 This argument is made by Chubb (1988) and is also found in Chubb and Moe (1987). A slightly different relationship is described by Meyer, Scott and Deal (1983), who suggest that communication may operate as part of the technical complexity of a school's links with its outside constituency. These links may be political or communal in nature.

120 As Chubb and Moe (1987) note, private school parents always have the option of removing their child from the school, should a serious disagreement arise. Such options are not as readily available in the public sector. Further, because the 'exit' option exists in private schools, it is often possible to negotiate a satisfactory resolution at the school site. In the public sector, serious disputes require political action 'downtown'.

121 This argument is the essence of the concept of 'loosely-coupled' systems (Bidwell, 1965; Weick, 1976). Little (1982b) and Rosenholtz (1985) both suggest links between this activity and effective school management.

122 See reference in note above. See also Meyer and Rowan (1978) and Gersten *et al.* (1982).
123 Martin and Willover (1981) provide case study evidence for this point.
124 Issues of leadership are especially complex in secondary schools because of the larger school size and diverse academic purposes often present in a single school. How the leadership function is actually addressed at this level has been little studied. Most of the recent research on this function has focused instructional leadership in elementary school. High schools are larger, more complex organizations, and instructional quality is more dependent on specific subject matter knowledge. Further, others such as the department head or a 'master teachers' may share this leadership function within a high school. Firestone and Herriott (1982) provide more elaborate discussion of this issue, as does the work of Murphy (1988); Purkey and Smith (1983); and Sizer (1984).
125 This argument is made by Meyer (1977), and elaborated in Meyer, Scott and Deal (1983). See also Firestone and Wilson (1985).
126 For a more elaborate discussion of school administration in a goal framework, see Brookover *et al.* (1979); Edmonds (1979); Hoy and Ferguson (1985); and Rutter *et al.* (1979).
127 See, for example, Bossert *et al.* (1982); Clark *et al.* (1984); and Hoy and Ferguson (1985).
128 See, for example, the case study on Carver High in Atlanta described by Lightfoot (1983).
129 Both Bryk and Driscoll (1988) and Newmann, Rutter and Smith (1989) address this point. See also the argument by Firestone and Rosenblum (1988).
130 This relationship between charismatic leadership and the operation of indirect management in loosely-coupled schools is suggested by Scott and Meyer (1988) and by Peterson (1989).
131 See Peterson (1989) for a review of literature relating to this argument.
132 See, for example, Barr and Dreeben (1983) and Stodolsky (1988).
133 This topic is taken up directly in the work of Neufeld (1984) and McLaughlin (in press). It is also alluded to in the case studies of Cusick (1983) and Powell *et al.*, (1985).
134 This argument is advanced in both Jackson (1968) and Lortie (1975). See also Rosenholtz (1985) and McLaughlin *et al.* (1986).
135 See Newmann, Rutter and Smith (1989) and Rutter (1987).
136 Unlike previous research which has viewed 'sense of community' as a climate characteristic, Bryk and Driscoll (1988) developed the concept of a communal school *organization*. Specifically, based on a review of research on effective schools and more general theoretical literature on the structure and function of communities, they argued that three core concepts comprise a communal school organization: (1) a system of shared values among the members of the organization, reflected primarily in beliefs and purposes of the institution, about what the students should learn, about how adults and students should behave, and about what kinds of people students are capable of becoming; (2) a common agenda of activities designed to foster meaningful

social interactions among school members and link them to the school's traditions; and (3) a distinctive pattern of social relations, embodying an ethos of caring that is visibly manifest in collegial relations among the adults of the institution and in an extended teacher role.

They created a set of twenty-three indicators of these three core concepts from *HS&B* data and combined them together into a single continuous index of communal school organization. In communally organized schools, teachers were much more likely to report satisfaction with their work, to be seen by students as enjoying their teaching, and to share a high level of staff morale. Teacher absenteeism was also lower. In terms of consequences for students, various forms of social misbehavior (class cutting, absenteeism, and classroom disorder) were all less prevalent in schools with a communal organization. The drop out rate was also lower, students' interest in schooling higher, and the gains in mathematics achievement from sophomore to senior year were greater.

137 The theory of bureaucratic organization as it applies to schools is laid out by Bidwell (1965). The functional division of labor and definition of staff roles are the first two criteria he establishes.

138 For an historical account of the forces contributing to the rapid expansion of high school activities in the 1960s and 1970s, see the 'Origins' chapter in Powell *et al.* (1985).

139 Another benefit of specialization, although perhaps unintended, is that it has afforded teachers greater freedom to determine the courses they will offer and the activities in which they will engage. The latter is the teacher side of inidvidualism and choice which characterizes the 'Shopping Mall High School' (Powell *et al.*, 1985). See also Cusick (1983) on the latter point.

140 For a more philosophical treatment of this topic see Bowers (1985).

141 Only recently, for example, has research focused on possible school effects on students' decisions to drop out (see Bryk and Thum, 1989; Coleman and Hoffer, 1987; Wehlage and Rutter, 1986). We know of no similar investigations on other aspects of youth disorder.

142 A similar concept of a diffuse teacher role has been described by Parsons (1960).

143 See Berlak and Berlak (1981) and Wehlage (1982). For a more general discussion of the ethic of caring and its implications for school organization see Noddings (1988).

144 See, for example, Schwartz, Merten and Bursik (1987).

145 This is a well established theme in the literature on the teaching profession. See, for example, Jackson (1968) and Feiman-Nemser and Floden (1986).

146 Coleman and Hoffer (1987) report that the probability of dropping out is substantially less in Catholic than in public schools, with the most pronounced differences existing for students from troubled families and students who have a history of discipline problems in their first years in high school. Bryk and Thum (1989) provide some statistical evidence linking school organization characteristics to the social distribution of dropping out (in terms of the student's social class and at-risk behavior).

147 Theoretical details for this argument are advanced in a number of places,

including Parsons (1960); Barr and Dreeben (1983); and Gamoran (1986).

148 Notable field studies here include Goodlad (1983); Lightfoot (1984); Powell *et al.* (1985); Oakes (1985); and Sizer (1984). More in-depth studies of high school instruction include Rosenbaum (1976); Cusick (1983); Page (1987); and McNeil (1988a; 1988b).

149 See Valli (1986). Supporting evidence is also reported in Bryk *et al.* (1984).

150 This topic has been treated by Alexander, Cook and McDill (1978); Bowles and Gintis (1976); Circourel and Kitsuse (1963); Heyns (1974); Jencks and Brown (1975); Oakes (1985); Rosenbaum (1976); Rosenbaum (1980); Shafer and Olexa (1971); and many others.

151 For a further discussion of this idea see Bryk and Raudenbush (1988). For a detailed empirical application of the concept see Lee and Bryk (1989).

152 The arguments about opportunity to learn are spelled out by Hallinan and Sorenson (1983); Sorenson (1970); and, most recently, by Sorenson (1987). In the context of school organization, closely related ideas are expressed by 'vacancy theory', dissussed earlier in this chapter. (See also the empirical study by Garet and Delaney, 1988.) The basic idea is that schools control access to learning by expanding or contracting the numbers of places in various learning environments (e.g., the top ability group, the college-preparatory track, or honors or advanced placement courses). Thus, access to these learning environments is an interactive process, involving both specific school policies and student characteristics such as ability and motivation.

153 Recent work by Powell *et al.* (1985); Cusick (1983); and Grant (1988) has described a 'vertical curriculum', consisting of a large number of courses with similar titles which are taught at different ability levels.

154 The simple correlation between advanced mathematics coursetaking and senior year achievement is about .65, which rivals the strength of the sophomore-senior achievement correlation of .78 (see Lee and Bryk, 1988). Course-taking and tracking have been shown to account for a large portion of the positive Catholic school effect on academic achievement (Hoffer, Greeley and Coleman, 1985; Lee and Bryk, 1988), and to have moderate structural effects in more detailed models of academic achievement (see, for example, Bryk *et al.*, 1984; Gamoran, 1987; Lee and Bryk, 1988). Results reported in Alexander *et al.* (1978); Alexander and Cook (1982); and Vanfossen *et al.* (1987) also support this conclusion.

155 This argument is made in a variety of places including Sebring (1987). For detailed discussions of the possible effects of heightened couse-taking requirements for graduation see McDill *et al.* (1986), as well as a recent field study on this topic by Clune *et al.* (1989).

156 National Coalition of Advocates for Children, 1985, p 115.

157 See, for example, Cusick (1983); Grant (1988); Powell *et al.* (1985).

158 This is the claim that student achievement in Catholic schools is less dependent upon family background than is student achievement in the public sector.

159 The statistical evidence consists of a hierarchical linear model relating school organizational characteristics to differentiation by class, race, and academic

backgound. Although they fit a combined model for public and Catholic schools, this single model accounts for a similar proportion of the variance in the two sectors. This is an unlikely result if the structural mechanisms were different in the two sectors.

160 For a further discussion of multilevel models and their applications in educational research see Bryk and Raudenbush (1988) or Raudenbush and Bryk (1988). The basic statistical theory for these models is reviewed in Raudenbush (1988).

161 For a further elaboration of this argument see Bidwell (1965).

162 For a further discussion of Dewey's writings as they bear on this idea of the small society of the school see Driscoll (1989).

163 We refer here to the work documenting the hyper-rationalization of schooling such as described by Wise (1979) and McNeil (1988b).

164 See, for example, the interpretative review by Purkey and Smith (1983); also Stevenson (1987b) and Corcoran (1985).

165 The classic reference here is Berman and McLaughlin (1978). See also Goodlad (1975).

166 See Clune (1988) for a synthesis of the research on school effectiveness, school improvement, and staff development in terms of models for school communication.

167 See, for example, Murphy, *et al.*, (1985).

168 These arguments are advanced principally in the research syntheses offered by Rosenholtz (1985, 1987), and also in work by Little (1982) and Bird and Little (1986). See also Fullan (1985) and Stevenson (1987).

169 This is a major theme in Grant's (1988) account of *The World We Created at Hamilton High*.

170 Recent studies on peer groups make an important distinction between the development of peer groups and the interaction which takes place between peers (Epstein, 1983). Studies on the development of peer groups have generally focused on the selection of friends. The studies involving schools are specifically concerned with organizational practices which might influence friendship selection, such as ability grouping within classrooms (Hallinan and Sorenson, 1985), tracking within schools (Hansell and Karweit, 1983), or the segregation/desegregation of racial groups in schools (Hallinan and Williams, 1989).

Interaction between peers, on the other hand, involves the influences peers have over each other's attitudes, values, and behaviors. Researchers examining the influence of peers on various outcomes (both educational and social) focus more on the mechanisms of social interaction, and how these contribute to individual outcomes (see, for example, Biddle, Bank and Marlin, 1980; Epstein, 1983; Ishiyama and Chabassol, 1985).

However, an examination of peer influence must take selection processes into account. Correlational studies attempt to demonstrate influence by examining similarities among peers, similarities which may have led to friendship selection initially. This methodological problem can lead to a considerable overestimation of the effects of peer groups on one's behaviors and attitudes. See, for additional discussion of this problem, Cohen (1983a) and Kandel (1978).

171 See, for example, Clasen and Brown (1985); and Maliphant (1979).

172 In addition to studying the impact of peer groups, recent research has also focused on the ways in which these effects occur. The primary mechanism for peer influence appears to be through the modeling of behavior, but there may be indirect influences of normative expectations which have yet to be adequately captured in quantitative research. The personal orientation of the inidvidual toward the group and the nonrecursive nature of peer interaction makes causal inferencing from group to individual conceptually and methodologically difficult. See Biddle, Bank and Marlin (1980) and Epstein (1983) for examination of specific influences.

173 The research by Hallinan and Sorensen (1983; 1985) and by Hallinan and Williams (1989) on the formation of peer groups provides evidence on this point.

174 See, for example, the descriptive accounts offered in Jackson (1968).

175 For an excellent theoretical exposition on the contribution of school organization to student alienation, see Newmann (1981). For recent statistical data supporting this concern, see Ekstrom *et al.*, (1987).

176 See, for example, Farber (1984) and Dworkin (1987).

177 For a review of the research on teacher expectations see Brophy (1983).

178 See for example Wehlage *et al.*, (1989).

179 See Firestone and Rosenblum (1988) for research citations on these various findings.

180 Coleman and Hoffer (1987) reported substantial differences in adjusted dropout rates between Catholic and public schools. Wehlage and Rutter (1986) provide the first published research which approaches the problem of dropping out of school from an organizational perspective. See also, Bryk and Thum (1989).

181 Newmann (1989a; 1989b) offers an interesting theoretical argument concerning students' engagement and the authenticity of students' academic experiences. He suggests that students become alienated from their academic environment when the 'work' of schooling does not have much meaning in terms of other social or psychological characteristics of an adolescent's role in society.

182 The edited volume by Natriello (1986) provides a broad discussion of the patterns of school dropouts and the school policies that may contribute to this. See also the introductory and concluding chapters in Wehlage *et al.*, (1989).

183 In a comparision of high school seniors in 1972 and 1980, Rock *et al.*, (1984) reported that average achievement declined in reading and mathematics, although slight gains were registered for blacks and Puerto Ricans. Conflicting evidence, however, appears in NAEP (1984) which reported general increases in reading ability between 1971 and 1984 especially for minority students. Since these increases were not sustained in the 1986 assessment, however, some doubts are raised about the significance of the earlier report.

184 It is important to note that, although such problems are particularly acute in disadvantaged urban schools, this phenomenon is pervasive among all types

of high schools. For a summary discussion of the research on this point see Sedlak *et al.*, (1986).

185 In J.G. March (Ed.) (1965) *Handbook of Organizations*, Chicago: Rand McNally, 972-1019.

186 See the essay by Willis Hawley (1976) entitled 'The possibility of nonbureaucratic organizations'. The term nonbureaucratic is itself interesting in that it defines the alternative by what it is not; rather than a positive, active vision of what it should be. In this very choice of words, Hawley demonstrate the liberal dilemma of how public institutions accommodate the more subjective, personal, and particularistic aspects of a pluralistic paideia.

187 This is the classic Aristotelian perspective on human nature. For a contemporary discussion of this topic from a humanitarian perspective see MacIntyre (1981).

188 For a more contemporary discussion of these ideas see Gutmann (1987) and Bryk (1988).

189 This description of a communally organized school is developed in more detail in Bryk and Driscoll (1988) and Driscoll (1989). They also present a review of related research and the *HS&B* analyses on the effects of a communal organization on teacher commitment and student engagement. Wehlage *et al.*, (1989) offer a similar conceptualization in describing successful high schools for at-risk youth.

190 The recent research on the structural effects of ability grouping in reading instruction is illustrative of this point. See, for example, Barr and Dreeben (1983).

191 See Noddings (1988). For a related argument in the case of effective postsecondary insitutions see Burton Clark's discussion of the organizational saga (1972). In this interpretative account of the institutional development of Reed, Antioch and Sawarthmore colleges, he describes the important role that beliefs and sentiments play in the development of these organizations.

192 This argument draws on the romanticist stream within anthropology, reflected for example in the work of Goertz, that ideas and practices fall beyond the scope of deductive and inductive reason. In this regard, they are neither rational nor irrational but rather nonrational. As Shweder (1984) points out, however, such arguments can be examined in terms of basic principles of internal consistency and logic. It is often difficult, however, to demonstrate that one is of necessity always better, leading to the dilemma of divergent realities (Shweder, 1986). A similar argument was raised by Fein (1970) in a discussion of the conflicts over community control of New York City schools. He argues that a movement toward community control is an affirmation of the parochial and a rejection of the universalism at the core liberal idelolgy. Much the same argument (and attendant concerns) can be raised about the push toward greater school autonomy.

193 Cohen (1982) provides a good discussion of the cumulative effects on schools of the various state and federal initiatives instituted in the 1960s and 1970s. While each new program or policy was a conscious response to a legitimate educational concern, the overall effect was to produce much more complex organizations with weakened internal social ties.

194 Coleman and Hoffer (1987).

195 Lee and Bryk (1986), using *HS&B* data, report positive effects for Catholic girls' schools on academic achievement, educational aspirations, locus of control, sex role stereotyping and academic attitudes and behaviors. Riordan (1985), using NLS72 data, also found positive effects on achievement for girls' schools. A report on recent field research in progress, however, (Lee and Marks, 1990) suggests that this pattern may not be generally characteristic of other non-Catholic schools. Should these findings be sustained by further analyses, they would confirm other evidence that private schools as a set are a very diverse enterprise with few generalization appropriate for the entire set.

196 Brief descriptions of life within Catholic schools appear in a number of places (Bryk *et al.*, 1984; NCEA, 1986; Benson and Guerra, 1985). Lesko (1988) offers an ethnographic account of Catholic schools which deepens this perspective. A summary of this research can be found in Wehlage *et al.*, (1989).

References

Alexander, K.L. and Cook, M.A. (1982) 'Curricula and coursework: A surprise ending to a familiar story', *American Sociological Review*, **47**, 5, pp. 626–40.

Alexander, K.L. and Eckland, B.K. (1975) 'Contextual effects in the high school attainment process', *American Sociological Review*, **40**, pp. 402–16.

Alexander, K.L., Cook, M. and McDill, E.L. (1978) 'Curriculum tracking and educational stratification: Some further evidence', *American Sociological Review*, **43**, pp. 47–66.

Alexander, K.L., McDill, E.L., Fennessy, J. and D'Amico, R.J. (1979) 'School SES influences — Composition or context?' *Sociology of Education*, **52**, pp. 222–37.

Alexander, K.L. and Pallas, A.M. (1985) 'School sector and cognitive performance: When is a little a little?' *Sociology of Education*, **58**, pp. 115–26.

Alwin, D.F. and Otto, L.B. (1977) 'High school context effects on aspirations', *Sociology of Education*, **50**, pp. 259–73.

Anderson, C.S. (1982) 'The search for school climate: A review of the research', *Review of Educational Research*, **52**, 3, pp. 368–420.

Ashton, P.T. and Webb, R.B. (1986) *Making a Difference: Teachers' Sense of Efficacy and Student Achievement*, New York: Longman.

Baker, D.P. and Stevenson, D.L. (1986) 'Mothers' strategies for children's achievement: Managing the transition to high school', *Sociology of Education*, **59**, pp. 156–66.

Barker, R. and Gump, P. (1964) *Big School, Small School: High School Size and Student Behavior*, Stanford, CA: Stanford University Press.

Barnett, B.G. (1984) 'Subordinate teacher power in school organizations', *Sociology of Education*, **57**, pp. 43–55.

Barr, R. and Dreeben, R. (1983) *How Schools Work*, Chicago: University of Chicago Press.

Barth, R.S. (1980) *Run School Run*, Cambridge, MA: Harvard University Press.

Becher, R.M. (1984) 'Parent involvement: A review of research and principles of successful practices', Washington, DC: National Institute of Education. [ED 247 032]

Becker, H.J. and Epstein, J.L. (1982) 'Parent involvement: A survey of teacher practices', *The Elementary School Journal*, **83**, pp. 86–102.

Becker, H.S., Geer, B. and Hughes, E.C. (1961) *Boys in White: Student Culture in the Medical School*, Chicago: University of Chicago Press.

Bellah, R., Tipton, S., Swidler, A. and Sullivan W. (1985) *Habits of the Heart: Individualism and Commitment in American Life*, New York: Basic Books.

Bell-Nathaniel, A. (1979) 'Facilitating parent-teacher interaction', *Elementary School Guidance & Counseling*, **14**, pp. 22–7.

Benson, P.L. and Guerra, M.J. (1985) *Sharing the Faith: The Beliefs and Values of Catholic High School Teachers*, Washington, D.C.: National Catholic Educational Association.

Berger, E.H. (1981) *Parents as Partners in Education: The School and Home Working Together*, St. Louis, MO: C.V. Mosby.

Berlak, A. and Berlak, H. (1981) *Dilemmas of Schooling*, London: Methuen.

Berman, P. and McLaughlin, M.W. (1978) *Federal Programs Supporting Educational Change*, Vol. III Implementing and sustaining innovations; Santa Monica, CA: Rand Corporation.

Biddle, B.J., Bank, B.J. and Marlin, M.M. (1980) 'Parental and peer influence on adolescents', *Social Forces*, **58**, pp. 1057–79.

Bidwell, C.E. (1965) 'The school as a formal organization', in March, J.G. (Ed.) *Handbook of Organizations*, Chicago: Rand McNally.

Bidwell, C.E. (1972) 'Schooling and socialization for moral commitment', *Interchange*, **3**, pp.1–26.

Bidwell, C.E. and Friedkin, N.E. (1988) 'The sociology of education', in Smelser, N. (Ed.) *The Handbook of Sociology*, New York: Sage Publications.

Bidwell, C.E. and Kasarda, J.D. (1975) 'School district organization and student achievement', *American Sociological Review*, **40**, pp.55–70.

Bidwell, C.E. and Kasarda J.D. (1980) 'Conceptualizing and measuring the effects of schools and schooling', *American Journal of Education*, **88**, pp.401–30.

Bird, T. and Little, J.W. (1986) 'How schools organize the teaching occupation', *Elementary School Journal*, **86**, pp. 493–511.

Bloch, M. (1984) 'Parent-teacher relationships: Complementary, supplementary, or conflicting?' in Grant, C.W. (Ed.) *Perparing for Reflective Teaching*, New York: Allyn & Bacon.

Bock, R.D. (Ed.) (1989) *Multilevel Analyses of Educational Data*, New York: Academic Press.

Bossert, S., Dwyer, D., Rowan, B. and Lee, G. (1982) 'The instructional management role of the principal', *Educational Administration Quarterly*, **18**, pp. 34–64.

Bowers, C.A. (1985) 'Culture against itself: Nihilism as an element in recent educational thought', *American Journal of Education*, **93**, pp. 465–90.

Bowles, S. and Gintis, H. (1976) *Schooling in Capitalist America: Educational Reform and the Contradictions of Economic Life*, New York: Basic Books.

BRIDGES, E.M. (1982) 'Research on the school administrator: The state of the art, 1967–1980', *Educational Administration Quarterly*, **18**, pp. 12–33.

BRIDGES, E.M. (1986) *The Incompetent Teacher: The Challenge and the Response*, Philadelphia: Falmer Press.

BRIDGES, E.M. and HALLINAN, M.T. (1978) 'Subunit size, work system interdependence, and employee absenteeism', *Educational Administration Quarterly*, **14**, 2, pp. 24–42.

BROOKOVER, W.B., BEADY, C., FLOOK, P., SCHWEITZER,, J. and WISENBAKER, J. (1979) *School Social Systems and Student Achievement: Schools Can Make a Difference*, New York: Praeger.

BROPHY, J.E. (1983) 'Research on the self-fulfilling prophecy and teacher expectations', *Journal of Educational Psychology*, **75**, pp. 631–61.

BROWN, B.W. and SAKS D.H. (1975) 'The production and distribution of cognitive skills within schools', *Journal of Political Education*, **83**, pp. 571–94.

BROWN, B.W. and SAKS, D.H. (1981) 'The microeconomics of schooling', *Review of Research in Education*, **9**, pp. 217–54.

BROWN, B.W. and SAKS, D.H. (1983) 'Spending for local public education: Income distribution and the aggregation of private demands', *Public Finance Quarterly*, **11**, pp. 21–45.

BROWN, B.W. and SAKS, D.H. (1985) 'The revealed influence of class, race, and ethnicity on local public school expenditures', *Sociology of Education*, **58**, pp. 186–90.

BRYK, A.S. (1988) 'Musings on the moral life of schools', *American Journal of Education*, **96**, pp. 231–55.

BRYK A.S. and DRISCOLL, M.E. (1988) *The School as Community: Theoretical Foundations, Contextual Influences, and Consequences for Students and Teachers*, Madison, WI: National Center on Effective Secondary Schools, University of Wisconsin.

BRYK, A.S., HOLLAND P.B., LEE, V.E. and CARRIEDO, R.A. (1984) *Effective Catholic Schools: An Exploration*, Washington DC: National Catholic Education Association.

BRYK, A.S. and RAUDENBUSH, S.W. (1988) 'Methodology for cross level organizational research', in *Handbook of Research in Organizational Behavior*, Greenwich, CT: JAI Press.

BRYK, A.S. and THUM, Y.M. (1989) 'The effects of high school organization on dropping out: An exploratory investigation', *American Educational Research Journal*, **26**, pp. 353–84.

BUELL, E.H. and BRISBEN, R.A. (1982) *School Desegregation and Defended Neighborhoods: The Boston Controversy*, Lexington, MA: D.C. Heath and Co.

BURSTEIN, L. (1980) 'The role of levels of analysis in the specification of educational effects', in DREEBAN, R. and THOMAS, J. (Eds) *The Analysis of Educational Productivity, Vol I: Issues in Microanalysis*, Cambridge, MA: Ballinger.

CALDWELL, W.E. and LUTZ, F.W. (1978) 'The measurement of principal rule administration behavior and its relationship to educational leadership', *Educational Administration Quarterly*, **14**, 2, pp. 63–79.

CALLAHAN, R.E. (1962) *Education and the Cult of Efficiency*, Chicago: University of Chicago Press.

CAMPBELL, W. (1970). *Scholars in Context: The Effects of Environments on Learning*, New York: John Wiley.

CAPLOW, T. (1957) 'Organization size', *Administrative Science Quarterly*, pp. 484–505.

CHAMBERS, J.G. (1981) 'An analysis of school size under a voucher system', *Educational Evaluation and Policy Analysis*, **3**, pp. 29–40.

CHAPMAN, D.W. and HUTCHESON, S.M. (1982) 'Attrition from teaching careers: A discriminant analysis', *American Educational Research Journal*, **19**, 1, pp. 93–105.

CHUBB, J.E. (1988) 'Why the current wave of school reform will fail', *The Public Interest*, **90**, pp. 28–49.

CHUBB, J.E. and MOE, T.M. (1987) 'No school is an island: Politics, markets, and education', *Politics of Education Association Yearbook*, pp. 131–41.

CHUBB, J.E. and MOE, T.M. (1988) 'Politics, markets, and organization of schools'. Unpublished manuscript.

CICOUREL, A.V. and KITUSE, J.I. (1963) *The Educational Decision-makers*, Indianapolis: Bobbs-Merrill.

CLARK, B.R. (1972) 'The organizational saga in higher education', *Administrative Science Quarterly*, **8**, pp.178–84.

CLARK, D.L., LOTTO, L.S. and ASTUTO, T.A. (1984) 'Effective schools and school improvement: A comparative analysis of two lines of inquiry', *Educational Administration Quarterly*, **20**, 3, pp. 41–68.

CLASEN, D.R. and BROWN, B.B. (1985) 'The multidimensionality of peer pressure in adolescence', *Journal of Youth and Adolescence*, **16**, pp. 451–68.

CLUNE, W. (1988) 'A communication model of school effectiveness, school improvement and staff development implications for policy and practice', Madison, WI: University of Wisconsin Center on Effective Secondary Schools.

CLUNE, W.H., WHITE, P. and PATTERSON, J. (1989) *The Implementation and Effects of High School Graduation Requirements: First Step Towards Curricular Reform,* Center for Educational Policy Research, Eagleton Institute of Politics, New Brunswick, NJ: Rutgers University.

COHEN, D.K. (1982) 'Policy and organization: The import of State and Federal educational policy on school governance', *Harvard Educational Review,* **52**, pp. 474–99.

COHEN, D.K. (1988) 'Knowledge of teaching: Plus que a change . . . ' in JACKSON, P.W. (Ed.) *Contributing to Educational Change*, Berkeley, CA: McCutchen.

COHEN, J. (1983a) 'Peer influence on college aspirations with initial aspirations controlled', *American Sociological Review*, **48**, pp. 728–34.

COHEN, J. (1983b) 'The relationship between friendship selection and peer influence', in EPSTEIN, J.L. and KARWEIT, N. (Eds.) *Friends in School: Patterns of Selection and Influence in Secondary Schools*, New York: Academic Press.

COHEN, M (1983) 'Instructional, management, and social conditions in effective schools', in WEBB, A.O. and WEBB, L.D. (Eds) *School Finance and School Improvement: Linkages in the 1980s*, Cambridge, MA: Ballinger.

COLEMAN, J.S. (1961) *The Adolescent Society*, New York: Cromwell-Collier.

COLEMAN, J.S. (1979) *The School Years: Current Issues in the Socialization of Young People*, London: Methuen.

COLEMAN, J.S. (1987) The relations between school and social structure. In

HALLINAN, M.T. (Ed.), *The Social Organization of Schools: New Conceptualizations of the Learning Process* (pp. 177–204). New York: Plenum Press.

COLEMAN, J.S. (1989) 'Social capital in the creation of human capital', *American Journal of Sociology*, **94**, pp. 95–120.

COLEMAN, J.S. CAMPBELL, E., HOBSON, C., MCPARTLAND, J., MOOD, A., WEINFELD, F. and YORK, R. (1966) *Equality of Educational Opportunity Report*, Washington DC: United States Government Printing Office.

COLEMAN, J.S. and HOFFER, T. (1987) *Public and Private High Schools: The Impact of Communities*, New York: Basic Books.

COLEMAN, J.S., HOFFER, T. and KILGORE, S. (1982) *High School Achievement: Public, Catholic, and Private Schools Compared*, New York: Basic Books.

COMER, J. (1980) *School Power: Implication of an Intervention Project*, New York: Free Press.

COMER, J. (1988) 'Educating poor minority children', *Scientific American*, **259**, 5, pp. 42–8.

CONANT, J.B. (1959) The American High School Today, New York: McGraw-Hill.

CORBETT, H.D., DAWSON, J.L. and FIRESTONE W.A. (1984) *School Context and School Change: Implications for Effective Planning*, New York: Teachers College Press.

CORCORAN, T.B. (1985) 'Effective secondary schools', in KYLE, R.M.J. (Ed.) *Reaching for Excellence: An Effective Schools Sourcebook*, Washington, DC: Government Printing Office.

CRAIN, R.L. and STRAUSS, J.K. (1986) 'Are smaller high schools more or less effective?' Unpublished paper, Center for Social Organization of Schools, Johns Hopkins Univ., Baltimore, MD.

CREMIN, L.A. (1988) *American Education: The Metropolitan Experience, 1876–1980*, New York: Harper and Row.

CRONBACH, L.J. (1976) *Research on Classrooms and Schools: Formulations of Questions, Design, and Analysis*, An occasional paper of the Stanford, CA: Stanford Evaluation Consortium, Stanford University.

CRONIN, J. (1973) *The Control of Urban Schools*, New York: Free Press.

CSIKSZENTMIHALYI, M. and LARSON, R. (1984) *Being Adolescent: Conflict and Growth in the Teenage Years*, New York: Basic Books.

CSIKSZENTMIHALYI, M. and MCCORMACK, J. (1986) 'The influence of teachers,' *Phi Delta Kappan*, **64**, pp. 415–19.

CUSICK, P.A. (1983) *The Egalitarian Ideal and the American High School*, New York: Longman.

DAFT, R.L. and BECKER, S.W. (1980) 'Managerial, institutional, and technical influences on administration: A longitudinal analysis', *Social Forces* **59**, pp. 392–413.

DAVIE, R. (1979) 'The home and the school', in COLEMAN, J.C. (Ed.) *The School Years: Current Issues in the Socialization of Young People*, London: Methuen.

DAVIS, J. (1966) 'The campus as a "frog pond", *American Journal of Sociology*, **72**, pp. 17–31.

DEAL, T.E. and CELOTTI, L. (1980) 'How much influence do (and can) educational administrations have on classrooms?' *Phi Delta Kappan*, **61**, pp. 471–3.

DEAL, T.E. and KENNEDY, A.A. (1982) *Corporate Culture: The Rites and Rituals of Corporate Life*, Reading, MA: Addison-Wesley.

DEVANEY,, K. (1987) *The Lead Teacher: Ways to Begin*. Paper commissioned by the Carnegie Forum on Education and the Economy: New York, NY.

DEWEY, J. (1966) *Democracy and Education*, New York: McMillan.

DEWEY, J. (1981) 'My pedagogic creed', in MCDERMOTT, J. (Ed.) *The Philosophy of John Dewey*, Chicago: University of Chicago Press.

DI PRETE, T. (1981) *Discipline and Order in American High Schools*, Report to National Center for Educational Statistics. Washington, DC: National Center for Educational Statistics.

DORNBUSCH, S.M. and RITTER, P.L. (1988) 'Parents of high school students: A neglected resource', *Educational Horizons*, **66**, pp. 75–7.

DREEBEN, R. (1970) *The Nature of Teaching: Schools and the Work of Teachers*, Glenview, IL: Scott, Foresman.

DREEBEN, R. (1988) 'The sociology of education: Its development in the United States', Unpublished manuscript. Chicago: University of Chicago Department of Education.

DRISCOLL, M.E. (1989) 'The school as community', Ph.D. Dissertation, University of Chicago.

DURKHEIM, E. (1961) *Moral Education*, Glencoe, IL: The Free Press.

DURKHEIM, E. (1956) *Education and Sociology*. Glencoe, IL: The Free Press.

DWORKIN, A.G. (1987) *Teachers Burnout in the Public Schools: Structural Courses and Consequences for Children*, Albany, NY: SUNY press.

EDMONDS, R. (1979) 'Effective schools for the urban poor', *Educational Leadership*, **37**, pp. 15–24.

EKSTROM, R.B., GOERTZ, M.E., POLLACK, J.M. and ROCK, D.A. (1987) 'Who drops out of high school and why: Findings from a National Study', in NATRIELLO, G. (Ed.) *School Dropouts: Patterns and Policies*, New York: Teachers College Press.

EPSTEIN J.L. (1983) 'The influence of friends on achievement and affective outcomes', in EPSTEIN, J.L. and KARWEIT, N. (Eds.) *Friends in School: Patterns of Selection and Influence in Secondary Schools*, New York: Academic Press.

EPSTEIN, J.L. (1985) 'Home and school connections in schools for the future: Implications of research on parental involvement', *Peabody Journal of Education*, **78**, pp. 18–41.

EPSTEIN, J.L. (1986) 'Friendship selection: Development and environmental influences', in MUELLER, E. and COOPER, C. (Eds) *Process and Outcome in Peer Relationships*, New York: Academic Press.

EPSTEIN, J.L. (1987) 'Toward a theory of family-school connections: Teacher practices and parent involvement', in HURRELMANN, K., KAUFMANN, F.X. and LOSEL, F. (Eds.) *Social Intervention: Potential and Constraints*, New York: Walter de Gruyter.

EPSTEIN, J.L. and KARWEIT, N. (1983) *Friends in School: Patterns of Selection and Influence in Secondary Schools*, New York: Academic Press.

EYLER, J., COOK, V.J. and WARD, L.E. (1983) 'Resegregation: Segregation within desegregated schools', in ROSSELL, C.H. and HAWLEY, W.D. (Eds.) *The Conse-*

quences of School Desegregation, Philadelphia: Temple University Press.

FARBER, B.A. (1984) 'Teacher burnout: Assumptions, myths, and issues', *Teacher's College Record*, **86**, 2, pp. 321–37.

FEIMAN-NEMSER, S. and FLODEN, R.E. (1986) 'The cultures of teaching', in WITTROCK, R. (Ed.) *Handbook of Research on Teaching*, 3rd edition NY: MacMillan, pp. 505–27.

FEIN, L.J. (1970) 'Community schools and social theory: The limits of universalism', in LEVIN, H. (Ed.) *Community Control of Schools*, Washington, DC: Brookings Institution.

FIRESTONE, W.A. and HERRIOT, R.E. (1982) 'Prescriptions for effective elementary schools don't fit secondary schools', *Educational Leadership*, (Dec), pp. 51–3.

FIRESTONE, W.A. and ROSENBLUM, S. (1988) 'Building commitment in urban schools', *Educational Evaluation and Policy Analysis*, **10**, pp. 285–300.

FIRESTONE, W. and WILSON, B.L. (1985) 'Using bureaucratic and cultural linkages to improve instruction: The principal's contribution', *Educational Administration Quarterly*, **21**, 2, pp. 7–30.

FISHER, R. (1984) *Let the people decide: Neighborhood organizing in America*. Boston: Twayne Publ.

FORSYTH, P.B. and HOY, W.K. (1978) 'Isolation and alienation in educational organizations', *Educational Administration Quarterly*, **14**, 1, pp. 80–96.

FOX, W.F. (1981) 'Reviewing economics of size in education', *Journal of Education Finance*, **6**, pp. 273–96.

FREDERIKSEN, N. (1984) 'The real test bias: Influences of testing on teaching and learning', *American Psychologist*, **39**, pp. 192–202.

FRIEDKIN, N.E. and NECOCHEA, J. (1988) 'School size and performance: A contingency perspective, *Educational Evaluation and Policy Analysis*, **10**, pp. 237–49.

FULLAN, M. (1985) 'Change processes and strategies at the local level', *The Elementary School Journal*, **85**, pp. 391–419.

FULLER, B. and IZU, J.A. (1986) 'Explaining school cohesion: What shapes the organizational beliefs of teachers?' *American Journal of Education*, **94**, August, pp. 501–35.

FULLER, B., WOOD, K., RAPOPORT, T. and DORNBUSCH, S.M. (1982) 'The organizational context of individual efficacy', *Review of Educational Reserach*, **52**, 1, pp. 7–30.

GAMORAN, A. (1986) 'Instructional and institutional aspects of ability grouping', *Sociology of Education*, **59**, pp. 185–98.

GAMORAN, A. (1989) 'Measuring curriculum differentiation', *American Journal of Education*, **97**, pp. 129–43.

GARET, M.S. and DELANEY, B. (1988) 'Student courses and stratification', *Sociology of Education*, **61**, pp. 61–77.

GERSTEN, R., CARNINE, D. and GREEN, S. (1982) 'The principal as instructional leader: A second look', *Educational Leadership*, **40**, 3, pp. 47–9.

GITTELL, M., BERUBE, M.R., GOTTFRIED, F., GUTTENTAG, M. and SPIER, A. (1972) *Local Control in Education: Three Demonstration School Districts in New York City*, New York: Praeger Publishers.

GLASMAN, N.S. (1984) 'Student achievement and the school principal', *Educational Evaluation and Policy Analysis*, **6**, pp. 283–96.

GODDING, R.Z. and WAGNER, J.A. (1985) 'A meta analytic review of the relationship between size and performance: The productivity and efficiency of organizations and their subunits', *Administrative Science Quarterly*, **30**, pp. 462–81.

GOOD, T.L. and BROPHY, J.E. (1984) *Looking in Classrooms*, New York: Harper & Row.

GOOD, T.L. and BROPHY, J.E. (1986) 'School effects', in WITTROCK, M.C. (Ed.) *Handbook of Research on Teaching*, New York: MacMillan Publishing.

GOODLAD, J. (1975) *The Dynamics of Educational Change: Toward Responsive Schools*, New York: McGraw-Hill.

GOODLAD, J. (1984) *A Place Called School: Prospects for the Future*, New York: McGraw-Hill.

GORDON, C.W. (1957) *The Social System of the High School*, Glencoe, IL: Free Press.

GOTTFREDSON, G.D. and DAIGER. D. (1979) *Disruption in Six Hundred Schools* (Report 289), Baltimore: Center for Social Organization of Schools, Johns Hopkins University.

GRANT, C.A. and SLEETER, C.E. (1988) 'Race, class, and gender and abandoned dreams', *Teacher's College Record*, **90**, 1, pp. 19–40.

GRANT, G. (1988) *The World We Created at Hamilton High*, Cambridge, MA: Harvard University Press.

GREELEY, A.M. (1982) *Catholic High Schools and Minority Students*, New Brunswick, NJ: Transaction Books.

GRIFFIN, G.A. (Ed.) (1983) *Staff Development*, Chicago: University of Chicago Press.

GUTHRIE, J. (1979) 'Organizational scale and school success', *Educational Evaluation and Policy Analysis*, **1**, 1, pp. 17–27.

GUTMAN, A.E. (1987) *Democratic Education*, Princeton, NJ: Princeton University Press.

HAERTEL, E. (1986) 'Measuring school performance to improve school practice', *Education and Urban Society*, **18**, pp. 312–25.

HALL, G.S. (1905) *Adolescence: Its Psychology and its Relations to Physiology, Anthropology, Sociology, Sex, Crime, Religion, and Education*. 2 vols. New York: D. Appleton.

HALLER, A.O. and WOELFEL, J. (1972) 'Significant others and their expectations: Concepts and instruments to measure interpersonal influence on status aspirations', *Rural Sociology*, **37**, pp. 591–621.

HALLINAN, M.T. (1983) 'Commentary: New directions for research on peer influence', in EPSTEIN, J.L. and KARWEIT, N. (Eds.) *Friends in School: Patterns of Selection and Influence in Secondary Schools*, New York: Academic Press.

HALLINAN, M.T. (Ed.) (1987) *The Social Organization of Schools*, New York: Plenum.

HALLINAN, M.T. and SORENSEN, A.B. (1983) 'The formation and stability of instructional groups', *American Sociological Review*, **48**, pp. 838–51.

HALLINAN, M.T. and SORENSEN, A.B. (1985) 'Ability grouping and student friendships', *American Educational Research Journal*, **22**, 4, pp. 485–99.

HALLINAN, M.T. and WILLIAMS, R.A. (1989) 'Interracial friendship choices in secondary schools', *American Sociological Review*, **54**, pp. 67–78.

HALLINGER, P. and MURPHY, J. (1983) 'Instructional leadership and school socio-economic status: A preliminary investigation', *Administrator's Notebook*, **31**, 5, pp. 1–4.

HALLINGER, P. and MURPHY, J.F. (1986) 'The social context of effective schools', *American Journal of Education*, **94**, pp. 328–55.

HAMMACK, F.M. (1986) 'Large school systems' dropout reports: An analysis of definitions procedures, and findings', in NATRIELLO, G. (Ed.) *School Dropouts: Patterns and Policies*, New York: Teacher's College Press.

HAMPEL, R. (1986) *The Last Little Citadel*, Boston: Houghton Miffin.

HANNAWAY, J. (1988) *Signals and Signalling: The Workings of an Administrative System*, Oxford: Oxford University Press.

HANSELL, S. and KARWEIT, N. (1983) 'Curricular placement, friendship networks, and status attainment', in EPSTEIN, J.L. and KARWEIT, N. (Eds.) *Friends in School: Patterns of Selection and Influence in Secondary Schools*, New York: Academic Press.

HART, V. (1981) *Mainstreaming Children with Speical Needs*, New York: Longman.

HATTON, B. (1979) 'Community control in retrospect: A review of strategies for community participation in education', In Grant C. (Ed.), *Community Participation in Education* (pp. 2–20). Boston: Allyn and Bacon.

HAWLEY, W.D. (1976) 'The possibility of nonbureaucratic organizations', in HAWLEY, W.D. and ROGERS, R.D. (Eds.) *Improving Urban Management*, Beverly Hills, CA: Sage Publications.

HENDERSON, A.T. (Ed.) (1987) *The Evidence Continues to Grow: Parent Involvement Improves Student Achievement*, Columbia, MD: National Committee for Citizens in Education.

HERRIOTT, R.E. and FIRESTONE, W.A. (1984) 'Two images of schools as organizations: A refinement and elaboration', *Educational Administration Quarterly*, **20**, pp. 41–57.

HEYNS, B.L. (1974) 'Social selection and stratification within schools', *American Journal of Sociology*, **79**, pp. 1934–51.

HOFFER, T., GREELEY, A.M. and COLEMAN, J.S. (1985) 'Achievement growth in public and private schools', *Sociology of Education*, **58**, pp. 74–97.

HOLLISTER, C.D. (1979) 'School bureaucratization as a response to parents' demands', *Urban Education*, **14**, pp. 221–35.

HOY, W.K. and FERGUSON, J. (1985) 'A theoretical framework and exploration of organizational effectiveness of schools', *Educational Administration Quarterly*, **21**, 2, pp. 117–34.

IDE, J.K., PARKERSON, J., HAERTEL, G.D. and WALBERG, H.J. (1981) 'Peer group influence on educational outcomes: A quantitative synthesis', *Journal of Educational Psychology*, **73**, 4, pp. 472–84.

ISHIYAMA, F.I. and CHABASSOL, D.J. (1985) 'Adolescents' fear of social consequences of academic success as a function of age and sex', *Journal of Youth and Adolescence*, **14**, 1, pp. 37–46.

JACKSON, P.W. (1968) *Life in Classrooms*, New York: Holt, Rinehart, Winston.

JAMES, T. and LEVIN, H.M. (Eds.) (1988) *Comparing Public and Private Schools, Vol. 1: Institutions and Organizations*, Philadelphia: Falmer Press.

JENCKS, C. (1985) 'How much do high school students learn?' *Sociology of Education*, **58**, pp. 128–35.

JENCKS, C. and BROWN, M.D. (1975) 'Effects of high schools on their students', *Harvard Educational Review*, **45**, pp. 273–324.

JENCKS, C., SMITH, M., BANE, M.J. COHEN, D., GINTIS, H., HEYNS, B. and MICHELSON, S. (1972) *Inequality: A Reassessment of the Effect of Family and Schooling in America*, New York: Basic Books.

JOHNSON, D. & RANSOM, E. (1983) Family and School. London: Croom Helm.

KAGAN, S.L. (1984) *Parent Involvement Research: A Field in Search of Itself*, Boston: Institute for Responsive Education.

KANDEL, D.B. (1978) 'Homophily, selection, and socialization in adolescent friendships', *American Journal of Sociology*, **84**, pp. 427–36.

KARWEIT, N. (1983) 'Extracurricular activities and friendship selection', in EPSTEIN, J.L. and KARWEIT, N. (Eds.) *Friends in School: Patterns of Selection and Influence in Secondary Schools*, New York: Academic Press.

KATZ, M. (1987) *Reconstructing American Education*, Cambridge, MA: Harvard University Press.

KATZ, M.B. (Ed.) (1973) *Education in American History: Readings on the Social Issues*, New York: Praeger.

KEITH, T.Z., REIMERS, T.M., FEHRMANN, P.G., POTTEBAUM, S.M. and AUBEY, L.W. (1986) 'Parental involvement, homework, and TV time: Direct and indirect effects on high school achievement', *Journal of Educational Psychology*, **78**, pp. 373–80.

KIMBERLY, J.R. (1976) 'Organization size and the structuralist perspective: A review, critique, and proposal', *Administrative Science Quarterly*, **21**, pp. 571–97.

KOTTKAMP, R.B. (1984) 'The Principal as cultural leader', *Planning and Changing*, **15**, pp. 152–60.

KOTTKAMP, R.B. and MULHERN, J.A. (1987) 'Teacher expectancy motivation, open to closed climate and pupil control ideology in high schools', *Journal of Research and Development in Education*, **20**, pp. 9–18.

LEE, V.E. and BRYK, A.S. (1988), 'Curriculum tracking as mediating the social distribution of high school achievement', *Sociology of Education*, **61**, pp. 78–94.

LEE, V.E. and BRYK, A.S. (1989) 'A multilevel model of the social distribution of high school achievement', *Sociology of Education*, **62**, pp. 172–92.

LEE, V.E., DEDRICK, R.F. and SMITH, J.B. (in press) 'The effect of the social organization of schools on teacher satisfaction', *Sociology of Education*.

LEE, V.E. and EKSTROM, R.B. (1987) 'Student access to guidance counseling in high school', *American Educational Research Journal*, **24**, pp. 287–310.

LEE, V.E. and MARKS, H.M. (1990) *Who Goes Where? Choice of Single-Sex and Coeducational Independent Secondary Schools*, Ann Arbor, MI: University of Michigan. Unpublished manuscript.

LESKO, N. (1988) *Symbolizing Society: Stories, Rites and Structures in a Catholic High School*, Philadelphia: Falmer Press.

LEVIN, H.M. (Ed.) (1970) *Community Control of Schools*, Washington, DC: The Brookings Institute.

LEVINE, D.W. and LEIBERT, R.E. (1987) 'Improving school improvement plans', *Elementary School Journal*, **87**, pp. 397–412.

LIEBERMAN, A. and MILLER, L. (1978) 'The social realities of teaching', *Teacher's College Record*, **80**, pp. 54–68.

LIEBERMAN, A. and MILLER, L. (1984) 'School improvement: Themes and variations', *Teacher's College Record,* **86**, 1, pp. 4–19.

LIGHTFOOT, S.L. (1983) *The Good High School: Portraits of Character and Culture*, New York: Basic Books.

LITTLE, J.W. (1982a) 'Norms of collegiality and experimentation: Workplace conditions of school success', *American Educational Research Journal,* **19**, pp. 325–40.

LITTLE, J.W. (1982b) 'The effective Principal', *American Education*, (Aug–Sept), pp. 38–43.

LORTIE, D.C. (1975) *Schoolteacher*, Chicago: University of Chicago Press.

MACINTYRE, A. (1981) *After virtue*, South Bend: University of Notre Dame Press.

MAHARD, R.E. and CRAIN, R.L. (1983) 'Research on minority achievement in desegregated schools', in ROSSELL, C.H. and HAWLEY, W.D. (Eds.) *The Consequences of School Desgregation*, Philadelphia: Temple Univ. Press, pp. 103–25.

MALEN, B. and OGAWA, R.T. (1988) 'Professional patron influence on site-based governance councils: A confronting case study', *Educational Evaluation and Policy Analysis*, **10**, pp. 251–70.

MALIPHANT, R. (1979) 'Juvenile delinquency', in COLEMAN, J.C. (Ed.) *The School Years: Current Issues in the Socialization of Young People*, London: Methuen.

MARCH, J.G. (Ed.) (1965) *Handbook of Organizations*, Chicago: Rand McNally.

MARCH, J.G. and OLSEN, J.P. (1976) *Ambiguity and Choice in Organizations*, Bergen: Universitets Forlaget.

MARTIN, W.J. and WILLOVER, D.J. (1981) 'The managerial behavior of high school principals', *Educational Administration Quarterly*, **17**, pp. 69–90.

McDILL, E.L., NATRIELLO, G. and PALLAS, A.M. (1986) 'A population at risk: Potential consequences of tougher school standards for student dropouts', in NATRIELLO, G. (Ed.) *School Dropouts*, New York: Teacher's College Press.

McGUIRE, J.B. (1984) 'Strategies of school district conflict', *Sociology of Education*, **57**, pp. 31–42.

McKENNA, T. and ORTIZ, F.I. (1988) *The Broken Web: The Educational Experience of Hispanic American Women*, Claremont, CA: The Tomas Riveria Center.

McKEY, R.H. CONDELLI, L., GANSON, H., BARRETT, B.J., McCONKEY, C. and PLANTZ, M.C. (1985) *The Impact of Head Start on Children, Families and Communities*, Final report of the Head Start Evaluation, Synthesis and Utilization Project. US Department of Health and Human Servies. Washington, DC: US Government Printing Office.

McLAUGHLIN, M.W. (in press) *Careers in Schools*, Stanford University School of Education.

McLAUGHLIN, M.W. & MARSH, D.D. (1978) 'Staff development and school change. *Teacher's College Record*, **80**, pp. 68–94.

McLAUGHLIN, M.W., PFEIFER, R.S., SWANSON-OWENS, D. and YEE, S. (1986) 'Why teachers won't teach', *Phi Delta Kappan*, **67**, pp. 420–5.

McNEIL, L.M. (1988a) 'Contradictions of control, Part 1: Administrators and teachers', *Phi Delta Kappan*, January, pp. 333–9.

McNEIL, L.M. (1988b) *Contradictions of Control: School Structure and School Knowledge*, New York: Routledge and Kegan Paul.

McPARTLAND, J.M. and McDILL, E.L. (1982) 'Control and differentiation in the structure of American education', *Sociology of Education*, **55**, pp. 77–88.

McPhee, J. (1966) *The Headmaster: Frank L. Boyden, of Deerfield*, New York: Farrar, Straus and Giroux.

Meier, A. and Rudwick, E. (1973). Early boycotts of segregated schools: The case of Springfield, Ohio, 1922–1923. In Katz, M. (Ed.), *Education in American History: Readings on the Social Issues.* (pp. 290–300), New York: Praeger.

Merton, R.K. (1949) *Social Theory and Social Structure: Toward a Codification of Theory and Research*, Glencoe: Free Press.

Metz, M.H. (1978) *Classrooms and Corridors: The Crisis of Authority in Desegregated Secondary Schools*, Berkeley, CA: University of California Press.

Metz, M.H. (1986) *Different by Design: The Context and Character of Three Magnet Schools*, London: Routledge and Kegan Paul.

Meyer, J.W. (1977) 'The effects of education as an institution', *American Journal of Sociology*, **83**, 1, pp. 55–77.

Meyer, J.W. (1987) 'Implications of an institutional view of education for the study of educational effects', in Hallinan, M.T. (Ed.) *The Social Organization of Schools*, New York: Plenum, pp. 157–75.

Meyer, J.W. and Rowan, B. (1983) 'The structure of educational organizations', in Meyer, J.W. and Scott, W.R. (Eds.) *Organizational Environments: Ritual and Rationality*, Beverly Hills, CA: Sage.

Meyer, J.W. and Scott, W.R. (1983) *Organizational Environments: Ritual and Rationality*, Beverly Hills, CA: Sage.

Meyer, J.W., Scott, W.R. and Deal, T.E. (1983) 'Institutional and technical sources of organizational structure: Explaining the structure of educational organizations', in Meyer, J.W. and Scott, W.R. (Eds.) *Organizational Environments: Ritual and Rationality*, Beverly Hills, CA: Sage.

Michelson, S. (1972) 'Equal school resource allocation', *Journal of Human Resources*, **7**, pp. 283–306.

Miller, Z.L. (1981) 'The role and concept of neighborhood in American cities', In Fisher R. & P. Romanofsky (Eds.), *Community Organization for Urban Social Change: A historical Perspective*, (pp. 3–32), Westport, CT: Greenwood Press.

Miller, N. (1983) 'Peer relations in desegregated schools', in Epstein, J.L. and Karweit, N. (Eds.) *Friends in School. Patterns of Selection and Influence in Secondary Schools*, New York: Academic Press.

Miller, L. & Wolf, T.E. (1978) Staff development for school change: Theory and practice. *Teacher's College Record*, **80**, pp. 140–156.

Minzey, J.D. (1981) Community education and community schools. In D. Davies (Ed.), *Communities and their schools* (pp. 269–295). New York: McGraw Hill.

Miskel, C.G., Fevurly, R. and Stewart, J. (1979) 'Organizational structures and processes, perceived school effectiveness, loyalty, and job satisfaction', *Educational Administration Quarterly*, **15**, pp. 97–118.

Mohrman, A.M. Jr., Cooke, R.A. and Mohrman, S.A. (1978) 'Participation in decision making: A multidimensional perspective', *Educational Administration Quarterly*, **14**, pp. 13–29.

Moles, O.C. (1987) 'Who wants parent involvement? Interest, skills, and opportunities among parents and educators', *Education and Urban Society*, **19**, pp. 137–45.

MORGAN, D.L. and ALWIN, D.F. (1980) 'When less is more: School size and student social participation', *Social Psychology Quarterly*, **43**, 2, pp. 241–52.

MOROCCO, J.C. (1978) 'The relationship between the size of elementary schools and pupils perceptions of their environment', *Education*, **98**, pp. 451–4.

MORTIMORE, P., SAMMONS, P., STOLL, L., LEWIS, D. and ECOB, R. (1988) *School Matters*, Berkeley, CA: University of California Press.

MOSHER, R.L. (1979) *Adolescents' Development and Education*, Berkeley, CA: McCutchan.

MOSTELLER, F. and MOYNIHAN, D.P. (Eds.) (1972) *On Equality of Educational Opportunity*, New York: Random House.

MOWRY, C. (1972) 'Investigations of the effects of parent participation in Head Start: Non-technical report', Washington, DC: Department of Health, Education, and Welfare. [ED 080 216]

MURNANE, R.J. (1981) 'Evidence, analysis, and unanswered questions', *Harvard Education Review*, **51**, pp. 483–9.

MURPHY, J. (1988) 'Methodological, measurement, and the conceptual problems in the study of instructional leadership', *Educational Evaluation and Policy Analysis*, **10**, 2, pp. 117–39.

MURPHY, J., WEIL, M., HALLINGER, P. and MITMAN, A. (1985) 'School effectiveness: A framework', *The Educational Forum*, **49**, pp. 361–74.

MYERS, D.E., BHOER, K., MILNE, A.M. and GINSBURG, A. (1987) 'Student discipline and high school performance', *Sociology of Education*, **60**, pp. 18–33.

NATIONAL ASSESSMENT FOR EDUCATIONAL PROGRESS (1984) *Reading Report Cards: Trends in Reading Over Four National Assessments, 1971–1984*, Princeton, NJ: Educational Testing Service.

NATIONAL CATHOLIC EDUCATIONAL ASSOCIATION (1985a) *The Catholic High School: A National Portrait*, Washington, DC: National Catholic Educational Association.

NATIONAL CATHOLIC EDUCATIONAL ASSOCIATION (1985b) *Sharing the Faith: The Beliefs and Values of Catholic High School Teachers*, Washington, DC: National Catholic Educational Association.

NATIONAL CATHOLIC EDUCATIONAL ASSOCIATION, (1986) *Catholic High Schools: Their Impact on Low-income Students*, Washington DC: National Catholic Educational Association.

NATIONAL COALITION OF ADVOCATES FOR CHILDREN (1985) *Barriers to Excellence: Our Children at Risk*, Boston: Author.

NATRIELLO, G. (Ed.) (1986) *School Dropouts*, New York: Teachers' College Press.

NEUFELD, B. (1984) 'Inside organization: High school teachers effort' to influence their work.' Doctoral Thesis, Graduate School of Education, Harvard University.

NEWMANN, F.M. (1981) 'Reducing student alienation in high schools: Implications of theory', *Harvard Educational Review*, **51**, 4, pp. 546–64.

NEWMANN, F.M. and OLIVER, D.W. (1967) 'Education and community', *Harvard Educational Review*, **37**, 1, pp. 61–106.

NEWMANN, F.M., RUTTER, R.A. and SMITH, M.S. (1989) 'Organizational factors affecting school sense of efficacy, community, and expectations', *Sociology of Education*, (in press).

NIESSER, U. (1986) *The School Achievement of Minority Children: New Perspectives*, Hillsdale, N.J.: Lawrence Erlbaum Associates.

NODDINGS, N. (1988) 'An ethic of caring and its implications for instructional arrangements', *American Journal of Education*, **96**, pp. 215–31.

OAKES, J. (1985) *Keeping Track: How Schools Structure Inequality*, New Haven: Yale University Press.

OGBU, J.U. (1974) *The Next Generation: An Ethnography of Education in an Urban Neighborhood*, New York: Academic Press.

OGBU, J.U. (1985) 'A cultural ecology of competence among inner-city blacks', in SPENCER, M.B. BROOKINS, G.K. and ALLEN, W.R. (Eds.) *Beginnings: The Social and Affective Development of Black Children*, Hillsdale, NJ: Lawrence Erlbaum Associates, Inc.

OGBU, J.U. (1986) 'The consequences of the American caste system', in NIESSER, U. (Ed.) *The School Achievement of Minority Children: New Perspectives*, Hillsdale, NJ: Lawrence Erlbaum Associates.

OGBU, J.U. (1988) 'Class stratification, racial stratification, and schooling', in WEIS, L. (Ed.) *Class, Race, and Gender in American Education*, Albany, NY: State University of New York Press.

OTTO, L.B. (1982) 'Extracurricular activities', in WALBERG, H.J. (Ed.) *Improving Educational Standards and Productivity*, Berkeley, CA: McCutchan, pp. 217–33.

PAGE, R.N. (1987) 'Lower-track classes at a college-preparatory high school: A caricature of educational encounters', in SPINDLER, G. and SPINDLER, L. (Eds.) *Interpretative Ethnography of Education*, Hillsdale, NJ: Erlbaum.

PALLAS, A.M. (1988) 'School climate in American high schools', *Teacher's College Record*, **89**, pp. 541–54.

PAPAGIANNIS, G.J., KLEES, S.J. and BICKEL, R.N. (1982) 'Toward a political economy of educational innovation', *Review of Educational Research*, **52**, 2, pp. 245–90.

PARSONS, T. (1951) *The Social System*, Glencoe: Free Press.

PARSONS, T. (1960) 'Some ingredients of a general theory of formal organization', in *Structure and Process in Modern Societies*, Glencoe, IL: Free Press.

PESHKIN, A. (1986) *God's Choice: The Total World of a Fundamental Christian School*. Chicago: University of Chicago Press.

PETERSON, K.D. (1989) Secondary school principals and instructional leadership: Complexities in a diverse role. Unpublished manuscript for the *National Center on Effective Secondary Schools*, University of Wisconsin-Madison.

PETERSON, P.L. WILKINSON, L. and HALLINAN, M. (Eds.) (1984) *The Social Context of Instruction*, New York: Academic Press.

PHILLIPS, S.D., SMITH, M.C. and WITTE, J.F. (1985) 'Parents and schools: Staff report to the study commission on the quality of education in metropolitan Milwaukee', in HENDERSON A.T. (Ed.) *The Evidence Continues to Grow: Parent Involvement Improves Student Achievement*, Washington DC: National Committee for Citizens in Education.

PINK, W. (1984) 'Creating effective schools', *The Educational Forum*, **49**, 1, pp. 91–107.

PITNER, N.J. (1986) 'Substitutes for principal leader behavior: An exploratory study', *Educational Administration Quarterly*, **22**, 2, pp. 23–42.

PITNER, N.J. and OGAWA, R.T. (1981) 'Organizational leadership: The case of the school superintendent', *Educational Administration Quarterly*, **17**, 2, pp. 45–65.

PORTER, A.C. (1983) 'The role of testing in effective schools: How can testing improve school effectiveness?' *American Education*, pp. 25–8.

POWELL, A.G., FARRAR, E. and COHEN, D.K. (1985) *The Shopping Mall High School: Winners and Losers in the Educational Marketplace*, Boston: Houghton Mifflin.

PURKEY, S.C. and SMITH, M.S. (1983) 'Effective schools: A review', *Elementary School Journal*, **83**, pp. 427–54.

PURKEY, S.C. and SMITH, M.S. (1985) 'School reform: The distinct policy implications of the effective schools literature', *Elementary School Journal*, **85**, pp. 353–89.

RALPH, J.H. and FENNESSEY, J. (1983) 'Science or reform: Some questions about the effective school model', *Phi Delta Kappan*, **64**, pp. 689–94.

RAUDENBUSH, S.W. (1988) 'Educational applications of hierarchical linear models: A review', *Journal of Educational Statistics*, **13**, pp. 85–116.

RAUDENBUSH, S.W. and BRYK, A.S. (1988) 'Methodological advances in analyzing the effects of schools and classrooms on student learning', in ROTHKOPF, E.Z. (Ed.) *Review of Research in Education 15*, Washington, DC: American Educational Research Association.

RAUDENBUSH, S.W. and BRYK, A.S. (1986) 'A hierarchical model for studying school effects', *Sociology of Education*, **59**(1), pp. 1–17.

RAVITCH, D. (1983) *The Troubled Crusade*, New York: Basic Books.

RAYWID, M.A. (1985) 'Family choice arrangements in public schools: A review of the literature', *Review of Educational Research*, **55**, pp. 435–67.

RESNICK, D.P. and RESNICK, L.B. (1985) 'Standards, curriculum, and performance: A historical and comparative perspective', *Educational Researcher*, **14**, 4, pp. 5–21.

RIORDAN, C. (1985) 'Public and catholic schooling: The effect of gender context policy', *American Journal of Education*, **93**, pp. 518–40.

ROCK, D.A., EKSTROM, R.B., GOERTZ, M.C., HILTON, T.L. and POLLACK, J. (1985) *Excellence in High School Education: Cross-sectional Study 1972–1980*, First report, Princeton, NJ: Educational Testing Service.

ROGERS, D. (1968) *110 Livingston Street: Politics and Bureaucracy in the New York City Schools*, New York: Random House,

ROGERS, D. and CHUNG, N.H. (1983) *110 Livingston Street Revisited: Decentralization in Action*, New York: New York University Press.

ROSENBAUM, J.E. (1976) *Inequality: The Hidden Curriculum of High School Tracking*, New York: John Wiley & Sons.

ROSENBAUM, J.E. (1980) 'Track misperceptions and frustrated college plans: An analysis of the effects of track and track perceptions in the NLS', *Sociology of Education*, **53**, pp. 74–88.

ROSENHOLTZ, S.J. (1985) 'Effective schools: Interpreting the evidence', *American Journal of Education*, **93**, pp. 352–88.

ROSENHOLTZ, S.J. (1987) 'Education reform strategies: Will they increase teacher commitment?' *American Journal of Education*, **95**, pp. 534–62.

ROUSSEAU, D.M. (1985) 'Issues of level in organizational research: Multilevel and crosslevel perspectives', *Research in Organizational Behavior* 7, Greenwich, CT: JIA Press.

ROSSMAN, G., CORBETT H.D. and FIRESTONE, W. (1988) *Change and Effectiveness in Schools: A Cultural Perspective*, New York: SUNY Albany Press.

ROWAN, B., BOSSART, S.T. and DWYER, D.C. (1983) 'Research on effective schools: A cautionary note', *Educational Researcher*, April, pp. 21–31.

RUTTER, M., MAUGHAN, B., MORTIMORE, P., OUTSON, J. and SMITH, A. (1979) *Fifteen Thousand Hours: Secondary Schools and their Effects on Children*, Cambridge, MA: Harvard University Press.

RUTTER, R. (1986) *Facilitating Teacher Engagement*, Madison, WI: National Center on Effective Secondary Schools.

SALGANIK, L.H. and KARWEIT, N. (1982) 'Volunteerism and governance in education', *Sociology of Education*, **55**, pp. 152–61.

SALMON, P. (1979) 'The role of the peer group', in COLEMAN, J.C. (Ed.) *The School Years: Current Issues in the Socialization of Young People*, London: Methuen.

SARASON, S.B. (1971) *The Culture of the School and the Problem of Change*, Boston: Allyn and Bacon.

SCHEIN, E.H. (1985) *Organizational Culture and Leadership*, San Francisco: Jossey Bass.

SCHOFIELD, J.W. and SAGAR, H.A. (1983) 'Desegregation, school practices, and student race relations', in ROSSELL, C.H. and HAWLEY, W.D. (Eds.) *The Consequences of School Desegregation*, Philadelphia: Temple University Press, pp. 58–102.

SCHUNK, D.H. and HANSON, A.R. (1983) 'Peer models: Influence on children's self-efficacy and achievement', *Journal of Educational Psychology*, **77**, 3, pp. 313–22.

SCHWAB, R.L. and IWANIKI, E.F. (1982) 'Perceived role conflict, role ambiguity, and teacher burnout', *Educational Administration Quarterly*, **18**, 1, pp. 60–74.

SCHWARTZ, G., MERTEN, D. and BURSIK, R.J., JR. (1987) 'Teaching styles and performance values in junior high school: The impersonal, nonpersonal and personal', *American Journal of Education*, **95**, pp. 346–70.

SCOTT, L.K. (1978) 'Charismatic authority in the rational organization', *Educational Administration Quarterly*, **14**, 2, pp. 43–62.

SCOTT, W.R. (1981) *Organizations: Rational, Natural, and Open Systems*, Englewood Cliffs, NJ: Prentice-Hall.

SCOTT, W.R. and MEYER, J.W. (1988) 'Environmental linkages and organizational complexity: Public and private schools', in JAMES, T. and LEVIN, H.M. (Eds.) *Comparing Public and Private Schools, Vol. 1: Institutions and Organizations*, Philadelphia: Falmer Press.

SEBRING, P.A. (1987) 'Consequences of differential amounts of high school coursework: Will the new graduation requirements help?' *Educational Evaluation and Policy Analysis*, **9**, pp. 258–73.

SEDLAK, M.W., WHEELER, C.W., PULLIN, D.C. and CUSIK, P.A. (1986) *Selling Students Short*, New York: Teachers College Press.

SEEMAN, M. (1975) 'Alienation studies', *Annual Review of Sociology* (Vol. 1). Palo Alto, CA: Annual Reviews.

SEWELL, W.H., HALLER, A.O. and PORTES, A. (1969) 'The educational and early occupational attainment process', *American Sociological Review*, pp. 82–92.

SEYFARTH, J.T. and BOST, W.A. (1986) 'Teacher turnover and the quality of worklife in schools: An empirical study', *Journal of Research and Development in Education*, **20**, pp. 1–6.

SHAFER, W.E. and OLEXA, C. (1971) *Tracking and Opportunity: The Locking-out Process and Beyond*, Scranton, PA: Chandler.

SHULMAN, L.S. (1986) 'Paradigms and research programs in the study of teaching: A contemporary perspective', In WITTROCK M.C. (Ed.), *Handbook of Research on Teaching*, (3rd Ed. — pp. 3–36).

SHWEDER, R.A. (1984) 'Anthropology's romantic rebellion against enlightment, or there is more to thinking than reason and evidence', in SHWEDER, R.A. and LE VINE, R.A. (Eds.) *Culture Theory: Essays on Mind, Self and Emotion*, New York: Cambridge University Press.

SHWEDER, R.A. (1986) 'Divergent realities', in FISHER, D.W. and SHWEDER, R.A. (Eds.) *Metatheory in Social Science: Pluralisms and Subjectivities*, Chicago: University of Chicago Press.

Sizer, T.R. (1984) *Horace's Compromise: The Dilemma of the American High School*, Boston: Houghton Miflin.

SIROTNIK, K.A. (1982) 'The contextual correlates of the relative expenditures of classroom time on instruction and behavior: An exploratory study of secondary schools and classes', *American Educational Research Journal*, **19**, pp. 275–92.

SLAVIN, R.E. (1983) *Cooperative Learning*, New York: Longman.

SOAR, R. and SOAR, R. (1979) 'Emotional climate and management', in PETERSON, P. and WALBERG, H. (Eds.) *Research on Teaching: Concepts, Findings, and Implications*, Berkeley, CA: McCutchan.

SORENSON, A.B. (1970) 'Organizational differentiation of students and educational opportunity', *Sociology of Education*, **43**, pp. 355–76.

SORENSON, A.B. (1987) 'The organizational differentiation of students in schools as an opportunity structure', in HALLINAN, M.T. (Ed.) *The Social Organization of Schools*, New York: Plenum Press, pp. 103–29.

SORENSON, A.B. and HALLINAN, M.T. (1986) 'Effects of ability grouping on growth in academic achievement', *American Educational Research Journal*, **23**, pp. 519–42.

SORENSON, A.B. & HALLINAN, M.T. (1977) 'A reconceptualization of school effects', *Sociology of Education*, **50**, (October), 273–289.

SPENCE, J.T. (Ed.) (1984) *Achievement and Achievement Motives*, San Francisco: W.H. Freeman & Co.

SPENCER, M.B., BROOKINS, G.K. and ALLEN, W.R. (1985) *Beginnings: The Social and Affective Development of Black Childarn*, Hillsdale, NJ: Lawrence Erlbaum Associates, Inc.

SOROKIN, P. (1928) *Contemporary Sociology Theories*, New York: Harper and Brothers.

SPRING, J. (1972) *Education and the Rise of the Corporate State*, Boston: Beacon Press.

STALLINGS, J. and MOHLMAN, G. (1981) 'School policy, leadership style, teacher change, and student behavior in eight schools', (Final report, Grant No. NIE-G-80-0010). Washington, DC: National Institute of Education. *Cited* in GOOD, T.L. and BROPHY, J.E. 'School effects', in WITTROCK, M.C. (Ed.) *Handbook of*

Research on Teaching, New York: MacMillan Publishing.
STARK, J.S. and LOWTHER, M.A. (1984) 'Predictors of teacher's preferences concerning their evaluation', *Educational Administration Quarterly*, **20**, 4, pp. 76–106.
STEVENSON, R.B. (1987a) 'Staff development for effective secondary schools: A synthesis of research', *Teaching and Teacher Education*, **3**.
STEVENSON, R.B. (1987b) 'Autonomy and support: The dual needs of urban high schools', *Urban Education*, **22**, pp. 366–86.
STODOLSKY, S. (1988) *The Subject Matters*, Chicago: University of Chicago Press.
SWAP, S.M. (1984) *Enhancing Parent Involvement in Schools*, Boston, MA: Center for parenting studies.
SWEENEY, J. (1982) 'Research synthesis on effective school leadership', *Educational Leadership*, **39**, pp. 346–52.
TALBERT, J.E. (1988) 'Conditions of public and private school organizations and notions of effective schools', in JAMES, T. and LEVIN, H.M. (Eds.) *Comparing Public and Private Schools, Vol. 1: Institutions and Organizations*, Philadelphia: Falmer Press.
TUCKMAN, B.W., STEBER, J.M. and HYMAN, R.T. (1979) 'Judging the effectiveness of teaching styles: The perceptions of principals', *Educational Administration Quarterly*, **15**, pp. 104–15.
TYACK, D. (1974) *The One Best System*. Cambridge, MA: Harvard University Press.
VALLI, L. (1986) 'Tracking: Can it benefit low achieving students?' Paper presented at the annual meeting of the American Educational Research Association, San Francisco, CA.
VANFOSSEN, B.C., JONES, J.D. and SPADE, J.Z. (1987) 'Curriculum tracking and status maintenance', *Sociology of Education*, **60**, pp. 104–22.
VIOLAS, P. (1978) *The training of the urban working class: A history of twentieth century American education*. Chicago: Rand McNally.
WAGENAAR, T.C. (1977) 'School achievement level viv-a-vis community involvement and support: An empirical assessment.' Paper presented at Annual Meeting of American Sociological Association (September).
WALBERG, H. (Ed.) (1982) *Improving Educational Standards and Productivity*, Berkeley, CA: McCutchan.
WALBERG, H. and FOWLER, W.J. (1987) 'Expenditure and size efficiencies of public school districts', *Educational Researcher*, **16**, pp. 5–13.
WALLER, W. (1932) *The Sociology of Teaching*, New York: Russell & Russell.
WAYLAND, S. (1958) 'The school as community center', in BERIDAY, G. and VOLPICELLI, L. (Eds.) *Public Education in America: A New Interpretation of Purpose and Practice*, New York: Harper and Row.
WAXMAN, H.C. and SULTON, L.D. (1984) 'Evaluating effects of nonclass experiences on students' educational aspirations and academic achievement', *Psychological Reports*, **54**, pp. 619–22.
WEBER, M. (1924) *The Theory of Social and Economic Organization*, in HENDERSON, A.M. and PARSONS, T. (Eds.) Glencoe, IL: Free Press (translated in 1947).
WEHLAGE, G. (1982) *Effective Programs for Marginal High School Students*, Madison, WI: Center for Effective Secondary Schools.
WEHLAGE, G. and RUTTER, R.A. (1986) 'Dropping out: How much do schools

contribute to the problem', in Natriello, G. (Ed.) *School Dropouts: Patterns and Policies*, New York: Teachers College Press.

Wehlage, G., Rutter, R.A., Smith, G.A., Lesko, N. and Fernandez, R.R. (1989) *Reducing the Risk: Schools as Communities of Support*, Philadelphia: Falmer Press.

Wehlage, G., Stone, C. and Kleibard, H.M. (1980) *Dropouts and Schools: Case Studies of the Dilemmas Educators Face*, Madison: University of Wisconsin.

Weick, K.E. (1976) 'Educational organizations as loosely coupled systems', *Adminsitrative Science Quarterly*, **21**, pp. 1–19.

Weinberg, I. (1967) The English Public Schools. New York: Atheron Press.

Weinberg, M. (1983) *The Search for Quality Integraded Education: Policy and Research on Minority Students in School and College*. Westport, CT: Greenwood press.

Weis, L. (Ed.) (1988) *Class, Race, and Gender in American Education*, Albany, NY: State University of New York Press.

Wellisch, J.B., MacQueen, A.H., Carriere, R.A. and Duck, C.A. (1978) 'School management and organization in successful schools', *Sociology of Education*, **51**, pp. 211–26.

Willie, C.V. (1978) *The Sociology of Urban Education*, Lexington, MA: D.C. Heath.

Wilkinson, R. (1964) *Gentlemanly power: British leadership and the public school tradition*. London: Oxford University Press.

Williams, M.R. (1989) *Neighborhood Organizing for Urban School Reform*, New York: Teacher's College Press.

Wilson, W.J. (1987) *The Truly Disadvantged: The Inner City, the Underclass, and Public Policy*, Chicago: University of Chicago Press.

Wilson, B.L., Herriot, R.E., & Firestone, W.A. (1988) Explaining differences between elementary and secondary schools: Individual, organizational, and institutional perspectives. To appear in P. Thurston & P. Zodhiates (Eds.), *Advances in Educational Administration*, Vol. 2. New York: JAI Press.

Wise, A. (1979) *Legislated Learning: The Bureaucratization of the American Classroom*, Berkeley: University of California Press.

Wolcott, H.F. (1973) *The Man in the Principal's Office: An Ethnography*, New York: Holt, Rinehart, & Winston.

Zirkel, P.A. and Greenwood, S.C. (1987) 'Effective schools and effective principals: Effective research?' *Teachers College Record*, **89**, pp. 255–67.

Commentary

Political Institutions and School Organization

John E. Chubb

Over the last decade or so researchers have made tremendous progress in solving one of the great puzzles in American education, the puzzle of school performance. For many years, dating from about 1966 when the first 'Coleman Report' appeared, researchers could find little systematic relationship between school performance — usually measured as student achievement — and the school characteristics commonly thought to produce it — for example, student-teacher ratios; expenditures per pupil; physical and material resources; and teacher compensation and education. Defying casual observation and common sense, schools themselves did not seem to matter. Performance seemed to be wholly determined by characteristics of students and student bodies and not — as puzzling as it might be — by characteristics of schools themselves.

With the emergence of a new kind of research, however, the puzzle began to be solved. School characteristics that had not received much attention in analyses of student achievement emerged in study after study as correlates of school performance. What was different about these characteristics was that they pertained mostly to the internal organization of the school. The characteristics that had previously attracted attention were primarily economic inputs. During the 1960s and 1970s research on student achievement tended to conceive of schooling in terms of a production function, an unspecified process that somehow converted economic inputs into educational outputs. The job of research was to gauge the sensitivity of important school outputs, such as student achievement, to major school inputs such as facilities, teachers, and supplies. Since the late 1970s, however, research has been reoriented — away from production functions and toward the production process itself. The result is an abundance of evidence, still rapidly accumulating, that schools really matter, and that school organization may hold the key to school performance.

It is the considerable burden of Bryk, Lee and Smith to weigh this new evidence and to assess the new perspective that lies behind it. I say considerable burden because recent research on school organization is remarkable for its diversity and its volume. To their great credit, Bryk, Lee and Smith examine roughly 300 books, articles, and monographs, and offer a balanced evaluation and integrated summary of them. Their chapter is the most ambitious effort to date to size up the burgeoning literature on school organization and its effects. And for that reason alone their chapter important. But it is also important, in my view, for helping to crystallize is another puzzle about school performance, one that like the original puzzle may require a reorientation of research and thinking, if it is to be solved.

Bryk, Lee and Smith reveal a major tension in the organization of American high schools. It is a tension that is manifest in every aspect of school organization — in leadership, goal setting, decisionmaking, staff relations, and teaching. It is also a tension that influences students. If it is severe, student achievement suffers. If the tension is somehow moderated, student achievement benefits from a more effective school. The tension, in essence, is between two forms of organization, one more classically bureaucratic and the other more professional and collegial, struggling to shape the modern high school. The tension is not new or unique. Charles Bidwell highlighted the tension in schools in a famous review essay published in 1965. And in her survey of theories of control in organizations, Weiss reveals that the tension is a general problem, affecting the management of many organizations. The tension in contemporary high schools is different, however. There is reason to believe it is getting progressively worse, and there is steadily mounting evidence that it is damaging school effectiveness.

The bulk of Bryk, Lee and Smith's chapter is devoted to reviewing this evidence. It must be said at the outset that the new research on school organization, despite its incredible volume and diversity, is far from conclusive. Research has often been narrowly focused, examining individual parts of school organization in isolation from other parts, when all of the parts are actually interdependent. Research has also relied very heavily on ethnographic methods that while highly revealing in crucial cases — for example, in effective urban schools — have disclosed much less that can be generalized with real confidence. Research using large quantitative data sets, particularly *High School and Beyond,* has been handicapped by a paucity of organizational measures and by statistical problems such as selection bias, reciprocal causality, and the variability of school effects within individual schools. The estimated influence of school organization on student achievement has therefore been unusually dependent on the specification of the statistical model used to gauge it. According to Bryk, Lee and Smith the most consistently important influence on student achievement that occurs within schools is course-taking. But even if that is true — and my research, with Terry Moe, suggests that that influence has been exaggerated — the finding that course-taking promotes achievement begs more than answers the question of school effectiveness.[1] The unanswered question of why some schools are so much more effective than others at getting students to take academic courses is not much different from the original and basic question of why some schools are more effective than others at getting students to learn.

These methodological problems do not obscure the central tension in school organization, however. At some risk of oversimplification, most of the research reviewed by Bryk, Lee and Smith can be placed into one of two categories. One category includes research on what might be called non-bureaucratic aspects of school organization. The research in this category, while perhaps more suspect methodologically, provides a lot of evidence that schools organized non-bureaucratically, or characterized by traits often missing in bureaucracies, have positive influences on teacher morale and efficacy and on student satisfaction and achievement. The organizational qualities falling into this category include shared values or 'value communities', parent-school bonding, strong educational leadership, vigorous school culture, staff collegiality, a true sense of school community, and other more specific traits of what Moe and I call team-like organization.

The second category of research includes studies, often more rigorous and numerous, of more classically bureaucratic aspects of school organization. These studies tend to show effects on teachers and students that are quite mixed. For example, increasing school size provides economic economies of scale and enables more schools to meet the specialized needs of more students. But increasing school size may also interfere with the development of a school community, and may exacerbate differences in student achievement as unmotivated students are accommodated in undemanding courses. Modern school personnel systems protect schools from certain forms of political influence and administrative caprice, but by sanctioning conflict between teachers and principals and among teachers themselves, these systems also interfere with the development of school communities. The departmentalization of teaching staffs and the differentiation of academic programs have positive effects for some teachers (depending on the particular department) and for some students (perhaps especially the students in the top academic track). But the overall effects of these two bureaucratic developments are unknown and may well be negative. Both interfere with the social integration of the school and may thereby exacerbate problems such as the alienation and isolation of teachers and students.

The tension between the organizational forces described in these two categories of research certainly constitutes one of the most serious problems facing American high schools today. As Bryk, Lee and Smith suggest in their conclusion, if the recent research on school organization is basically correct — if effective schools need to organize more along the lines of communities or teams and less according to the hierarchical principles of bureaucratic organization — American high schools may be in deep trouble. The reason is that the history of school organization has tended to follow the classic principles of consolidation, centralization, standardization, and routinization. Organizational trends reflecting these principles continue apace today. If these trends continue, it is possible that they could force the establishment of a new model of effective schooling based on classic bureaucratic principles — for example, a model like the stereotype of Japanese education. But since the tension between bureaucratic and non-bureaucratic organizational forces has persisted so long, it is more likely that it will simply continue to cause problems for school effectiveness.

This pessimistic conclusion is not shared by everyone. There is considerable enthusiasm among certain researchers and many school reformers that the tension can be overcome. Schools can be made to develop the requisite organizational attributes of effectiveness. Principals and teachers can be trained to function more professionally and collegially. Schools can be freed from some of their hierarchical constraints and permitted to shape their goals more internally and consensually. Yet, there is little reason for any confidence that these things can be done. And there is ample reason to believe they cannot. The reason for pessimism is that research on school organization has really not solved the puzzle of school performance. Research appears to be well on the way to solving part of the puzzle, the part that links school organization, and the tension within it, to student achievement. But research has scarcely addressed the other major part of the puzzle: why schools have generally not become effectively organized and have generally failed to reduce the basic tensions that impair them. Until that part of the puzzle is solved, it is presumptuous to believe that researchers and reformers, armed with new evidence on the organization of effective schools, can accomplish what researchers and reformers in the past could not.

So, what does the new organizational research have to say about this part of the puzzle? What accounts for the variation in the organization of

American high schools? Why are some schools organized so much more effectively than others? The truth is, the new organizational research has not paid serious attention to the causes of school organization. To be sure, there is recognition in the literature that organizational tensions have resulted from increasing demands from the school environment. As more interests, representing more social, professional, and business groups, have asked the schools to do more for them, governments at all levels have imposed more rules and regulations on schools and monitored their operations more closely. These interventions have often conflicted with the efforts of teachers and principals within particular schools to organize themselves in the manner that they consider most effective for meeting the needs and demands of their immediate clients — including clients who may have pressured the government for assistance.

Of course, it is only natural that the new organizational literature would look outside the school, to the school environment, for an explanation of school organization. It is received wisdom among organization theorists that schools are 'open systems' and consequently products of their environment. Schools, like any organization, survive through exchanges with their environment, taking in resources, support, and demands, and putting forth products that the environment values. It would stand to reason, then, that organization research would carefully probe the school environment for sources of organizational ineffectiveness. Yet, that has not been the case.

In Bryk, Lee and Smith's chapter, the discussion of research on the school 'environment' looks at school size, student bodies, family involvement, and school governance. Two things are especially interesting about this research. The first is that the influences of school size, student bodies, and family involvement should be classified as external or exogenous influences, essentially beyond the control of schools. This implies that schools cannot affect their size, influence their student bodies, or structure their relationships with families in order to enhance their effectiveness. While this may widely be true, the possibility that it is ought to raise questions. But such questions would have to be directed to the system of governance that puts such matters beyond school control.

That brings up the second interesting thing about Bryk, Lee and Smith's review of research on the school environment. There is scarcely any serious research on the influence of government on school organization. To be fair, Bryk, Lee and Smith leave much of the task of reviewing this research to other contributors to this book. But as Weiss reveals in her chapter, there is simply not much to review — at least not much that focuses on the problems of school organization per se. As Weiss's chapter makes abundantly clear, there is good reason to take a close look at how governments control schools. By her count there are five different methods that governments may use to control organizations under their jurisdiction. And there are almost countless ways in which these methods can come into conflict with one another and cause debilitating problems for organizations. Unfortunately, Weiss is compelled to discuss these problems in the abstract, because research on school organization has simply not examined the consequences of government control very carefully or seriously.

Partly I suspect this dearth of attention has occurred for the same reason that school organization received so little attention for so long in analyses of student achievement. Just as economists, oriented little by organizational concerns, once dominated research on student achievement and focused on production functions, sociologists, oriented little by political and governmental concerns, now dominate research on school effectiveness and focus on matters that are more narrowly organizational. This is all part of the inevitable, though sometimes regrettable, division of labor in social science research. If and when political scientists become more interested in school organization and performance, the role of government will come into somewhat sharper focus. Yet even then it is possible that the role of government will not be adequately revealed. Partly this is because political science does not have a great track record in this field. It has produced a lot of rigorous research on the often minimal organizational consequences of such reforms as non-partisan and at-large school board elections, and a lot of less rigorous but much more interesting research on the problems of implementing special education programs. But the more serious problem with research on the influence of government on school organization is that the largest role of government is fundamentally difficult to discern.

The reason that the role of government is so difficult to appreciate fully is that in very basic ways the role of government does not vary from one public school to the next. All public schools are governed by democratic institutions of the same basic form at the local level and then organized into larger systems of schools governed by institutions, again of the same basic form, at the state level. All of these systems are then subject to the influence and control of one set of democratic insitutions at the national level. It has been said that public schools are governed by the 'one best system', and in formal respects this is nearly so: there is basically one system, though it is not necessarily best. This makes research on the role of government tough. While any researcher would probably acknowledge that government institutions shape the behavior of the individuals and organizations that must function within them, it is difficult for researchers to analyze or even conceptualize the influence of institutions when the structure of those instutions does not vary.

There are good reasons to believe, however, that researchers should try. One reason is historical. The history of school governance and organization is in part a story of growing tension between increasingly bureaucratic methods of government control of schools and ongoing efforts by teachers and principals to perform educational tasks that resist bureaucratic control. To put it simply, researchers ought to be more impressed than they apparently are by the longevity and entrenchment of the organizational tension that now plagues so many public schools. Researchers ought to at least suspect that this chronic tension is inherent in the traditional structure of public school governance and control.

A second reason why researchers should show greater curiosity in the institutions of school control is empirical. The research that Moe and I have now completed using the *High School and Beyond* and the *Administrator and Teacher Survey* data sets provides considerable evidence of the importance of the institutional structure governing public schools. In that research we found that, all things being equal, schools with greater control over school policies and personnel — or schools subject to less external authority over these matters — are more effectively organized than schools that have less organizational autonomy. We also found that autonomy from control is the most important determinant of the effectiveness of school organization. The specific reasons for concern about school control in the public sector are that, all things being equal, public schools are substantially less likely to be granted autonomy from authoritative external control (i.e., from superintendents, district offices, and boards) than are private schools; and as important, schools in urban systems — where the problems of school performance are most grave and where the efforts to solve them have been the most bureaucratic — are much less likely, all else being equal, to enjoy autonomy.

There is another reason for researchers to be more concerned about the one best system, though, and that reason is theoretical. Autonomy from excessive external control, which may be vital to effective school organization, is to an important degree incompatible with the direct governance of schools. Public schools are not supposed to be governed by the desires of parents and students or directed by the judgment of teachers and principals. To simply state the obvious, public schools are organized to satisfy the needs and interests of society generally and of a host of social and professional groups besides those with a stake in a particular school. This does not mean that it will be impossible to strike a balance between society's need for control over schools and a school's need for sufficient autonomy to organize itself into an effective teaching institution. But it does mean that a proper balance will be difficult to strike. Especially if striking that balance implies the provision of greater school-site autonomy, the interests that have long prospered from greater centralization will see the interests that have long prospered from greater centralization will see such changes for what they are — reallocations of power over education — and will resist them strenuously.

It is for all of these reasons that we believe serious analyses of the influence of school governance on school organization should consider the basic structure of political institutions, and serious efforts at reform should consider alternatives to those institutions. One institutional alternative is the market, an institution that would enable public education to be governed with less reliance on troublesome bureaucratic controls. The advantages and disadvantages of market controls are well beyond the scope of this commentary, but one advantage merits brief mention. It is said by Bryk, Lee and Smith that 'the micro-economic argument [for market control] bears little relation to ideas about schools as communities'. This assessment is simply wrong. Perhaps the greatest advantage of a system of market controls is that it would encourage school authorities to structure educational decision-making in a way that responds most efficiently to the demands of clients, who would now enjoy the freedom to choose their schools. This would inevitably lead to a restructuring of school authority toward greater school autonomy. And greater school autonomy would, in turn, permit schools to develop the kinds of team-like or collegial organizations that seem to be essential for effectiveness. Far from being antithetical to school communities, market institutions may provide the only methods of school control that permit communities to flourish. But be this as it may, political institutions, for reasons that research has yet to adequately illuminate, have not generally encouraged the development of effective school organizations.

Note

1 All personal research referenced in this commentary is reported in John E. Chubb and Terry M. Moe (1990) *Politics, Markets and America's Schools*, Washington, D.C.: The Brookings Institution.

Reference

BIDWELL, C.E. (1965) 'The school as a formal organization', in MARCH, J.G. (Ed.) *Handbook of Organizations*, Chicago: Rand McNally.

Commentary

School Organization and the Quest for Community

Cora B. Marrett

Questions about choice and control invariably raise questions about organization, about the appropriate ways for structuring the world of formal education. But discussions on appropriate forms cannot — or at least should not — proceed, oblivious to the matter of goals. It would be foolhardy to design a structure with no regard for the ends it is to achieve and the kinds of activities it is to incorporate.

Using a model based on goals to plan an educational system could prove difficult, given the myriad of objectives assigned to that system. The objectives are not necessarily overly diffuse, however. Levin (1990) reminds us that in American society schools, and especially public schools, have had two general missions: to foster the development of individuals, and to promote the general welfare. Much of the effort to restructure schools stems from dissatisfaction with the ability of these institutions to serve both missions. The missions are not always compatible, however, nor do they necessarily require the same structure. We can spur performance through close monitoring and autocratic procedures, but at costs we might deem excessive (for more on this point, see Bryk, Lee and Smith, in this volume; and the classic study on leadership styles and their consequences, White and Lippitt, 1960). To frame that discussion, I have chosen to emphasize the social goals of education. I do so, given the criticism often raised that schools have failed as communities, as settings in which individuals learn about one another and learn to work cooperatively. Schools, according to this argument, operate all too often as alienating environments, dividing teachers from administrators, students from teachers, and students from the contexts they know. But so chaotic are these contexts at times, that if the school fails to provide opportunities for shared experiences, the student will not have them. The school 'must be in some respects a haven for its students, capable of shutting out some of the most destructive aspects of city life'. It must be as well an enterprise in which young people 'learn to take responsibility for the well-being of any group they are in' (Gardner, 1989).

The Structure of Education in the United States

One can view education in the United States as constituting a system: a set of units linked formally to one another. The school represents one of the units, although it, too, consists of its own parts. Schools generally are aggregated into a larger unit, such as a district, which may itself report to a higher level. The system is vertically integrated, with each level in some way responsible to the level above it. Discussions on control generally have to do with this question: at what level within this system should responsibility rest?

Weiss (1990), as well as Bryk, Lee and Smith (1990), contends that the issue of control cannot be confined to the formal hierarchy of education and represents the school system as an open system. Schools are linked to segments which, at least formally, have no direct line of authority over what takes place within the system itself. Some groups are more intimately involved than are others. Parents, businesses, professional associations all shape in some way the course of events within schools. Weiss maintains, consequently, that the study of control should recognize market control, parental control, and political control; that administrative or managerial control — control over divisions within the bureaucracy — is not the sole type that can be exercised. The distinction among types of influence is useful, for it draws our attention to the fact that the educational system is not isolated from its social context, even if elements in that context have no managerial role to play.

I have omitted the fifth category in the Weiss assessment — control through values and ideas — for it strikes me as somewhat different from the other four. Weiss defines control as the ability of an actor — an individual or institutional actor — to limit the range of behaviors of others. Her comments about professional associations, political elites, educational leaders, and parents focus on identifiable actors. Actors are not so readily evident in the instance of values and ideas. Most of her observations, then, have to do with sectors or segments that set limits. The limits may operate in various ways: as constraints on the actions that are possible, or as influences on the premises used. 'Control through values and ideas' possibly illustrates a means professionals, administrators, and others can use to shape options.

I would favor the term 'influence' over control to refer to the impact on the system had by those who stand outside of its formal borders. Control, in my view, has to do with behaviors that direct, evaluate, reward and punish the actions taken within a system (see Edwards, 1979, for an elaboration of control of coordinated systems). I choose 'influence' rather than control in the instance of schools and outside forces for certain reasons. First, if we assume that parents already exercise control, then we render moot much of the debate over the question: who should control schools? The debate rages — at least in part — because some observers regard parents as marginal actors in the distribution of rewards and punishments within the educational systems. Second, discussions about who should control schools rarely revolve around the role to be played by businesses and other potential employers. Hence, it probably adds little to the debate to introduce too wide a range of other actors. Finally, no matter where within the system formal responsibility rests, outside influences are likely to continue to matter. In the American milieu, with its array of interests, groups and actors, some influences on schools will remain, whether formal authority rests at the aggregate or at the site of the individual school.

The proposals call first and foremost for decentralization, usually meaning the granting of authority over decisions — about pedagogy, curriculum — to levels below the aggregated ones. But the proposals differ on how or if they would integrate those units who exercise influence but not authority into the system. Some would incorporate parents or their representatives directly into the decision making hierarchy, giving them direct control not only over the choices available to their own offspring but to those of the peers of their children as well. Other proposals seem to assume that the mere shift of authority from the central level to lower ones would increase participation from the outside. The assumption rests on the belief that the closer are the decision makers — to parents, in particular — the more likely are parents to contact those decision makers.

What marks the Weiss overview is its conception of the school system as an open system. She demands that we acknowledge the effects of missiles and missives from without.

The Internal Structure of the School

A change in the location of authority within the system need not bring with it modifications in the nature and type of influence used at the school site. The organization of the school does not always parallel the organization of the district. One can have a highly centralized school, with decisions made primarily by the principal, in a decentralized district. Likewise, even the most oligarchical system can contain units with multiple centers of influence (Fliegel, 1990).

Essentially, then, an analysis of school organization must consider not only the wider system but the complex that the school itself constitutes. As Bryk, Lee and Smith indicate, the outcomes — for students, teachers, and other school personnel — flow more directly from forces within the school than from those in the larger educational setting. If decentralization enhances involvement, one should expect increased teacher, parent, and student commitment, only if the school itself promotes involvement.

Bryk *et al.*, offer a framework that integrates social goals with individual level ones. The research, they suggest, shows that the attitudes of teachers, as well as the behaviors and performance of students vary, depending on the 'communal' characteristics of schools. The more closely the school approximates a community, the more positive the results from those within it. What the authors note is that research is richer and more consistent on the relationships of some organizational conditions to outcomes than on others.

Bringing the Public In

I have dwelt thus far on life interior to the school, on the conditions that further and flow from the school as a commonwealth. But the discussions about choice and control do not limit the notion of community to the world the school makes. They often mean by 'community' the wider public, particularly those citizens who are located within a specific district. The question for these analyses: through what mechanisms can the larger community sway its schools?

Two rather different ideas about the nature of this larger community appear. The first sees the community as an array of groups and individuals, some of whom have greater difficulty than do others penetrating the educational systems, as that system currently is structured. Certain parents intervene in the schooling of their children, but others do not; some individuals — not all — have the resources to shop around for educational programs and practices. This approach to community and control aims to widen the circle who can exercise options. It supposes that no place of education should be so daunting that only a few members of the public should dare cross its portals.

The second treats the community as a locus of shared interests. Those who take this view intend to involve the collectivity — not separate individuals — in affairs of the school. From this perspective, the task must be to draw segments together for common educational purposes, not to enlarge the net of persons who pursue their special interests.

Let me return to an earlier point: organizational arrangements should take account of the purposes sought. Organizing education to diversify the kinds of persons who can make meaningful choices may call for changes primarily at the level of the larger district. If one wants to reorganize education with diversification in mind, then mechanisms directed towards individuals — vouchers, for example — are the tools. If education is a social goal, however, whose benefits accrue to more than the individual student, mechanisms for assembling the 'community', for identifying and responding to joint concerns are imperative.

The political process represents a means through which parents and others can express their joys and frustrations, their ideas and ideals about education in general and a school system in particular. That process is indirect and rarely allows citizens to comment on the direction any given school should take. Moreover, it does not always encourage discussion, or promote shared understandings within the populace. Organizing to mobilize a community proceeds from a framework that departs from the one the 'diversification' model requires.

One may question the extent to which shared interests in fact appear in the heterogeneous society that is the United States. Bryk, Lee and Smith see in the calls for educational reforms 'attacks on underlying values such as universalism which have driven the development of our public institutions'. The attackers, I contend, wish us to note that the values some see as universal are rather parochial; they are the ideas of the few and not the many. As one source has observed: 'Things in life that appear to be universal often are local, temporary, and artificial' (Klinkenborg, 1989).

The Paths to be Traveled

Bryk, Lee and Smith set before us an ambitious research agenda, the completion of which should add substantially to our knowledge about the organization of schools and its consequences for the lives of persons within them. Weiss cautions us against too narrow a treatment of the sources of influence within the complicated world of formal schooling. Whether or not they are given formal authority, parents, employers, professional associations affect schools and will continue to do so, whatever reorganization takes place within the system. When we add her concerns to those of Bryk, Lee and Smith we arrive at a program of research, with a strong conceptual base, that considers the effect of organization — on the school as a community. I hope that the program would attend as well to the community of interests that potentially exists outside of the school. We cannot mean 'community' as it operated in the somewhat homogeneous world of rural America, for ours is a many-sided society whose variety should be neither denied nor denigrated. The idea of community must accommodate this variety, acknowledge the significance of both the liberty of the individual and the importance of the collectivity, and embrace universals, attentive to the dangers of elevating particular interests to that status.

References

BRYK, A., LEE. V. and SMITH, J.B. (1990) 'High school organization and its effects on teachers and students: An interpretive summary of the research', prepared for Conference on Choice and Control in American Education (in this volume).

EDWARDS, R. (1979) *Contested Terrain: The Transformation of the Workplace in the Twentieth Century*, New York: Basic Books.

FLIEGEL, S. (1990) 'Creative non-compliance in East Harlem Schools', prepared for Conference on Choice and Control in American Education in CLUNE, W. and WITTE, J. (Eds.) Volume 2: *The Practice of Choice, Decentralization and School Restructuring*, of this collection.

GARDNER, J. (1989) 'Building community', unpublished.

KLINKENBORG, V. (1989) 'Review of *The Road from Coorain* (by Jill Ker Conway)', *New York Times Book Review*, 7 May, p. 3.

LEVIN, H. (1990) 'The theory of choice applied to education', prepared for Conference on Choice and Control in American Education (in this volume).

WEISS, J. (1990) 'Theories of control in organizations: Lessons for schools', prepared for Conference on Choice and Control in American Education (in this volume).

WHITE, R. and LIPPITT, R. (1960) 'Leader behavior and member reactions in three 'social climates', in CARTWRIGHT, D. and Zander, A. *Group Dynamics*, New York: Harper and Row, Chapter 28.

Commentary

The Prospects for Communal School Organization

Fred M. Newmann

The topics tackled by Bryk *et al.*, and Weiss could form a potentially powerful duet. Ideally, one chapter would identify those features of school organizations that produce desired effects. The other would explain how to control schools so as to develop and maintain the required organizational features. Knowledge of this sort would presumably enable administrators and policymakers to take more effective strides toward school improvement. Unfortunately, the authors show that knowledge on these matters cannot be packaged so conveniently. A variety of complicated issues obstruct the path to straightforward lessons.

The interpretive summary by Bryk, Lee and Smith is the most useful comprehensive review of literature on the effects of high school organization to date. It synthesizes findings from a diverse body of analytic, quantitative and ethnographic work, and it translates its own theoretical perspective into a novel model for conceptualizing the organization itself, how it is affected by the external environment, and how its organizational qualities produce effects for teachers and students.

The authors show that within the last twenty five years, we have learned much about what happens inside the 'black box' of school, and how the workings of these organizations are tied to their external environments. But it is a complex story; we have to pay attention to the simultaneous interaction of many variables. External factors include school size, student body composition, parent and community involvement; and school governance. Internal characteristics include the cultural system; the role of administration in management, mediation and leadership; the formal organization of work for teachers and students; and the structure of social relations. Still, the large number of variables and the lack of adequate data make it difficult to identify the particular *independent* impact that specific organizational features have on particular outcomes.

In spite of these uncertainties, I draw several main conclusions from the chapter. First, evidence is rapidly mounting which challenges the long-standing rational-bureaucratic model for effective school organization. This model represents many assumptions, but one of its central pillars is the premise that diverse needs of diverse people are best served by creating organizations that differentiate official roles and services to respond to the different people and their needs. This premise has led to schools characterized by large enrollments, fragmentation and conflict in organizational goals, proliferation of specialized courses and services that are difficult to coordinate administratively, pervasive isolation among both students and staff who interact only within parochial activities, and escalating demands from external groups who claim the right to an expanding array of special services.

Such organizations produce at least two major effects: alienation for large proportions of students, parents and staff; and substantial differentiation in academic achievement among students. Some would also argue that these organizational characteristics tend to depress the overall *level* of achievement, but this is harder to demonstrate with available evidence.

In contrast to the rational-bureaucratic model, Bryk *et al.*, revive consideration of an alternative pattern; namely, communal school organization. The central premise of the communal model is shared and common, rather than differentiated, purposes and activities. A good deal of evidence indicates that schools with these qualities have more positive effects on social outcomes; they minimize alienation of students, parents and staff. For high schools, evidence on the academic outcomes of communal organizations is supportive, but, because of limited measures of achievement, less conclusive. At this stage, the single most robust factor for enhancing academic achievement seems to be the number of academic courses taken. But communal organizational qualities tend to intensify the positive impact of academic courses.

Let us assume that, on balance, communal school organizations do in fact have more positive effects on both the social and academic outcomes of schooling for most students and staff. If we wish consciously to work toward this vision, it is important to ask *why* the rational-bureaucratic model that previously seemed so useful for the schooling of youth in the United States now seems inappropriate. This puzzle can be solved, I think, by considering two major historical developments: the decline in social consensus on educational goals and the loss of social capital required for student learning. Each of these signals the need in this historical period for more vigorous efforts to create communal organizations.

As background for discussion of these developments, we must keep in mind a fundamental distinction between precollegiate schools and other client-serving organizations that operate on the rational-bureaucratic model, such as hospitals, insurance companies, automotive corporations, or social service agencies. Schools coerce their clients (students) into accepting the service of human betterment, but to benefit from the school's service the student must generate enormous personal commitment and effort. In contrast, clients of other bureaucratic organizations participate voluntarily; they autonomously seek the organizations' help and, usually, they can benefit without such a substantial commitment of effort. A central problem for the school, then, is how to generate committed effort from its clients.

Until about 1940, schools served a relatively homogeneous group of students, which helped to reinforce widespread consensus about the academic goals of schooling. Youth who chose not to pursue these goals had other options. Since the high school diploma was less necessary for securing minimal material needs later in life, society put less pressure on high schools to serve all students. Although schools were technically organized under the general premise of rational-bureaucracy, in practice, they functioned more as communal organizations, because there was relatively low demand for differentiated services and programs. As the high school diploma became more universally required as a credential for future economic opportunity, however, this brought a greater diversity of students into schools, and the diversity has been recently accentuated by escalating proportions of racial and ethnic minorites. The natural response of the rational-bureaucracy already in place was increased specialization and fragmentation. In the 1960s such specialization was defended as a way of enhancing student engagement, without anticipating the ways in which increased ambiguity and confusion in educational purpose may actually have undermined student engagement. In contrast, less specialized communal organizations, by sending clearer, more unified messages about the goals and processes of school, would seem to have a better chance of inspiring student effort.

In an ideal world it would be possible for a school to offer highly specialized educational programs and services to students with quite different aspirations. If all students came to school eager to develop their competence and with sufficient support in the home and community to sustain the personal effort that school requires, we might expect the bureaucracy to serve a variety of academic, personal and vocational agendas quite successfully (large universities operate on this expectation). But along with the decline in consensus over the goals of schooling came a breakdown in social capital. Monumental changes in community and family life have removed this essential support for millions of young people, making it virtually impossible for the school to instruct them without simultaneously also trying to meet a number of other personal needs which are critical to children's engagement in academic tasks. The rational-bureaucracy now operates special programs for feeding, for counseling (drugs, pregnancy, vocation, physical and sexual abuse), for study skills, for minority services. Regrettably, the kaleidoscope of specialized services fails to offer the kind of nurturance, challenge and hope that comes only from sustained, continuous contact with a few adults who can be counted on to respond to students as whole persons. Communal forms of organization are more likely to compensate for the loss in social capital in the society at large.

If research on organizational features of schools, supplemented by historical analysis, suggests the need for a shift to more communal organizational forms, can the research on control in organizations offer guidance on how to shape schools in this direction? Janet Weiss provides a wide-ranging exposition of five types of control that must be considered in formulating education policy: professional norms and styles of work, political processes and institutions, administrative direction, market forces, and the articulation of values. Weiss explains how each of the sources of control may try to exert influence in varied, even inconsistent, directions and how, because of countervailing forces, no single source is unilaterally capable of controlling the entire system. Further, she implies that because there are serious disadvantages to each type, it would be undesirable to enhance the potency of any of these sources to exercise more comprehensive control.

The chapter suggests two major conclusions relevant to the challenge of deliberate planning to reinforce communal school organization. Ultimately, Weiss' interpretation of the literature conveys a strong implication that, pardon the expression, the educational enterprise is basically out of control. Second, the basic reason for this state of affairs is not the absence of adequate theory, but instead a multitude of incongruities or contradictions among the fundamental values which actually guide the exercise of control within any of the other four dimensions.

To exert more constructive forms of control in educational organizations I think we need to focus more systematically on the dimension of control that Weiss labels as 'values and ideas'. These should be seen not as a separate arena of control, but instead as the fundamental cultural energy that influences how all the other types of control are exercised. Authors of both chapters recognize the considerable organizational inefficiency that results from social disagreement on valued educational outcomes.

Whether we operate primarily from a concern for national and organizational efficiency or from an effort to create more communally organized schools, we must face the issue of goal consensus. At the same time, we must recognize that the building of greater consensus *merely* to exercise more efficient control cannot itself be considered a legitimate policy objective. Since control can be exercised in moral or immoral ways, to achieve or to deny noble human purposes, any attempt to increase control must itself be subject to persistent moral scrutiny. Even communal educational organizations with high goal consensus, common activities, shared rituals, and a vigorous work ethic can indoctrinate rather than educate, can perpetuate caste-like inequalities and can discriminate against outsiders. Thus, the control we exercise must affirm or at least not violate, more fundamental values such as human dignity, equality, fairness, and liberty.

The problem is that these values, used as ends to justify particular forms of control and consensus, themselves lead to the advocacy and advancement of diverse educational outcomes such as the mastery of academic subjects, training for specific vocations, the teaching of thinking, cultivation of the arts, the prevention of drug abuse and teenage pregnancy, nurturing of self-esteem, and preservation of cultural heritage. As indicated above, vigorous support for pluralism in educational values, while customarily celebrated as evidence of the nation's commitment to liberty and local self-determination, may, in these times, need to be re-examined. Again, historical perspective might help — in this case to understand how organizations deal with pluralistic values.

In the United States, we have relied upon two major mechanisms for responding to pluralism in educational values. One is to create large comprehensive high schools that try to cater to all needs through highly differentiated rational-bureaucracies. But as indicated earlier, the evidence casts increasing doubt on the viability of this approach: lack of consensus within comprehensive schools undermines student engagement, and the bureaucratic model is usually incapable of compensating for the loss in social capital.

The second mechanism, represented more recently by 'schools of choice', is to create separate schools that limit their services to more homogeneous interests of distinct groups. Within schools of choice there is likely to be less differentiation and more value consensus (except for those schools that continue as comprehensive schools), and this could be expected to enhance student engagement. But even schools of choice will probably lack certain important communal qualities necessary to compensate for the loss of social capital, because they are most likely to be organized around narrow educational interests, rather than more complete functional communities (see Coleman and Hoffer, 1987).

While the comprehensive high school and schools of choice offer alternative responses to educational pluralism, neither will necessarily help to rebuild the social capital required for students' educational engagement. Furthermore, neither can necessarily be counted on to advance educational equity. Equity of educational opportunity will require an historically novel response to educational pluralism, namely, the building of a coherent national consensus on educational goals that can serve as a baseline for judgment about the achievement of equity.

In summary, these two chapters suggest several lessons. First, the rational-bureaucratic model of school organization offers an inadequate mechanism for stimulating student engagement and for rebuilding social capital; communal forms can offer more promise. Second, efforts to develop more communally organized schools will be continually frustrated by the multiple sources of control in educational organizations. Third, the difficulties of deliberate, intentional institutional control in education are exacerbated most profoundly by the lack of societal consensus on educational goals. Fourth, even communally organized schools are unlikely to serve the cause of educational equity without a new approach to educational pluralism in the United States, namely, the forging of a more coherent consensus on national standards. In short, the agenda of researchers, practitioners and policymakers ought to focus more vigorously on (1) building a greater national consensus on educational goals for all students and (2) creating communal school organizations that generate the social capital and engagement that students need to achieve these goals.

Reference

Coleman, J.S. and Hoffer, T. (1987) *Public and Private High Schools: The Impact of Communities*, New York: Basic Books.

Chapter 5

The Theory of Choice Applied to Education

Henry M. Levin

This chapter places the recent debate over choice in education into a theoretical framework. It begins by considering both private and social purposes of education and their implications for a common educational experience *versus* choice by families. It proceeds to an examination of two systems of choice: market choice and public choice. Market choice refers to the use of an educational marketplace with a voucher financing mechanism. Public choice refers to a system of choice within the public domain in its many variants. At the heart of the discussion is the need to sustain social and democratic benefits of education while promoting choice in those areas that confer private and family benefits. The final part of the chapter compares market and public choice systems in education for their ability to confer social and private benefits as well as their relative efficiency. As might be expected, a market approach to education would appear to be superior in terms of private benefits, while the public choice approach appears to be superior in terms of social benefits. It is difficult to find an advantage for either system in terms of efficiency. The market system appears to be more efficient in terms of meeting private tastes for education, and there is evidence of a slight superiority in terms of student achievement. However, the overall costs for sustaining the information, regulation, and other parts of the market system while providing, at least, minimum social protections look high to prohibitive relative to a public choice approach.

Introduction

One of the major themes of educational reform in the 1980s is that of educational choice. The call for greater parental and student choice in education has taken many forms including educational vouchers and tuition tax credits which could be used to finance education in public or private schools or systems of greater choice among public alternatives. Although the many different choice proposals differ in their features and priorities and are often in conflict with each other, they share the common element of agreement that greater choice is desirable in the US system of education.

Choice is one of the major tenets of both a market economy and democratic society. Indeed, the lack of choice is usually associated with centrally administered and authoritarian regimes. Thus, choice is con sidered to be something that is good in itself and that is a crucial indicator of the freedom of a people. The expansion of choices is likely to be viewed — at least in the abstract — as a strike in favor of a better society.

But, at a more applied level, choice can have both good aspects and bad aspects, both progenitors and detractors. Some choices are considered to be bad for both individuals and for the rest of society by at least some constituencies. Many persons would restrict both the consumption of alcohol and tobacco and the ownership of certain types of firearms, and all but the most die-hard libertarians would restrict drug use and child pornography. The right to terminate a pregnancy by induced abortion is hotly contested, even though it provides a strategic choice to women who must address the decision of whether they wish to bear a child. The important point is that when we move from choice as an abstract process to an concrete one, things are more complicated politically (Boyd and Kerchner, 1988), and in some cases the entire legitimacy of particular choices is questioned.

To illustrate the complexity of the choice issue in education, it is useful to note the existence of a powerful anti-choice movement in education. Some feel that social competence and cultural cohesion in the United States require a relatively fixed set of formative experiences for all members of the society. But, such competence and cohesion are threatened by the provision of numerous elective subjects that create great diversity in student learning experiences. These critics suggest that the schools have capitulated their responsibilities to define and require a common and essential educational experience (Adler, 1982; Bloom, 1987; Hirsch, 1987; Sizer 1984). In a related vein, Butts (1989) argues that the schools must attend to the promotion of a common civic culture. In contrast, contemporary high schools have been characterized as 'shopping malls' containing a hodge-podge of course offerings with little articulation, a system of too much choice (Powell, Farrar and Cohen, 1985). These critics proceed to define the elements of an appropriate education or the minimal knowledge that they believe an education ought to confer on all of society's members and to seek greater uniformity rather than choice.

The quest for greater educational choice is anything but simple. To illustrate the complexity of the movement, consider that former US Secretary of Education, William Bennett, and his followers were in the forefront of the crusade for greater choice and diversity among schools while being equally vocal advocates of a standard curriculum requirement for elementary and secondary schools (Bennett, 1987; US Department of Education, 1988b). It is also ironic that many advocates for greater school choice in the US are the same persons who have singled out West Germany and Japan as exemplars of educational success. Yet, the educational systems of these two countries are among the most rigid and uniform in the world, with far less choice than exists in the US at the present time.

The purpose of this chapter is to examine theories of choice in the context of education. In doing this we will place primary emphasis on comparing a system of market choice with a system of public choice. Less attention will be devoted to the evaluation of choices under the present system which, while far more restricted in options than either a market or public school approach, shares some elements of both. We should bear in mind that even the present organization of education with its 16,000 local educational agencies, 84,000 public schools, and 28,000 private schools (US Department of Education 1988a: p. 83) provides considerable choice to those who are able to move their residences (Tiebout, 1956) or are able to attend private schools. Beyond this, many districts offer magnet schools or alternative schools of choice, individual schools offer a considerable choice in student programs, some schools permit choice in teacher assignment, and virtually all local educational agencies provide a voice in the governance of the local schools.

The next section will delineate the salient characteristics of education that make choice an important issue. The following sections will introduce two choice systems — choice in the private market and choice in the public arena — as conceptual frameworks for viewing choice in education. The final section of the chapter will compare the impacts of the two approaches on the functioning and outcome of the educational system.

Choice in Education

Why is choice in education important in the US at the present time? In the debate on the subject, at least three major reasons are given, each with different implications. First, there is the argument that families should have the right to choose the *type* of education that they want for their children. Of special importance in this regard are differences in philosophic and religious values among families. Just as parents have rights to raise their children with a particular set of traditions and value orientations, they should have the right to select schools which transmit and reinforce those dimensions. In order to exercise that right, they need to be able to have a choice among schools which reflects the universe of values among families rather than a single approach (Coons and Sugarman, 1978).

Second, even among schools of the same type, families should be able to choose the school which best fits the specific educational needs of their child. Some students do better in small schools than large ones or in schools with a particular pedagogical approach, organization, or curriculum. The ability to choose a particular school or teacher and curriculum within a school is likely to improve the likelihood of matching the school experience to the child's needs, producing better educational outcomes.

Third, there is the more general argument that choice among schools will lead to greater competition for students and improvements in school efficiency with respect to student achievement. This argument is predicated on the view that in most respects schools have a monopoly with regard to the student clientele in their attendance areas, and monopolies do not have the competitive pressures to use resources efficiently. It is grounded particularly in the poor educational results associated with students who are considered to be educationally at-risk — those who are at risk of academic failure because they lack the home and community resources to benefit from conventional schooling practices. Such students are especially concentrated among minority groups, immigrants, non-English speaking families and economically disadvantaged populations (Levin, 1986; Pallas, Natriello and McDill, 1988).

Private and Social Purposes of Education

To the degree that these arguments call for an unrestricted system of educational choice, they make a very strong assumption about the purposes of education. They assume that the societal purpose of education is satisfied when families choose the education of their children on the basis of their own tastes and judgments. If each family chooses its most preferred option and the system of schooling responds in the long run by reflecting favored options and eliminating those without adequate demand, the social purposes of schooling will be met.

There can be no doubt that schooling can confer important private benefits that ought to be subject to some degree of private choice. For example, the schooling experience itself can be a source of inspiration, excitement, and personal development or a source of boredom, repression, and emptiness. Clearly many families would rather choose the former for their children than have them fall subject to the latter. Further, families may wish to choose schools for their children that they feel will maximize other private benefits such as knowledge and contribution to adult well-being. It has long been established that schooling enhances individual production and earnings, trainability, health, efficiency in consumption, access to information, and a wide variety of other private outcomes (Becker, 1964; Haveman and Wolfe, 1984). Education also contributes to political efficacy and civic participation (Campbell, 1962; Torney-Purta and Schwille, 1986). Finally, schooling can contribute to social status and personal knowledge as well as the reinforcement and transmission of personal values.

There are few who would limit the purposes of schooling to only those aspects that enhance private lives and that should be matters of family or student choice. It is widely recognized that democratic and capitalist societies must rely heavily upon their schools to provide an education that will preserve and support the fundamental political, social, and economic institutions that comprise those societies (Butts, 1978; Carnoy and Levin, 1985; Levin, 1985) and that make it possible to change those societies in a democratic fashion (Dewey, 1966). Beyond the fulfillment of private needs, schools must provide students with a common set of values and knowledge to create citizens who can function democratically (Butts, 1989; Gutmann, 1987; pp. 50–64). They must contribute to equality of social, economic, and political opportunities among persons drawn from different racial and social class origins. They must contribute to economic growth and full employment, both nationally and regionally. They must provide the intellectual foundation for cultural and scientific progress, and they must produce graduates with the commitment and skills to defend the Nation.

To a large extent these requirements suggest that all students be exposed to a common educational experience that cannot be left to the vagaries of individual or family choice. For example, the children of the Nation must learn that we are a society of laws that entail both rights and obligations for all citizens; that there exist political processes for resolving public conflict; that participation in such political processes requires knowledge of issues and exposure to other points of view as well as productive discourse; that social and political conflict can be resolved legitimately by reliance on acceptable political, legal, and social mechanisms; and that ultimately one must act on one's political views through the exercise of free speech and association as well as through the electoral process and direct forms of political participation.

In a nation that has welcomed continuous waves of immigration, students must learn a common language that can be fully understood and used for social, cultural, and commercial intercourse throughout the

Republic. This does not mean the exclusion of other languages as much as it means the affirmation that a single language will be the official one that will be used widely and will be assumed to be known by all citizens. Literacy in that langauge will include the ability to read, write, speak, and understand it in its daily applications in the political, social, and economic arenas. At least a minimum of literacy in science, technology, and mathematics for effective participation in society is also expected as is knowledge of music and arts that contribute to the understanding of a common culture and that are required for the full development of a social entity.

Finally, it is expected that all students understand the basis for a capitalist economy and their potential roles in such an economic setting. This means that they must be familiar not only with the philosophical and institutional basis for the US economy, but also the requirements for participating productively in economic institutions. They must understand the basis for modern work organizations with their principles of hierarchy and supervision, division of labor, labor markets, role of technology, and wages and salaries. They must understand the functions of investment and savings as well as consumption and both the potential and limits of government intervention in the economy.

While this list of social benefits that we expect from the educational system is not exhaustive, it illustrates the degree to which we share common expectations of outcomes for schooling that are subject to social rather than private choice. And, indeed, that is the heart of the dilemma. Education lies at the intersection of two sets of competing rights. The first is the right of parents to choose the experiences, influences, and values to which they expose their children, the right to rear their children in the manner that they see fit. The second is the right of a democratic society to use the educational system as a means to reproduce its most essential political, economic, and social institutions through a common schooling experience. In essence, the challenge is that of preserving the shared educational experience that is necessary for establishing a foundation of shared knowledge and values for preserving the existing economic, political, and social order while allowing some range of choice within that.

I have emphasized elsewhere (Levin, 1983) that this dilemma has challenged the common school movement in the US since its origins in the middle of the nineteenth century. Although the states established common schools and compulsory attendance laws, they also permitted extraordinary diversity and choice that violated much of the spirit of commonality. Families could send their children to private schools, avoiding completely the specter of a democratic education. Even more important, schools were treated by the states as local institutions that were subject to local governance, even though they were the constitutional responsibility of the states. Because individual communities were often relatively homogeneous in terms of occupation, wealth, income, race, ethnicity, politics, and religion, the schools also reflected those attributes. Hiring patterns, curriculum, religious practices, political content, the language of instruction, and the values expressed in the schools tended to mirror those of the surrounding community in the spirit of democratic localism rather than universalism (Katz, 1971; Levin, 1983; pp. 21–8; Tyack, 1974; pp. 104–9). Local financing also meant that what was spent on schools closely reflected differences in state and local wealth (Coons, Clune and Sugarman, 1970) as well as social and racial discrimination with respect to schools attended by nonwhites and the poor (Kluger, 1975).

The conflict between the private interests of citizens and the public interest of the commonwealth was resolved in the educational arena through a compromise of sorts. Private differences were permitted in an overall system of local common schools established within a broad institutional structure of formal educational standards and compulsory attendance requirements adopted by each state.

But, legal and political challenges to these practices in the twentieth century — and particularly after World War II — narrowed such differences considerably. These challenges were mounted through social movements that attempted to increase democratic participation, equality, and greater extension of constitutional rights into the public schools (Carnoy and Levin, 1985). Private schools faced early attacks on their legitimacy in meeting the compulsory attendance requirements of the states. These disputes were ultimately resolved in 1925 by the decision of the US Supreme Court in *Pierce v. Society of Sisters*, which ensured the freedom of citizens to send their children to schools outside the public system. But within the public system, movement towards equality and uniformity proceeded more slowly until the decades of the fifties and sixties.

In less than thirty years many of the systematic differences based upon private privilege and preferences were obliterated from the operations of the public schools through enforcement of existing laws, passage of new ones, and drastic shifts in educational policy towards greater uniformity (Levin, 1983; pp. 23–8). Court challenges to property-tax based inequalities in school finance among communities resulted in greater equality of educational expenditures within states; all religious practices were proscribed from public schools; teachers and pupils were given protection against suspension or dismissal for exercising their constitutional rights to free expression; new state and federal laws were established and funding provided to more nearly equalize the educational opportunities of female, handicapped, bilingual, and economically disadvantaged students; affirmative action in both hiring and admissions decisions were applied to underrepresented groups at all levels of education; and racial segregation was no longer sanctioned legally as the courts pushed for racial integration of schools wherever possible.

As schools became more uniform, egalitarian, and secular in their practices, such changes occurred at the expense of 'private' interests that had previously been reflected in the public schools. This loss was greatest among those with the highest incomes, social status, and political resources as well as among those with strong political and religious views who had taken for granted the responsibility of their schools to foster their views or provide certain educational advantages to their offspring. For example, school finance equalization tended to restrict educational expenditures in high wealth school districts and reduce their educational advantage over poorer ones. These groups are largely at the forefront in the present quest for greater choice along with those who believe that choice will improve school quality more generally through the tonic of competition.

Expanding School Choice Once Again

I have argued that there is inherently a tension between common schools for the reinforcement of democratic institutions in society and the provision of individual and family choice to meet narrower parochial and private goals, worthy as those goals may be to individual families. The question is how to resolve such a tension. Basically, there are two potential approaches to establishing systems of choice, a market system and a public choice system. A market system relies upon permitting the establishment of schools that meet criteria set out by the state where such entities can compete for students. The best-known version of such an approach is that proposed by Friedman (1955 and 1962) in the form of educational vouchers. Under a voucher approach, families would be provided with educational certificates by the state for all eligible students that could be used to pay tuition at any school that met the minimal requirements for participation in the voucher system.

The alternative to a market system for promoting greater educational choice is a system of greater public choice through the promotion of more public schooling alternatives. These can include the provision of greater choice within schools in terms of programs and curriculum or among schools in terms of a larger number of public schools to choose from.

The distinction between market systems and public systems of choice is not strictly a public/private distinction. Even under market systems such as educational vouchers, the funding and regulation are likely to be the responsibility of public authorities, and government sponsored alternatives might be eligible for inclusion. And various forms of public choice approaches make use of private alternatives such as contracted services. Thus, I will not focus here on differences between public and private sponsorship of schools as much as on the implications of the two different choice mechanisms for education as a public and private good (Levin, 1987).

The next section will review the market approach to choice, and the following section will review the public choice approach. The final section will evaluate the implicatons of each for a range of performance criteria.

Market Choice in Education

Obviously, a limited private market exists in education within the independent school sector for those with adequate incomes or the ability to secure scholarships. However, the purpose of this section is to discuss the extension of that market to a much more comprehensive system of private choices such as those that would be promoted by educational vouchers or tuition tax credits. The ensuing discussion will be devoted primarily to the voucher mechanism because it represents a far more general approach than tuition tax credits. Tuition tax credits refer to the ability to obtain a credit against taxes that are owed for some portion of the tuition paid in behalf of the education of offspring (James and Levin, 1983). It is a complicated mechanism with widely differing effects according to the structure and level of the tax credit as well as the taxable liability of the family. It has been mainly of interest in public policy discussions because of the success of a tuition tax deduction law in Minnesota to meet the constitutional standard for approval as determined by the US Supreme Court (Darling-Hammond, Kirby and Schlegel, 1985; Jensen, 1983).

In contrast, the educational voucher mechanism is more general in its potential for promoting a broad educational market for all families, even those with little or no tax liability. The concept of an educational system in which at least some of the payment would be made directly from the parent to the school was proposed as early as 1776 by Adam Smith in *The Wealth of Nations*. Smith reasoned that if the state paid all of the costs, the teacher ' . . . would soon learn to neglect his business' (Smith, 1937; p. 737). Tom Paine proposed a voucher plan in *The Rights of Man* in which every family would receive a specified amount for each child under the age of fourteen, and children would be subject to compulsory attendance (West, 1967). Local ministers would certify compliance with the law.

Present discussions of voucher plans derive primarily from the provocative proposal of Friedman (1955 and 1962), its refinement by Jencks (Center for the Study of Public Policy, 1970) for a voucher experiment, and the use of the voucher mechanism by Coons and Sugarman (1978) as a basis for a family choice approach in education. A voucher plan would relegate the production of education to a marketplace in which both public and private schools would compete for students. Each parent of a school-age child would receive a voucher that could be used to pay a specified level of tuition at any 'approved' school. Schools would become eligible to receive and redeem vouchers by meeting certain requirements set out by the state. Schools would compete for students by meeting the needs of their clientele in a sufficient manner to attract and retain enrollments. Parents would seek that school that best met their own concerns with respect to the education of their children.

The role of the state would be that of: (1) providing funds in the form of educational vouchers for all school-age children; (2) establishing criteria for eligibility of schools to receive and redeem vouchers; and (3) assuring that the educational marketplace functions efficiently and effectively by setting out mechanisms for providing information on schools to parents, adjudicating conflicts between parents and schools, and ensuring that all children were enrolled in an approved school.

In the late 1960s and early 1970s, the US Office of Economic Opportunity (OEO) sought to implement an experiment utilizing educational vouchers (Center for the Study of Public Policy, 1970). That experiment was aimed at testing the educational consequences of providing educational vouchers in a large, urban area, with specific attention to the process and outcomes of parental choice, the types of schools that would emerge, and the effects of those schools on student achievement and on racial and social stratification of students. The OEO version of educational vouchers was designed to be 'pro-poor' in providing higher or compensatory vouchers to persons from low-income backgrounds and in utilizing a lottery for selecting students for those schools when the number of applicants exceed available spaces. Because of the inability to obtain enabling changes in state laws, it was not possible to test the OEO voucher plan. A modified version was attempted in a school district located in San Jose, California, but all of the alternatives were restricted to the public schools rather than permitting the development of non-public alternatives (Weiler *et al.*, 1974).

Understanding Vouchers

A crucial tenet for understanding vouchers is that there is no single voucher system, but a large number of different approaches using the voucher mechanism. For example, the voucher versions of Friedman (1955 and 1962), Jencks (1966), the Center for the Study of Public Policy (1970) that was prepared for the proposed voucher experiment by the US Office of

Economic Opportunity (OEO), and Coons and Sugarman (1978) differ substantially from each other in ways that have different implications for choice and educational outcomes. Voucher plans differ on three dimensions: (1) finance; (2) regulation; and (3) information (Levin, 1980).

Finance

The finance component of a voucher plan refers to such factors as the size of the educational voucher, what it can be used for, whether a school can charge more than the voucher or obtain additional funding through gifts, whether costs of transportation are covered, and the basic sources of funding. The treatment of each of these aspects will have different impacts on choice, in general, but specifically among groups with different private capabilities to use their resources for schooling.

For example, Friedman would provide a uniform voucher to parents for each child, and parents could provide 'add-ons' to the voucher to purchase more expensive education for their children. Obviously, wealthier families and those with fewer children would benefit the most from this arrangement. In contrast, the voucher proposal that was the basis for the proposed voucher experiment would have provided the largest vouchers to children in poorer families to help compensate for the lack of educational resources in their homes. Other approaches might also set the level of the voucher according to grade level, curriculum, bilingualism, special needs and handicaps, variations in local cost, or other social priorities as in a prospective state constitutional initiative proposed by Coons and Sugarman for the State of California in 1979 and summarized in Levin (1980).

Differences in provision for the costs of transportation are also important determinants of the impact of a voucher plan. In the absence of transportation allowances, the poor will be limited to schools in their immediate neighborhoods relative to those with more substantial family resources. But, transportation costs can be very high, diluting the amount of educational expenditure that can be assigned to the costs of instruction. Accordingly, a plan with substantial transportation provision can provide greater equality in choices among families with different family incomes; but the cost of greater equality in choice will be a smaller portion of educational expenditures for instruction.

Regulation

Although the voucher approach represents a shift from government production of educational services to the private marketplace, that market would consist of schools that had to meet particular regulations in order to be eligible to receive vouchers. Differences in regulatory requirements will create differences in the range of choices. Among the major areas of regulation are those of curriculum content, personnel, and admissions standards.

Regulation of schools under a voucher system is designed to make certain that the social benefits of schooling are captured under the market approach. Any given definition of social benefits such as those associated with a common educational experience will generate a set of regulations for all schools to ensure that those benefits are generated. Obviously, the greater the degree of regulation, the less diverse will be voucher-eligible schools in the educational marketplace.

The present system of public education provides a highly detailed and articulated set of curriculum requirements with respect to the areas in which instruction must be provided and students must have instructional experiences. In addition, there are a large number of areas in which teaching is proscribed, the most notable area being that of religious instruction. Different voucher plans vary with respect to curriculum requirements. Friedman (1962) is not specific on this dimension, but it is apparent from his short discussion that such requirements would be minimal with emphasis on instruction in basic skills and a common set of civic values. The OEO voucher plan (Center for the Study of Public Policy, 1970) is more detailed, but leaves the specifics to the state that might adopt a voucher experiment. The California Initiative tended to limit curriculum requirements to those that were required of private schools in the State, a fairly minimal standard.

Both the Friedman (1962) and Coons and Sugarman versions would permit a large diversity of schools with respect to underlying values and content in curriculum. The State would not intervene or attempt to regulate instruction, except to assure that no laws were being violated. Since the constitutional protection of free expression is the implicit standard, public support for schools could extend to fairly extreme political, religious, philosophical, and ideological sponsorship and content as long as the Supreme Court interpreted an educational voucher plan as aiding children and families rather than institutions. Separation of church and state would preclude direct public support for religious instruction.

Personnel requirements for voucher plans vary from no state requirements — permitting each school to set its own standards — to the use of existing standards for licensing of public school teachers and administrators. The regulation of admission practices shows similar diversity. Friedman would permit schools to have complete rein in setting admissions policies. The OEO plan would set fairly detailed requirements including non-discriminatory practices, possible quotas for racial composition, and a lottery approach to choosing some portion of the student body for schools that had more applications than places.

Information

The competitive efficiency of market systems of choice depends crucially upon knowledge of alternatives. In fact, the perfectly competitive market assumes the existence of perfect knowledge of all pertinent information for making efficient decisions on the part of both potential consumers and producers. Unfortunately, the educational marketplace presents an unusual challenge in this regard as delineated in the work of both Bridge (1978) and Klees (1974).

Two particular difficulties emerge in the area of educational information, whether provided in the context of the educational marketplace or that of public choice. First, education represents a rather complex service that can not be easily summarized in ways that will reflect accurately the nature of the educational experience that a particular child might face. Second, available methods of providing appropriate information on a large number of educational alternatives to a wide variety of audiences in a constantly changing situation as new schools open and others fail is likely to be costly and problematic. This challenge is particularly severe for the least-advantaged families such as those where parents are poorly educated, do not speak English, and who tend to move frequently because of marginality in housing markets.

With respect to the first of these dimensions, it is probably possible to provide accurate information on such prominent dimensions as religious, political, or ideological sponsorship or orientation of a school as well as emphases on particular curricula such as the arts, sciences, sports, and so on. However, qualitative aspects of education are much more difficult to characterize. For example, a reading of college catalogs suggests that from the largest state universities to the smallest liberal arts colleges there is a common descriptive vocabulary that includes references to 'academic excellence, outstanding faculties and facilities, and concern for the individual student'. It is difficult to ascertain how well educational institutions carry out their missions and how appropriate a particular environment is for a particular student. Unfortunately, it is difficult for students to sample different schools before making a choice, and there is also the problem of advertising and promotional distortions such as those found among post-secondary proprietary institutions by the US Federal Trade Commission (1976).

The second problem is the cost of establishing and maintaining an up-to-date system of information in a form that will be understandable and accessible to potential producers and consumers. This challenge is especially important for addressing the information needs of disadvantaged populations. Such persons are characterized by low educational attainments, higher probabilities of speaking a language other than English, and a higher incidence of mobility because of a lack of housing and job stability. In essence, the system of information will have to be constructed according to the needs of local populations and the specific options in each of hundreds of local educational markets in each state. Bilingual services need to be available in many settings, and counselors will need to be available to interpret the information. Such a decentralized approach to information with its many services and data collection is likely to have a high cost. Alternatively, as with an adequate transportation system, the cost of a suitable information system may discourage its provision because of the substantial resources that it drains away from the level of the voucher and instructional resources.

Summary of Voucher Arrangements

Any attempt to understand the implications of a market system of choice in education using educational vouchers must address the particular attributes of the voucher plan that is under consideration. Different specifics can lead to radically different results. Of particular importance are the arrangements for financing, regulating, and providing information for the educational marketplace. Clearly a voucher plan with 'compensatory' vouchers for the poor, no 'add-ons', extensive provisions for transportation and information, and regulation of admissions to assure participation of the poor will have vastly different consequences than one which provides a uniform voucher with parental 'add-ons', a poor information system, no transportation, and a laissez-faire approach to admissions.

Public Choice in Education

Systems of public choice in education can take many different forms (Elmore, 1986; Nathan, 1989; Raywid, 1985). However, they share two common features. First, schools are always sponsored by the government under a public choice system. Such sponsorship may take the form of direct government operation, or it can build on a contractual relation with a non-profit or profit-making sponsor within the scope of a particular agreement set out by the government. Second, within any public choice system there exists a common core of educational experiences and practices for all students that are based upon the social aims of education. The challenge of public choice is to establish a common core of educational experiences for all children, but to allow choice in how these are to be attained and in the schooling activities beyond this core.

The establishment of the common core of educational experiences is a matter for the electorate. Such a core may entail curriculum requirements, organizational practices (for example, student composition and grouping), instructional strategies, and personnel qualifications. Clearly, these should be based upon the requirements for producing social benefits beyond those that benefit only individual students and their families. Tyack and Hansot (1982) have argued that the public schools provide the most important opportunity for initiating and maintaining democratic debate, not only about education, but about the society itself. The schools represent a concrete arena of discourse on what type of society we want, what types of experience our children should be exposed to, and what we value as citizens. In contrast to virtually all other public and private institutions, 'public schools are everywhere close at hand and open to all children. They generate valuable debates over matters of immediate concern, and offer a potential for community of purpose that is unparalleled in our society' (Tyack and Hansot, 1982, p. 23).

Hirschman (1970) has analyzed and contrasted two mechanisms for getting organizations to produce services efficiently and be responsive to their clientele: exit and voice. 'Exit' refers to the act of shifting from one provider to another. When one is dissatisfied with one product and replaces it with another, or shifts purchases from one supplier to another, one is using the exit option. These impersonal shifts signal to producers important patterns of demand that must be responded to if the suppliers are to survive. In contrast, 'voice' refers to protest, discussion, negotiation, voting, and other forms of political or client participation to obtain one's goals. These acts tend to be more personal in nature and often require individuals to work with other individuals and groups to achieve their ends.

On the surface, the notion of a common educational core would suggest the use of voice, while the notion of choice within that common core would suggest exit. In fact, this is an oversimplification, since voice can also be used to obtain choice, as in the case of having one's child switched to a different class or given more homework assignments. As Hirschman emphasizes, the two mechanisms can be used to reinforce each other. If a supplier knows that a consumer might exit, it is likely that the supplier will be more responsive to protest.

Under the existing organization of education, both mechanisms prevail. As we noted, voice can be used at the local level by individual parents to obtain services for their children, and it can also be used collectively to alter local school and school district practices. Exit mechanisms are reflected in the option of migrating to other neighborhoods or school districts, or shifting to private schools or other private options such as home schools.

But, as noted above, the private mechanisms may violate the common core of democratic schooling, and the public ones may not offer a very wide range of options relative to others that can be provided within a common core. Further, they may be cumbersome, indirect, and costly, as in the case of having to move one's residence to obtain better or more appropriate educational services. Thus, the overall goal ought to be to increase educational options for everyone, while retaining the basic democratic or common core of educational experiences. This means that all schools should be organized to as great a degree as possible to meet the various democratic requirements of schooling, and violations of these requirements would not be choice options.

The use of public options as an alternative to market ones in expanding meaningful choice is supported by an empirical study that found that the larger the range of public educational choices in a geographical area, the smaller the number of private enrollments, *ceteris paribus* (Martinez-Vazquez and Seaman, 1985). Among the variety of political and organizational arrangements for increasing public educational options are the following:

School-Site Governance

One way of making schools more responsive is to create meaningful parental governance around smaller schooling units, such as individual schools rather than school districts. This can be especially significant in larger school districts that have dozens of schools, since uniform policies of such districts inhibit the response of schools to meeting the specific needs of their particular clientele (Levin, 1970). The decentralization of governance would presumably place school decisions closer to the families affected by them and permit a greater impact of families on the schooling of their own children in those areas of education that do not impinge on the common core. Such matters as budgetary allocations within the school, curriculum, personnel selection, and instructional materials could be influenced by local governing boards within the limits of the common core. This approach is presently being pursued in Chicago (Moore, 1990).

Open Enrollment

One traditional method of increasing choice within school districts is the practice of open enrollment. Families would have the choice of sending their children to neighborhood schools or to any other school with openings. To a certain degree this would foster competition among schools, since staffing and other resources for individual schools are a function of their enrollments. The open enrollment approach is likely to be most effective where there are meaningful choices and when the cost of transportation to other schools is low, as in cities with well-developed public transportation.

The effectiveness of this approach for choice could be enhanced considerably by requiring schools to permit interdistrict transfers upon request of parents and availability of space in receiving districts. In this context, districts could compete for students, a particularly important incentive in situations of declining enrollment. The district of residence would be required to provide a transfer of funds equal to the 'marginal' cost of educating an additional student in the receiving district. The state legislature would have to establish these practices by law as well as the overall definition of what should be included in marginal cost accounting.

Schools of Choice

A more elaborate framework for promoting school choice is to provide a system of schools within a district that specialize in major areas of concern (Bass, 1978). This approach has been used by school districts to reduce segregation in neighborhood schools by creating 'magnet schools' that will draw student representation from all neighborhoods (Blank, 1990). Such schools usually have specialized themes to create attractive alternatives to their neighborhood institutions. Examples of these themes include basic academics, art, music, science, multicultural enrichment, and so on.

Mini-Schools

The schools-of-choice framework can be expanded considerably by the establishment of mini-schools within existing school plants. This is an especially attractive option in urban areas where both elementary and secondary schools are often far too large to provide an effective educational experience (Chambers, 1981). Evidence suggests that large schools seem to have negative effects on student participation and achievement, especially among students who are from lower socioeconomic origins (Chambers, 1981; Holland and Andre, 1987). But, mini-schools would have the additional advantage of offering meaningful choices among alternatives at a single school site such as a neighborhood school. Each school plant would be divided into a number of relatively independent 'schools' from which parents could choose a particular one for their child. An attempt would be made to provide a diversity of themes among the mini-schools to create salient differences along the lines of parental interests.

The so-called voucher demonstration in the Alum Rock School District of San Jose, California was actually an example of a public choice approach in which mini-schools and open enrollments were combined. Students could choose any mini-school among the demonstration schools (over fifty choices emerged among the thirteen participating schools), and resource flows were guided by student choice to the particular schools whose enrollments were expanding. Fortunately, there were extensive evaluations of this approach from which perceptive insights can be derived regarding the design and implementation of mini-schools (Haggart, Rapp and Wuchitech, 1974).

Post-Secondary Options

One way of providing a richer set of options for high school students is to permit them to take courses at local post-secondary institutions as part of their high school program. Even at the community college level, there exist courses in foreign languages, sciences, literature, art, history, and the social sciences that are not available in local high schools. Almost every high school is within a reasonable distance of a community college. But, in addition, secondary schools ought to seek agreements with four year colleges with respect to the establishment of a list of courses that are accessible to high school students as additional options to their normal secondary school menu. While such agreements can be forged at the local level, it is probably best that the state establish an enabling mechanism that includes financial arrangements. Particularly in sparsely populated areas with very small secondary schools, high school curricula can be enhanced considerably by providing access to post-secondary institutions. Minnesota has been the pioneer in establishing such an arrangement (Montano, 1989).

Mini-Vouchers

'Mini-vouchers' are certificates that students can use for a selected range of educational services. They fit rather well the conceptual separation of a common educational experience from the domain of individual and family choice in that the mini-vouchers would apply only to the areas of choice. For example, all students would be expected to have exposure to the common educational core. Beyond that, students and their families could choose among different types of educational offerings both within and outside the public schools.

These options might be limited to 'enrichment' areas, such as creative writing, computer programming, and specialized scientific and artistic subjects; or they might be used for ancillary educational services such as those for handicapped, disadvantaged, and bilingual students. For example, an unusually promising tutoring program for students who are educationally at-risk such as Reading Recovery (Boehnlein, 1987) could be funded from mini-vouchers for services for at-risk students. Of course, the question might be raised that if the program is effective for all such children, why should it be an option? Moreover, such services must be closely integrated with classroom instruction to be fully effective, so this challenge is also one that must be addressed. Nevertheless, there are probably a large range of educational options that can be funded through mini-vouchers.

Private Contractors

The prospect of using private contractors to address particular portions of the educational program has been posed for the last two decades (Coleman, 1967; Lessinger, 1970). One version of this alternative would be to let contractors compete with the public schools to provide instruction in specified subjects as alternatives for parents who were not satisfied with the progress of their children in regular classes (Coleman, 1967). An alternative is for schools to hire private contractors to provide educational services in those areas where the school system did not have a strong record of success or the immediate ability to improve matters (Lessinger, 1970). In both cases, the contractual agreement might call for payment on the basis of improvement in student performance according to specified criteria, creating a strong incentive to produce results.

In general, this approach would seem to be most attractive for those students who have had the least success in existing schools in learning basic and problem-solving skills, particularly ones from minority and low-income backgrounds. However, an experiment in the early 1970s with performance contracting that was sponsored by the OEO did not show promising results (Gramlich and Koshel, 1975). Whether the poor results were due to the hurried nature of the experimental planning or an intrinsic flaw in the contracting mechanism cannot be determined from the data.

The results do suggest, however, that the predictability of outcomes from educational contracting is not as straightforward as some of its advocates have argued.

Summary of Public Choice Mechanisms

Each of the public choice mechanisms that was described is premised on choice within a common educational framework. Further, each requires substantial elaboration on its specific design and provisions for implementation that are appropriate in a particular setting. Many of these issues have been discussed in the literature (Bass, 1978; Bridge and Blackman, 1978; Thomas, 1978; Fantini, 1973). Together they offer a variety of possibilities for expanding educational choice within the public sector.

In the final sections I will attempt to compare market and public choice approaches with respect to several criteria. These criteria will include: (1) implications for addressing the social purposes of schooling; (2) implications for addressing private purposes of schooling; and (3) issues of social efficiency in the use of educational resources. In marking these comparisons it is important to bear in mind that the discussion will be kept to a fairly general level. The reason for this generality is that specific consequences flow from particular choice alternatives, whether public or private. As I tried to demonstrate in the section on market choice, different voucher plans have rather different consequences. The same is true of different public choice approaches. Nevertheless, I believe that it is possible to make some generalizations about differences between the two approaches in terms of their educational consequences.

Choice Approaches and the Social Purposes of Schooling

In general, we can argue for two social purposes of schooling on which there seems to be wide agreement. First, there is the standard of a common educational experience that is necessary to provide a common set of values and knowledge that is needed for the functioning of a democratic society. Second, there is the requirement of equality of some sort in terms of access to and/or educational results among the different races, genders, and social groupings.

On the first of these, public choice approaches have a strong advantage over market approaches. A public choice approach can define the common educational experience and implement a system of choice within that framework. The situation is much more problematic with market approaches for two reasons. First, the advantage of a market approach is the ability to satisfy a wide range of preferences by encouraging individual schools to differentiate their offerings to appeal to a particular set of clientele. Parents could then choose schools according to their own cultural, academic, social, political, ethnic, racial, and religious values.

In this respect, the very appeal of the market approach to maximize choice and to create schools that will compete for clientele with particular views must necessarily create a divisive system of education rather than one that converges on a common educational experience. Some market advocates argue that it is possible to set out 'protections' against such balkanization and stratification by regulating the private market place. But, the more regulations that one places upon schools in order to ensure their democratic contributions, the more cumbersome and costly the overall apparatus and the less likely that there will be significant differences among schools. One cannot ensure both an unfettered or slightly fettered system of choice and a common educational experience at the same time.

But, there is also the issue of whether a system of regulation for ensuring the democratic content of schooling is even feasible. Friedman argues for minimum standards for all participating schools in a voucher system because ' . . . a stable and democratic society is impossible without a minimum degree of literacy and knowledge on the part of most citizens and without widespread acceptance of some common set of values' (Friedman, 1962, p. 86). This concern is also implicit in the critiques by Bloom (1987), Hirsch (1987), and Adler (1982) that there is some minimum body of knowledge or set of educational experiences that are fundamental to reproducing a literate society. Somehow the state must assure that at least a minimum of social outputs are produced to satisfy the democratic standard. Whether this can be done through mandating minimum personnel, curriculum, or output requirements is problematic. Surely personnel must be competent to impart the necessary social values and knowledge, the curriculum must include the appropriate subjects and experiences, and the result must be reflected in school outcomes.

Yet to assure that this is so would require an unusual amount of regulation that would be costly and cumbersome (Murnane, 1986) and probably unconstitutional to the degree that the state would become entangled in religion when evaluating whether schools meet these regulations (Yudof, Kirp, van Geel, and Levin, 1982, pp. 88–108). Furthermore, it is not clear that the art of measurement of values and attitudes is sufficient to assure accountability with respect to these outcomes. Even a system that began with a minimum of regulation would likely find itself experiencing increased monitoring and regulation over time, following the pattern of other private activities that have received government subsidies (Encarnation, 1983).

Even more serious is the strong possibility that it is the educational process itself that must be regulated. That is, many of the social benefits of education are related to the process itself. For example, effective participation in a democracy requires a willingness to tolerate diversity. This process must acknowledge the existence of different views on a subject and accept a set of procedures for resolving such differences in reaching social decisions. This requirement suggests that schooling for democracy must ensure exposure to different views in controversial areas, a discourse among those views, and the acceptance of a mechanism for reconciling the debate. Research on political socialization has shown that tolerance for diversity is related to the degree to which different children are exposed to different viewpoints on controversial subjects in both the home and school (Torney-Purta, 1984).

But, a major advantage of the market approach to choice is the ability of families to choose the type of schooling that reflects their political and religious values. It would be unrealistic to expect that Catholic schools will expose their students to both sides of the abortion issue; that evangelical schools would provide a disinterested comparison of creation and evolution; that military academies would debate the value of disarmament and peace movements; that leftist schools would provide a balanced presentation of the positive and negative aspects of capitalism; or that white academies would explore different views towards race in the US. Their curriculum and faculty would be selected in order to make them efficient competitors in a differentiated market for students in which the views of parents would be reinforced and others excluded or derided.

A related social purpose of schools in a democracy is to provide equality of access to educational benefits. Presumably, this means that persons from different social groups should have equal access to the types of resources that they need to succeed educationally. Clearly there are a number of standards that can be applied to translating this general principle into educational practice (Coleman, 1968; Rawls, 1971; pp. 100–1; Levin, 1976; Gutmann, 1987; pp. 127–71). But, at a minimum one might set two requirements: First, educational resources available for each student should favor those with greater educational need — for example, educationally disadvantaged or the mentally and physically handicapped — and those with fewer private resources in the home and community to be able to meet educational needs — for example, low income and single parent families. Second, families from different social origins ought to have at least equal ability to exercise choices among all of the available alternatives. This requires equal access to information about alternatives as well as equal ability to exercise choice.

Under both market and public choice plans, it is possible to meet the first criterion. With respect to market choice, the size of vouchers should be greater for those with greater educational needs and those from more modest economic origins. Further, 'add-ons' from families should not be permitted either through payment of higher tuition than the voucher or through 'donations' to eligible voucher schools. This view is consistent with principles set out in both the OEO design (Center for the Study of Public Policy, 1970) and with some of the principles set out by Coons and Sugarman (1978). Public choice arrangements can also provide greater educational resources for redressing 'undeserved' inequalities by setting out programs according to educational need.

The second criterion represents more of an obstacle because persons with less education and income and racial minorities have less access to information and seem less able to use it to make educational decisions. The crucial role of information in educational decision-making is developed extensively by Friedman and Sugarman (1988). Both access to information and its efficient use in making choices require experience in choosing among alternatives as well as a level of education that provides the capacity for making rational choices. In both respects parents in economically and educationally disadvantaged circumstances will be handicapped, whether facing a system of market choice or public choice.

The OEO voucher demonstration made a substantial investment to saturate the community with information through school bulletins, newspapers, mailings, radio announcements, neighborhood meetings, and information counselors. Even with such a costly effort, one-quarter of the parents were totally unaware of the availability of alternatives over the four year period (Bridge, 1978; pp. 514–16). Further, income and education were positively related to awareness of alternatives, and minorities had lower levels of awareness than Anglos. At a more specific level, only 50–60 per cent of the parents were aware that transportation was free and that they had a right to transfer their child to another school (Bridge and Blackman, 1978; p. 34).

A similar pattern was found in the analysis of parental choice among magnet schools in Milwaukee with substantially lower awareness of the availability of magnet schools among non-whites and low income parents (Archbald, 1988; pp. 60–1). Further, inner-city parents who were aware of the magnet school alternatives seemed to have almost no substantive idea of their purposes, specializations, or even their names. In fact, proximity was the dominant factor in determining both awareness and demand for magnet schools in the inner city (Archbald, 1988; pp. 78–110).

A further complication is raised by the criteria that parents from different social background might choose for educating their children. It is reasonable to believe that parents will choose those school environments that they believe will maximize the probability of success as defined within the context of their experience. Kohn (1969) has shown that working-class families seem to emphasize conformity in their children (obedience to rules) while parents in relatively higher occupational positions stress independence and the ability to choose among available alternatives. This pattern is substantiated in research on maternal interactions with children (Hess, Shipman, and Jackson, 1965).

If we extrapolate these findings to the choice of schools for their children, it is likely that working-class parents will select highly structured schools for their children that emphasize a high degree of discipline, concentration on basic skills, and following orders — the requirements for holding jobs at low occupational levels. In contrast, parents from the upper middle class will choose the kinds of schools that are perceived by them to contribute to success in their careers. Such parents will stress greater freedom of student choice in curriculum and scheduling as well as development beyond basic skills in conceptual, thinking, scientific, art, and communication skills. These educational attributes are functional in contributing to professional and managerial development such as the ability to consider alternative production techniques, products, marketing strategies, and personnel; to create the rules and regulations which define work organization; to maintain relatively great flexibility in work schedules; and to have the ability to supervise others. The result is that parents will choose schooling for their offspring that will reinforce their own occupational standing.

The distinguished sociologist Kohn has concluded on the basis of extensive empirical research:

> At lower levels of the stratification order, parents are likely to be ill-equipped and ill-disposed to train their children in the skills needed at higher class levels . . . No matter how dramatic the exceptions, it is usual that families prepare their offspring for the world as they know it and that the conditions of life eventually faced by the offspring are not very different from those for which they have been prepared. (Kohn, 1969; pp. 200–1)

In summary, it appears that choice mechanisms are not likely to be 'neutral' with respect to social class and other background factors. The ability to use educational choice effectively depends heavily upon occupational experience, education, and other resources such as the capacity to obtain and interpret information in a useful way. Empirical evidence supports the interpretation that choice schemes in education, whether market or public, will tend to favor more advantaged families.

The exercising of choice in education also means the ability to transport one's children to the school of choice. In this respect, any market or public choice plan which does not provide substantial free or low-cost transportation options will work against lower income families. The higher the family income, the more able the family is to be able to afford transportation to schools that are not within walking distance. Lower income families may not have such options in the absence of accessible, convenient, and low-cost public transportation.

In summary, there are some differences between the market choice and public choice approaches with respect to the three democratic criteria. In terms of providing a common core of experiences, the public choice approach would seem to have a distinct advantage. In contrast, it appears that both approaches can create mechanisms to ensure that those with greater educational need obtain more educational resources than those with less educational need. Finally, both approaches appear to have a differential impact in favor of more advantaged families with respect to the effects of educational choice on the distribution of actual educational choices. This is probably a more serious problem for market choice schemes with their likelihood of greater numbers of small schools and greater differentiation among schools. Sheer numbers and differences complicate the ability to disseminate useful information in a parsimonious manner to less-advantaged persons. Finally, the provision of transportation for lower income families is crucial for any choice approach.

Choice Approaches and the Private Purposes of Schooling

A second major category for comparison is the ability of each system of choice to satisfy the private purposes of schooling. More specifically, how does each approach serve to provide responsiveness to the private concerns of families with respect to their educational goals including philosophic, academic, religious, and political dimensions of schooling. In this respect it appears that market choice mechanisms are superior because they are likely to provide greater flexibility and more choices.

Greater flexibility of the private market is provided through greater decentralization of decision-making in terms of the establishment of schools. Any potential entrepreneur or special interest group could establish schools according to the perceived demand for that type of schooling, as long as the eligibility requirements were met to redeem vouchers. This freedom to establish schools subject only to eligibility guidelines provides potential incentives to a wide range of potential school sponsors with diverse orientations. In contrast, most public choice plans build on the decisions to provide alternatives by school districts or states in which choices will be made among district schools and/or school districts.

This advantage in meeting private goals of schooling is further reinforced by the likelihood that market systems of choice are likely to provide greater numbers of schools to choose from. Chambers (1981) showed that private schools are considerably smaller than public schools. There are at least two reasons that this is the case. First, private schools tend to emphasize 'product differentiation' in terms of appealing to a particular market niche. Program focus tends to be narrow in serving a particular clientele or educational community, a point emphasized by both Coleman (1987) and Coons and Sugarman (1978). With a relatively narrow focus in terms of grade levels and programs, it is possible to reach economies of scale at relatively low enrollment levels. In contrast, public schools must serve a broad range of clientele including a wide range of abilities, physically and mentally handicapped students, and those who are academically-oriented or vocationally-oriented. The high fixed costs to provide minimal programs for meeting all of these needs requires a much larger scale of enrollments to provide enough students for each program to bring average cost per student to a reasonable level.

Second, governance and control of public schools takes place at a more centralized level than in the marketplace. There are limits to control of large numbers of small units by central authorities, even when much of the school-site decision-making is relegated to individual schools. Accordingly, a public choice approach would likely be based upon relatively fewer and larger schools in contrast to a market approach with its greater potential for decentralized sponsorship which would encourage more and smaller units. In the middle eighties, the average public school in the US had an enrollment of about 482 students in contrast with an average enrollment of 206 students in private schools (US Department of Education, 1988a; pp. 62 and 94). If these size differences were to hold under a market system, it would take about 217,000 private schools to accommodate the enrollments of the present 111,000 public and private schools in the US.

I conclude that a market approach to educational choice is likely to show greater diversity of choices and more choices for meeting the private goals of families than a public choice approach. Of course, we should bear in mind that it is exactly this capacity to provide greater diversity and choice in meeting private needs that creates an obstacle to addressing the democratic goals of schooling in the form of a common educational experience.

Choice Approaches and Social Efficiency

In this final section I wish to review the social efficiency of market and public choice approaches in education. By social efficiency I am referring to the comparative ability of each approach to maximize educational outcomes for any given set of resources. There are two levels at which such a comparison might be made. The first is a micro-level approach in which one might compare the ability of schools under each choice system to produce educational results for any given level of resource use. That is, does either of the two choice systems have an advantage in using resources efficiently at the school level. The second is a macro-level approach in which the requirements for promoting and maintaining the system of choice in which schools are situated is also taken into account. We will review each of these separately.

Micro-Level Efficiency

One of the major claims of educational market advocates is that the mechanisms of market choice and competition among providers will create greater efficiency than any publicly-controlled approach to schooling. One part of this claim is undoubtedly true as concluded in the previous section. That is, a market approach will be more responsive to the private goals of families in the sense that such an approach will provide more options and more diverse options than a public choice approach. If the only criterion were that of consumer sovereignty, we would view the market choice approach as more efficient than the public choice one.

However, there is also the related issue of whether the incentives and decision flexibility of schools in the private market might be more efficient in addressing a given set of social goals such as that of school achievement. Clearly, school achievement is not the only social objective of schooling, but it is a major one that is of great concern at the present time when it has been argued that the Nation is At-Risk because of its low level performance on tests of educational achievement (National Commission on Excellence in Education, 1983). Two types of evidence have been used in the recent past to provide support for the claim that private schools are more efficient than public schools. First, it has been asserted that private schools show a lower cost per student than public schools (American Enterprise Institute, 1978; p. 28; West, 1981). Second, it has been asserted that they produce higher levels of academic achievement, at least at the high school level. Taken together, these assertions suggest that a market choice approach would provide education more efficiently than a public choice approach.

But, in fact, the cost comparisons are biased in that they understate the costs of private schools relative to public ones (Sullivan, 1983). Such comparisons usually compare per-student expenditures in public schools with tuition charges in Catholic schools. But tuition reflects only a portion of expenditures for Catholic schools. Extensive fund raising and periodic fees are used to supplement tuition, and many other resources are donated or subsidized (Bartell, 1968). For example, Catholic parochial schools often rely heavily upon teaching clergy whose salaries understate substantially their market value. The Church typically provides facilities that are not charged to the school. As a result, much of the apparent disparity in costs is due to massive gaps in cost accounting in private school data rather than to real cost differences.

But, beyond this the service mix is quite different for public and private schools (Sullivan, 1983). Public schools must provide many mandated services and educate 'high cost' students who are often excluded from private schools through admissions policies or lack of appropriate programs. Public schools are required by law to provide special educational services for handicapped students, while private schools are not obligated to do so and rarely provide such services. Special education students typically cost at least twice as much as regular students (Kakalik *et al.*, 1981; Hartman, 1981). At the secondary level, the vocational courses sponsored by public schools are rarely found in private schools, and such courses are considerably more expensive than academic ones (Hu and Stromsdorfer, 1979). Public schools must provide more high cost services and educational services to 'high cost' students than private schools. Thus, the present evidence comparing per-student cost differences is not adequate for comparing efficiency between public and private schools.

Chambers (1985) found that private schools paid lower salaries than public schools, but more than half of the gap was due to the private schools employing teachers with less experience and education and under more favorable working conditions than the public schools. Further, it is likely that some of the remaining gap was due to the higher cost of attracting teachers to public schools in which there are high proportions of educationally disadvantaged and handicapped students, a situation that is much less prevalent among private schools. Chambers suggests that a movement to a market-based educational system with public funding would probably raise salaries in the private schools, since teachers in those schools would no longer be willing to make the sacrifices that they must do in the present situation.

But, if the evidence comparing costs between public and private schools is too weak to be conclusive, what can be said about the differences in academic achievement? In cross-sectional statistical analysis comparing achievement between public and private schools (mainly Catholic schools because of the small sample of other private schools), while adjusting for student race and socioeconomic background, James Coleman, Thomas Hoffer, and Sally Kilgore (1982) found that students in private schools had between a 0.12 to 0.29 standard deviation advantage in achievement. Their results were criticized as overstatements of private-school effects because of the treatment of tracking, inadequate controls for self-selection — that is families with strong educational concerns within race and social class whose efforts raise the achievement of their children and who choose private schools as part of those efforts — and other flaws in the statistical design (Goldberger and Cain, 1982). Purported adjustments for some of these problems reduced considerably or eliminated estimated private-school advantages (Willms, 1983).

Longitudinal results based on sophomore-to-senior changes found even smaller estimated private-school effects (Alexander and Pallas, 1985; Haertel, James and Levin, 1987; Hoffer, Greeley and Coleman, 1985; Willms, 1985). Depending upon the statistical model, the maximum private-school advantage varied from nothing to about 0.1 standard deviations. If we assume the maximum private school advantage of 0.1 standard deviations, we can explore the practical significance of such a difference. As Alexander and Pallas (1985) note, such a difference would place private school students of similar race and socioeconomic status at the 52th percentile relative to public school students at the 50th percentile. What is remarkable about this comparison is the similarity in test scores rather than the differences. For example, this is equivalent to saying that about 48 per cent of private school students score below the average of similar public school students.

Further, a 0.1 standard deviation difference is equal to about 10 points on the Scholastic Aptitude Test for college admissions. Since the difference in average scores between a non-competitive institution and a highly competitive one is about 300 points, a 10 point advantage is unlikely to make much difference in college admissions. Finally, using statistical analyses for 1976 from Meyer and Wise (1982), such an advantage in achievement translates into less than 5 cents an hour for high school graduates some four years after graduation and about one *day* less unemployment a year among a cohort that experienced about 10 *weeks* of annual unemployment (Levin, 1987; p. 634).

In terms of efficiency in the production of schooling between public and private schools, we conclude the following: (1) There is no systematic evidence of differences in costs for similar students and services and a given level of educational outcome; (2) There is some systematic — though contested — evidence that private schools produce superior results in student achievement for otherwise similar students. However, the differences in results are very small on the average with little practical significance, and almost half of private school students have achievement scores below the average for public schools. Thus, the overall conclusion is that private schools have a very slight advantage over public schools in terms of efficiency at the school level. Whether this very nominal difference would be exacerbated with greater competition in a market choice system is a matter of speculation.

Macro-Level Efficiency

The two different choice mechanisms cannot be evaluated for efficiency only at the micro or school level. Each system requires a range of institutions at the macro-level to make choice effective and workable. For example, a market choice system based upon educational vouchers requires a regulatory system for schools, adjudication and information systems for parents, and a mechanism for assuring that students receive vouchers that are appropriate to their educational needs and that they are meeting compulsory attendance laws. A public choice system requires at least a strong information system to apprise families of alternatives and a transportation system to make school choices accessible. Each of these functions represents an additional cost to the overall system of education to make choice work.

From a private efficiency perspective, the market choice approach is the most decentralized one, leaving decisions on schooling to individual schools and individual families. Thus, it is a paradox that at the macro-level a voucher system would require far more centralization than a public choice approach. Presumably, the state would be responsible for sponsoring and constructing institutional mechanisms to assure meaningful choice and participation of both schools and families. To give a picture of what types of institutions might be required to do this, I will refer to the California Initiative for Family Choice in Education that was proposed by John Coons and Steve Sugarman in 1978 and reproduced in Levin (1980).

(1) Information

The California Initiative specified that reasonable requirements of disclosure be established by law with respect to curriculum and teaching methods, qualifications of teachers, and resource use as well as the possible requirement of standardized test results. All of these would have to be reported to a voucher information agency for dissemination. This information would be made available through sources independent of the schools, and nonliterate parents and others with special information needs would receive a grant redeemable for the services of independent counselors. Presumably, the information agency would have offices throughout the state so that parents could obtain information regarding their local market options. The deliberate provision of false or misleading information by schools would be forbidden, so the information agency would also have some role in validating information and in checking out complaints that information was inaccurate or misleading.

(2) Regulation

The voucher agency would be responsible for ascertaining that schools meet the regulatory requirements with respect to admissions, curriculum, and educational practices that are necessary for eligibility to redeem vouchers. The California Initiative required only that voucher schools meet the existing private school requirements, but these were never designed to take into account the social purposes of schooling and would be unlikely to be acceptable as the marketplace was extended to all schooling. At the present time the State of California must monitor about 1,000 school districts with respect to compliance with the educational code. In contrast, the state would be responsible for establishing eligibility and monitoring some 10,000–20,000 schools, depending upon the average size of a voucher school. For terms of reference, there were about 7,300 public schools in California in 1986–87 and about 5,700 private schools (Policy Analysis for California Education, 1988, pp. 51–2). As schools entered the market, left the market, or altered their activities to meet competition, a watchdog function would have to be maintained by the State. As I noted in the section on the democratic aspects of schooling, any monitoring to assure the social purposes of schools would entail considerable observation. At the present time there are economies because existing school districts both monitor and operate schools under the state law, thus interpreting the law and educational policy and applying it to the children in the district. In contrast, an intermediate agency between the state and individual schools under a voucher plan would have to be independent of schools in developing and maintaining its own data base and monitoring function, a far more expensive approach.

(3) Adjudication

A mechanism is necessary to address parental complaints about misleading information or other practices which they found to be inappropriate for their children as well as to determine the financial and other conditions for transfer from one school to another. For example, schools may make financial obligations at the beginning of the year on the basis of their enrollments and may oppose refunds during the year of any portion of tuition. An adjudication procedure will need to be established to balance the rights of families and schools.

(4) Attendance and voucher levels

At the present time the State of California relies on its approximately 1000 school districts to make sure that children meet compulsory attendance requirements and that educational outlays for each student reflect educational needs. The voucher plan would shift these responsibilities so that the State would have to address over 5 million students rather than 1000 public school districts. The state will have to ascertain whether each student is enrolled in an approved school as well as to diagnose the educational characteristics of each child in order to ascertain how large the voucher would be. The California Initiative would have awarded different vouchers according to grade level, curriculum, bilingualism, special needs and handicaps, variations in local costs, need to encourage racial desegregation, and other factors. Presumably, each child would have to be located by the state and screened for voucher eligibility. Further, the state would have to establish relations with individual schools rather than school districts in order to confirm child attendance.

(5) Transportation

Financial provision for transportation is a central consideration, since the number of educational alternatives available to families will depend upon their ability to obtain ready geographical access to different schools. Schooling must be consumed at the site of production, in contrast to most goods that can be distributed to consumers at other sites. Public choice plans are likely to include fewer school sites than market choice approaches. This arrangement allows a more compact and orderly set of transportation plans with fixed routes and high levels of utilization. In contrast, a market approach would require flexible routes depending upon the residences and choices of each student, and they would have to change over time to accommodate changing student patterns. The latter would require relatively more buses and drivers in order to provide flexibility in routes relative to a fixed route system.

National data show average costs at about $258 per transported student in 1984–85 (US Department of Education 1988a, p. 56). Costs of transportation would rise considerably under any school choice plan and most precipitously under a market plan because of the increase in students who would need transportation and the high cost of 'customized' transportation routes for relatively small groups of students who will be distributed idiosyncratically within the school market.

Far from decentralizing the administration of funding and administration of educational activities, the market approach would require a monumental centralization of such activities at the state level. The state would be charged with working directly with individual families and individual schools rather than school districts. Public choice plans would also require some additional administrative apparatus at the school district level to provide useful information about choices. But, this expansion of administrative responsibilities would be relatively small in comparison to the expansion and centralization of activities required of a market choice plan.

Summary of Macro-Efficiency

With respect to macro-efficiency, it appears that a market approach would require an expansion and centralization of educational activities at the state level that would be vastly greater than public choice plans. The very diversity promoted by a market approach as well as the larger number of schools has the effect of expanding immensely the difficulties of oversight. Further, the fact that the state would have to shift to families, students, and schools as decision-making units would increase by a multiple of thousands the numbers of units that must be evaluated and monitored on a continuing basis. It is this additional drain on societal resources through an expansion of transaction costs for obtaining a given educational result that has led Krashinsky (1986) to reject the market approach.

In summary, the market choice approach promises some improvement in micro-efficiency by increasing the range of choice for families and by showing slightly higher achievement test scores on the basis of available evidence. Presumably, the market system would also provide greater competitive benefits towards efficiency for any given output. However, at the macro-efficiency level these advantages must be weighed agair[illegible] the very high costs of centralized administration and intrusion into the

tional process. On balance, it is not clear which system of choice is likely to be more efficient, *in toto*, without an explicit comparison of the particular versions of public and market choice that are being posited.

References

ADLER M.J. (1982) *The Paideia Proposal: An Educational Manifesto*, New York: Macmillan Publishing Co.

ALEXANDER, K.L. and PALLAS, A.M. (1985) 'School sector and cognitive performance: When is a little a little?' *Sociology of Education*, **58**, April, pp. 115–28.

AMERICAN ENTERPRISE INSTITUTE (1978) *Tuition Tax Credits and Alternatives*, Washington, DC: AEI.

ARCHBALD, D.A. (1988) *Magnet Schools, Voluntary Desegregation, and Public Choice Theory: Limits and Possibilities in a Big City School System*. Unpublished doctoral dissertation, School of Education, University of Wisconsin–Madison.

BARTELL, E. (c. 1968). *Costs and Benefits of Catholic Elementary and Secondary Schools*, Notre Dame, IN: Notre Dame University Press, (no date).

BASS, G.V. (1978). *A Study of Alternatives in American Education, Vol. I: District Policies and the Implementation of Change*, R-2170/1-NIE, April, Santa Monica, CA: The Rand Corporation.

BECKER, G.S. (1964) *Human Captial*, New York: Columbia University Press.

BENNETT, W.J. (1987) *James Madison High School: A Curriculum for American Students*. Washington DC: US Department of Education.

BLANK, R. (1990) 'Educational effects of magnet schools'. Paper prepared for Conference on Choice and Control in American Education, Robert La Follette Institute of Public Affairs, University of Wisconsin–Madison, 17–19 May and in Volume 2 of this collection.

BLOOM, A. (1987) *The Closing of the American Mind*, New York: Simon and Schuster.

BOEHNLEIN, M. (1987) 'Reading intervention for high-risk first graders', *Educational Leadership*, **44**, 6, March, pp. 32–7.

BOYD, W.L. and KERCHNER. C.T. (1988) *The Politics of Excellence and Choice in Education*, Philadelphia: Falmer Press.

BRIDGE, G. (1978) 'Information imperfections: The Achilles' heel of entitlement plans', *School Review*, **86**, 3, May, pp. 504–29.

BRIDGE, G. and BLACKMAN. J. (1978) *A Study of Alternatives in American Education, Vol. IV: Family Choice in Education*, April, R-2170/4-NIE, Santa Monica, CA: The Rand Corporation.

BUTTS, R.F. (1978) *Public Education in the United States*, New York: Holt, Rinehart and Winston.

BUTTS, R.F. (1989) *The Civic Mission in Educational Reform*, Stanford, CA.: Hoover Institution Press.

CAMPBELL, A. (1962) 'The passive citizen', *Acta Sociologica*, **VI** (fasc. 1–2), pp. 9–21.

CARNOY, M. and LEVIN, H.M. (1985) *Schooling and Work in the Democratic State*, Stanford, CA: Stanford University Press.

CENTER FOR THE STUDY OF PUBLIC POLICY (1970) *Education Vouchers*, A Report on Financing Elementary Education by Grants to Parents, December, Cambridge, MA.

CHAMBERS, J.G. (1981) 'An analysis of school size under a voucher system', *Educational Evaluation and Policy Analysis*, **3**, 2, March–April, pp. 29–40.

CHAMBERS, J.G. (1985) 'Patterns of compensation of public and private school teachers', *Economies of Education Review*, **4**, 4, pp. 291–310.

COLEMAN, J.S. (1967) 'Towards open schools', *The Public Interest*, **9**, pp. 20–7.

COLEMAN, J.S. (1968) 'The concept of equality of educational opportunity', *Harvard Educational Review*, **38**, 1, pp. 7–22.

COLEMAN, J.S. (1987) 'Families and schools', *Educational Researcher*, **16**, 6, August–September, pp. 32–8.

COLEMAN, J.S., HOFFER, T. and KILGORE, S. (1982) *High School Achievement: Public, Catholic, and Private Schools Compared*, New York: Basic Books.

COONS, J.E., CLUNE, W. and SUGARMAN, S. (1970) *Private Wealth and Public Education*, Cambridge, MA: Belknap Press of Harvard University Press.

COONS, J.E. and SUGARMAN, S.D. (1978) *Education by Choice*, Berkeley, CA: University of California Press.

DARLING-HAMMOND, L. and KIRBY S.N. with SCHLEGEL, P.M. (1985) *Tuition Tax Deductions and Parent School Choice: A Case Study of Minnesota*, Santa Monica, CA: The Rand Corporation.

DEWEY, J. (1966) *Democracy and Education*, New York: The Free Press.

ELMORE, R.F. (1986) *Choice in Public Education*, JNE-01. December, New Brunswick, NJ: Center for Policy Research in Education.

ENCARNATION, D.J. (1983) 'Public finance and regulation of nonpublic education: Retrospect and prospect', in JAMES, T. and LEVIN, H.M. (Eds.) *Public Dollars for Private Schools*, Philadelphia: Temple University Press, Chapter 10.

FANTINI, M.D. (1973) *Public Schools of Choice*, New York: Simon and Schuster.

FRIEDMAN, L.S. and SUGARMAN, S.D. (1988a) 'School sorting and disclosure: Disclosure to families as a school reform strategy. Part I: Existing practices and the social interests in school information disclosure', *Journal of Law and Education*, **17**, 1, winter, pp. 53–89.

FRIEDMAN, L.S. and SUGARMAN, S.D. (1988b) 'School sorting and disclosure: Disclosure to families as a school reform strategy. Part II: Policy and legal analysis', *Journal of Law and Education*, **17**, 2, spring, pp. 147–201.

FRIEDMAN, M. (1955) 'The role of government in education', in SOLO, R.A. (Ed.) *Economics and the Public Interest*, New Brunswick, NJ: Rutgers University Press.

FRIEDMAN, M. (1962) 'The role of government in education', in *Capitalism and Freedom*, Chicago: University of Chicago Press, Chapter VI.

GOLDBERGER, A.S. and CAIN, G.G. (1982) 'The causal analysis of outcomes in the Coleman, Hoffer, and Kilgore report', *Sociology of Education*, **55**, pp. 103–22.

GRAMLICH, E.M. and KOSHEL, P.P. (1975) *Educational Performance Contracting*, Washington, DC: The Brookings Institution.

GUTMANN, A. (1987) *Democratic Education*, Princeton: Princeton University Press.

HAERTEL, E.H., JAMES, T. and LEVIN H.M. (Eds.) (1987) *Comparing Public and Private Schools: School Achievement*, (Volume 2), Philadelphia: Falmer Press.

HAGGART, S., RAPP, M. and WUCHITECH, J. (1974) *Instructional Aspects of the 1972–73 Mini-school Programs in the Alum Rock Voucher Demonstration*, Santa Monica, CA: The Rand Corporation.

HARTMAN, W.T. (1981) 'Estimating the costs of educating handicapped children: A resource cost model approach — Summary Report', *Educational Eval — Nation and Policy Analysis*, **3**, (4), pp. 33–48.

HAVEMAN, R.H. and WOLFE, B.L. (1984) 'Schooling and economic well-being: The role of nonmarket effects', *The Journal of Human Resources*, **XIX**, 3, summer, pp. 377–407.

HESS, R.D., SHIPMAN, V. and JACKSON, D. (1965) 'Early experience and the socialization of cognitive modes in children', *Child Development*, **36**, pp. 869–86.

HIRSCH, E.D. JR., (1987) *Cultural Literacy: What Every American Needs to Know*, New York: Houghton Mifflin.

HIRSCHMAN, A.O. (1970) *Exit, Voice, and Loyalty*, Cambridge, MA: Harvard University Press.

HOFFER, T., GREELEY, A. and COLEMAN, J.S. (1985) 'Achievement growth in Public and Catholic schools', Sociology of Education, **58**, pp. 79–97.

HOLLAND, A. and ANDRE, T. (1987) 'Participation in extracurricular activities in secondary school: What is known, what needs to be known', *Review of Educational Reserach*, **57**, 4, winter, pp. 437–66.

HU, T. and STROMSDORFER, E.W. (1979) 'Cost-benefit analysis of vocational education', in ABRAHMSON, T., TITTLE, C.K. and COHEN, L. (Eds.) *Handbook of Vocational Education Evaluation*, Beverly Hills: Sage Publications, Chapter 8.

JAMES, T. and LEVIN, H.M. (1983) *Public Dollars for Private Schools: The Case of Tuition Tax Credits*, Philadelphia: Temple University Press.

JENCKS, C. (1966) 'Is the public school obsolete?' *The Public Interest*, **2**, winter, pp. 18–27.

JENSEN, D.N. (1983) 'Constitutional and legal implications of tuition tax credits', in JAMES, T. and LEVIN, H.M. (Eds.) *Public Dollars for Private Schools: The Case of Tuition Tax Credits*, Philadelphia: Temple University Press, pp. 151–74.

KAKALIK, J.S., FURRY, W.S., THOMAS, M.A. and CARNEY, M.F. (1981) *The Cost of Special Education*, Santa Monica, CA: The Rand Corporation.

KATZ, M. (1971) *Class, Bureaucracy and Schools: The American Illusion of Education Change*, New York: Praeger Publishers.

KLEES, S. (1974) 'The role of information in the market for educational services', *Occasional Papers on Economics and Politics of Education, 74-1*, Stanford, CA: Stanford University School of Education.

KLUGER, R. (1975) *Simple Justice*, two volumes. New York: Alfred A. Knopf, Inc.

KOHN, M.L. (1969) *Class and Conformity: A Study in Values*, Homewood, IL: Dorsey Press.

KRASHINSKY, M. (1986), 'Why educational vouchers may be bad economics', *Teachers College Record*, **88**, 2, winter, pp. 163–8.

LESSINGER, L. (1970) *Every Kid a Winner: Accountability in Education*, New York: Simon and Schuster.

LEVIN, H.M. (Ed.) (1970) *Community Control of Schools*, Washington, DC: The

Brookings Institution.
LEVIN, H.M. (1976) 'Educational opportunity and social inequality in Western Europe', *Social Problems*, **24**, 2, December, pp. 148–72.
LEVIN, H.M. (1980) 'Educational vouchers and social policy', in HASKINS, R. and GALLAGHER, J.J. and HASKINS, R. (Eds.) (1980) *Care and Education of Young Children in America*, Norwood, NJ: Ablex Publishing Co, pp. 103–32.
LEVIN, H.M. (1983) 'Educational choice and the pains of democracy', in JAMES, T. and LEVIN, H.M. (Eds.) *Public Dollars for Private Schools: The Case of Tuition Tax Credits*, Philadelphia: Temple University Press, pp. 17–38.
LEVIN, H.M. (1985) 'Are block grants the answer to the federal role in education?' *Economics of Education Review*, **4**, 3, pp. 261–70.
LEVIN, H.M. (1986) *Educational Reform for Disadvantaged Students: An Emerging Crisis*, West Haven, CT: NEA Professional Library.
LEVIN, H.M. (1987) 'Education as a public and private good', *Journal of Policy Analysis and Management*, **6**, 4, pp. 628–41.
MARTINEZ-VAZQUEZ, J. and SEAMAN, B. (1985) 'Private schooling at the Tiebout hypothesis' *Public Finance Quarterly*, **13**, 3, July, pp. 293–318.
MEYER, R. and WISE, D.A. (1982) 'High school preparation and early labor force experience', in FREEMAN, R.B. and WISE, D.A. (Eds.) *The Youth Labor Market Problem: Its Nature, Causes, and Consequences*, Chicago: University of Chicago Press, Chapter 9.
MONTANO, J. (1989) 'Choice comes to Minnesota', in NATHAN, J. (Ed.) *Public Schools by Choice*, St. Paul, MN: Institute for Teaching and Learning.
MOORE, D. (1990) 'Voice and choice in Chicago', in CLINE, W. HAND WITTE, J.F. (Eds) *Choice and Control in American Education, Volume 2: The Practice of Choice, Decentralization and School Restruchuring*, Lewes, Falmer Press.
MURNANE, R. (1986) 'Comparisons of private and public schools: The critical role of regulation', in LEVY, D.C. (Ed.) *Private Education: Studies in Choice and Public Policy*, New York: Oxford University Press, Chapter 5.
NATHAN, J. (1989) *Public Schools by Choice*, St. Paul, MN: The Institute for Teaching and Learning.
NATIONAL COMMISSION ON EXCELLENCE IN EDUCATION (1983) *A Nation at Risk: The Imperative for Education Reform*, Washington, DC: US Department of Education.
PALLAS, A.M., NATRIELLO, G. and MCDILL, E.L. (1988) 'Who falls behind: Defining the 'at-risk' population — current dimensions and future trends'. Paper presented at Annual Meeting of the American Educational Research Association, New Orleans, Louisiana, April.
Policy Analysis in California Education (1988) *Conditions of Education in California*, Berkeley, CA: Author.
POWELL, A.G., FARRAR, E. and COHEN, D.K. (1985) *The Shopping Mall High School: Winners and Losers in the Educational Marketplace*, Boston: Houghton Mifflin.
RAWLS, J. (1971) *A Theory of Justice*, Cambridge, MA: The Belknap Press.
RAYWID, M.A. (1985) 'Family choice arrangements in public schools: A review of the literature', *Review of Educational Research*, **55**, winter, pp. 435–68.
SIZER, R.R. (1984) *Horace's Compromise: The Dilemma of the American High School*,

Boston: Houghton Mifflin.

Smith, A. (1937) *The Wealth of Nations*, Modern Library Edition, New York: Random House.

Sullivan, D.J. (1983) *Comparing Efficiency Between Public and Private Schools, TTC-15*, Stanford, CA: Stanford University School of Education, Institute for Research on Educational Finance and Governance.

Thomas, M.A. (1978) *A Study of Alternatives in American Education, Vol. II: The Role of the Principal*, R-2170/2-NIE, April, Santa Monica, CA: The Rand Corporation.

Tiebout, C.M. (1956) 'A pure theory of local expenditures', *Journal of Political Economy*, **64**, pp. 416–24.

Torney-Purta, J. (1984) 'Political socialization and policy: The United States in a cross-national context', in Stevenson, H. and Siegel, A. (Eds.) *Child Development Research and Social Policy*, Chicago: University of Chicago Press.

Torney-Purta, J. and Schwille, J. (1986) 'Civic values learned in school: Policy and practice in industrialized nations', *Comparative Education Review*, **30**, 1, pp. 30–49.

Tyack, D.B. (1974) *The One Best System*, Cambridge, MA: Harvard University Press.

Tyack, D.B. and Hansot, E. (1982) *Managers of Virtue: Public School Leadership in America, 1820–1980*, New York: Basic Books.

US Department of Education (1988a) *Digest of Educational Statistics*, CS 88-600. Washington, DC: US Government Printing Office.

US Department of Education (1988b) *James Madison Elementary School: A Curriculum for American Students*, Washington, DC: US Government Printing Office.

US Federal Trade Commission (1976) *Proprietary Vocational and Home Study Schools*, Bureau of Consumer Protection. Washington, DC: Government Printing Office.

Weiler, D. *et al.*, (1974) *A Public School Voucher Demonstration: The First Year at Alum Rock*, Santa Monica, CA: The Rand Corporation.

West, E.G. (1967) 'Tom Paine's voucher scheme for public education', *Southern Economic Journal*, **33**, January, pp. 378–82.

West, E.G. (1981) *The Economics of Education Tax Credits*, Washington, DC: The Heritage Foundation.

Willms, J.D. (1983) 'Do private schools produce higher levels of academic achievement? New evidence for the tuition tax credit debate', in James, T. and Levin, H.M. (Eds.) *Public Dollars for Private Schools: The Case of Tuition Tax Credits*, Philadelphia: Temple University Press, pp. 223–34.

Willms, J.D. (1985) 'Catholic school effects on academic achievement: New evidence from the high school and beyond follow-up study', *Sociology of Education*, **58**, April, pp. 98–114.

Yudof, M.G., Kirp, D.L., van Geel, T. and Levin, B. (1982) *Educational Policy and the Law: Cases and Materials*, Second Edition, Berkeley, CA: McCutchan Pub lishing Corporation.

Chapter 6

Choice as an Instrument of Public Policy: Evidence from Education and Health Care[1]

Richard F. Elmore

A major strategic problem confronting public policymakers is the degree to which client and provider choice should shape the nature and distribution of public services. Advocates of choice stress its beneficial effects on efficiency — in both the allocative and technical sense. Critics stress the adverse distributional consequences of enhanced choice. This chapter argues that issues of choice in the design of public policy cannot be resolved by resorting to theory, but must be resolved by examining the political and social construction of choice by institutions. Evidence from health and education suggests that the effects of choice policies are heavily contingent on the existence of information enhancing policy implements, on client preferences that have little to do with quality of services, and on institutional constraints on quality.

The Problem of Choice in the Design of Public Policy

All public policies that involve the delivery of services must confront the problem of client and provider choice. Solutions to this problem vary considerably from one policy sector to another, and are typically embedded in the institutional structures of those sectors. In elementary and secondary education, for example, all but a small share of schooling is provided through local public agencies, and most students are assigned to schools on the basis of residence. In the health care sector, on the other hand, public involvement takes the form largely of reimbursements to private providers for care given to individuals. In the one sector, most services are provided directly by public agencies and most client choice, if it occurs at all, takes place within the structures of those agencies. In the other sector, most services are provided by private practitioners, and clients use public subsidies to choose among alternative providers.

Public policy in each of these areas represents a different solution to the strategic problem of client and provider choice. Elementary and secondary education operates, for the most part, on the assumption that students and educators should be assigned to schools by a centrally-administered process, and that decisions about what gets taught to whom should be heavily influenced, if not completely controlled, by a combination of state and local policy, rather than the preferences of clients and providers. The health care sector operates, for the most part, on the assumption that people will seek the type and amount of health care they need, financed with the assistance of third-party insurers, and that private practitioners will provide care consistent with consumer preferences and professional standards. Public intervention in the health care sector is predicated mainly on protecting people who, because of income, age, or disabling conditions are unable to provide adequate protection for themselves.

This chapter examines the problem of client and provider choice in the design of public policies from the perspective of evidence on elementary and secondary education and health care. In both education and health care, experiments have been conducted with client and provider choice. In both areas, there is a suggestive body of evidence available on the effects of using policy to influence client and provider choice.

Furthermore, the contrast between education and health care sheds some light on the current policy debate about choice in education. Advocates of greater client and provider choice in education often propose alternative structures that entail schools composed of teachers engaging in educational practice jointly with students and parents, both sides having chosen their affiliation voluntarily, both sides subsidized by direct public payments either to families or to schools (see, for example, Coons and Sugarman, 1978; Nathan, 1983). These proposals can be seen as a form of public subsidy for private, or quasi-public, practice of teaching, distinguished from the present system for organizing education by the increased latitude of choice offered both clients and practitioners. This form of organization, and the problems of policy design that attend it, are analogous to organizational forms and problems that arise in the public subsidy of medical practice.

From an analytic perspective, the arguments for greater client and provider choice are relatively straightforward. These arguments take at least two forms. One line of argument is that sectors based on the direct provision of public services, like education, can be made more responsive by increasing client and provider choice. For example, advocates argue that allowing educators to devise programs tailored to the needs and preferences of students and parents and allowing parents and students to choose among these alternatives will increase the 'fit' between educators and students, the satisfaction of students and parents, and the learning that occurs in schools.

A second line of argument is that public subsidies to privately-provided services, like health care, can be made more cost-effective by giving consumers a greater role in selecting their services, by making them better-informed consumers, and by increasing competition among providers. Consumers are the best judges of the nature and level of health care they require, the argument states, and providers are more likely to respond to clients' particular needs when the client chooses which practitioners he or she will patronize.

These arguments around the issue of client and provider choice have been heavily influenced by economic theory. In simple terms, the economic argument is that, other things being equal, government services are more efficient when the mode of their provision least constrains the choices of providers and clients. Efficiency, in this context, has two closely related meanings. The first is a technical meaning: the ratio of cost to output. The simpler and more direct the transaction between client and provider, the greater the level of service for a given level of expenditure. The second meaning of efficiency is a broader allocative one, based on the principle of welfare maximization. People have variable preferences and needs, the argument goes, and they are better off when the form of the service allows them to choose the combination of attributes that most closely matches their preferences. Taken together, these principles suggest, to paraphrase Schultze, that there should be a 'rebuttable presumption' against forms of public policy that involve direct public service provision, that entail high transaction costs, or that constrain the choices of recipients, and in favor of those that provide the most direct transfer to recipients and that least constrain their choices (Schultze, 1977).

The problems of applying these abstract principles to the design of operating public policies are of two general types. The first set of problems has to do with the 'macro-structure' within which policy decisions are made and implemented.

One part of this macro-structure is the institutional framework within which policy decisions are made about client and provider choice. As a number of analysts have observed, policy decisions are not only choices among courses of action, but also choices among institutions (Clune, 1987; Gormley, 1987). Every policy decision involves some implicit or explicit choice among the competing claims, interests, and capacities of existing institutions. Schools and hospitals, and the people who work in them, for example, are not simply passive recipients of public directives; they are active agents in shaping their own mandates, they have their own organizational interests, they have histories, and they have capacities to do some things and not others.

Policy decisions are rarely, if ever, taken in the hypothetical mode — 'What would be the ideal institutional arrangement for solving this problem?' They are almost always taken in the pragmatic mode — 'How can existing institutions be influenced to act consistently with the purposes of public policy?' Policy initiatives designed to enhance parent choice in education, for example, typically do not replace existing local school boards or administrative structures, nor do they replace the institutions that implement policy on such matters as teacher qualifications, curriculum requirements, graduation requirements, or university entry requirements. Yet all these institutional structures would have a significant bearing on what parents could choose and what educators could provide under policies designed to enhance parent choice. Likewise, policies designed to enhance consumer choice and cost-effectiveness in medical care typically do not alter the structure of medical specialties or the organizations through which medical practitioners find their niche in the market. Yet these structures affect what consumers can choose, and what practitioners will provide, under health care policies.

Another part of the macro-structure is the purposes of public policy and the politics that surround those purposes. Policies typically carry complex purposes that are not adequately represented by simple principles of welfare maximization. As we shall see, advocates of client and provider choice carry complex agendas and interests to the political arena that are often concealed by simple claims of efficiency. Furthermore, the most difficult issues that policymakers confront in deciding on the role of client and provider choice are not simple efficiency questions, but questions that require balancing efficiency with equity.

The second set of policy design problems has to do with what might be called the 'micro-structure' — that is, the individual factors that operate on client and provider choice within a given institutional framework. Any given institutional structure, for example, entails a particular conception of knowledge and expertise for practitioners, creates particular information costs for clients, and generates particular patterns of preferences among clients. In order to design policies that move institutional structures in one direction or another, and in order to produce results of one kind or another, one must understand how these forces operate.

In general, then, simple notions of technical and allocative efficiency, abstracted from purposes, institutions, and individual factors, are not very useful in designing policies. Whether more client choice is 'better', by whatever criteria, depends not on general normative principles but rather on the specific political, institutional, and individual context within which choice occurs. Let us examine how these contextual factors operate in education and health care.

Macro-Structure: Institutions, Modes of Practice, and Political Agendas

Institutions

American elementary and secondary education has, at least since the late nineteenth-century, been organized around a locally-centralized administrative structure, reinforced by state and federal systems of governance and finance. Peterson (in this volume) argues that this locally-centralized structure evolved into a public monopoly, which restricted client and provider choice in the interest of equity and uniformity, and then, in the latter half of this century, it evolved into a system in which choice accrues to those affluent enough to buy residences in high quality school districts and uniformity to those too poor to move (see also Coons and Sugarman, 1978). Witte (in this volume) takes exception to this argument, observing that the seeming uniformity of school organization conceals a high level of diversity among schools, within districts, and among states and localities, which is attuned to the local political environment. Peterson sees uniformity in the foreground and diversity in the background; Witte sees diversity in the foreground and uniformity in the background.

Whether one calls the institutional structure of American elementary and secondary education 'monopoly' or 'polyarchy', certain features remain constant. These features have a decisive impact on the way choice is constructed, organizationally and politically, in public school systems (Elmore, 1988). Virtually all students and teachers, once inside a given school district, arrive in a given school through some centrally-controlled process of assignment. Increasingly, these assignment processes involve some acknowledgment of parent and student preferences, but, on the margin, assignments are made administratively rather than through independent transactions between clients and providers. Virtually all schools receive their funding through a locally centralized process of allocation and control. Sometimes these allocation systems are based on principles that attempt to promote school-level decision making (Malen, Ogawa and Kranz in Volume 2 of this collection), but, on the margin, funding decisions are determined by district-level decisions, not by client demand for services. Finally, what teachers actually teach and what students are actually allowed to learn within a given school are significantly influenced and constrained by local and state policies. Teacher certification, curriculum controls, testing, and graduation requirements significantly affect what goes on inside schools, on the margin, as opposed to professional standards or client preferences. In the language of institutional choice, then, American public elementary and secondary education locates the authority for decisions on access, funding, and content of services with locally-centralized administrative structures which are, at least nominally, accountable to locally-elected boards.

Within this institutional structure, school board members, district administrators, principals, and teachers play relatively well-defined roles defined by predictable constraints and operating routines. These roles, structures, and routines are, for the most part, expressed in bureaucratic terms. Someone in the central district office, for example, is responsible for pupil assignment and, unless attendance boundaries are changed or schools are closed, students are typically assigned to schools in a more or less routine way based on their place of residence. Likewise, within buildings, teachers receive students through a more or less predictable process that involves first being assigned to teach certain grade levels and subjects, and then being given a share of the students who fall into that category.

Client and provider choice in public education occur on the margins of these bureaucratic routines. District administrators, for example, modify standard pupil and teacher assignment practices in the name of district-wide priorities. Magnet schools and examination schools, drawing pupils from district-wide attendance areas, are designed to enhance racial balance and give visibility to traditional academic subject matter. Alert parents often exert significant influence on the assignment of their children to teachers within elementary schools and on their children's access to teachers and courses at the secondary level. Students exercise considerable influence over which courses they take from which teachers within a school's established curriculum, especially elective courses. Teachers who understand the bureaucratic norms of assignment exercise considerable influence, as they advance in tenure, over which grade levels and courses they will teach. Those teachers with a strong commitment to a particular view of knowledge and teaching, and the skill to translate it into practice, also exercise considerable influence over the subject matter and pedagogy within their classrooms. So while the institutional structure of education is mainly one of local centralization, it permits significant choices on the margin.

But the structure favors those with the knowledge, influence, and resources to seek exceptions to bureaucratic routines. Virtually all large urban systems now use either residence or racial balance to allocate students and teachers to elementary schools, and most have developed a system of academically stratified assignment at the high school level. One recent study identified a number of distinctive types of high schools in large cities, which vary systematically in income and academic achievement depending on their degree of selectivity. The 'non-selective' schools, which enroll the largest proportion of students overall and the largest proportion of poor and minority students, operate mainly on residential assignment and exercise little or no control over the composition of their student bodies. The 'selective' schools, which enroll a small proportion of students overall and smaller proportions of poor and minority students, operate mainly on district-wide assignment systems and exercise a high degree of control over the composition of their student bodies (Moore and Davenport, 1988). This evidence matches within-school studies that demonstrate systematic variations in course-taking within comprehensive high schools and significant differences in students' opportunities to learn by race and income (Oakes, 1985).

The existence of local bureaucratic centralization in education, then, does not mean the absence of choice for either clients or providers. It does mean, however, that choices are highly constrained, that the structure rewards choosers who are willing to invest the resources necessary to seek exceptions to bureaucratic rules and routines, and that central authorities determine, for the most part, what the legitimate range of choice is for teachers, parents, and students.

Medical care in the US, by contrast, has traditionally been organized around private practice, with public subsidies appearing in the 1930s and increasing markedly after the 1960s (Davis and Schoen, 1978, pp. 50ff). The present structure of medical practice in the US evolved through a gradual process of professional consolidation and dominance in the late nineteenth and early twentieth centuries (Starr, 1982). Health care is still largely provided by solo practitioners operating on a fee-for-service basis. Practitioners have created networks of organizations of convenience — professional partnerships, billing agencies, referral networks, hospital corporations, malpractice insurance pools, etc., — which allow them to capture many of the economies of cooperation without seriously undermining their professional or economic autonomy. Competition among practitioners, while surely present in many forms, is still considered unprofessional, even unethical, and often antithetical to quality care. This private market of solo practitioners is complemented by third party insurers, operating between clients and providers to pool risk among clients and reduce uncertainty in the payment of fees

This structure of private practice is nested within a complex web of public policy, which attempts to provide access to health care for those unable to purchase it in sufficient quantity in the private market. Public policy toward health care takes three essential forms: one is direct subsidies to private practitioners for activities like hospital construction; the second is subsidies to the aged (Medicare), which provide universal access for those over age sixty-five and are financed through a social insurance fund generated by a payroll tax; and the third is subsidies to the dependent and disabled (Medicaid) which provide rationed access to selected groups of beneficiaries, whose eligibility is determined by criteria tied to welfare policies, and is financed by direct expenditures from federal and state governments. These policies are mandated and regulated by the federal government, but on the Medicaid side they are heavily influenced by state-administered welfare policies. The dominant mode of public involvement in health care, then, with important exceptions that will be dealt with momentarily, is subsidies to consumers based on services used.

Lately, mounting political pressure for cost control has prompted the federal and state governments to press for a number of innovations in the organization and finance of publicly-subsidized health care delivery. One model is 'capitation plans', or health maintenance organizations (HMOs), in which a group of practitioners combines to form an integrated practice, delivering a range of medical service for which clients pay a flat fee based on pooled risk. The distinctive institutional character of HMOs is, first, they combine insurance and health care provision in a single organization; and, second, the flat fee structure creates strong internal incentives to control the cost and utilization of health care. Another model is Preferred Provider Organizations (PPOs), in which an insurance company contracts with doctors and hospitals selectively on behalf of clients. Clients are then given a list of preferred providers covered by the plan; if they use others, they pay a larger fraction of the cost. The distinctive character of PPOs is, first, they are able to aggregate client demand; second, they exert significant influence over choice of providers on behalf of clients; and, third, because of their market power, they are able to negotiate price. Still another model is the Primary Care Network (PCN), in which clients are enrolled in a capitation plan and assigned to a primary care physician. The primary care physician is given two accounts, one for his own services and a second for specialty referrals and hospitalization. The physician is allowed to keep the unspent portion of the second account. The distinctive character of PCNs is the strong incentives they introduce for primary care and reduction in utilization of high-cost treatment (Luft, 1981; Starr, 1986; Enthoven, 1985). Each of these innovations has been tried in selected settings. But this high level of organizational innovation has had a limited impact on the overall delivery of publicly-subsidized health care. Less than 2 per cent of Medicare patients, for example, are enrolled in HMOs (Starr, 1986, p. 128).

Like education, health care has its own distinctive institutional biases. From the origins of publicly-subsidized health care, the medical profession has used its influence to limit direct provision of medical services by public agencies. Those public health care organizations that do exist — veterans' hospitals, state and county public health agencies, and publicly-funded community health centers — operate under highly restrictive mandates, very limited funding, or both (Starr, 1986; Davis and Schoen, 1978).

Furthermore, the history of direct public subsidies to clients for health care has a decided 'institutional tilt' (Starr, 1986, p. 131) in favor of the interests of traditional providers and away from cost controls and innovative forms of medical practice. Until 1983, payment under Medicare and Medicaid was based on retrospective billing by physicians, constrained only by the requirement that charges be 'usual, customary, and reasonable'. This system preserved the fee-for-service system of solo providers and, of course, introduced significant incentives for cost inflation (*ibid.* p. 121). It has now been replaced by a system of prospective payment based on a set fee schedule for specific procedures (Diagnostic Related Groups, or DRGs). Established health care organizations have responded to this new system by shifting the mix of clients toward DRGs with higher fees, by rationing access of publicly-subsidized patients, and by pushing marginal diagnoses up the fee schedule (so-called DRG-creep). Squeezing greater efficiencies out of the fee-for-service system has also had ironic effects on voluntary provision of health care by hospitals to the indigent. This care was traditionally financed by cross-subsidies — using surpluses generated on private, third-party payments and on direct public subsidies to cover the cost of free care to the indigent. As cost controls mounted, these surpluses decreased, making voluntary provision of free care increasingly difficult. Finally, Medicare and Medicaid payment systems have systematically favored traditional providers over HMOs, despite several attempts to change the law and several state experiments designed to introduce capitation plans for publicly-subsidized clients (*ibid.*).

The institutional structure of publicly-subsidized health care creates severe cross-pressures on federal and state policymakers which in turn affect clients' access to health care. The institutional tilt of health care policy means that policymakers tend to resolve trade-offs between cost and access in favor of decreased access. As total costs of health care have risen, policymakers have consistently chosen to limit access by controlling eligibility and authorized treatments, rather than reducing payments to practitioners or relying increasingly on more efficient forms of delivery.

This form of rationing disproportionately affects the poor, since Medicaid, which is funded by direct public expenditures, is more sensitive to budget-cutting than Medicare, which serves a broader population and is funded as social insurance. When Medicare and Medicaid were initially introduced, the medically uninsured population dropped significantly and stayed at a relatively low level until cost inflation began to create pressures for expenditure control, at which point the uninsured population began to grow. Recent estimates suggest that about one-quarter of those below the poverty line, about 30 per cent of the unemployed, and about 10 per cent of all persons in the US were without health coverage (*ibid.* p. 115).

The existence of a structure based on direct subsidies of clients and providers in health care, then, does not mean that client and provider preferences determine access, utilization, and treatment in the health care system. Federal and state governments have altered the form of subsidies, promoted alternative forms of medical practice, and rationed access — all in the name of controlling expenditures and increasing efficiency. Nor does it appear that direct subsidies of clients and providers produce a technically or allocatively efficient solution to the problem of how to spend public health care dollars. Indeed, public policy toward health care in the US has, until quite recently, been based on the principle that providers should be able to name their own price, substituting pricing conventions and professional judgment for price competition. Even the solutions to cost inflation that have been introduced, through DRGs, for example, are not competitive solutions; they are, in effect, uniform pricing agreements. One analyst estimates that health care expenditures could be reduced as much as 20 per cent with no appreciable decline in welfare if the health care system were operated efficiently (*ibid.* p. 121).

Modes of Practice

Education and health care institutions also construct choices by the way they define the nature of practice. The range of alternatives that practitioners can offer to clients is heavily influenced by what practitioners are required to know in order to practice, and by how the work of practitioners is socially defined. The knowledge requirements for entry to elementary and secondary teaching are high relative to most occupations in society, but low relative to other human service professions (medicine and social work, for example). The knowledge requirements for teaching are driven by the practical necessities of staffing a mass institution in which the participation of clients is mandatory. Because public schools are unable to ration access to services in any systematic way, fluctuations in school enrollment have historically been accommodated by raising and lowering entry requirements to the occupation of teaching. While entry requirements have steadily increased with each cycle of enrollment increase and decline, the locus of decisionmaking about entry requirements does not reside with educators. Decisions about entry requirements for teaching are, for the most part, made by public agencies in response to enrollment fluctuations, rather than by the education professions acting in any institutional capacity.

The knowledge requirements for entry to medical practice, on the other hand, are high relative to most other occupations, and are driven by a professional services market in which practitioners play a large role in determining the level of service offered and consumed. Decisions about entry requirements are lodged largely with professional organizations, acting under public authority. Control over the conditions of entry to medical practice, and control over the level of medical services and the terms under which they are offered, mean that medical practitioners exercise greater influence over their own labor supply than do educators.

The relatively low entry requirements for teaching and the relatively high public management of supply and demand mean that individual teachers typically do not play an influential role in deciding on the conditions of their practice. They exercise relatively little influence, for example, in deciding who their colleagues will be or in evaluating colleagues' practice, and when they do, it is at the pleasure of administrators. While teachers exercise considerable influence over what goes on in their classrooms, they typically have little formal authority, and highly variable influence, over school-wide decisions about what will be taught, how, and to whom. For most teachers, influence over the content and organization of their practice is low.

Medical practitioners, on the other hand, are expected to exercise relatively high influence over the content and organization of their practice, both individually and collectively. They routinely select their colleagues, they are required to serve on professional standards bodies to evaluate the practice of their peers, they affiliate with and gain privileges from a number of different types of professional organizations, and they are expected to participate in the decisions of those organizations that affect their practice. Only recently, with the introduction of forms of 'managed practice', have the tensions between health care managers and medical practitioners begun to emerge.

The range of alternative forms of practice that might emerge in response to increased public pressure for client choice will be heavily influenced by the way practice is socially constructed. The lower the knowledge requirements, the greater the public management of entry requirements, and the more heavily constrained the terms of practice, the less likely practitioners will be respond to external pressures with significantly different alternative forms of practice. The higher the knowledge requirements, the greater professional management of entry requirements, and the less constrained professional influence over the terms of practice, the greater the range of alternative forms of practice that are likely to emerge in response to external pressures.

Political Agendas

The institutional structures and modes of practice in education and health care are, of course, not just random events. They are the result of political interests acting on public agendas. Broad questions of how public services should be organized and what role choice should play in their design and operation are always mediated by specific political contexts, and specific interest groups, acting on specific institutions.

In education, for example, the issue of student and parent choice never appears on the political agenda of states or localities without the sponsorship of some interest group. Often, but not always, the dominant interests are those of the established service providers. Choice has been used, for example, by parochial school interests to press for public support of parochial schools. It has been used by laissez-faire conservatives to press for direct public aid to private schools and greater public-private competition. It has used by liberals to press for access by poor parents to the same quality of education that well-to-do parents achieve by living in expensive residential communities or by paying private school tuition. It has been used by good government interests to prod public school bureaucracy into being more effective and responsive. And it has been used by urban school systems to promote selectivity and racial balance simultaneously in a few settings. In health care, choice has been used by advocates of alternatives to fee-for-service medical practice to introduce public support for HMOs and other alternative forms of practice. It has been used by private firms and insurers to introduce pressures for cost-containment. And it has been used by the fee-for-service medical establishment to argue for the preservation of traditional forms of practice. Of course, introducing 'more choice' for clients and providers can not possibly satisfy all these competing objectives. What the advocates for choice typically mean when they say 'more choice' is more choice of a particular, structured around a particular incentive, to have a particular effect on an existing system of political and institutional relations.

As a political issue, then, client and provider choice means a variety of different things to different interests. Choice, by itself, does not lead to any predictable political or social result. The meaning of choice proposals can only be understood in the context of specific alterations of institutional structures within specific constraints on organization, money, and information. While it sounds good for advocates to say that increased client and provider choice will lead predictably to greater client satisfaction, greater efficiency in the use of resources, or better distribution of public benefits, these claims are based largely on political interest rather than on empirical reality. The empirical reality, as we shall see shortly, is considerably more complex than the assertions of advocates.

Macro-Structure: Some Conclusions About Policy Design

As noted earlier, advocates of educational choice describe the ideal educational system as one in which students and parents are free to choose among schools with different types of educational programs, and in which teachers are free to form the kind of schools that parents and students demand. A few advocates of educational choice propose direct payments to parents, which can then be used to purchase education in the market; most advocates propose choice within the public system, in which payments from clients to providers are implicit in the choices that clients make among alternative programs. In other words, advocates of educational choice propose some form of publicly subsidized market for professional services analogous to the market for health care. In this sense, then, the parallels between education and health care are instructive.

What is striking about these comparisons between education and health care is the degree to which the problems of client and provider choice in the two systems seem to be mirror images of each other. In education, locally-centralized assignment of teachers and students, coupled with controls over finance and curriculum, produces a relatively standardized service, but this uniformity means that client preferences are frequently ignored. In health care, the system of solo practitioners produces little variation in the form of medical practice offered to clients, and while major structural alternatives are more likely to arise in this institutional setting, established patterns of practice dominate. In education, the form of funding and administration makes efficiency, in either the technical or allocative sense, difficult to achieve. Money passes from central authorities to schools with relatively strict budget controls, but little or no regard for how effectively it is being used or whether it is being allocated to activities that clients value. In health care, the costs of public subsidies are largely driven by professional judgments about acceptable treatments and the costs that attach to them. Even under newer, more rigid, cost controls the decisions that drive the total cost of public health care subsidies are made largely by hospital administrators and medical practitioners, not by clients shopping in a competitive market for the lowest cost, highest quality care. In education, where the institutional structure allows little or no rationing of entry, access to high quality academic programs is differentially allocated by central administrators and access to academic courses is allocated by building administrators. Almost everyone gets some level of service, but some clients in a given system get a much high level of service than others. In health care, the institutional structure allows considerable rationing of both entry and access to different kinds of services. In health care policy, trade-offs between efficiency and coverage are typically resolved by allowing the existing institutional structure to determine the cost of services and limiting coverage to meet *a priori* budget targets. The result is that large portions of the public are uninsured, which limits or excludes them from entry or access to services. Both systems have rationing mechanisms — one inclusive, the other exclusive.

Hence, it seems dubious to argue that any major problems of organization, efficiency, or access will be solved by moving the education system to something that more closely resembles a professional services market. The same problems that now affect education will occur in slightly modified form in a new macro-structure.

The key problems of policy design, then, lie not in getting the macro-structure of education to look more like a professional services market, but in finding solutions to the specific problems that arise when any system tries to represent client preferences in the nature and organization of services. These are problems of micro-structure.

Micro-Structure: Information, Preferences, and Effects

In order for client and provider choice to be useful as an instrument of public policy, we must understand how they work in specific institutional structures. Among the important issues of policy design that surround choice are at least three major ones: (1) the level and type of information that clients have and that providers produce about the nature of the service they offer; (2) the preferences of clients and the way those preferences operate on the distribution of services; and (3) the effects of client choice on policy-relevant outcomes.

Information

A major problem underlying policies designed to enhance client and provider choice is whether clients are able to make informed choices among alternative services. In education and medical care there are at least two *a priori* reasons for skepticism about informed choice (see Weisbrod, 1983). One reason is that the practice of education and medicine, and the organization of that practice, are relatively complex. Making an informed judgment under these conditions requires a high level of information and a relatively high degree of sophistication in using it.

A second reason to be skeptical of informed choice is that providers in both education and medicine have relatively strong incentives to limit clients' access to information. Bureaucratic monopolies, like public education, place a high priority on maintaining central control over clients' access to information, in the name of impartiality, procedural fairness, and equal treatment. Professional services markets, like medicine, also have strong incentives to limit information, in the name of professional standards and peer control over the terms of practice. In both sectors, one would expect clients to be at a relative disadvantage to providers in access to information.

Information in health care

One line of research on client information in health care examines basic knowledge of medical practice and its relationship to client characteristics. Participants in the federally-sponsored health insurance experiment[2] were asked a series of questions designed to measure aspects of their knowledge of medical practice that could be expected to affect their sophistication as clients. Most respondents were aware that they could get a second opinion in a medical diagnosis and most were aware that getting an appropriate response to a medical problem often depends on finding the right specialist. On the other hand, most respondents did not know that board certification was an important indicator of a physician's qualifications, that choosing a doctor constrains a patient's choice of hospitals, or that doctors are not routinely re-examined for renewal of their licenses to practice (Newhouse *et al.*, 1981b, pp. 325–6). A study comparing surgery rates between medical school faculty and people in other occupations of similar status (attorneys, ministers, and business school graduates) showed little difference, suggesting that physicians' professional knowledge does not result in patterns of surgery different from those of other well-educated professionals (Bunker and Brown, 1974).

Another line of research examines clients' knowledge of their health insurance coverage. Participants in the health insurance experiment were asked a series of questions about their health coverage. Virtually all respondents were able to say accurately whether they had insurance or not, and whether their insurance covered hospitalization. However, respondents substantially under-reported their coverage for physician out-patient services and for drugs. Respondents' knowledge was also found to vary significantly with the form of insurance. Participants in pre-paid group practice (HMO) were likely to report their coverage more accurately than those with reimbursement insurance. Among those with reimbursement coverage, those with deductibles were more likely to under-report their coverage than those with first-dollar coverage. The study also found that clients' knowledge was inversely related to the complexity of their coverage and that knowledge was positively related to education (Marquis, 1981).

A third line of research examines the degree to which health care clients engage in behaviors associated with active consumer choice. Hibbard and Weeks (1987) argue that there are significant contradictions between the behaviors of a 'good patient' in the health care sector and a 'good consumer'. A good patient is expected to be 'compliant, trusting, and uncomplaining'. A good consumer is expected to be 'questioning, willing to make independent judgments . . . and seeks out alternative sources of information' (*ibid.* p. 1020). In a sample of state government employees and Medicare enrollees in Oregon, researchers found less than 40 per cent of respondents reported engaging in active price-seeking, information-seeking, or use of independent judgment in dealing with physicians. Respondents were found to differ significantly by age, sex, income, and education in their reported willingness to engage in active consumer behavior. For example, older people were less likely to be cost-sensitive than younger people, females were much more likely to be information seekers than males, and those with more education and larger families were found to be more likely to exercise independent judgment. In general, the researchers concluded that 'those with the greatest risk for using services and incurring costs are the least prepared to behave as critical consumers'. (*ibid.* p. 1030).

Client information in education

One line of research on client information in education deals with parents' awareness of and their reported willingness to exercise choice. A 1984 Minnesota survey found that 62 per cent of public school parents reported themselves to be 'active choosers', either in the sense of considering alternatives to their children's present school or choosing a place of residence based on the quality of a school (Darling-Hammond and Kirby, 1988, pp. 247–8). A nationwide household survey found that about half of public school parents reported school quality influenced their choice of residence, and about 18 per cent cited it as the most important factor in their choice. Parents with higher income and more education were more likely to consider school quality in choice of residence; black parents were less likely (Sherman *et al.*, 1983, p. 50).

Another line of research on parents' information in education grows out of the Alum Rock voucher demonstration.[3] The demonstration was conducted over a five-year period, beginning in 1972–73. Over the first four years of the demonstration, parents were allowed to choose among a number of 'minischools', alternative educational programs organized within schools. The number of programs increased from twenty-two in six schools during the first year to fifty-one in fourteen schools during the fourth year. Parents in 'voucher school' attendance areas were allowed to choose among programs in any voucher school; parents in 'non-voucher schools' were treated as controls during the demonstration. For voucher participants, free transportation was provided to non-neighborhood schools, transfers were permitted during the year, preferential access was granted to students enrolled in the schools the previous year and to kindergartners and first graders with older siblings enrolled in a given school, and a lottery was used to assign admissions to oversubscribed programs. In the fifth year of the demonstration, the district disbanded the voucher system in favor of an open enrollment plan. Under the open enrollment system the number of alternative programs was severely reduced and mid-year transfers were made more difficult (Bridge and Blackman, 1978, pp. 17–19).

Surveys done during the demonstration showed that voucher parents were consistently more knowledgeable about the existence of program options, transportation, and transfer rights than those who did not participate. The accuracy of voucher participants' information increased over time. Parents' knowledge of options, transportation, and transfer rights were positively related to their expectations and aspirations for their children. Education and income were positively related to parents' information about their options, but not to their information about transportation and transfer rights. Anglo and black parents showed greater awareness of the existence of options than did Mexican-American parents. Better-educated parents were more likely to rely on official information sources and printed material, while less-educated parents were more likely to rely on face-to-face contacts for information. When the voucher demonstration was abandoned in favor of open enrollment all parents' information about options, transportation, and transfer rights dropped precipitously (*ibid.* pp. 27–42).

These studies suggest a number of implications for the role of information in the design of policies affecting client and provider choice. One implication is that what clients know about their choices seems to be heavily influenced by the institutional structure within which choice occurs. When significant incentives exist for providers to limit client information, as is the case in both education and health care, then it seems unlikely that the level of information supplied by providers will be adequate by itself to insure informed choices. In health care, the existence of third-party insurers operates to limit the advantages of providers. Choice plans in education should probably include third-party sources of information on schooling alternatives.

A second implication is that what clients know about a given institutional structure, and the sources of information they use, seem to differ significantly for different types of clients. So in order to know what kind and level of information is effective, one must know something about the information-seeking behavior of different types of clients.

And a third implication is that the level of information possessed by a given client seems to be heavily influenced by the complexity of the structure within which clients are expected to choose and by opportunities provided by the structure to engage in information-seeking behavior. Highly complex structures require more knowledge and skill to negotiate. It takes time for individual clients and clients in the aggregate to learn about the complexity of structures. Opportunities to engage the structures provide opportunities to learn. Changing key structural features increases the level and cost of learning.

Each of these implications has at least two sides. On the one hand, structures inhibit acquisition of information by creating barriers and controls; on the other hand, it seems likely that inequities of information — between providers and clients, as well as among different types of clients — can be reduced by the design of institutional structures.

The view that client choice increases the responsiveness and efficiency of public institutions is subject to serious qualifications. It seems unlikely, for example, that giving clients greater choice in highly complex, inscrutable structures will result in anything other than a reshuffling of opportunity in favor of those who are willing to incur the costs of information-seeking. It also seems unlikely that making greater choice available to clients, in absence of changes in the structure of institutions, will by itself make clients into more avid information seekers.

Existing research on information and choice in health care and education has not begun to tap the level of information required to be a critical consumer in either sector. The research typically asks clients very simple factual questions about the characteristics of their choices that have right and wrong answers. In both education and health care, the level of information required to be a critical consumer is far beyond that tapped by the surveys done thus far. In health care, for example, clients are typically presented with choices that are characterized not just by fees, benefit levels, and various forms of cost-sharing, but they are also confronted by choices of practitioners, service mixes, service qualities, and philosophies of medical practice. To be an informed and critical consumer, in other words, requires not just readily available information on complex subjects but also the ability to engage, observe, and interrogate the system. In education, clients are typically presented with simple descriptions of their procedural rights and sketches of the educational options available to them. But they are in fact choosing a complex combination of practitioners, curriculum content, and some sort of agreed-upon mode of interaction among educators, parents, and children (even if the agreement is to leave such matters to individuals). Differences on these dimensions can hardly be tapped by simple description. Again, being an informed and critical consumer would seem to depend on some kind of sustained engagement, observation, and interrogation.

Preference and Composition

Another major problem underlying policies designed to enhance client and provider choice has to do with the role that client preference and selection play in determining the composition of provider organizations. This problem occurs in two different but closely-related forms in health care and education. In health care, the problem arises mainly in the form of 'adverse selection'. The financial viability of alternative forms of health care, and the organizations that provide them, depends heavily on the ability of those organizations to maintain a certain client mix. An HMO, for example, must maintain a mix of high- and low-utilization clients in order to be competitive with conventional insurance and fee-for-service providers.

In education, the problem centers mainly on the racial and socio-economic composition of schools. Actions on the part of state and local school officials that increase racial and socio-economic stratification are often legally and politically suspect. They may also be educationally suspect. School achievement is related to race and social class. When parents are allowed to choose among schools, they 'may succeed in raising their child's achievement by placing the child in a school with a socio-economically advantaged student body. In contrast, . . . the public policy goal of providing all students with a good education cannot be achieved by providing all students with the option of attending a school with a socioeconomically advantaged student body' (Murnane, 1986, p. 146).

Preference and composition in health care

From the client's perspective, the choice of prepaid-HMO versus reimbursement of fee-for-service presents a complex problem. The monthly premium costs for prepaid-HMO coverage are relatively high, and total costs do not vary much with utilization. Fee-for-service reimbursement typically entails relatively lower premium costs, but total costs vary significantly with utilization (Buchanan and Cretin, 1986; p. 5). Hence, one might predict that clients who expect to have high medical costs would select HMOs on the expectation that their long-run out-of-pocket costs would be lower than reimbursement insurance. This, of course, is a formula for adverse selection into HMOs.

The evidence on HMO versus fee-for-service choice is considerably more ambiguous than this expectation suggests. There is some evidence that health risk and utilization patterns of clients play a role in selection of health care (Luft, 1981) and that there may be adverse selection into HMOs (Manning *et al.*, 1984). But a more important finding is that client choice is quite 'sticky'. That is, clients with strong ties to certain providers and longer tenure in a given system are less likely to change delivery systems than those with weaker ties and shorter tenure. Likewise, the clients who are most likely to leave one delivery system for another are those with weaker ties and shorter tenure (Buchanan and Cretin, 1986; p. 4; see also Juba *et al.*, 1980; and Garfinkel *et al.*, 1986).

The complexity of these patterns of choice is exemplified in a selection of studies. One study found that when an HMO option was introduced by a large California aerospace firm as an alternative to existing fee-for-service reimbursement coverage, the families selecting the HMO option were younger, had less time on the job, and had lower medical costs than those with fee-for-service coverage. Families who switched out of HMO coverage during subsequent enrollment periods had higher total claims than those who switched into HMOs (*ibid*, pp. 2, 39, 40).

Another study examined patterns of choice between two different types of prepaid plans for Stanford University employees. One plan was an established HMO, the other — called the clinic plan — was a prepaid plan administered by a multi-specialty physicians' group whose main practice was fee-for-service. The HMO took the traditional organizational form: prepayment, closed-panel (no selective coverage), integrated primary and hospital care. The physicians' group shared receipts from the prepaid plan as part of its larger practice and incorporated a conventional hospitalization policy to cover clients' use of a neighboring university hospital. The HMO plan had slightly lower premiums than the clinic plan, but the HMO had negligible utilization charges while the clinic plan had a 25 per cent coinsurance charge for all outpatient and inpatient services. The clinic plan had been operating since the 1950s, while the HMO had been offered to employees since 1969. The study found that family income, convenience, and prior experience were the chief determinants of choice of plan. Higher income families tended to choose the clinic plan over the HMO and tended to cite as reasons for their choice the proximity of clinic facilities and the convenience of access to physicians and medical records. Lower income families tended to choose the HMO plan and to cite cost as a major reason. Furthermore, families enrolled in the clinic program before the HMO enrollment option was introduced tended to stay with the clinic program even when their family income would predict that they would switch to the HMO (Scitovsky, McCall and Benham, 1978).

A final study examined the response of employees in a large California bank to the addition of a new option to their health care coverage. Employees had access to multiple HMOs and to a standard fee-for-service reimbursement scheme prior to the introduction of a preferred provider organization (PPO), a contracting arrangement between an employer and a network of physicians to deliver health care according to a negotiated fee schedule (see Enthoven, 1985). The study found that the new system was used initially by individuals who required little health care and was used most extensively for low-risk services requiring little treatment. The likelihood of joining the PPO decreased with the number of prior visits to a physician, and clients were more likely to switch to the PPO if their physician switched (Wouter and Hester, 1988).

These studies suggest that there are preference and selection effects associated with various health care options, but that they are not easily predicted by the formal characteristics of the options. The kind of factors that account for choices, at least in the short term, are not ones that are easily engineered through the construction of economic incentives.

Another feature of preference and selection in the health care sector, noted earlier in this chapter, is the diversification of organizational forms. As private firms and governmental agencies have increased pressure for cost-control, the number and variety of organizational alternatives for the delivery of health care has increased markedly. Distinctions between fee-for-service and pre-paid group practice have been blurred by a variety of arrangements in which employers contract directly with panels of physicians and in which HMOs introduce copayment and diversified coverage plans to capture specific segments of the market. As noted above, this kind of diversification is more likely when the sector starts from an organizational base of solo practitioners than when it starts, as in education, from a base of public monopoly.

Preference and composition in education

From the client's perspective, choices in education are largely defined by residential location and by the availability and relative price of private schools. In a some select instances, attempts have been made to create options within existing public schools, in which the nature of the educational program is a larger factor in choice than cost.

As noted above, more than 60 per cent of parents in Minnesota and over half of the parents in a national sample reported that public school quality played an important role in their choice of residence (Darling-Hammond and Kirby, 1988; Sherman *et al.*, 1983). In a national sample, there were significant differences in reported reasons for choice between parents of public and private school children. Public school parents were more likely to cite cost and convenience as key factors in their decisions. Parochial school parents were more likely to cite values and religious instruction as key factors. Independent school parents were more likely to cite purely academic factors as decisive in their choice (Sherman *et al.*, 1983; p. 53).[4]

When parents are asked about their willingness to exercise choice within the existing public school system, substantial proportions support the availability of alternative programs but substantial portions also report that they would be unwilling to have their children transported long distances to take advantage of those options. In Minneapolis, for example, well over 70 per cent of parents in one area supported the provision of alternative programs, but 44 per cent said they would be unwilling to have their children transported beyond the adjacent attendance area for such a program, and more than one quarter said they would choose the nearest available school regardless of its educational program (Farnam *et al.*, 1975, quoted in Glenn, 1988a, pp. 26–7).

Parent surveys conducted in the Alum Rock voucher demonstration found that the geographical location of alternative programs was the single most important factor in parent choice. More than half the parents responded positively to a statement citing location as the most important factor in choosing a school and more than 7 per cent of parents in the first year of the demonstration responded to an open-ended question about the reason for their choice with location. On the other hand, parents in voucher schools showed a decreased attachment to location over time.

There is also some evidence to suggest that as parents perceive the alternatives to be more differentiated, they are more likely to choose non-neighborhood schools. And the willingness of parents to choose schools outside their neighborhoods increases with the age of their children. While parents manifested considerable resistance to choosing schools outside their immediate neighborhood, on balance the proportion of children attending non-neighborhood schools increased each year of the voucher experiment, from about 11 per cent in the first year of the demonstration to about 22 per cent in the third year (Bridge and Blackman, 1978, pp. 47, 100–1).

Curriculum and instruction played a less important role than location, general perceptions of staff, and whether a child would be comfortable with the school in parents' reported reasons for choosing schools in Alum Rock. About one-third of parents reported factors related to educational program as influencing their choice of school in the first year of the voucher demonstration (*ibid.* pp. 51, 101).

When parents were asked a series of specific questions about what kind of educational program they preferred for their children — on dimensions such as broad versus narrow coverage, level of tolerance for controversy, and classroom behavior — their responses varied by ethnicity, education, and occupational status. Anglos and English-speaking Mexican Americans preferred a broader curriculum than Spanish-speaking Mexican Americans. Blacks, Anglos, and English-speaking Mexican Americans preferred less structured classrooms than Spanish-speaking Mexican Americans; white collar workers preferred less structured classrooms than blue collar workers; and parents with more than a high school education preferred less structured classrooms than those with less. The relationship between social class and program content was corroborated by comparison data collected in Minneapolis and Mamaroneck, New York (*ibid.* pp. 53–5, 102).

Another perspective on the role of preference and selection can be gained from attempts to use choice as a tool of desegregation in urban districts. A number of cities have begun to use open-enrollment schemes, which operate by allowing parents to state a preference for schools and then assigning pupils based on parental preference and racial balance. In Cambridge, for example, 73 per cent of new students were assigned to the school ranked first by their parents, and 18 per cent were assigned to their second choice. This system resulted in 42 per cent of students attending the school that would have been their neighborhood school. More minority parents chose schools outside their neighborhoods than non-minority parents, by 64 per cent to 52 per cent. The plan has resulted in substantial reductions of racial isolation and substantial reduction in the previous racial identification of schools. Schools in Cambridge are encouraged to take different educational approaches, yet evidence of parents' school preferences do not show significant differences by race (Rossell and Glenn, 1987).

An example of how preference and selection can operate in a system that encourages parental choice over a long period of time comes from Holland. Since 1917, Holland has guaranteed full public funding for any school that meets certain basic enrollment and quality standards. Parents are allowed to choose any such school. According to Glenn (1988b, p. 15), the resulting 'diversity in Dutch education owes more to the accommodations reached among [competing religious and social] groups than to any principled commitment to foster individual choice'. All operating costs of schools are directly subsidized by the state. Each school is governed by a 'responsible authority', which might be a local government in the case of public schools, a religious body in the case of a church school, or a board in the case of an independent school. The state requires schools to meet minimum size requirements, based on the population of the area and the availability of alternatives, to employ teachers who meet certain standards, and to meet certain class size and subject matter requirements.

This system has resulted in a proliferation of small, sectorally-identified schools. The average elementary school enrolls 159 students and has a capacity for 199. Public schools enroll 31 per cent of the students, Protestant schools enroll 28 per cent, Catholic schools about 37 per cent, and independent or 'non-confessional' private schools about 3 per cent (*ibid.* p. 3). Overall, parents' expressed preference for denominational education has been declining steadily for the past twenty years. Since 1966, for example, the proportion of Catholic parents expressing a preference for Catholic schools has declined from 86 per cent to about 65 per cent. For some denominations, evangelicals and mainline Protestants in certain areas, preferences for denominational education has been increasing (*ibid.* p. 31). Recent opinion data show that the proportion of parents who think it is important for schools to represent their religious preferences in the educational program is about equal to those who think it is unimportant — roughly 40 per cent on each side (*ibid.* p. 22). There is a lively political debate in Holland over the nature and significance of this 'secularization'. Advocates of public education argue that it means religious differences are increasingly irrelevant and should be erased by a universal public system. Advocates of non-public education argue that it means schools are not doing a good enough job of defining their unique mission. Whatever the significance of these arguments, there is substantial opinion, both inside Holland and outside, that the particular combination of sectarian organization and state regulation that characterizes Dutch schooling has not resulted in much innovation or attention to differences in the educational needs and preferences of children or their parents. There is some agreement that the system does not operate as a quasi-competitive market offering options to its clients, but rather as a cartel of interlocking interests supported by the state which limits competition and improvements in quality (*ibid.* p. 55).

In education, as in health care, there is some evidence of preference and selection effects associated with changes in the structure of client and provider choice. Offering choice to clients results in some redistribution of opportunities, but the exact nature of this redistribution depends, as in health care, on the institutional structure within which choice occurs, the purposes for which choice is being used, and on client preferences that often have little to do with the content of education. There is also evidence that clients adapt over time to opportunities to choose. The Dutch case seems to illustrate how a combination of state regulation and parent choice can produce a result that does not necessarily result in greater attention to client preferences and needs or to innovation.

This research suggests at least three implications for the design of policies on client and provider choice and their effects on composition of providers. The first implication is that institutional structure defines choices. The more diverse the structure, the greater the range of choice. But the more diverse the structure, the greater the complexity and cost of choosing. In health care, there are strong incentives built into policy and institutional structure — largely having to do with cost control — for increasing the diversity of organizational forms. In education, incentives for diversity are weak and would have to be strengthened if diversity is to be increased.

The second implication is that there is no compelling *a priori* case that increased choice leads to adverse selection in health care or stratification by race or class in education. The evidence is mixed, in large part, because the structures defining choices vary in the degree to which they acknowledge and deal explicitly with problems of preference and selection.

The third implication is that the preferences that actually operate on client choice often are not the ones that policy makers regard as central to effective servies, but are instrumental in clients' minds to their use of the service. Location is one example of such an instrumental factor. The 'stickiness' of client choices is another. Understanding how client preferences would affect the nature and composition of service organizations means understanding a lot about the specific preferences of clients for specific attributes of services.

Effects

A final problem of policies designed to affect client and provider choice is the relationship between increased choice and client outcomes. The arguments of advocates of increased choice rest on the assumption that providers must satisfy client demands and, in turn, must produce positive effects for clients. Increased client and provider choice, in this view, should result in greater client satisfaction, positive client outcomes, and greater efficiency in the delivery of services. Considering the centrality of this argument to policy debates about client and provider choice, there is surprisingly little evidence available on the actual effects of increased choice.

Health care effects

The national health insurance experiment was designed mainly to estimate the effects of various types and levels of cost-sharing on utilization of services and health status (Newhouse, 1974). Not surprisingly, the experiment found that as cost-sharing increases total expenditures for both ambulatory and hospital care decrease, from about $400 per person for free care to about $250 per person for 95 per cent coinsurance, as does the frequency of utilization. The experiment also found that low-income people are not more sensitive to cost-sharing, adjusted for their income, than middle- or high-income people. Nor did cost-sharing for ambulatory care cause clients to defer treatment and hence increase later hospitalization costs (Newhouse *et al.*, 1981a). These results suggest that changes in the economic conditions under which clients choose seems to affect health care utilization in predictable ways.

The effects of different forms of health insurance on health status present a somewhat different picture. Since utilization rates vary as much as 50 per cent with cost-sharing, it makes sense to ask whether those who receive free care have better health than those with cost-sharing. Examination of a broad battery of health status indicators revealed that free care was associated with improvement only of blood pressure and vision, and had no discernible effect on general health, health habits, or risk of dying (Brook *et al.*, 1984). A closer examination of hypertension revealed that free care did result in significant reductions in hypertension but that there were significantly more efficient ways to achieve the same result through screening and education rather than free general health care (Keeler *et al.*, 1985).

Outside the health insurance experiment, studies of the relationship between the level of medical resources in a given area and the health status of people in that area consistently show little effect of medical resources on health status. These studies are typically interpreted as saying that 'what the individual does (or does not) do for himself affects health more than do additional medical resources' in the surrounding area (Newhouse and Friedlander, 1980). Hence, the conditions under which people choose to seek health care are a more influential determinant of overall health than the level of resources within which they choose.

Education effects

Direct evidence on the effects of choice in education is quite weak. The Alum Rock demonstration was predicated on the dual assumptions that alternative programs would offer parents distinctively different options for their children and that these choices would improve student learning. Neither of these assumptions proved to be well-founded. Structured classroom observations revealed no significant differences among voucher classrooms, or between voucher and non-voucher classrooms, on such dimensions as pacing of content, use of Spanish in instruction, the degree of teacher initiation of instruction, or the degree of student initiation (Barker *et al.*, 1981). Likewise, analysis of reading scores revealed no significant differences among voucher classrooms or between voucher and non-voucher classrooms, nor were differences found between the reading scores of children whose parents saw themselves as active choosers and those who were non-choosers (Capell, 1981).

While evidence of the direct relationship between client choice and student effects is lacking, researchers point to what they regard as persuasive circumstantial evidence that choice increases diversity in educational offerings and positively affects student outcomes. In a number of districts that have adopted open enrollment choice plans, advocates argue, student test scores have risen. In some cases, the evidence is relatively persuasive (see, for example, Rossell and Glenn, 1987). Also there is substantial evidence that educators who work in alternative educational programs have more positive views of their work and have constructed conditions for learning that would seem to bear a presumptive relationship to better student outcomes (Raywid, 1984; 1985). But despite this strong circum stantial evidence, research directly linking choice with program diversity and program diversity with student effects does not exist beyond the disappointing results of the Alum Rock demonstration.

A related line of evidence deals with public-private school comparisons. If one assumes that a major difference between public and private schools rests on parental choice,[5] then it seems reasonable to predict that public and private schools would have different organizational cultures and different effects on student achievement. Catholic high schools appear to exceed public high schools in student achievement, controlling for student composition, and in fact appear to have greater effects for minority and low-income students than for others (Coleman *et al.*, 1982; Goldberger and Cain, 1982). In addition, there seem to be systematic differences in the way educators in public and non-public schools perceive their roles, their expectations of parents and students, and their control over key resources in the school environment (Chubb and Moe, 1985). Murnane, however, has observed about this literature that 'even the largest estimates of private school advantage are small relative to the variation in quality among different public schools, among different Catholic schools, and among different non-Catholic private schools. Consequently, in predicting the quality of a student's education, it is less important to know whether the student attended a public school or a private school, than it is to know which school within a particular sector the student attended' (Murnane, 1984, p. 270). Hence, the public-private school literature presents a less-than-compelling case for the relationship between choice and achievement.

The lack of persuasive connections between choice and effects in the research on education and health care is more a function of the state of research than of the state of practice. There are strong presumptive reasons, for example, to expect that as instructional programs become more highly focused, and as students and teachers become more invested in their work by virtue of having chosen the setting in which they work, that learning will improve. There is also substantial evidence that structural variations in schools, aside from their impact on choice, result in different patterns of student achievement (Bryk, Lee and Smith, in this volume). Likewise there are strong presumptive reasons to believe that if clients make informed choices about their health care under conditions that promote cost and quality, they will become more intelligent users, and hence healthier people. The problem is not that causal connections between choice and effects do not exist; the problem is that these effects are mediated by specific factors — notably, information, client preferences, the structure of services — that can vary greatly across contexts. So it makes little sense to say that 'choice works', without describing the conditions under which it might be expected to work. The main implication of this research for policy design, then, is that policymakers and researchers should focus in a more detailed way on the relations between client choice, contextual factors, and client outcomes, rather than on the simple connection between choice and outcomes.

Conclusion

I have argued that the simple view of choice as an instrument of public policy, based on technical and allocative efficiency, should be elaborated into a more complex view that takes account of institutional structures, political interests, and specific contextual factors that operate on client choice. This alternative view is agnostic on whether increased choice results in greater efficiency or responsiveness of public services. It asks instead what sort of political and institutional conditions would have to exist in order for increased client and provider choice to increase the efficency and responsiveness of public services, and what are the likely unanticipated effects of policies designed to increase choice.

The range of alternative forms of organization and practice that will emerge in response to policies designed to increase client and provider choice will be heavily constrained by institutional factors, including the knowledge requirements for practitioners' entry into organized practice, the degree of bureaucratic versus professional management of entry, and the degree of bureaucratic versus professional regulation of the terms of practice. Sectors which are knowledge-driven in their entry requirements, and which rely more heavily on professional controls, are more likely to respond to policies enhancing choice with a wider array of alternatives than sectors in which entry and practice are driven by bureaucratic norms. Using policy to stimulate alternative forms of organization and practice means not simply altering the conditions of client and provider choice but also, in many instances, changing the conditions of entry and practice in provider organizations.

But the existence of structural variations in practice is no guarantee that clients will necessarily gain increased choice. In both health care and education, the policy that surrounds practice constrains clients' access to alternative forms of service even after they are established. So the creation of alternative forms of practice must be accompanied by changes in the policies that affect client access in order for choice to operate effectively.

Left to their own devices, clients seem to know little about the institutional conditions that underlie their choices. Clients' knowledge and the type of information they use vary significantly by ethnicity and social class. Knowledge seems to be a function of the complexity of the insitutional structures in which clients are required to make choices. And knowledge increases with experience in structures that require them to make choices. On balance, these conditions seem to argue for a relatively active public role in the management of information in policies designed to encourage client and provider choice.

It seems unlikely that policies designed to give clients greater choice in highly complex, inscrutable structures will result in anything other than a reshuffling of opportunities in favor of those who are willing to incur the costs of information-seeking. It also seems unlikely that making greater choice available to clients, without increasing opportunities for clients to engage and interrogate institutions, will do anything other than increase the random movement of clients among providers.

Clients often choose services on the basis of criteria — location, previous loyalites, etc., — that have little to do with the objectives that policymakers are trying to accomplish with enhanced choice. Clients' attachments to these preferences seem to decrease with experience and exposure to alternative forms of practice. If client preference and selection alone operate on choice of service, then social stratification is likely to increase, but in the presence of relatively simple controls, choice can increase social integration. Again, these conditions seem to argue for a relatively active public role in managing the terms of choice.

There is no necessary relationship in existing empirical evidence between increased client and provider choice and increased effectiveness of services. Such evidence as exists suggests that choice, in combination with a number of as yet poorly-specified factors, may have beneficial effects for clients. But the evidence also suggests that the degree of variation among providers in the nature of services and the level of information possessed by clients are likely to heavily influence the degree to which choice increases effectiveness. In institutional settings, like education, where the degree of variation and the level of information is heavily constrained, it is unlikely that increasing choice will result in significant increases in effectiveness.

Notes

1 The author is indebted to William Clune, John Witte, John Coons, Richard Murnane, Susan Fuhrman and Barbara Wolfe for comments on an earlier version of this chapter.

2 The national health insurance experiment was conducted between 1974 and 1982 in six geographically dispersed sites in the US. Each of about 3,000 families were randomly assigned to one of fourteen health insurance plans, representing a range of coverage from free care through various combinations of deductibles (fixed dollar liability to patient), coinsurance (patient pays a fraction of all expenses), and copayment (patient pays a flat fee for each use). Some control group participants in one site were members of an HMO. The plans were evaluated on the basis of their effects on utilization of health care, cost, and health status. For a detailed discussion of design issues, see Newhouse (1974) and Marquis (1981).

3 For more detailed accounts of the Alum Rock demonstration see Bass (1978) and Cohen and Farrar (1977).

4 I am indebted to Charles Glenn for his summary of this evidence.

5 This assumption is more problematical than is apparent at first blush. A survey of Minnesota parents, for example, found that a significantly smaller proportion of private school parents considered themselves to be 'active choosers' than public school parents — 53 per cent versus 62 per cent. (Darling-Hammond and Kirby, 1988, pp. 247–8, cited in Glenn, 1988a, p. 25) Glenn explains this finding by arguing that 'the relatively low proportion of private school parents who are "active choosers"' seems to be attributable to the fact that 'many are Catholics for whom the local parochial school is simply a part of the parish affiliation, and others have a family tradition of using a particular private school', (Glenn, 1988a, p. 25). It is at least as plausible to hypothesize that some significant proportion of private-school parents are not active choosers as it is to hypothesize that some significant proportion of public-school parents are active choosers. School affiliation, in other words, is a far from perfect proxy for parent choice.

References

BARKER, P. *et al.*, (1981) *A Study of Alternatives in American Education, Vol. V: Diversity in the Classroom*, Santa Monica, CA: The Rand Corporation.

BASS, G. (1978) *Alternatives in American Education, Vol. 1, District Policies and the Implementation of Change*, Santa Monica, CA: The Rand Corporation.

BRIDGE, R.G. and BLACKMAN, J. (1978) *A Study of Alternatives in American Education, Vol. IV: Family Choice in Education*, April, R-2170/4 NIE, Santa Monica, CA: The Rand Corporation.

BROOK, R. *et al.*, (1984) *The Effect of Coinsurance on the Health of Adults*, Santa Monica, CA: The Rand Corporation.

BUCHANAN, J. and CRETIN, S. (1986) *Fee-for-Service Health Care Expenditures: Evidence of Selection Effects Among Subscribers Who Choose HMOs*, Santa Monica, CA: The Rand Corporation.

BUNKER, J.P. and BROWN, B.W., JR. (1974) 'The physician-patient as an informed consumer of surgical services', *New England Journal of Medicine*, **290**, p. 1051.

CAPELL, F. (1981) *A Study of Alternatives in American Education, Vol. VI: Student Outcomes at Alum Rock, 1974–1976*, Santa Monica, CA: The Rand Corporation.

CHUBB, J. and MOE, T. (1985) 'Politics, markets and the organization of schools', Paper delivered to the Annual Meeting of the American Political Science Association.

CLUNE, W. (1987) 'Institutional choice as a theoretical framework for research on educational policy', *Educational Evaluation and Policy Analysis*, **9**, 2, pp. 117–32.

COHEN, D. and FARRAR, E. (1977) 'Power to the parents? The story of educational vouchers', *Public Interest*, **48**, pp. 72–97.

COLEMAN, J. *et al.*, (1982) *High School Achievement: Public, Catholic, and Private Schools Compared*, New York: Basic Books.

COONS, J. and SUGARMAN, S. (1978) *Education by Choice: The Case for Family Control*, Berkeley, CA: University of California Press.

DARLING-HAMMOND, L. and KIRBY, S.N. (1988) 'Public policy and private choice: The case of Minnesota', in JAMES, T. and LEVIN, H. (Eds.) *Comparing Public and Private Schools, Volume 1: Institutions and Organizations*, Philadelphia: Falmer Press.

DAVIS, K. (1977) 'A decade of policy developments in providing health care for low-income families', in HAVEMAN, R. (Ed.) *A Decade of Federal Antipoverty Programs: Achievements, Failures, and Lessons*, New York: Academic Press.

DAVIS, K. and SCHOEN, C. (1978) *Health and the War on Poverty: A Ten-Year Appraisal*, Washington, DC: Brookings Institution.

ELMORE, R. (1988) 'Choice in public education', in BOYD, W. and KIRCHNER, C. (Eds.) *The Politics of Excellence and Choice in Education*, Philadelphia: Falmer Press.

ENTHOVEN, A. (1985) 'An economic analysis of the "Preferred Provider Organization" concept', in BOLAND, P. (Ed.) *The New Health Care Market: A Guide to PPOs for Purchasers, Payors, and Providers*, Homewood, IL: Dow Jones-Irwin.

FARNAM, J. *et al.*, (1975) *A Survey of Parent Opinons About Educational Alternatives in Minneapolis North Area Elementary Schools*, Minneapolis, MN: Minneapolis Public Schools.

GARFINKEL, S. *et al.*, (1986) 'Choice of payment plan in the Medicare capitation demonstration', *Medical Care*, **24**, p. 628.

GLENN, C. (1988a) *Why Parents in Five Nations Choose Schools*, Massachusetts Department of Education, Office of Educational Equity.

GLENN, C. (1988b) 'Choice in Dutch education'. Unpublished paper, Massachusetts Department of Education, Office of Educational Equity.

GOLDBERGER, A. and CAIN, G. (1982) 'The causal analysis of cognitive outcomes in the Coleman, Hoffer and Kilgore report', *Sociology of Education*, **55**, pp. 103–22.

GORMLEY, W.I. JR. (1987) 'Institutional policy analysis: a critical review'. *Journal of Policy Analysis and Management*, **6**, 2, pp. 153–69.

HIBBARD, J. and WEEKS, E. (1987) 'Consumerism in health care: Prevalence and predictors', *Medical Care*, **25**, 11, pp. 1019–32.

JUBA, D., LAVE, J. and SHADDY, J. (1980) 'Analysis of the choice of health benefits plans', *Inquiry*, **17**, p. 172.

KEELER, E. *et al.*, (1985) *How Free Care Reduced Hypertension of Participants in the Rand Health Insurance Experiment*, Santa Monica, CA: The Rand Corporation.

LUFT, H. (1981) *Health Maintenance Organizations: Dimensions of Performance*, New York: Wiley.

MANNING, W.G. *et al.*, (1984) 'A controlled trial of the effect of prepaid group practice on the use of services', *New England Journal of Medicine*, **310**, p. 23.

MARQUIS, M.S. (1981) *Comsumers' Knowledge About Their Health Insurance Coverage*, Santa Monica, CA: The Rand Corporation.

MOORE, D. and DAVENPORT, S. (1988) 'The new improved sorting machine'. A Paper Prepared for the National Center on Effective Secondary Schools, University of Wisconsin-Madison.

MURNANE, R. (1984) 'A review essay: Comparisons of public and private schools:

Lessons from the uproar', *Journal of Human Resources*, **19**, pp. 263–77.

MURNANE, R. (1986) 'Comparisons of private and public schools: The critical role of regulations', in LEVY, D. (Ed.) *Private Education: Studies in Choice and Public Policy*, New York: Oxford University Press.

NATARAJ KIRBY, S. and DARLING-HAMMOND, L. (1988) 'Parental schooling choice: A case study of Minnesota', *Journal of Policy Analysis and Management*, **7**, 3, pp. 506–17.

NATHAN, J. (1983) *Free to Teach: Achieving Equity and Excellence in Schools*, New York: Pilgrim Press.

NEWHOUSE, J. (1974) 'A design for a health insurance experiment', *Inquiry*, **11**, pp. 5–27.

NEWHOUSE, J. *et al.*, (1981a) 'Some interim results from a controlled trial of cost sharing in health insurance', *New England Journal of Medicine*, **305,** 25, pp. 1501–7.

NEWHOUSE, J. *et al.*, (1981b) 'How sophisticated are consumers about the medical care delivery system?' *Medical Care*, **19**, 3, pp. 316–28.

NEWHOUSE, J. and FRIEDLANDER, L. (1980) 'The relationship between medical resources and measures of health: Some additional evidence', *Journal of Human Resources*, **15**, 2, pp. 200–18.

OAKES, J. (1985) *Keeping Track: How Schools Structure Inequality*, New Haven, CN: Yale University Press.

RAYWID, M.A. (1984) 'Synthesis of research on schools of choice', *Educational Leadership*, **41**, 7, pp. 70–8.

RAYWID, M.A. (1985) 'Family choice arrangements in public schools: A review of the literature', *Review of Educational Research*, **55**, 4, pp. 435–67.

ROSSELL, C. and GLENN, C. (1987) 'The benefits and costs of parent choice of schools: The Cambridge and Buffalo models', Unpublished paper, Massachusetts Department of Education, Office of Educational Equity.

SCHULTZE, C. (1977) *Public Use of Private Interest*, Washington: Brookings Institution.

SCITORSKY, A., MCCALL, N. and BENHAM, L. (1978) 'Use of physician services under two prepaid plans', *Medical Care*, **17**, (5), pp. 441–60.

SHERMAN, J. *et al.*, (1983) *Congressionally Mandated Study of School Finance, Volume 2: Private Elementary and Secondary Education*, Washington, DC: Office of Educational Research and Improvement, US Department of Education.

STARR, P. (1982) *The Social Transformation of American Medicine*, New York: Basic Books.

STARR, P. (1986) 'Health care for the poor: The past twenty years', in DANZIGER, S. and WEINBERG, D. (Eds.) *Fighting Poverty: What Works and What Doesn't*, Cambridge, MA: Harvard University Press.

WEISBROD, B. (1983) 'Competition in health care: A cautionary view', in MEYER, J. (Ed.) *Market Reforms in Health Care: Current Issues, New Directions, Strategic Decisions*, Washington, DC: American Enterprise Institute, pp. 61–71.

WOUTER, A. and HESTER, J. (1988) 'Patient choice of providers in a preferred provider organization', *Medical Care*, **26**, 3, pp. 240–55.

Commentary

As Arrows in the Hand

John E. Coons

I have a friend who opposes any educational subsidy to parents that could be used in private schools. His reasons are democratic. He says that too many parents, and especially the poor, would pick schools that teach intolerance. He sends his own children to an expensive private school. That's different; the school is secular, and the families who use it are liberal minded.

Another friend of mine recently bought a home in Piedmont. He tells us that the atmosphere in that opulent retreat is tolerant and humane. He wishes there were some way that every child could attend a school as good as Piedmont High. But, he too opposes government support for parental choice. He says it might hurt the public schools which are the foundation of our democratic order.

A civil-rights lawyer I know recently won a desegregation case in a town where the school population is only 25% white. His black clients thereupon signed up in large numbers for voluntary transfers to nearby white suburban public schools that the court had found innocent; the court ordered the guilty defendants to finance the transfers. Unfortunately the suburban districts will not admit any outsiders. Meanwhile thousands of spaces have been offered to these same black children by racially integrated private schools located in and around the segregated district; these schools would admit the children on standards more liberal than those applied by the defendant. Because their costs are about one-third that of public schools each transfer could save the taxpayers several thousands of dollars. The lawyer and the school board president concede that the schools would be good for the children and would promote desegregation. However, they decline to ask the judge to order the defendant to subsidize the choice of integrated private schools, because this would be undemocratic.

From a certain point of view these true stories make sense. Any society that hopes to take a systematic approach to education faces the threshold question addressed by Plato in *The Republic*. He asked — and necessarily we still ask — whom do we trust to choose the particular forms of education for the individual child? My stories are intelligible, only because implicitly they represent a common answer to this question. These friends of mine operate on an ancient precept: trust only the rich. For them wealthy parents alone can be expected to make the right decisions for society. And, when the rich have successfully clustered in Piedmont and in the fancy private academies, society must conscript the rest for public schools in order to ensure their democratic education. This familiar policy once was known as Aristocracy. It is a plain idea about who knows best, and of course there is something to be said for it. Indeed, these excellent papers by Elmore and Levin have said it all.

In the few pages allowed me I will focus upon this curious premise that economic compulsion of the non-rich in government schools will nourish the civic virtue of their children. To do so, however, I must first deal with a vexing issue of form that makes communication on this issue painfully difficult. My little trilogy illustrates the problem. My friends in these stories suffer from an irresistible impulse to convert what is a plausible argument for plutocracy into an impossible argument for democracy. Somehow in their minds rich parents are transformed into agents of brotherhood; and the familiar government school is made to seem as open as a public library or a park where all children are welcome. In benign complicity the rich and the government somehow nourish the 'core values' of the republic. The result is a kind of alchemy. Our elitist schools are put to the proverbial duck test, and they emerge as a canard.

Gone in this revisionist tale is the history of separate but equal education; gone are the religious compulsion of the dissenter and the exclusion of aliens; gone is the *Serrano* problem and class segregation. In their place stands a public school that is the cradle of community and human brotherhood, the ideal provider of social glue. Only here will the child of the ordinary family learn tolerance and the other civic virtues.

You will forgive my skepticism. I do agree that there have been occasional stirrings of democracy in some of these places. We have come a distance since 1954. Deliberate segregation is at last forbidden; so is compulsory prayer; and financial inequity is more often tempered. Are the democratic credentials of the system thereby established? I fear not. Each of those positive alterations had to be imposed upon an unwilling school system by judges. And even the judges remain unwilling to challenge the class segregation that continues to drive the system. My friends nevertheless recommend these government schools as the incubator of democratic values; bring them your tired and your poor — especially your poor.

To put it plainly democracy has been one of the chief casualties of the school system. Depending upon one's starting premise this could all be for the good, but, whatever the case, we should adapt our language to the reality. When we do, there will be plenty left to argue about. The honest critic cannot rest until he has compared this undemocratic calamity to alternatives that are based upon a different premise. It is thus wholly proper for Levin to turn our imagination to a world of choice in which low income families go blundering about seeking a place among private schools. These schools are not all so nice it seems; they are, indeed, places from which 'outsiders' are 'excluded'. There is at least some truth to this, but what is its relevance? Surely this observation about exclusion cannot be intended to distinguish private schools from public; no school could be more exclusive and more unfriendly to outsiders than are Piedmont High and the thousand other elite high schools just like it. By contrast, no schools more nearly qualify as public than those that will admit anyone who can pay a small tuition. To be fair, however, exclusion is a phenomenon that is more complex than either Levin or I are able to describe. Elmore is right; to clarify such an issue one has to be very specific about his assumptions including their institutional setting. By Elmore's prudent standard, alas, we lack sufficient context to make sense of the question of exclusivity. We seem even to lack a definition.

In any case the more important claim advanced against choice has little to do with the relative degree of exclusion to be expected in public and private schools. The real complaint is that private schools chosen by non-rich families ' . . . must necessarily create a divisive experience rather than one that converges on a common educational experience'. There are many passages to this same effect in Levin's paper. Note the antinomy: education of common families either is conducted 'in common', or it is 'divisive'. Ordinary kids must, therefore, be made to go to school together in a place that many might not have chosen. Otherwise we will sow the seeds of social division.

This traditional attitude still strikes me as overconfident and aggressive. I suggest that our very familiarity with the system masks its radical conservatism. Some of this leaks through, however, in passages like the following:

> [T]he challenge is that of preserving the shared educational experience that is necessary for establishing a foundation of shared knowledge and for preserving the existing economic, political and social order while allowing some range of choice . . .

Were I a marxist, this would be Exhibit A. 'Comrade, this system is no accident; observe how it preserves the existing economic, political and social order.' In truth it has always astounded me that marxist analysis has so seldom troubled to portray American education as an epiphenomenon of the market. There would be only one flaw in such an assertion; it would be wrong. The causes are much more complex and chaotic than this, even if the result is so class segregated. But I will leave that story to someone else.

So far as appears in his chapter, Levin accepts the historic magisterium of the rich. Otherwise he would call for the reversal of *Pierce* v. *The Society of Sisters*, which remains the principal barrier to our hailing the aristocracy into the schools they reject. He also seems to take as a given the continuation of that efficient mechanism of class separation — the school district. In short, even before he begins, he has surrendered the necessary conditions for giving rich children the 'common educational experience'. His disparagement of parental judgment is left to apply only to the ordinary family and to the poor and thus reduces to this proposition: people from these social classes can learn the civic virtues only from a prescribed curriculum and forced association. Left to their own devices they would choose against the public interest. There is inevitable conflict between the right of non-rich parents to choose and the right of a democratic society to teach us to be good citizens.

The evidence for this grim conclusion is not obvious to me, and none is cited. The reality that I do observe and the research that I do know can be read quite the other way round. The major threat to core values comes, not from choices made by the reckless poor but from anti-democratic practices of the schools. First of all, it is no small offense to civility that the system cripples the authority of ordinary parents over the one medium in which many can effectively express their identity — their own child. For better or worse every parent I have encountered hopes to represent his ideal self to the future through his children. The psalmist got it right: 'As arrows in the hand of a mighty man, so are the children of one's youth'. This is exquisitely true for you and me — that is for every professional who struggles to get his daughter into the one best school where she can learn to recapitulate the virtues or at least avoid the catastrophes of the parent. Happily, for public people like us, children are but one instrument of our proxy immortality; we also write books and make speeches. We have many arrows in our quiver beside our children. With all these opportunities for impact on the future, we nevertheless worry that we will fail to reproduce our moral selves. What must that same worry be like for those who are not so lucky — for the ordinary parent who seldom gets to a microphone or a publisher? Children are the poor man's principal gift to the future; they are both medium and message to the outside and to the world of tomorrow. Every parent enjoys this one hope to be heard in the forum. This political aspect of parenting is intimately linked to the values of free expression protected by the First Amendment. One day lawyers may make something of this, but not yet.

Remember that I am still addressing the question of whether there is a natural conflict between parental choice and the civic virtues. If I have read the profoundly political motivation of the ordinary parent correctly, something relevant may follow. The greatest folly for the social engineer could be to frustrate deliberately this parental hope to sculpt the soul of his own child. Nothing could be more destructive of social trust than to restrict to the rich the realization of this hope for an earthly immortality. The present regime is thus the classic recipe for division. We rub the noses of ordinary parents in their impotence to transmit their basic attitudes through formal schooling.

May I add that nothing could be more corrosive of family life itself. From infancy, the child of the middle class family experiences the parents' capacity to decide it is the foundation of personal trust. This capacity is confirmed and extended in the parents' choice of a school and in their continuing option to seek alternatives. By contrast, for the poor, the capacity to choose disappears at age five when the child is delivered to an alien institution to which the parent is subordinate. This seems to me a precarious social policy. It risks not only parental resentment but the effective end of the child's confidence both in the parents and in an ordered and protective society. This act of disempowerment is antithetic to stable community. It is deeply resented.

In your imagination experiment with the alternative possibility. Consider the effect upon parents of being told that this society specifically values their ideals and their hopes for their own children. Who could prescribe a more effective lesson in democracy for those parents now left apathetic by their encounters with compulsory institutions? Is it so strange to believe that the effective way to create social trust is for society itself to display that trust? It could be that our institutions will finally begin to generate allegiance to core values when they have come to deserve it by respecting the dignity of ordinary persons.

What the citizen-child would actually learn in a humane system of choice would, I concede, be affected by the kind of school actually chosen. Some schools that would be chosen neither Levin nor I would like. In our calculus of overall effects, however, even these decisions would represent a net gain. If I am correct in my reading of family and school dynamics, these schools that present a focused and insistent message — including sectarian schools — can be as democratic as any secular or mainline religious institution. There is not a great deal of systematic evidence for this, but there is some, and there is experience. The key, as Coleman's work suggests, is the school's production of a consistent atmosphere and a life-theme about which a community of shared beliefs can cluster. By contrast, the most debilitating education for the citizen-child is the daily message that the right and proper attitude toward important ideas is a cool neutrality. The risk of this occurring is very great in public schools that try to address their notion of 'core values' to a captive clientele. Our society has specialized in such schools, hence in rapid and inoffensive stuff of the sort that can survive school politics and recapitulate the compromising shallowness of the media. In a rural nineteenth century that was marked by parochial religion and geographic isolation this 'common experience' in school may have been plausible as a broadening influence. Today it guarantees cultural anaesthesia.

By a curious historic inversion civic vitality in our time may well depend upon schools in which children experience adult educators picked out by the family and gripped by commitment to a specific ideal. That this ideal be religious or secular, Muslim or Montessori is of less moment than that the child be witness daily to the consistent moral concern of the family's chosen agents. If he learns early and consistently that it is human to care about truth and justice in a very particular way, he is more likely as an adult to care about them in a general way. Perhaps one must learn to love something before he can learn to love everything. In any case I am quite content to live with adults who have very particular views of the good life that differ from my own. In a system driven by choice these ideological competitors of mine will have experienced tolerance for their own views. They will wish to preserve that system of tolerance by supporting the larger society which has made it possible.

I grant that these merely plausible notions of the sources of social trust have been little tested. How could they be tested? There has been no subsidizing mechanism by which most families could make a choice. What we can say on the present evidence is that poor families that have somehow managed to pay for private schools seem as keen as their public school brothers to be good Americans. They work, they vote, they avoid prison in at least their representative numbers. There is more to communal life than this. But just how that extra something is to be defined is a matter on which people can fairly disagree. I certainly do not know any universal answer.

Those who would impose a common curriculum and a common experience upon the non-rich in the name of tolerance and civic virtue should also ask themselves how much we really know about the instrumental value of force. Just who is it that possesses the wisdom to prescribe the effective forms of this social therapy? There have been many proposals for imparting the civic virtues; their most common characteristic (aside from compulsion) is that they conflict with one another in content.

One sometimes has the impression that each of their authors has drawn upon some private inspiration of his own. Such idiosyncratic proposals can be valuable, but only on the condition that they remain in mutual competition and not be provided a monopoly status. Otherwise our selection of the best universal prescription from this grab-bag of ideas would be simply a matter of chance. Some of us remember the triumph of 'progressive education'.

The proponents of choice generally take the modest, and I think realistic, position that nobody really is certain how to achieve these various goals or even to define them. More accurately, they concede that different enthusiasts know different and contradictory things. Well-intentioned elitists think they can identify positive programs that will make us tolerant, but Choiceniks claim to know no such thing. They simply like a society that respects their own ideas, and they assume that others will like it for the very same reason. I'm not sure that one need go much farther than this in order to support parental choice as the system most likely to succeed in producing good citizens. The short of it is that the assertion that choice and public values conflict is unsupported. Meanwhile, as Levin himself insists, parental choice best secures all those benefits of education for the child that he calls 'private'. In this state of the argument I see little to be said for continuing a system marked neither by choice nor by tolerance for the values of the ordinary family. Should we preserve the worst of both worlds simply to satisfy an ancient prejudice?

In any case it is of very great importance that academics not lose confidence in the common man. That they might actually come to distrust the upper class is perhaps too much to hope; given all the temptations that burden the rich, their mistakes are simply too forgivable. There is, nonetheless, reason to expect something better than this from the common family, and I note a depressing tendency even in Elmore's splendid chapter to see the family in static terms. When we assess the potential acumen of non-rich parents, it should be remembered that they have had very little experience so far with authentic educational choice (with one exception that I will shortly note). Alum Rock scarcely qualified as such an experience, and the other analogies, as Elmore properly observes, are very remote. There has not been in modern times a sufficiently proximate example in which the non-rich — and especially the minority poor of the United States — have been given a significant educational market in which to shop with real money. What, then, can we predict for them under a system of real choice? At least we can say that inexperienced choosers would, like the rest of us, be liberated to do their best. They would learn by their mistakes and adjust as they go. That's life. And, given the chance, life is something that even the poor might turn out to be rather good at. I know no other way of bringing persons from a state of tutelage to that of autonomy. And I assume that this is a crucial part of everyone's goal. Who is prepared to write off the poor as invincibly irresponsible?

There is one exception to the historic vacuum of experience with choice; this is the present private sector. Here we have some information about behavior, and I suggest that the peculiar history of these institutions constitutes a natural experiment infinitely more powerful than Alum Rock. Over time hordes of parents from the most disadvantaged circumstances have provided their own 'voucher' to enroll in private schools. This element of self-help makes the inferences to be drawn all the more reliable. These actors have shown extraordinary acumen at great personal cost. This claim holds good whether these low-budget, mostly religious, schools are doing only a little better than public schools or a lot better, and it is so whether their cost is one half or a little more than one half. These people have clearly found the right place for their children. They did not find it by conscription.

Some say these families are a self-selected sample. Of course they are. Indeed, that's the point. In a system of choice, it is true by definition. In a way this is the most telling of all the data. It says very simply that many poor parents are good choosers. Further, both the waiting lists at these schools and the polls about parental preferences are additional data that suggest just how many more low-income parents would like this same opportunity to swell that self-selected sample. We have no reason to suppose that poverty has canceled the family's natural capacity for effective choice. Obviously we should be prudent and frugal in the instruments we adopt to animate that capacity. There was little opportunity at our meeting to consider the most promising mechanisms. Whatever answers we propose, we should never submit to the despairing and contradictory premise that only the rich among us can be trusted with educating our children for democratic life.

Commentary

Parent Choice: A State Perspective

Charles L. Glenn

Much of the discussion at the conference, while stimulating, was pretty theoretical, and the lack of reliable data about the actual results of parent choice of schools has been lamented. For a number of the social scientists participating in the conference, however, this lack of research was not a reason to reserve judgment or to seek experiential data from those of us who are working directly with choice policies; perhaps they consider us blinded and confused by too much reality!

One fundamental concern was expressed again and again, in various forms: that ordinary people, and especially poor people, could not be trusted to make decisions about the education of their children. Coons expressed with characteristic bluntness the fundamental disagreement: do you trust parents, or don't you?

I suggested that in Massachusetts we possess a rich experience, stretching over twenty years now, with publicly-sponsored parent choice of schools. Some of that experience is bad, has produced new inequities, but much of it — especially recently — is very good indeed. This September one public school pupil in six in the Commonwealth will attend a school which enrolls its pupils on the basis of parent choice. Three out of four Black pupils, and three out of four Hispanic pupils, will attend such schools of choice.

My office has approved and funded plans for equitable parent choice for seventeen cities, and has monitored their effects. Thirty-nine suburbs enroll, on a voluntary basis, minority pupils from two of these cities, and have for more than two decades. So we are not speculating or theorizing when we talk about what the effects of parent choice plans are, for good and ill. Nor are we speculating when we say that poor parents are interested in choosing and capable of choosing well, when given the right information and counseling; my office provides more than two million dollars a year to fund support for decisions by urban parents.

Fliegel and Peterkin made the point even more strongly, when they said that they had never met parents who didn't want to choose, or who felt incapable of doing so! So why do some very bright social scientists assume that such parent choice is at best irrelevant, and at worst profoundly harmful? It would make a nice study in the sociology of knowledge.

Choice can — often does — operate in a way which is harmful, but it is our job to find ways to make it work positively, to go forward rather than back. As Peterkin said, it is up to him and other urban superintendents to assure that there are no bad choices among urban schools. After all, why is it worse for a parent to make a bad choice of a school than for a child to be assigned to that school involuntarily? And as I pointed out, it is up to state and other equity officials to devise strategies that assure that the way choice operates maximizes positive and minimizes negative effects. Willie and Alves provided the conference with a rich and detailed information-base on the precise details of such a choice policy for a large city, but there was little impulse to come to grips with those details (surely a case study in control as well as in choice) in lieu of continued speculation. Peterkin was available to describe precisely how a superintendent made choice work for equity and educational improvement in a smaller city, but the discussion quickly slipped back into speculation.

I focused my remarks on the challenge of what we can learn from experience and from the Levin and Elmore chapters about doing choice. There is a prior question, of course, about the desirability of parent choice, based upon what I call 'the myth of the common school'. In my book by that title (University of Massachusetts Press, 1988) I explore the historical roots of this myth, which has dominated thinking about popular education in this country. The myth is alive and well, and is invoked continually by opponents of parent choice within the education establishment.

But let us begin by assuming that parent choice is a good thing, that it tends to generate in pupils, parents and teachers what Newmann referred to as 'committed effort', and that the question is how to do it, and how to answer the practical criticisms which are also continually raised.

Four challenges arise in the design and implementation of any program of educational choice:

1 equity (including equal access and integration) on the basis of class and language as well as race;
2 the public interest in the appropriate education of all with whom we will be sharing tomorrow;
3 the inertia of the staffs of public schools as sub-units of routinized bureaucracies; and

4 the ideal and material interests of the various actors, in local and state government, in school systems, in organizations, and among both the restricted group of parents and the broader group of voters.

We know how to deal effectively with the equity issues, though at a considerable cost to anyone's theories of pure market mechanisms. It requires both state regulation and state incentives, whether choice is to operate (as in Coons' proposal) within an open market or (as in my efforts) within the public sector alone. Elmore stresses (page 314) that choice can increase social integration if there is 'a relatively active public role in managing the terms'.

Levin's discussion of such regulation is helpful, though he may, in detailing the greater costs of regulation in a market, understate the need for such efforts in the public sector. There is no reason to be complacent about the extent to which public education is equitable — think of the contrast between the public schools of the City of Lawrence and its suburb Andover, and of how much more wealth it requires to get your child into Andover Public High School than into Phillips Andover Academy in the same town — or to which public schools are successfully imparting 'the necessary social values and knowledge, . . . the appropriate subjects and experiences, and . . . school outcomes' (page 267).

The second issue requires defining clearly what is non-negotiable and cannot be given away in the euphoria of letting 'a thousand flowers bloom, a hundred schools contend'. Levin refers to this as 'a common core of educational experiences and practices for all students that are based upon the social aims of education' (page 261). He seems to assume that this is a problem only with respect to non-public schools, and that there is an irony to former Secretary Bennett's advocacy of both choice and content.

Without endorsing Bennett's specific proposals (which I have not read), I would argue that it is essential for us to become far clearer than we are now about what we expect every pupil to demonstrate mastery of, not each year, but at certain gate-ways in the educational process. That kind of clarity is necessary precisely to permit real diversity in how they get there, so that we set result requirements rather than the present process requirements. Sizer is my guru on this, and I won't expand upon it further, except to stress that millions of both public and non-public pupils already measure themselves against the common standard of the SATs. Perhaps we should have a common standard that we expect all pupils to reach (at whatever age) before they begin the specialized portion of their secondary schooling. That would free schools up to be much more diverse.

But will they be? The third issue is how to overcome the inertia which grips most public schools even when they are given the opportunity to become distinctive and to seek out and serve those parents and children who share their vision of education. Quite apart from the debate over choice, there is a growing recognition that we must find a way not only to empower but also to incite teams of teachers to work in ways that are less passive, less isolated, less routinized. This is fundamental to real effectiveness.

Parent choice cannot function meaningfully until that begins to happen. Oh, you can have a few elite magnet schools — everyone sings, everyone dances — and leave other schools (and pupils) to stultify even further, but if you want to make every school a school of choice and every parent an active decision-maker, you have to find ways of inciting a divine impatience among teachers and principals. That's hard. Most people don't go into education because they want to be entrepreneurs or take risks. Elmore's paper (pages 295–6) helps me to understand that 'the lower the knowledge requirements, the greater the public management of entry requirements, and the more heavily constrained the terms of practice, the less likely practitioners will be [to] respond to pressure for increased client choice with significantly different alternative forms of practice'.

But if real choice depends upon energy and daring to make schools distinctively effective, a good case can be made that the reverse is true as well. Centralized specification of process leads to passivity which leads to poor education which leads to more centralized requirements which leads to more passivity and so on. A system of assigning all pupils by choice rather than by residence can be a powerful way to break out of that vicious circle.

Sometimes I compare school reform to Frankenstein's monster stretched on the table, all the parts neatly sewn together but no life to make it get up and walk until the lightning is hitched up; parent choice can be that jolt of lightning.

Do non-public schools (as Chubb has argued) have more scope to exhibit the qualities associated with effectiveness because (as Levin concludes) they have greater 'capacity to provide greater diversity and choice in meeting private needs' (page 272)? Is there an inherent limitation (other than 'the myth of the common school') to how distinctive and responsive public schools can be?

Certainly the First Amendment is a significant limitation along one of the dimensions of choice (it seems unlikely that we will follow the example of the other Western democracies in accommodating religious conviction within publicly-supported pre-university education). But many parents who 'choose out' of public schools do so for reasons which, while they may be associated with religious beliefs, do not have to be satisfied with explicit religious instruction. And many parents of equal religious fervor keep their children in particular public schools which they find satisfactory. We in public education have not explored sufficiently what parents really want; we have not listened to what their decisions should tell us. We are not bold enough, and perhaps we grow timid in part because social scientists discourage us from trusting the instincts and the values of parents.

The fourth challenge of designing and implementing educational choice is to overcome the countless particular interests in maintenance of the present system. This includes 'ideal interests' rooted in the 'myth of the common school'; these can be extremely stubborn to overcome since they involve how educators think about themselves and their mission. And it includes material interests, jobs, tax rates, bus contracts, voters and much more. I have recently spent six months wrestling with such interests, to develop for Governor Dukakis a program for inter-district parent choice, and my head is bloody and not a little bowed! Elmore identifies some of the diverse interests pressing for parent choice, but I wish that our authors had described the many other interests entrenched against the extension, even the universalizing, of parent choice, and suggested which of these can be accommodated and which cannot. On the basis of what principles and what priorities shall we make compromises between liberty and the interests — other than justice itself — that call for restrictions upon liberty? These are the questions we need to grapple with.

Commentary

Family Choice

Richard J. Murnane

There are two seminal lessons that I take away from the interesting chapters by Elmore and Levin. First, it is naive to address the question of whether an expansion of family choice is good for American education without considering a host of prior questions. These antecedent questions concern the nature of the institutional setting into which family choice might be introduced, and the details of the design of the family choice system. Only after achieving clarity about the answers to these questions, is it sensible to evaluate the merits of expanding family choice in education.

The second lesson is that there are difficult tradeoffs in the design of a family choice plan. For example, choosing a design that maximizes the diversity of options is likely to come at the expense of a reduction in the teaching of core democratic values. It is difficult to overemphasize the importance of these two related lessons, particularly since they rarely inform debates about the value of extending family choice in education.

While the two chapters differ in many respects, the two key lessons run through both chapters. I would like to commend the authors for finding interesting, and in some cases, novel ways to clarify these two lessons. Given the large number of papers that have been written about family choice over the last twenty years, and the paucity of solid evidence concerning the effects of particular choice plans, writing in 1989 anything new about family choice is a considerable accomplishment. Both authors have done this.

I would like to focus my comments on extending, and probing, a few of the examples that the authors use in clarifying what I take to be the two key lessons of the papers. I turn, first, to Elmore's point that

> The higher the knowledge requirements [for teachers], the greater professional management of entry requirements, and the less con-

> strained professional influence over the terms of practice, the greater the range of alternative forms of practice that are likely to emerge in response to external pressures. (p. 296)

This seems to me to be a powerful example of the theme that the outcomes of choice depend critically on aspects of the governance structure of the educational system. In particular, without talented, energetic, entrepreneur ial teachers, expansion of choice options is unlikely to result in interesting educational options. Consequently, the results of expanding choice are likely to depend on the rules concerning who can enter teaching. While this seems right, I wonder whether small scale choice plans might help to keep in teaching the minority of teachers who appear willing to trade extra work for increased autonomy. In other words, not only do the consequences of choice depend on the presence of able, energetic, indeed entrepreneurial teachers, it may also be the case that artfully designed choice plans might make public education more attractive for some such teachers.

A second point worthy of discussion concerns information requirements. Both authors emphasize the importance of providing families with good information about the attributes of the school programs among which they choose. They also point out that in many demonstrations with family choice, a relatively large percentage of eligible families were not aware of their options, not to speak of the quality of the programs among which they could choose (Levin, p. 269). Thus, if knowledge of options by all families is a criterion for a successful choice program, past demonstrations are not promising.

While I agree with the authors that information is important, it may be useful to clarify why the criterion of knowledge of options *by all families* is appropriate. The reason I raise this issue is that knowledge of options by all families is not necessary to 'make the market work'. As a result of poor information, consumers frequently make mistakes and buy products that they don't like — bread that doesn't taste good, and VCRs that wear out quickly. These results are quite consistent with the operation of relatively well functioning markets, in which, over time, firms die out that do not provide at reasonable prices products that consumers value. The only requirement for this to happen is that some consumers are well informed, and that consumers learn from their mistakes.

In evaluating the attractiveness of family choice plans, why do we adopt the criterion that *all families* should be well informed? As is the case with bread and VCRs, a much less stringent criterion, that some families are well informed and that families learn from their mistakes, is compatible with a process of Darwinian selection whereby schools that do not provide programs that informed consumers value die out over time. The reason for the strict criterion, I believe, is that mistakes about education are more costly than mistakes about bread and VCRs. Purchase of a VCR that wears out quickly does not diminsh the consumer's potential for purchasing a better VCR next time. However, choosing an elementary school program in which a child does not learn to read may diminish the child's options for a lifetime.

It is useful to sort out the reasons we care about the quality of information families have about their educational options because it helps in interpreting the implications of survey evidence. For example, a survey indicating that a significant proportion of families are not aware of their educational options is still compatible with a process whereby weak programs lose support over time. It probably also means, however, that some families are not getting the best available education for their children. I would argue that, by itself, the survey evidence does not imply a condemnation of choice. To evaluate the merits of family choice versus, for example, a system in which professional educators make program choices for students, it is necessary to compare the frequency of poor decisions under the two sytems. This is way beyond any research that we have done, or indeed, that we know how to do.

Another important issue in the design of choice plans concerns transfers. At first blush, it seems sensible that parents be able to transfer their child in midyear out of a program that does not seem satisfactory into a program that holds more promise. However, in Alum Rock and elsewhere, faculties of choice programs strongly resisted midyear transfers. The source of this tension stems from a characteristic of education that lies at the center of many problems in designing delivery systems, namely, that a child cannot 'demand' education without being part of the 'supply' process. In other words, a child's midyear change in educational program not only affects the quality of the education he or she receives, it may also influence the quality of the education other participants receive. For example, the attempt to build an instructional program in which the Spring curriculum builds heavily on material taught in the Fall term (and thereby avoids the 'spiral curriculum' in which material is frequently repeated) can be seriously undermined by the entry into the program in midyear of children who have not experienced the Fall program.

This is but one example of the many ways that the dual role of the student as consumer of education and part of the 'supply' process complicates the design of choice plans. Another example concerns the incentives that parents have to choose programs serving children whom they feel will be desirable peers, and that providers of educational services have to recruit into their programs children who will contribute positively to the education of their peers. This does not mean that choice cannot work. It does mean, however, that the incentives for sorting of students with different attributes into different types of schools are quite strong. As Jencks argued almost twenty years ago, a system that protects the options of children from disadvantaged families is likely to be a highly regulated system of choice.

Finally, I would like to comment on Levin's interesting observation that William Bennett and others who have argued for greater choice have also advocated a standard curriculum for elementary and secondary schools. In other words, they want both more choice and less choice. I think it is worth thinking about the source of this apparent paradox. I conjecture that the interest in a standard curriculum stems, at least in part, from the international test score comparisons, showing that the average scores of US students are substantially below the average scores of students in countries such as Japan that have a relatively standardized curriculum. An inference one might draw from this quite limited evidence is that the way to improve the test scores of US students, especially in mathematics and the sciences, is to reduce choice and expose all students to a standard curriculum.

I find it interesting that, while the low test scores of American students are of great concern to the National Science Foundation and some other national organizations, they do not seem to be of central concern to many parents. Bishop has an interesting hypothesis to explain parents' relative indifference to test scores. He argues that for high school graduates who do not go on to college, how much they learn in high school has no impact on the wages they earn in their first jobs.[1] Students know this, and consequently, they have no incentive to take demanding courses or to work hard in school, nor do their parents have incentives to urge them to do so.

This strikes me as an interesting example of Elmore's point that the consequences of expanding family choice will depend on the institutional setting. The aspect of the setting that matters here is the interface between the educational system and the labor market for high school graduates. Seen from this perspective, expanding family choice, or for that matter, contracting choice, is a weak instrument for improving the academic achievement of American students. What is needed is a change in the relation between the skills of high school graduates and their treatment in the labor market.

Returning once again to the central lessons of these two chapters, advocating, or opposing, family choice in the abstract is foolish. The consequences of any choice plan will depend on its details and on the institutional setting in which it is embedded. Moreover, no choice plan will further all legitimate goals of American education. There will always be tradeoffs. This does not mean that expanding choice is a bad idea, only that its defenders and detractors need to get beyond rhetoric, and focus their discussions on the operational details of particular plans for particular settings.

Note

1 Bishop, J.H. (1989) 'Why the apathy in American high schools?' *Educational Researcher*, **18**, 1, (Jan.–Feb.), pp. 6–10.

Chapter 7

Governance and Instruction: The Promise of Decentralization and Choice

David K. Cohen

Decentralization is one of America's oldest and most treasured political remedies. Most government functions were left to the states by the Federal constitution, partly in hope of forestalling a home-grown version of European tyranny. Most states followed suit: by constitution or custom they left most government to localities, including many functions for which states were constitutionally responsible. The result, described in many tidy textbooks as The Federal System, actually is a great congeries of jurisdictions that sprawl across this vast land.

Markets also are a venerable American solution for political problems. Jacksonian Democrats accepted Jefferson's view, that that government is best which governs least, but they extended the idea from politics to economics. Jacksonians attacked government ownership, subsidy, and regulation of economic enterprises, complaining that such arrangements favored the wealthy or politically connected few, but limited economic opportunity for everyone else. Champions of the masses against the upper-classes, the Jacksonians tried to get government out of banking, transportation, and other enterprises. One result was to make free markets into a sort of liberal populist dogma, and government regulation into an elitist object of suspicion. Another was to make monopoly one of the dirtier words in the US political vocabulary. Still another was to help create a tradition in which Americans of all political persuasions could favor more markets and less government as a solution to economic and social problems.

American ideas about politics have changed in some important ways since the days of Jefferson and Jackson, and government has grown enormously. But decentralization and markets still have powerful appeal, despite or perhaps partly because of these changes. Indeed, the last few years have seen especially hostile attacks on government, and great enthusiasm for markets and decentralization. These ideas have popped up in many sectors of American society, but education has been especially favored. President Reagan probably would have endorsed decentralization and choice in nearly any circumstances, for ideological reasons. But why have many state officials, newly engaged in education, followed suit? Why have some local districts embraced the ideas? And why have some old opponents even changed their minds?

Part of the answer is pure political appeal. America is a vast society with immense organizations. Any reform that promises accessible government, or social services on a human scale would seem a breath of fresh air. Another part of the answer is effective advocacy. Proponents of these reforms have fed a steady stream of arguments into public discourse over two decades, and a few states and localities have tried modest versions of the reforms without disastrous results. Still another part of the answer is circumstances. Many Americans feel that their nation's leadership in the world is slipping, and that stern measures must be taken in response. In such times Americans often turn to schools, to change the tide of events. Another part of the answer is history. For as we turn to the schools just now, we do so in light of a popular belief that liberal reforms of education failed, and that different approaches must be tried. The dramatic growth of government since the 1930s makes it an especially visible target, and our history makes it particularly attractive. After all, American schoolchildren learn about the evils of big government in their lessons on Independence and The Constitution. Finally, governance reform is especially appealing just now, when many commentators and officials believe there is little money for more expensive and familiar approaches.

These considerations make it a bit easier to understand the remarkable interest in these reforms. But they hardly diminish the uniqueness of the moment. It seems an opportune time to re-visit the arguments for decentralization and choice.

One key idea in both reform proposals is that when government is remote, teaching and learning stultify (Gittel, 1970; Fantini, 1970; Coons and Sugarman, 1978). Some analysts believe that centralized power paralyses schools and teachers, or promotes indifference. Others argue that state school monopolies encourage unresponsiveness to students and families. On either account, remote government is seen as a source of school failure. The key to improvement is to move political influence closer to those who deliver, support, and receive instruction. The assumption is that such changes will open schooling to more constructive educational influences. Some hope to accomplish this by redistributing power within the extant political structure, while others prefer to change the political structure to a market system.

Does governance stultify education in these ways? Will such reforms have the desired effects? If one focuses on schools in the slums of most big cities, decentralization and choice seem appealing. For the educational problems in such schools are immense, and the schools' responses often appalling. Any change that promised more energy, a departure from established routines, and more concern with teaching and learning would be welcome. But one also wants to know if these reforms would address the fundamental problems of education. For freshness and energy will wane, as successive generations of reformers have discovered.

Despite their appeal, there is little reason to believe that choice or decentralization alone would broadly or dramatically improve education. One set of reasons for this view concerns the political problems these reforms are supposed to solve. Reformers see the source of educational problems in centralized school monoliths, or state education monopolies. They see school government as a huge and self-centered monster, satisfying its own appetites at the expense of those it is supposed to serve. But if American school government has grown large, it also is remarkably diverse and disjointed: fragmentation seems at least as pronounced as centralization. Education governance more closely resembles many busy colonies of Liliputians, working in many different ways toward many different ends, than a single clumsy giant doggedly pursuing its own selfish purposes at the expense of its clients. There is fragmentation and incoherence at many levels of education, which often have damaging effects. By themselves, decentralization and choice would exacerbate these problems of educational organization, even if they mobilized energy for improvement.

A second set of reasons for doubt about these reforms concerns their promise of instructional improvement. Reformers see politics and economics as potent educational influences; they believe that structural change in these departments will make a big difference in education. The key idea is that new governance or market mechanisms will open schools to the influence of those who care most about children. Schools that respond with good education will be rewarded, and others will be penalized. This prospect abounds with theoretical appeal. But in practice I doubt that decentralization or market structures would broadly or dramatically improve instruction. For most of the agencies that guide instruction in the US lie outside the present scope of school government: school systems have little leverage on these agencies. In addition, though these agencies offer immense amounts of instructional guidance to schools, it is inconsistent and generally weak. Hence, each school that wishes to offer effective instruction must decide on its goals, and on how to achieve them. And they must find ways not only to implement these decisions, but also to insulate them from the blizzard of advice that swirls in their vicinity. Deciding such basic issues is difficult in any circumstance, and it is particularly difficult in a diverse and contentious society like our own. Additionally, this sort of work is most arduous for the schools most in need of improvement. For basic overhaul of learning and teaching is a difficult and protracted endeavor, even in quite advantaged schools. It is much more difficult in the schools that need such improvement most, for they have fewer of the social and educational resources that improvement requires.

Decentralization and choice are appealing ideas. They probably would be quite fruitful, in a relatively modest number of relatively exceptional schools. But schools, families, and politics being what they are, these reforms alone are not likely to produce broad or dramatic educational improvement.

Formal Governance

Some reformers argue that schooling has been paralyzed and degraded by state monopoly. They believe that US public schools deliver a standard brand of education, which is not adjusted to family preferences or children's needs. Though such schooling is unlikely to be either valued or effective, schools that provide it still prosper under monopoly control. For most consumers have nowhere else to go. Only a fundamental change could correct this problem: the creation of markets for schooling. Such markets would break the state monopoly. Families would be able to secure education that responded to their educational values and needs, for unresponsive schools would have to either change their tune or go out of business.

Choice and its Effects

Though advocates of choice contend that education is a state monopoly, the meaning of this assertion varies. In some contexts it seems to mean that the state or its agents have too much influence on decisions about education. In others it seems to mean that school offerings are too homogenous. In still other contexts it seems to mean that public schools have a captive market, and an unfair competitive advantage (Coons and Sugarman, 1978; West, 1976; Center for the Study of Public Policy, 1970; Friedman, 1962).

Does the state monopolize decisions about schooling in the US? One cannot answer sensibly without first asking: compared to what? If other nations are the comparison standard, the state's influence in US education looks relatively modest. Take the extreme case: state influence on non-state schools. In many countries, 'independent' education is extensively subsidized and regulated, often nearly as much as state schools. In places as different as France, Singapore, and New South Wales [Australia], for instance, state and independent schools are stitched together with common leaving exams, curricula, and requirements for teacher qualification. Administrative arrangements vary among nations: in some cases non-state schools have considerable administrative autonomy, while in others they have little. These schools are fairly free to vary the religious and cultural context of schooling. But the key elements of education — curriculum, examinations, teacher qualification, and sometimes even discipline requirements — differ little between state and non-state schools. The state's influence in non-state schools is profound and pervasive in such cases. That, after all, is part of the social contract that enables state subventions to such schools.[1]

In the US, by contrast, government's hand lies much more lightly on independent education. For one thing, state regulation of non-state education is relatively spare here. Licensing requirements for schools are quite modest, with nearly as much attention to health and safety as educational program. Regulatory oversight also is relatively light. Schools must supply state agencies with data on enrollments, staffing, and the like. And schools must satisfy requirements on course offerings. But none of this regulation reaches the content or style of education. Curricula that link non-public and public schools are only very broadly specified, and there are no common leaving or promotion examinations. For another thing, nearly all regulation occurs as a distance, on paper. Enforcement is modest at best, and often it occurs only in response to public provocation. So, if state influence on non-state schools is our standard of monopoly power, and if the world is our stage, we would have to say that education in the US is relatively non-monopolistic.[2]

Do public schools offer a standard brand of education — are school offerings too homogenous in the US? Again, a sensible answer requires that we ask: compared to what? By a cross-national comparison standard, variability in offerings among state schools seems considerable, often greater than in many other developed nations. For one thing, curriculum here is not closely prescribed. State and local school agencies require courses and choose textbooks in the US, but most decisions about content and coverage are left to schools and teachers. In contrast, French, Singaporean, and New South Wales school agencies prescribe not only courses but also content and coverage for entire systems. Additionally, teachers and students in these and other systems work toward system-wide promotion and school-leaving examinations.[3] These national exams exert a powerful homogenizing influence on curriculum content, but they have few counterparts in US instruction. Finally, consistency among the teachers who deliver instruction varies greatly among nations. Teacher qualification and preparation are quite uneven in the US: Teachers are examined and licensed in crazy-quilt patterns across and within the fifty states. They are educated in many different, often radically diverse ways. And whatever the fifty states do, all teacher hiring and assignment are local (Darling-Hammond and Berry, 1988). In contrast, teacher preparation and qualification are quite homogeneous in many other nations. Teachers are licensed, examined, hired, assigned, and often educated in uniform, system-wide fashion. For all of these reasons, educational offerings seem more varied in US state schools than in many other nations. If homogeneity of offerings in state schools is our standard of monopoly, then education in the US seems less monopolistic than in other developed nations.

Do US state schools have a captive market, and an unfair competitive advantage? If we judge by the results — i.e., the range of educational alternatives available — American education looks quite competitive. There are many different sorts of schools: Religious establishments for various persuasions and denominations; public and proprietary vocational schools; special-purpose public and non-public schools for those with unusual needs or abilities; and non-public schools that distinguish themselves by academic program, extra-curricular activities, or clientele, among other things. Additionally, schools within the state sector are more decentralized in the US than nearly anywhere else in the world. Public schools and school systems compete among themselves by offering different sorts of educational programs, or cultivating particular reputations, or attracting a particular clientele. Parents can choose among public schools simply by moving into their attendance area, while school admission in many other nations, especially in secondary education, is only by application and/or examination. One likely reason for this variability in schooling is the unusual diversity of American culture and society. But another is American political traditions, which give a relatively large role to individual rights and liberties. In contrast, the political traditions of many other nations that have fewer educational alternatives are much more communal or corporatist. So, if we judge the state schools' competitive advantage by the range of their offerings, the market for US education seems relatively un-captive, and the state's competitive advantage seems relatively modest.

But that is only part of the story, for there are constraints on competition and choice among US state schools. One such constraint is economic and social inequality. Public schools with strong reputations and programs are disproportionately located in communities with steep housing prices, or some sort of exclusionary zoning, or both. Working class, poor, and minority group Americans have less access to such schools. Schools in relatively disadvantaged neighborhoods therefore have a perverse competitive advantage over better schools in more privileged communities: For families in disadvantaged neighborhoods are less able to use residential change to find better schools. The pressure for school improvement that their exit from neighborhood schools might exert is therefore negligible. This competitive advantage for poor schools is compounded by the relative lack of resources that residents in such communities have for voice — i.e., to exert political pressure on schools (Hirschman, 1970). Hence, while public schools in the US do compete for clients, and clients do choose among such schools, such competition and choice are unequally distributed within the public sector. This difference cannot be justified by reference to the special place that public education occupies in American politics, for it only reflects the influence of private economic and social inequalities on the provision and use of public education.

Another constraint on competition and choice is the financial disadvantage that would be encountered by many families who might choose independent schools. For such families would have to pay public school taxes, and then also pay private school tuition. This situation weakens the demand for independent schooling, and thus also limits the supply of such schooling, though it would be difficult to estimate the magnitude of this effect. Some commentators justify the advantage for state schools on the ground that public education has a special role in American politics, and that families should be discouraged from leaving. But this justification loses some force from judicial decisions that establish family rights to enroll children in non-public schools. And it loses more force from economic inequalities in the operation of this constraint. Well-to-do families are not much impeded economically by 'double taxation', in efforts to move outside the state schools, but families with moderate or very limited incomes are less able to pay both taxes and tuition. This problem is compounded by high tuition in many US non-state schools. For unlike many other nations, in which non-public school tuition is held down by direct state subventions, most US independent schools must support themselves entirely or nearly entirely from tuition.

Some readers may object to parts of this account, thinking that it is foolish to judge monopoly by relative standards. Even if American schools seem less of a state monopoly than those in France or Singapore, perhaps they are still a monopoly. Perhaps we should say that monopoly is absent when there is a host of independent suppliers, and none control the market. Is there a monopoly in US education by this criterion? This seems to reduce to another question: Is the school board in Scarsdale, New York part of the same cartel as the school board in Cleveland, Ohio? Answers to this question will vary. Mine is negative. Though I can see similarities in management, I cannot see any of the other classical elements of monopoly, such as price-fixing, conspiracies to drive competition out of business, shadowy common ownership, and the like. These systems are of course all run by public school educators, most of whom had roughly similar educations and experience. But if that is the index of monopoly, then American business is fast becoming a great monopoly, for it is all run by private-sector managers, more and more of whom have had similar education and experience.

Other readers may think that all of these considerations are beside the point. They would say that the key question is whether choice improves schooling, and students' school performance. The evidence on this point, however, is not encouraging. American schools have had only one deliberate trial with a choice scheme, in Alum Rock, California. The district was small and poor; conditions were difficult; and the experiment lasted only for five years (RAND, 1981; Cohen and Farrar, 1977). Nonetheless, parents were strongly encouraged to choose among educational programs, within and among elementary schools, and schools were strongly encouraged to respond constructively to parent choice. Only a small fraction of parents chose programs other than those in which their children were already enrolled, though by the experiment's end there had been a modest increase in choice (RAND, 1981; Cohen and Farrar, 1977). Most parents' knowledge about schools and educational programs was exceedingly modest, and increased only a little as a result of the experiment. Teachers whose schools were part of the experiment were enthusiastic about it, and worked hard to improve education. But an extensive and careful evaluation found little difference between these classes and others, otherwise similarly situated, that were not in the experiment. No differences in achievement were found (RAND, 1981).

Of course, a modest fraction of American schools do entail choice — i.e., parochial and independent schools. But research on these is no more convincing. Some researchers report a small advantage for schools of choice — i.e., Catholic schools (Coleman, Hoffer and Kilgore, 1982), but most re-analyses cast doubt even on this small advantage (Levin, this volume). The most convincing analyses suggest that the advantage of Catholic schools may be less a consequence of choice than of specific policies concerning tracking, curriculum coherence, and insistence on academic standards. These policies can be found in some public high schools, as well as in Catholic schools (Bryk, Lee and Smith, this volume), which suggests that they could be adopted more broadly, apart from parent choice.

What does this account imply for efforts to increase choice in education? From one angle it suggests caution concerning what we might expect from such reforms. For educational offerings in the US already appear to be quite variable, at least when compared with those in other developed societies. State regulation of schooling certainly is much less pronounced and pervasive here, and there are various sorts of choice and competition within the public sector. Indeed, one could plausibly argue that there is a rough trade-off between subsidy and variety in schooling. Some nations have relatively extensive regulation and support of schooling, both in the state and independent sectors. In many such cases, non-state schools receive extensive support. In some such cases, independent schools seem to be able to start up relatively easily, and in some of those, economic inequality in access to independent education may be somewhat reduced. But there also is extensive state regulation of all schools in these cases, and rather uniform educational programs. In contrast, some other nations have little or no state support for independent schools, but less regulation and more variability in educational offerings. In such cases many independent schools have less fiscal security, but there also is less state intervention, and more variability in offerings. It is precisely this trade-off that has made so many non-state schools in the US so chary of state subventions.

These considerations seem to suggest that more state support for independent education might not produce much more varied school programs. And research on the effects of choice suggests that the improvements in student performance would be quite modest at best. But from another angle my account suggests the virtues of greater choice. For many American families who desire alternative public or private schooling must struggle against large and sometimes impossible obstacles. Family choice in education is restricted by economic and social inequalities, and the supply of schools to choose among also may be restricted. Most troublesome, the families who most need the educational leverage that choice could offer are the most handicapped in efforts to use choice to improve education for their children. Since they also are handicapped in many other ways, and since schools in their communities are especially likely to be weak, their situation is particularly difficult. These considerations suggest that choice might be an appropriate way to make schools more responsive to families' preferences.

Decentralization and its Effects

Some reformers argue that centralization has paralyzed local school systems. They assert that education has failed because power and decision making are located far from teachers, parents, and neighborhoods. Decentralization, they say, could break the influence of central school agencies. It would open schools to the influence of those most concerned with education: Parents, teachers, and local school administrators (Fantini, 1970; Gittell, 1970).

Is this account correct? Is centralized bureaucracy the cause of schools' unresponsiveness to parents and communities? Would decentralization cure this problem?

Many decentralization schemes would sufficiently change school governance structures to increase opportunities for parents to influence schools. And in most cities there are some neighborhoods that could turn nearly any decentralization plan to advantage. But would decentralization broadly boost schools' responsiveness? There are several reasons to doubt it. First, many governance problems in city schools arise from the larger structure of US school governance. These problems are not caused by city schools, and would persist after decentralization. Second, many of the problems that do arise within city schools' organization do not stem chiefly from centralization. Decentralization schemes would be unlikely to affect these problems, and they probably would crop up in new governing units. Third, to be broadly effective, decentralization requires that a new local politics of education be created and sustained in many new local government units. But that seems inconsistent with much else in local politics. And it would require political resources that are most scarce in the neighborhoods most in need of change.

The education landscape

Consider first the larger political landscape in which decentralization would occur. Schooling in the US is extraordinarily fragmented and highly politicized. Unlike centralized systems in other nations, educational organization in the US is in many ways a non-system, a congeries of weakly coordinated but increasingly overlapping centers of educational provision, influence, and governance.

One prominent feature of this landscape is that agencies and authorities are spread everywhere.[4] Individual schools are the basic unit of organization and provision, as in any educational system. Recent estimates place their number at about 80,000 (Center for Education Statistics, 1987, p. 70). In the US, many important educational decisions are made at the school level, including those bearing on educational program, student assignment, and resource allocation among students (Wirt and Kirst, 1982). In many nations with centralized systems, individual schools have much less influence on such decisions (Meyer, 1983; Ramirez and Rubison, 1979).

Local school districts are the fundamental unit of governance in the US; they now number about 15,000. Many important decisions also are made at the district level, including those that bear on funding, educational program, and teacher hiring. In contrast, most nations with centralized systems simply have no local school districts: Central ministries deal directly with each school, though in some cases they work through regional offices. Local governance builds many sources of variation into US education, in everything from finance to educational program. Such variation usually is much less marked in centralized systems (Meyer, 1983; Ramirez and Rubison, 1979).

State governments hold most constitutional authority in US education, though, with the exception of Hawaii, they directly operate few schools. These agencies always have made some important decisions, though historically most states delegated most authority to localities. That delegation of state power is a striking contrast to some other nations with federal systems. In Australia, for instance, the state governments hold most constitutional authority in education, but they also are the basic operating unit. Local districts simply do not exist. Each state operates all the public schools within its boundaries, performing all the functions that we associate with both state and local school governance (Boyd and Smart, 1987). Since the 1960s our own states have expanded their decision making in such areas as school finance reform, the improvement of instruction, school evaluation, and revisions in teacher qualification.

The federal government is the junior partner in US education. It directly operates few schools, and, on average, contributes about six per cent of school operating budgets. In centralized systems, of course, things are very different: The national ministry is the senior and often sole partner, managing all educational programs and paying most or all operating costs. But the US government is not powerless. Since World War II it has accumulated increasing influence on state and local decisions about funding and educational program. In addition, federal agencies have powerfully affected state and local decisions about education for disadvantaged groups, civil rights and civil liberties in schools, and curriculum improvement. But these influences are exerted in a piecemeal fashion, through individual programs and policies, rather than in a coordinated fashion through a central ministry that regulates instruction and controls core support (Meyer, 1983; Scott and Meyer, 1983).

Few nations have such dispersed authority and operations in education. This is not surprising, for few nations are so large, politically so decentralized, and so committed to federalism. This is not to say that schools here look wildly different, as though some were run by people from Mars. There are many important elements of commonality across government boundaries in US schooling. But many of these owe a great deal to cultural or market influences, as in widely shared views of teacher education arising in professional associations, or the influence of college and university entrance requirements on high school studies, or the influence of privately published texts on public school studies. But in these cases we see little evidence of coherent action in a system of public agencies (Clark, 1965; Peterson, 1974). Though Americans seem to complain more than any other people about state interference and centralizing forces in schooling, authority is much more dispersed here than in most other nations. Perhaps that is why we complain more.

A second feature of the US educational landscape is that nearly all of these centers of organization and governance are very active. For Americans attach great importance to education, and have used it to solve more and more problems. Especially in the years since WW II, policymaking has increased in nearly every corner of education. Federal policymaking grew dramatically between the mid-1950s and the mid-1970s, in areas as diverse as high school curriculum, civil rights for Blacks and other minorities, and improving education for the disadvantaged. In a mere twenty years the national government had intervened in state and local educational affairs in ways that few had imagined it could. Similarly, the last decade has seen a rapid and remarkable expansion of state policymaking. Many states have moved aggressively into regulation of curriculum, assessment of student performance and school effectiveness, school finance reform, and many other areas. Owing partly to these changes, and partly to increasing political activity around education generally, local districts also have taken on many more responsibilities in the decades since 1950. Many now operate programs that would have seemed unimaginable three decades ago, including advanced placement classes, education for disadvantaged and handicapped students, and programs for pregnant girls (Ravitch, 1983; Powell, Farrar and Cohen, 1985).

These changes have made education agencies much busier and more complicated places. One reason is that more responsibilities have been assumed everywhere in education. But another is that many of these responsibilities have been assumed jointly and therefore partially, by many different agencies in the education system. For instance, Chapter I is a federal program, but it operates through state and local governments. Local Chapter I budget decisions therefore depend on state and federal Chapter I decisions. But Chapter I is only one of many federal programs, and relations among these programs also make a difference within governments. Hence local Chapter I fund allocations also may depend on local PL

94–142 allocations, partly because the two programs' coverage often overlaps, and partly for general budgetary reasons. And many of these complications cut both ways at once: Local budget and personnel decisions for Chapter I may depend both on local evaluations of Chapter I programs and on state and federal reviews of the evaluations. The growth of policymaking means that more educational decisions are made, but in our system of dispersed authority and operations, it also means that more of these decisions are made partially, in a growing pattern of overlapping responsibilities. Policymaking has produced a greatly expanded system of check-offs and consultation, within and across levels of government. There are many more links and points of contact, within and among educational agencies. Workers in every organization must make more adjustments in their operations, in response to operations elsewhere (Cohen, 1982).

The combination of dispersed authority and organization with intense political activity has added a distinctive complexity to US education. It also contains an ironic twist. As educational policy has grown, the claims to competence of all education governments also have grown: The education problems which governments address have increased dramatically, along with the promised solutions. But the problems of coordination — among governments, and across policies and programs within governments — also have increased, in part because this expanded social problem solving occurs within an extraordinarily fragmented system of government. Hence political and administrative irrationalities have grown in the wake of growing claims to competence.

A third feature of the educational landscape is that all centers of governance and organization enjoy considerable autonomy, despite the general increase in policymaking. One source of autonomy is tradition and law. States long have been accustomed to operating with little federal interference, a habit sanctioned in the US Constitution. Many localities also are accustomed to operating with modest state interference, a habit hardened in long use, and sanctioned by many statutory delegations of state authority. A second source of autonomy is the difficulty of effective surveillance and enforcement. It is much easier for education agencies to issue directions than to figure out how well they have been followed, or to take action if they have not been. Educational surveillance has proved quite difficult even for relatively simple things like accounting. This point has been richly displayed in the long, sorry history of federal efforts to gather accurate statistics on rudimentary features of state and local schooling (Weiss and Gruber, 1987). Surveillance is many times more difficult for such matters as the nature of instruction, or its quality, or its effects. For there is an enormous range of things that might reasonably be monitored.

Many are difficult to specify, and even more difficult to observe. And there is much dispute about what should be observed, how it should be observed, and what the observed phenomena might mean. In addition to these problems, most US educational agencies lack the staff to even monitor the gross features of schooling. None, including those agencies specifically devoted to surveillance, have the staff, money, or time to closely monitor such things as the nature of instruction, or its quality.[4] Additionally, even if these agencies had armies of monitoring researchers, none have the resources that would be required to take action on the results of surveillance. There is no US educational inspectorate to check on compliance, nor is there much organized capacity to help education agencies learn how to correct any offending behavior, were it brought to light.[5] Recall the most vigorous federal enforcement efforts to date: The use of Title VI of the 1964 Civil Rights Act to disestablish the dual school system in the South. Even this unusual effort relied heavily on private agencies to monitor state and local compliance, report violations, and support efforts to change (Orfield, 1969).

For these reasons among others, the expansion of policymaking has not commensurately reduced autonomy. For instance, the states depend on localities for political support and policy execution, as any higher-level agent depends on subordinates. Hence state governments are often constrained by what localities will accept. Yet despite this, the states often act with remarkable independence. The last ten year's state education reforms are a case in point. The reforms often were quite offensive to local educators, but were still enacted with little difficulty (Fuhrman, Clune and Elmore, 1988). Similarly, the national government has only a modest constitutional role in education, and it has long deferred to state and local authorities. But federal agencies nonetheless have taken various dramatic initiatives designed to greatly change state and local education. Many were taken over local and state opposition, some over fierce and even violent opposition. Until they were taken, most of these initiatives had been thought impossible. The *Brown* decisions were one case in point, and the curriculum reforms of the later 1950s were another. Title VI of the 1964 Civil Rights Act, which helped to dis-establish the racially dual school system in the South, was still another (Orfield, 1969). Despite the constraints that lower-level agencies can impose on their superiors, state and federal agencies have regularly pushed far beyond the presumed limits.

The same phenomenon also seems to obtain in reverse. For state and local autonomy appear to be only modestly constrained by higher level policymaking. Researchers have documented the states' great flexibility, even in responding to the dramatic federal policies and programs noted just above. Researchers also have shown that local schools and districts retain considerable latitude in coping with state and federal policies. Despite the increasing flow of higher level directives, lower level agencies seem to have much elbow-room in interpreting and responding to them (McLaughlin, 1987).

Is this not a contradiction? How can higher level authorities have great autonomy in dealing with lower level agencies, while lower level agencies have similar autonomy in responding to higher level actions? It may seem illogical, but it makes perfect American political sense. For while policy-making is very active, centers of organization and governance also are widely dispersed and weakly linked. Any agency can make serious demands on others, if it can only mobilize the requisite political resources to enunciate a policy, or begin a new program. But because the governance system is so dispersed, the costs of enforcing demands are very much greater than the costs of making them. The costs of monitoring compliance are much greater than the costs of enunciating demands. Hence the agencies on which demands are made ordinarily retain great autonomy in responding to them.

A fourth feature of the US education landscape concerns the coordination of higher-level policy. State and federal policies and programs have increased dramatically, but most coordination among them falls to local schools and districts. This arrangement owes something to the shape of state and federal power in education: It is expressed in discrete policies and programs, not in general governance capacity. Despite much government activity in public education, the dispersion of authority has inhibited the growth of general government capacity in federal education agencies and in most state governments. The arrangement also owes something to the enormous tasks of managing each higher-level program. For state and federal education executives must try to shape the work of thousands or tens of thousands of unknown educators, in hundreds or thousands of different and often remote jurisdictions. Since programs and policies are primary, much time and money have been applied to that formidable task. Little has been left for coordination across programs.

How do local schools cope with this situation? One favorite approach is to ignore the matter. Inattention is a common management tool (Sproull and Kiesler, 1982), especially when authority is dispersed and capacity is limited in higher level agencies. But in highly politicized situations, agencies and interest groups regularly attempt to use higher-level policies and programs for their own ends. In the process they often draw attention to local management problems that higher-level agencies might otherwise miss, or wish to avoid. In such cases ignorance can be dangerous for local managers. Hence in the most politicized localities — i.e., urban districts — there has been increasingly attentive coordination of state and federal programs. Much of this occurs at the district level. Various semi-autonomous sub-units manage many different program requirements, regulations, and funding arrangements. Typically they deal with accounting, organizational, legal, and related matters. Substantive educational matters are only a modest concern. These sub-units also carry on extensive liaison with other governments, and with private agencies and groups. These offices cause many problems for schools and teachers, because they increase the difficulty of central decision making. But these bureaus also solve problems for schools and teachers, because they buffer them from many adminsitrative and legal difficulties.

But even at their most effective, central offices pass on many coordination problems to schools and teachers — often with little or no notice. Some of these matters are organizational, but few overtly involve matters of accounting or law. Many concern substantive educational issues. For instance, schools or teachers regularly are left to figure out the instructional content and organization of Chapter I and PL 94–142 programs. They also are regularly left to determine the relations between these two instructional programs. And they are frequently left to work out the relations between these programs and similar or related state programs (Peterson, Rabe and Wong, 1986; Peterson, 1983; Cohen, 1982). Principals and teachers regularly manage such work by inattention, but local politics can make that risky as well. These difficulties are complicated by higher-level inattention. For even when some guidance is offered, few or no management resources are provided.

This approach to policy and program coordination makes good sense from one perspective, for it fits with the structure of education governance. It also has many advantages for state and federal agencies, for they can reap the political advantages from initiating policies and programs, while tacitly delegating responsibility for many problems to local districts, schools, and teachers. But from another perspective, there are real problems. One is the the growing clutter in education agencies due to the accumulation of disparate policies and programs. Another is the coordination problems that local districts inherit, which can be immense. This is another case in which political and administrative irrationalities grow along with claims to competence.

A fifth notable feature of the US education landscape is the extraordinary prominence of non-government agencies. Private publishing firms design and produce the books and other materials that teachers and students use. Private agencies also design and sell the tests that, willy-nilly, become the goals that we set for schooling, and are used to decide how well schools have done. But text publishers and testing agencies are not part of the school governance system. Similarly, universities and colleges set their own admissions standards. But since these affect high school programs, and teachers' and students' work, they also are standards for high schools, even though many universities and colleges are private, and none are part of the school governance system. Business firms are similarly situated: They hire many employees straight from high schools, and so their job entry arrangements also affect high school programs and work. Yet they are not part of the formal school governance system. Additionally, private interest groups of many sorts press schools to respond to their special concerns, which include such varied things as tough academic standards, education for capitalism, better treatment for handicapped students or minority groups, teachers' rights and working conditions, and many more. Such interest groups also monitor and comment on the schools' performance in such matters, and regularly press for continuing adjustments in policy and practice (Peterson, 1974; Peterson and Rabe, 1983).

One way to summarize this account of the educational landscape is to say that it has become more politicized and more populous. As in many other sectors of public life, there are more issues to debate and decide, more organizations active in debate and decision, and more contact among issues and organizations. The political space of education has grown as the scope of problem solving and policy has expanded. But there also is more political movement within that space, more moving things, and more contacts and collisions among them.

Thus the universe of American education is not like the expanding universe of Big Bang theorists, in which a fixed amount of matter thins as the boundaries of the cosmos rush away from each other. Instead, the space and the 'matter' of education — issues, political activity, policymaking and organization — all have multiplied. The boundaries of education have pushed outward to embrace new concerns and types of service, but the sector itself also has become more densely populated. Contact and overlap among agencies have multiplied at the same time as the world of education has expanded.

These developments have greatly increased the organizational overhead — the various costs of getting things done — in US education. Educational systems have become larger, more complex, and more densely populated, with more contact in and among organizations, and more overlapping concerns. But this growth has been singularly dis-integrated.[6] Educational organization has grown rather as jungle creepers grow: Beginning from various widely separated small centers, educational policies and organizations have spread outward in many directions. Some agencies are of course centralized in some respects, and bureaucracy also has grown. But these are threads in a larger, increasingly dense and highly politicized tangle of organization and governance. Many commentators mistake these things for bureaucracy, or centralized government.

What does my account imply for decentralization? This reform is aimed only at local politics, after all. But local politics are not conducted in a vacuum; decentralization will be shaped by the larger landscape. One example is politicization. Advocates of decentralization argue that city school governance is insufficiently politicized: Schools are said to be dominated by bureaucracies that block political expression of family and community interests. The purpose of this reform is precisely to politicize local education. But can politicization be restricted to neighborhood or sub-district boards? It seems unlikely. For establishing new local governance entities would unsettle political and social relations all around. Decentralization would mandate new structures and revise old relationships. New political opportunities would open up, but — it comes to the same thing — old political relationships would be unsettled. Politics probably would therefore intensify. Local interest groups and government agencies would be drawn in to re-negotiate relationships, to defend their interests, to assert new interests, or to support allies. State agencies and interest groups also would probably be drawn in, either to exercise their own responsibilities in an unsettled situation, or because unresolved local con flicts would tend to percolate upward, creating additional pressures for higher-level involvment.

Experience supports this view. Previous efforts to implement decentralization and choice schemes have increased conflict and uncertainty. Hence political and regulatory activities also have increased, making governance more complex and difficult. Advocates of decentralization often argue that it would simplify school governance by clarifying accountability and breaking up central bureaucracies. But because American education is so fragmented and highly politicized, efforts to simplify it would bring new complications.[7]

Local organization

Advocates of decentralization often argue that the organizational problems of city schools stem chiefly from centralized bureaucracy. But most city school systems display the same patterns of dispersed authority and fragmented organization that mark the larger landscape in which they subsist.

These jurisdictions are formally centralized. They all have hierarchical organization charts, with superintendents and school boards resting comfortably at the pinnacle. Most are richly endowed with administrators, and seem mired in bureaucratic procedures. It also is true that hierarchical, 'rational' administration is a long-cherished administrative ideal, especially in urban districts. Since the turn of our century, superintendents and their university advocates have sought to create agencies in which the top administrator would reign supreme, and in which authority would flow tidily downward (Tyack, 1974; Tyack and Hansot, 1982).

But this ideal has been difficult to realize. One reason is that individual schools typically enjoy considerable autonomy within districts, for some of the same reasons that local districts enjoy autonomy from state and federal agencies. Fashions in educational administration change, of course, variously heralding central office and school 'leadership'. But however the prevailing winds blow, most schools seem to retain considerable latitude. Indeed, it is in the presumably most calcified districts, like New York City, where the most fruitful as well as the most depressing examples of school or sub-district autonomy regularly seem to turn up.

Administrative specialization is a second reason that local centralization has been elusive. Central offices look more like loose collections of semi-autonomous fiefdoms than centrally coordinated hierarchies. Evaluation is the most recent example of functional specialization, and budgeting is perhaps the most venerable. Personnel is the special function with the largest claim on operating budgets, but purchasing, curriculum, and transportation also are prominent. In most medium sized and larger districts, each functional specialty is incarnate in a semi-autonomous sub-agency within the central administration. Each is staffed by professionals with specialized education or experience, who therefore also have a special perspective on educational matters, and a commitment to making that perspective count in school management. And because this differentiation is functional, most sub-units have responsibilities that cut across educational operations in the entire district (Zimet, 1973; Rowan, 1982a, 1982b; Cohen, 1982). These developments have been reinforced by the 'professionalization' of school administration and administrative education. For in this field as in many others, professionalism has been identified with the cultivation of many learned sub-specialties.

Functional differentiation is commonly described as a form of decentralization by researchers who study government and business organizations (Kaufman, 1969; Jennergren, 1981), but this point seems to have escaped many students of education. In any event, such organization fragments organization and decision-making. Actions that seem a coherent package at the school level splinter in many different directions at higher levels. Take the case of a principal who wishes to begin a program for gifted students in her school. She and the school's teachers can take a single decision to initiate such a program, perhaps in consultation with parents.

But in order to implement this seemingly straightforward decision, the principal would have to deal with many different central office units — unless her district was quite unusual. For one sub-unit would have authority to re-arrange curriculum, while another would be in charge of releasing students from regular classroom commitments. Each sub-unit would have different concerns and procedures, different criteria for decisions, and different schedules. And this would only be the beginning. Still another sub-unit would regulate or control new teacher hiring, or reassignment of a teacher on staff, while yet another unit would be concerned with hiring an additional teacher's aide. These units also would have different concerns, procedures, and schedules, among other reasons because they deal with different internal and external constituencies. Still another sub-unit would be concerned with community relations, and another with purchasing any new equipment that might be needed. This is a formidable array of organizational baronies, each with its own perspective on the proposed school program, and each with its own approach to administration. Such specialization enhances expertise, reduces the demands on top administrators, and is often reported to improve effectiveness in business organizations. But it also inhibits the development of general administrative capacity, and fragments organization and decision making.

State and federal policymaking reinforces this fragmentation. For higher-level policies and programs have created or strengthened specialized sub-units within state and local education agencies. For instance, Chapter I or PL 94–142 greatly increase lower-level responsibilities for various sorts of oversight and regulation, in the effort to manage effectively across several levels of government and thousands of jurisdictions. But most of these increased responsibilities are specialized. PL 94–142, for instance, carries very complex regulations that define procedures to safeguard the rights of handicapped students, and to insure that they receive an appropriate education. State and local agencies are required to use those procedures, and to use and submit to evaluation, auditing, and program review as management instruments. Chapter I also has complex regulations, but they are aimed at improving education for the educationally disadvantaged. Chapter I also uses evaluation, auditing, and program review as oversight instruments for states and localities, but the content and procedures are quite different than PL 94–142. Chapter I has different ends, means, and clients than PL 94–142, and so managing the two programs is quite different. It seems entirely reasonable that specialized sub-units would grow up to deal with these and other state and federal programs (Peterson, 1983; Peterson, Rabe and Wong, 1986; Cohen, 1982; Stackhouse, 1982).

Additionally, some policies and programs are not just specialized, but also divergent. For instance, in the 1960s many state, federal and local education agencies created bureaus intended to monitor and push compliance with various anti-discrimination requirements. But during the same period many of the same agencies also devised or implemented programs and policies to improve education for disadvantaged or handicapped children. There was frequent tension between anti-discrimination policies that stressed racial and ethnic integration of students, and compensatory education policies and programs that offered specialized educational services for disadvantaged students. There also was tension between programs for handicapped students that encouraged 'mainstreaming' in regular classrooms, and compensatory policies that stressed special treatment in special classrooms. The sub-units that administered or monitored compliance with anti-discrimination efforts thus had different and sometimes divergent charters from those charged with the operation of compensatory or special education programs.

In these cases and many others, the program or policy has been the primary unit of higher-level action. Regulation and oversight requirements within individual policies and programs aim to coordinate work across many levels of government, and many hundreds or even thousands of jurisdictions. Special budgeting, personnel, curriculum or evaluation procedures are mandated or encouraged by each program or policy, and each is different than every other. Most of the added work associated with higher-level policies and programs has been confined within specialized administrative sub-units (Bankston, 1982; Cohen, 1982; Peterson, 1983; Peterson, Rabe and Wong, 1986; Scott and Meyer, 1983; Thomas, 1975).

These developments make sense in US politics. For many state and federal education policies seek to solve broad social problems, yet they do so in a system of government that was not designed to handle problems that cut across levels of the federal system, or spread beyond the boundaries of single local jurisdictions, or both. Programs like PL 94-142 or Chapter I cannot work unless they bridge many artfully designed chasms in American government. For effective initiation and implementation of such policies require coordinated action among many agents. Yet in a fragmented polity, the extant education agencies have few general means of coordination. Most higher-level policies and programs therefore must create their own system of coordination. One common artifice is semi-autonomous networks of agencies that span several levels of government, many different jurisdictions, and boundaries between public and private agencies. These networks bridge the political chasms in several different ways. For instance, they help to mobilize support for new programs and policies across several levels of government, and many sorts of agencies.

An example is the loose network of community organizations, advocacy groups, legislators, and others that helped to build support for the legislation that became PL 94-142. Such networks also help to secure and stabilize funding for state or national educational policies, once they are established. Continuing Congressional support for vocational education and Chapter I owes a good deal to the networks that grew up around these programs. Policy networks also play a part in revising and evaluating policies and programs. Members of the Chapter I network contributed to various evaluations and revisions of that program (Peterson, 1983; Scott and Meyer, 1983; Peterson, Rabe and Wong, 1986; Cohen, 1982).

Policy networks thus support state and national problem solving in a political system that was designed to frustrate it (Kaufman, 1969). But efforts to manage fragmentation in the larger landscape also compound it within local school organizations. For specialized policies and programs disperse authority and fragment organization within local school agencies. Sponsors, operators, and advocates of particular programs often see those sub-units as a key support for their programs' integrity and political stability, and a requirement for program operations. They are probably correct. But the sub-units also inhibit the growth of general government capacity.

One can think about these developments as the expansion of bureaucracy: There are more rules, more regulation, and more efforts to prescribe conduct. But the added regulation and oversight follow policy and program lines. They are centered in specialized sub-units for evaluation, or budget, or Chapter I, or Federal Programs. Regulations, rules, and oversight multiply within policy networks and administrative sub-units, not across them. Government has become more busy and complex, but it has done so in a variety of semi-autonomous subsectors. Bureaucracy has increased, but it has done so in a uniquely segmented fashion (Clark, 1965; Scott and Meyer, 1983).

What does my account imply for decentralization?

First, most arguments for this reform offer an inadequate account of local school organization. City school systems are a curious hybrid of organizational sprawl and formal hierarchy. Not surprisingly, this unusual beast often is seen in radically different ways by people who work in and around local schools. Many administrators think they see unresponsiveness that is due to fragmented organization and dispersed authority; they regularly argue for more centralization and streamlining. In contrast, many teachers and parents think they see unresponsiveness and resistance to change due to centralized bureaucratic hierarchy; they often argue for greater decentralization.

But if my analysis differs from those offered in support of decentralization, do they not add up to the same thing? On both accounts, city schools are overgrown with organization. On both accounts, governance seems clumsy, and a barrier to education. Would not decentralization eliminate these problems, whatever their source? If central school agencies were greatly pared back, and most of their authority handed over to individual schools or sub-districts, would not most of the present political clutter disappear? Or, if systems like those in New York or Chicago simply were dissolved and replaced by scores of smaller systems, would not governance be shrunk to a manageable scale? In either case, would not the organizational barriers to more responsive schools and better education be greatly reduced?

I think not. Decentralization would bring some such improvements, in some cases. But it would be unlikely to bring many of these improvements in many cases. For most approaches to decentralization would not affect the fragmented organization of local schools. Instead it seems likely that the organizational patterns described above would be reproduced in new governance units.

Consider the most 'radical' approach to decentralization: Existing city school jurisdictions would be dissolved, and replaced with many smaller, independent governing units. The absolute amount of administration in each new district would decrease due to the district's smaller size, but this does not mean that administrative problems would be reduced. One reason is that the fragmented organization described above would most likely be reproduced in the smaller jurisdictions. Functional specialization is deeply ingrained in US administrative practice. Additionally, each new district's administrative capacity would decrease with decentralization: Even though smaller districts would have fewer problems to deal with, they also would have less administrative capacity. It therefore seems likely that many administrative problems — such as coordinating higher-level programs and policies — would occupy a constant or increasing proportion of administrative capacity through decentralization. It is difficult to see how the proportional burdens could decrease, unless one supposed that administrative capacity would grow as districts became smaller. But there is no evidence of such an effect (Freeman, Hannan and Hannaway, 1978). Hence the same difficult coordination problems would be presented to governing entities that had less administrative capacity.

Further, if we shift attention from individual districts to the aggregate of governing entities, it seems quite likely that net administrative problems would increase. For the coordination problems that the old district had managed would be reproduced many times over in many new districts. Decentralization would create a larger local administrative burden, spread over many more units. Additionally, many administrative problems would shift upward in this approach, since state and federal agencies would have to deal with many more local entities, each trying to coordinate state and federal programs and policies.

Alternatively, consider a more conservative and common approach to decentralization: Big-city school districts would be retained as legal and administrative entities, while central authority and organization would be shifted to individual schools or sub-districts. Such schemes vary, depending on how much authority would be retained in central offices. But most versions entail some sort of shared power, in which both the central agency and local schools would have an important voice in decisions. Schools or sub-districts would have more authority than in the past, but the central administration would retain considerable authority as well.

Such schemes would enhance the authority of local schools or sub-districts, and increase opportunities for popular participation in school governance. But they also would further complicate local education governance. For basic authority and a large share of operations would remain at the center, while a new layer of governance and administration was added at the school or sub-district level. Such power-sharing arrangements also would be likely to increase conflict within districts, as schools or sub-districts struggled with central offices over policy and programs. They also would be likely to increase the check-offs and consultation required for many decisions, simply because power was being shared. Overlap in administrative operations probably would increase as well, as local or sub-district administrators took a larger share of decisions formerly held at the center.

If we compare conservative with radical school decentralization schemes, neither seems likely to produce a net simplification of local governance. But each would complicate it in a different way. In either case there would be new administrative costs and complexities. But in one case they would be parcelled out among new jurisdictions and passed upward to state and federal governments, while in the other they would be reallocated within extant jurisdictions. In either case there is a real potential for increasing political and administrative problems.

Is this result inevitable? One can imagine a different sort of scheme: Most authority and operations would be devolved to individual schools or sub-districts, but a few general functions — resource allocation, quality control, and fiscal accountability — would remain at the center. Such a scheme would simplify local governance while also increasing the opportunities for popular participation. But it also would produce some additional complications. Individual schools or sub-districts would gain considerable independence from complex central office decision making. But, barring revolutionary changes in state and federal policymaking, local schools or sub-districts also would inherit many of the governance and administration problems formerly managed at the center. These would include much coordination of higher-level policies and programs, liasion with other governments and with local interest groups, and all the attendant political conflict. These developments would make local governance more complex. No decentralization scheme can obviate the fragementation of higher-level policies and programs, or the tugging and hauling among various interest groups about the conduct of schooling. Additionally, even the most wisely designed division of local responsibility seems unlikely to avoid considerable friction between central and local school authorities over resource allocation and quality control. Responsiveness or educational quality might be enhanced by a scheme of this sort. And the combination of general governance authority at the center, with considerable autonomy in schools seems salutary. But better government is not necessarily simpler or easier government. Gains in schools' autonomy and control of resources probably would come at the cost of additional administrative work and political difficulty.

My analysis points to a difficulty in the rhetoric of decentralization.[8] Arguments for this reform often suggest that it is a scheme to greatly simplify local education governance while also making it more responsive to parents and communities. But most decentralization schemes would pare back one sort of local government while expanding other sorts. The net amount of local government and governance problems probably would not diminish. Under some schemes they would almost surely increase. Additionally, the centers of political influence in education would greatly multiply under any scheme for decentralization. That would increase local political fragmentation, and hence would increase the burdens of government at higher levels.

A new politics of education?

Advocates of decentralization see local politics as a way to enliven stultified school systems. They argue that if local school governance is opened up to parents, teachers, and community members, they will exert more vigorous educational leadership, and will focus schools on improved teaching and learning. Local politics is thus endowed with the purifying, vitalizing force that neutral administrative competence once was thought to have.

Would a new politics of school improvement arise in the wake of decentralization? In some cases it would. But a new politics seems unlikely to spring up on a large scale. One reason concerns political organization: Decentralization would quickly create new local political vacuums, simply by creating new offices, power, and authorities. These would create new opportunities for political organizing, and new avenues to political advancement. All of these things would offer new actors incentives to mobilize, but they also would be attractive to existing political agencies and actors. If new political organizations were strong and well organized, they could move into these vacuums. But building political organization is not easy. People must be found to do it, and they must be put in motion. They must learn how politics works, and how to work in it. Leaders must emerge and develop, and political networks coalesce. All of this can be exciting, but it also is difficult. Existing political organizations could move much more quickly. New school governance arrangements could become an expansion league for existing political organizations.

Such results can be found in the debris of earlier reforms. When a cautious decentralization scheme was adopted more than two decades ago in New York City, it created new political opportunities. But these opportunities all had the costs mentioned above: Recruiting new people, building new organizations, and the like. In some cases this was done, but in others there was little interest, and the promise of decentralization languished. In still other cases, the opportunities for a new politics seemed to be swallowed up by existing politics. One was the politics of the city's poverty program. Another was local politicians' everlasting search for patronage jobs and contracts. Still another was the political ambitions of various educational groups that were still at war over decentralization. In a few cases an autonomous politics of educational improvement seemed to develop. But in most cases, existing political organizations with existing concerns moved into the new political opportunities that decentralization had created. Many of these organizations were concerned with educational quality in some sense. But some saw quality as a by-product of having the correct position on the inherited decentralization issues, and thus electing people to defend those positions on the new boards. Others saw it as a matter of getting jobs and contracts for political friends and relations. Still others saw quality as a matter of defending the *status quo* on issues of race, or participation in special programs. In these ways and others, various versions of old politics seemed to dominate the new politics of school improvement (Zimet, 1973). Decentralization creates new opportunities, but it does not vaporize everything else in local politics.[8]

A second constraint on the development of a new local politics of school improvement is the political culture and educational values of city dwellers. Education is highly valued by most Americans, and many are involved in politics somehow. But these values and involvements are expressed in different ways. Highly educated cosmopolitan professionals are relatively concerned and knowledgable about educational issues. They also are relatively likely to hold progressive opinions on those issues, and to want education that challenges their children and encourages independence. They are relatively willing to work closely with professionals, to argue with them, and even to supervise their work. And they are relatively likely to organize community politics that are focused on educational quality, to use political institutions to maintain a focus on quality, and to organize reform crusades to improve school quality. Working class, lower-middle class, and poor Americans are less well informed about educational issues. They are more likely to leave most educational matters to the professionals, rather than trying to challenge or oversee them. Blacks, Hispanics and working class whites are more deferential toward educational authorities than better educated and more affluent whites. These Americans are more likely to hold traditional positions on educational issues, and to want traditional, even rigid education for their children (Masotti, 1967: Boyd, 1973; Zimmer and Hawley, 1968). Finally, working and lower-middle class Americans are more likely than cosmopolitans to approach politics with an eye on patronage and finance, rather than on broad issues and reform crusades (Banfield and Wilson, 1965; Peterson, 1981).

These differences show up in various ways. But one common manifestation has been the creation of different sorts of political organization in different sorts of communities. Affluent neighborhoods with many resident professionals (mostly suburban), have been the special locale of a reform oriented, 'non-partisan' and universalistic politics of educational quality. In some of these communities an independent politics of education has been created, that is distinct from local politics more generally and targeted on educational quality. But such an independent and focused politics of education is a relatively scarce commodity, even in well-to-do suburbs. In contrast, older industrial towns and cities commonly have been the home of a patronage oriented, partisan, particularistic politics of education. These places are of course the chief candidates for school decentralization. Most have large concentrations of working-class and poor families, many of them Black or Hispanic. Sociology is not destiny: Blacks, Hispanics, and working class whites have organized reform crusades. But that has not been their dominant pattern of local political organization. It would be surprising if these habits changed dramatically just because a new political opportunity was presented (Masotti, 1967; Boyd, 1973; Banfield and Wilson, 1965; Peterson, 1981).[9]

A third constraint on the development of a new education politics is the remarkable vulnerability of education as a field of political action. It has been difficult for Americans to sustain an enduring focus on any educational issue, quality included. Educational ideas, issues, and problems are persistently imported from other social and political arenas, or are shaped by ideas and actions in other arenas. This was true at the outset of public education, during Horace Mann's early administrations in Massachusetts. Support for free public education then was fed by anti-Irish bigotry, worries about industrialism, fear of urban crime, the belief that a growing democracy could not survive popular ignorance, and the conviction that family and church were everywhere dissolving and must be replaced by some new agency of moral instruction. Arguments for state schooling were mostly discussions of these other developments, and how state schools might ameliorate them. Conceptions of educational quality varied wildly across these various concerns. The same patterns hold today. In the early Reagan administration, education was the vehicle for a conservative religious revival, for worries about domestic economic strength, and for anxiety about America's world position. Several different conceptions of educational reform developed, along with different visions of educational quality. In the Kennedy and Johnson years education was no less passionately entangled with a larger politics — in that case, of Black civil rights and poverty. Conceptions of educational quality mirrored those concerns. Even when educational quality itself seems to be the issue, as in the Sputnik era and again today, it has largely been a surrogate for much broader worries about national security, economic vitality, or the collapse of traditional values. The politics of education is everywhere infused with, driven by, and even created by issues arising outside education. These issues change, sometimes with blinding speed. And since education in the US is highly politicized, its political focus changes in response.

The permeability of education politics is as common in local as in national education affairs. School districts are regularly convulsed by citizen crusades against Huck Finn, Holden Caulfield, and other harbungers of immorality. Efforts to vote new local school taxes are increasingly the victim of an aging population. And since the end of WW II, education politics in the cities has been powerfully shaped by demographic changes that arise outside city and even national borders. One might even argue that Americans have little in the way of a distinctive politics of education. Education politics are instead driven largely by winds that blow from elsewhere. The winds blow fiercely, and change direction quickly. This phenomenon is not distinctive to education, but it seems uniquely potent there. New decentralized districts would have as much difficulty holding fast to a focus on quality as the old districts have had.

One moral of my story about decentralization concerns the problems of school governance. This reform is premised on the idea that city schools are politically unresponsive because they are centralized bureaucracies. I have argued to the contrary that city schools are unresponsive largely because they are extraordinarily fragmented, and that in this respect they resemble the larger structure of US education. This fragmentation owes something to the size and social history of the US: It is, after all, is a vast nation in which nearly everything, including much organizational invention, occurred in a fragmented fashion for much of our history. There was little social infrastructure to do it any other way. But even if communications and social organization had been no barrier, our system of government was carefully designed to disperse power and authority. When educational policy began to expand, shortly after the Republic was founded, it expressed a powerful faith in the good that public institutions could do. But it expanded within a political system that expressed great skepticism about strong government. Hence the growth of educational policy produced repeated collisions between an optimistic and expansive faith in the power of government to solve social problems through education, and a political system designed to incarnate great caution about government in general, and coordinated action of government in particular.

The fragmented organization of education owes a good deal to those collisions. They have helped to produce a congeries of organizations intended to coordinate state and national initiatives in education, within a system that was designed to frustrate such coordination. The result has been a distinctive species of educational non-system, which abounds with a vast population of somewhat autonomous, often overlapping, and usually weakly and often indirectly coordinated organizations. It is ingenious in many ways, and often flexible and forgiving. It has helped to promote state and national education priorities. But the more we have asked education to do, the more difficult it has become to get things done. It is often maddening, but it should be no surprise. American government was designed to produce just that result.

School decentralization will not repair these problems. Indeed, the schemes that are most likely to be adopted — i.e., those that devolve power without strengthening central controls over resource allocation and quality control — would compound fragmentation. That is the second moral of my story: Efforts to simplify local school governance probably would complicate it. For decentralization would not change the larger organization of education governance. It would not suspend politics in education more generally. Nor could decentralized schools or districts be well-insulated against local political circumstances. The rhetoric of decentralization in these senses is misleading, for it promises major political and educational change in return only for changes in local education governance. But in a pluralistic society with highly developed politics of education at all levels of governance, the politics of local education does not transpire in a bell jar.

The last moral of my decentralization story is that a new local politics of educational quality would require a major program of political development, not just the creation of new governance structures. For new neighborhood political movements or elites would have to be constructed. They would have to invent a new politics. And they would have to sustain that politics as a winning combination. These things would take many resources, including the time to devote to the matter, the knowledge to manage the educational enterprise in the interests of quality, the tenacity to outlast opposing paid professionals, the organization to outfight contending interests with less noble purposes, and the capacity to do all this for few immediate rewards, and much immediate difficulty and heartache. In some cities, in some neighborhoods, some of these resources have been mobilized and some important changes made. Under any reasonable decentralization scheme, similar developments would occur in some other neighborhoods. But it is unlikely that a new politics would spontaneously or broadly arise. For the resources mentioned here are in short supply everywhere in US education. Even in very privileged communities, where adults have many cultural and economic advantages, creating and sustaining the necessary political organization and culture are formidable tasks. And such resources are especially difficult to mobilize in poor and working class neighborhoods, precisely because of the economic and social problems that bedevil their inhabitants. Even with capable assistance from advocacy groups, creating and sustaining a new politics are immense tasks.[10]

Decentralization alone is not enough. Yet many advocates of this reform seem to assume that it is. They argue that changes in local political structure will open access to influence, and that — perhaps with a bit of assistance — the schools will improve. But this approach to reform would end perversely, much like the 'de-institutionalization' of mental hospitals. If decentralization is to work, the schools and neighborhoods most sorely in need of improvement will need a major, long-term infusion of new political and organizational resources. Lacking that, some opportunities will languish, and others will be seized by existing political agencies. Those agencies that already have power will accumulate more. This too has happened before (Cohen, 1978).

Instructional Guidance

Advocates of decentralization and choice hold that changing governance will improve teaching and learning. If power is shifted to those who care most about children, it is said that schools will respond and education will improve. Is that assumption correct? Would structural changes in governance broadly improve instruction?

It seems unlikely. One reason is that the mechanisms for instructional guidance are unusually weak in the US. Instruction is guided in many ways in any system of schooling, including course requirements, texts, curriculum guides, teachers' education, and educational criteria for entry to universities and work. But in the US, the guidance that issues from these sources is diffuse, vague, and often inconsistent. For instance, the topics covered in textbooks vary considerably, from one text to another, in the same subject and the same grade. Similarly, the content that turns up on tests does not seem to be strongly related to the content that is covered in texts. Choice and decentralization would not change this situation, because these reforms are aimed at the gross structure of school governance, not at the fine structure of instructional guidance. Hence new school managers would confront the same inconsistent guidance for instruction with which school managers, teachers, and students presently must cope.

A second reason that decentralization and choice seem unlikely to broadly improve instruction is that governance is weakly linked to instruction in the US. Some of the agencies that offer the most crucial guidance for teaching and learning — like text publishers, or testing firms — lie largely outside the ambit of government. Some others — like accreditation agencies — are only marginally related to government. Decentralization or choice would not offer school managers any firmer grip on the many different types of instructional guidance, simply because so many instructional guidance agencies are so weakly connected to government of any sort. The decoupling of school governance from instructional guidance is a unique feature of US education.

School reformers often write as though any good principal, school board, or alert consumers could steer a school to better instruction, simply by focusing teachers' and students' attention on texts, tests, homework, and lessons. Like stagecoach drivers in the Old West, school leaders need only gather the reins and spur the team — or so reformers seem to believe.[11] But schools are no longer like stagecoaches, if ever they were. Instructional improvement is difficult in US schools partly because there are so many different instructional reins, that are both distant from government and tugged by many different hands.[12]

The relations between government and instruction vary enormously school systems among national. Some offer relatively coherent guidance for instruction, while others offer relatively incoherent guidance. The effects of any reform that seeks to influence instruction are mediated through these instructional guidance systems.[13] Relatively coherent systems offer government more opportunities to influence instruction than relatively diffuse systems.

This is not to say that teaching and learning are easy to guide in either sort of school system. For one thing, instruction is laced with uncertainty. Its purposes are difficult to specify and easy to dispute. There are no very reliable means to most instructional ends. For another, instruction of any sort is jointly produced. It is authored by learners as well as teachers, and in school systems it is authored by large groups of learners. Such groups can be difficult to guide, partly because their members often have many different wills, capacities, values, and ways of thinking about any given topic. But if instruction is difficult to guide in any system, those difficulties can be eased or enhanced by the instructional guidance systems within which teachers and students work.

Coherent Guidance Systems

One common feature of coherent instructional guidance systems is the detailed prescription of curriculum. At the most general level this includes course requirements. Many schools systems offer teachers and students relatively little choice in course offering and selection. At a somewhat greater level of specificity it includes the desired content for each course. Many systems closely prescribe the topics to be covered in courses, rather than offering general guidelines, or a menu of possible topics. At an even greater level of specificity, guidance includes texts or other materials that contain the topics to be covered, and the means of treating each. School systems often prescribe the material to be mastered in great detail. Curriculum requirements and texts offer extensive and focused guidance about instructional content.[14]

A second attribute of coherent systems is that they monitor compliance. One focus of such monitoring is instructional inputs and processes. In some systems, central school agencies include an inspectorate, whose members check on such things as the topics that teachers cover and the materials they use (Lawton and Gordon, 1987). In such systems, students often keep workbooks in each subject, in which they record their daily work. School principals intermittently read these work-books to monitor student's progress and check on teachers' work. And school inspectors can read them, to monitor the work of teachers and principals. Such monitoring tends to support the guidance for instruction that issues from texts and curriculum guides.[15]

Another focus of monitoring is instructional results. School systems with coherent guidance arrangements usually administer promotion and school leaving exams to all students. There are a few examinations, offered at key transition points in schooling. These exams ordinarily are referenced to the system's curriculum, and the curriculum is designed with the exams in view as well. The examinations thus provide a visible target for instruction, and a means of checking on its results. Instructional guidance agencies can influence instruction by defining the targets at which teachers and students aim.[16]

A third attribute of coherent systems is that teacher education tends to be integrated with the schools' educational program. In part this is because entrance to professional education in such systems is conditioned on candidates having done at least reasonably well in that very school system — for instance, making decent scores on the school leaving examinations. Additionally, professional courses often focus on the schools' curricula and operations in systems of this sort. Teachers are specifically prepared to offer instruction in the schools they will enter. Finally, since many of these systems are centralized, the requirements for teacher education tend to be uniform within them. Teachers educated in one tertiary institution would be prepared in roughly the same way as those educated in any other tertiary institution. In each of these ways, teacher education tends to support guidance that teachers receive from other sources.

Finally, such systems often have strong incentives for academic performance.[17] For instance, university entrance depends heavily on school leaving exam scores in many nations. Hence it pays students who wish to enter university to work hard in school, and perhaps also in after school exam preparation sessions (Clark, 1985). Similarly, students' employment opportunities on leaving high school depend on their school records in some nations (Rosenbaum and Kariya, 1989). In New South Wales [Australia] for example, employers routinely review transcripts and teacher references when high school graduates or earlier school leavers apply for jobs. Teachers know this, as do students. It is taken for granted that students who do not apply themselves and behave decently in school will have difficulty finding good jobs. Hence there are important rewards for academic effort and good behavior, even for students who have no ambitions for further education. Roughly the same sort of situation seems to exist in Singapore and West Germany, among other nations. In such systems, students receive strong messages from firms and universities about the value of attending to the instructional guidance they receive elsewhere (Bishop, 1987; Bishop, 1989).

Though many school systems offer coherent guidance for instruction, they do not all do it in the same way. Some rely more on examinations than on curriculum guides and texts, while others reverse that emphasis. Some systems have abandoned the inspectorate, while others continue to use it. And contrary to the views of many researchers, centralization is not necessarily the key feature of coherent guidance. Indeed, the arrangements for governing instructional guidance vary. Some countries manage all or nearly all of it from central ministries. Others delegate text writing, or curriculum design, or examinations, or various combinations of these to quasi-governmental bodies. Some nations combine ministry oversight with direct management by quasi-government agencies. The Singaporean system is largely managed by the Ministry, but the Dutch system, in which instructional guidance also is quite integrated, is much less centralized. The key point is that whatever the formal arrangements, instructional guidance issues from a system of agencies acting in concert.

Andrew Porter and his colleagues (Schwille, Porter, Alford, Floden, Freeman, Irwin and Schmidt, 1986), have developed a useful framework for analyzing instructional guidance. They identify four attributes of instructional guidance — consistency, prescription, authority, and power. These attributes are a useful way to summarize my account of coherent guidance systems.

Consistency: The content of curriculum guides is closely tied to the content of texts, in coherent systems. Texts and guides also are aligned with examinations. Hence students, teachers, and administrators hear the same or similar messages about content coverage from different sources.

Prescription: Guidance is specific rather than global, detailed rather than sketchy. It includes specification of what topics to cover, what will be examined, what form the examinations will take, and the like. Hence teachers, students, and others concerned can have a relatively clear idea of what compliance with guidance means.

Authority: Guidance comes with the blessing of agencies and persons who count, in coherent systems. This might include university academics, or the ministry, or fundamental school laws.

Power: Compliance with guidance has tangible benefits, and deviation has tangible costs. For students this refers to potential employers' interest in their school records or teachers' references, or universities' interest in their examination scores. For teachers this refers to the inspectorate, if it decides promotion, or to teacher education agencies, if they control access to job assignments.

Instructional Guidance in the US

How does this compare with instructional guidance in the US? The contrasts are marked. There are some similarities in instruction across classrooms, but these do not arise chiefly from the coordinated action of a system of agencies that seek to guide instruction.

One leading feature of the US approach to instructional guidance is that curriculum is not prescribed in detail. It is prescribed at the most general level, in course requirements. But even within these requirements, US students and teachers have unusual latitude. Required English courses can, for instance, be satisfied in different ways in many secondary schools. There is much less prescription at the next level of specificity, which is topic coverage. Few state and local systems in the US prescribe topics in detail, though some issue advisories. And at the next level of specificity — guidelines concerning topic coverage — one finds few states or districts that issue detailed curriculum guides. Additionally, most texts contain a great range of topics, many of which cannot be covered in any given course. Teachers and students are offered many possibilities. But they have little guidance from state or local school agencies concerning priorities among topics within subjects (Schwille, Porter, Alford, Floden, Freeman, Irwin and Schmidt, 1986).

Additionally, there are many different texts for most subjects at any grade level. These are published privately, by firms that compete for adoption in relatively unregulated markets. As might be expected in the absence of strong guidance about topic coverage, there seems to be only modest overlap in content coverage among texts within fields (Freeman, Kuhs, Porter, Floden, Schmidt and Schwille, 1983). Additionally, though some states adopt approved texts or lists of texts, many do not. And even in states that do decide on adopted texts, districts often may deviate. They might lose some state aid, but often they lose nothing. To the extent that curriculum requirements and texts offer instructional guidance, then, they seem to offer vague, diverse, and often inconsistent guidance.

A second leading feature of instructional guidance in the US is modest and inconsistent monitoring of instruction. Only a few states and localities actually monitor schools' compliance with either texts or curriculum guides — South Carolina is the outstanding case. There are no education inspectorates in US states or localities. It also is uncommon for principals to read students' workbooks; indeed, it is quite uncommon for students to keep the detailed records of work that would permit such reading by principals. It also is unusual for principals to involve themselves in instruction. Few principals seem to visit classrooms, and when they do, it often is in connection with a discipline problem or a mandated teacher evaluation. Hence there are few checks on what materials are used, or on how they are used, or on what instruction is provided. It is thus quite common to find that even when teachers use required texts, they use them very differently as respects content coverage. In some cases teachers use mandated materials little or not at all (Freeman, Kuhs, Porter, Floden,

Schmidt, and Schwille, 1983). To the extent that monitoring offers any guidance for instruction, then, the common message seems to be that teachers can make their own decisions.

Monitoring of results follows a similar pattern. There are few examinations in US schools, the Advanced Placement exams being perhaps the chief exception. There are, however, many different standardized tests. But unlike examinations, standardized tests are not referenced to specific curricula. The tests are designed, published, and marketed by many different private testing agencies. Though these tests are sometimes thought to be interchangeable because they cover the same content in the same fields in the same formats, the content they actually cover in any given field seems to vary a good deal from one test to another. One of the few careful US studies of the matter focused on fourth grade mathematics textbooks and tests. Its authors observed that '. . . our findings challenge . . . th[e] assumption . . . that standardized achievement tests may be used interchangeably' (Freeman, Kuhs, Porter, Floden, Schmidt and Schwille, 1983, p. 511).

Additionally, the content of standardized tests seems to map weakly onto the content of texts. The study just cited scrutinized the relations between fourth grade mathematics textbooks and tests. The authors concluded:

> The proportion of topics covered on a standardized test that received more than cursory treatment in a textbook was never more than 50 per cent. In other words, if a fourth-grade teacher limits instruction to one of the four books analyzed, students will have an adequate opportunity to learn or to review less than half of all topics that will be tested . . . (Freeman *et al.*, 1983, p. 511)

In most cases, then — with the possible exception of South Carolina and Florida — it seems reasonable to conclude that there is only modest consistency between texts and tests. This would limit the leverage that US in structional guidance agencies would be able to exert on instruction from the results side. To the extent that testing offers instructional guidance, for the most part it seems to offer diverse and inconsistent guidance.

A third leading feature of instructional guidance in the US is unconsistency in teachers' education. As I noted earlier, teacher education requirements vary among states. They also seem to vary across institutions of higher education within states — for instance, between public and private institutions. Nor is teacher education aligned with specific school systems' curricula. In fact, schools' curriculum generally seems to be ignored in teacher education, in favor of curricula that teacher educators want schools to use. There seems to be only modest consistency within teacher education, and only modest consistency between teacher education and school instruction. To the extent that teacher education offers instructional guidance to schools, it seems to be diverse and often inconsistent.

A final feature of instructional guidance in the US is inconsistent and weak incentives for academic performance. One reason for this lies in the structure of US higher education. A large fraction of US colleges and universities have very modest admissions requirements (Clark, 1985; Powell, Farrar and Cohen, 1985; Trow, 1961). Students need only a weak record of academic accomplishment in high school, often only a 'C' or low 'B' average, to be acceptable candidates for admission. In still another large fraction of institutions, only high school graduation is required for admission, and many do not even require that. There is something to celebrate in this, for it means that students can have a second or third chance to make good, despite previous difficulties. But these arrangements also mean that high school students need not work hard in order to get into college or university. America has one of the most successful tertiary education systems in the world, but its growth has been achieved at the expense of incentives for instructional effort. Under the existing arrangements it is irrational for most students who aspire to the middle or lower strata of higher education to work hard and make sacrifices in high school. It is therefore irrational for high school teachers to press students to try hard and do their best work, for the students not need push themselves in order to push ahead. This situation also affects academic work in colleges and universities. For they are unable to require or elicit good work from many students, having admitted them with marginal academic preparation. The institutional successes of higher education discourage instructional successes.

The employment practices of business firms are another source of weak and inconsistent incentives for academic performance. Few US firms seem to request transcripts of high school grades, when contemplating employment of their graduates. And even when firms do request transcripts, only a tiny fraction are actually sent by schools (Bishop, 1987; Bishop, 1989; Rosenbaum and Kariya, 1989). The lack of employer interest deters students from thinking that grades would count for jobs, and deters teachers from trying to convince them to the contrary. Similarly, few firms ask teachers for references on former students who are being considered for positions. This deters students' belief that grades or effort count for work. It also deters teachers from thinking that their judgments about students could make a difference for their employment. In US education, then, most students and teachers seem to receive weak or negative messages from firms and universities about the value of academic effort and good behavior.

How does instructional guidance in the US stack up? Consider the categories used earlier.

> *Consistency*: There is a great volume of guidance, from many different sources. But the content of curriculum guides often is weakly related to the content of texts. Texts and guides usually are little aligned with measures of results. Hence students, teachers, and administrators may hear many different messages about content coverage, from many different sources.
>
> *Prescription*: Guidance typically is global rather than specific, sketchy rather than detailed. There is little specification of what topics to cover, and what will be examined. Hence teachers, students, and others concerned with instruction often have only a vague idea of what compliance with guidance means.
>
> *Authority*: Guidance comes with many different blessings, from many different agencies and persons. Many of them count in some way, but their authority tends to diverge or compete, rather than reinforcing each other. Taken with the inconsistency of guidance mentioned above, this reduces the incentives for students and teachers take guidance seriously.
>
> *Power*: Compliance with guidance typically has few tangible benefits, and deviation has few tangible costs. Most potential employers are not interested in students' school records, nor in teachers' references. Many universities and other institutions of higher education will accept students with little or no reference to their prior academic achievement. In either case, many teachers have few incentives to press students for their best performance.

In some societies, guidance for instruction flows from the coherent actions of coordinated agencies. In these cases guidance is relatively prescriptive, consistent, authoritative and powerful. But in the US, guidance for instruction flows from the inconsistent actions of many little-coordinated agencies. They produce guidance in prolific quantities, more than in most societies with much more potent guidance systems. But what they produce is weakly prescriptive, inconsistent, and rarely has more than modest authority and power.

My argument might be summed up in a paradox: Great quantities of instructional guidance are directed at US schools and teachers, but they do not press instruction in any consistent direction. Difficult though it is to guide teaching and learning, schools in some societies are part of a relatively coherent instructional guidance system. In such cases teachers and students labor within relatively clear and authoritative guidelines. In the US, by contrast, schools are part of a relatively incoherent instructional guidance system. Teachers and administrators resemble consumers wandering in a carnival of instructional concessions. They can deal consistently with a few booths if they like. Or they can amble down the midway taking bits from many concessions, as their whims, habits, or the pressures of the crowd dictate.

In this carnival, many teachers and administrators are aware of many different sorts of advice. But few are keenly aware of most of it, partly because few voices can cut clearly through the din of a multitude. But many teachers know that most guidance is either weakly supported or contradicted by other adivce. That much they can learn from experience. Most also know that much instructional guidance can safely be ignored.

What falls out for instruction in US schools? One consequence is that in such a carnival, students and teachers can make up their own minds about many matters. The din of diverse, often inconsistent, and generally weak guidance offers considerable latitude to those who work within it.

Teachers' habits and decisions are important in any system of instruction. But absent strong guidance, they become unusally important. The result in US classrooms is curiously mixed: The forms of instruction are generally traditional, and the intellectual level usually is low; but the specific content is remarkably variable. On the one hand, lecture and recitation are still very common, as they were generations ago. Textbooks still are the chief grist for most instructional mills. Teaching still is telling, as it was generations ago. Knowledge still is offered in small bits and discrete skills, and much of it is neither interesting nor intellectually challenging. In these ways and others, teachers teach as they were taught.

On the other hand, there are significant differences in the content that teachers cover, and in the ways they cover it. Most teachers rely extensively on textbooks, for example, and many of these are officially adopted. But each teacher relies on the text in her own way. Even teachers in the same grade, in the same school, using the same text in the same subject, teach somewhat different topics. And when they teach the same topics, they teach them differently. The reasons for these variations include differences in students' inclinations and capacities from one class to another, and differences in teachers' judgments about appropriate actions in complex situations. But one additional reason for variability in content coverage is that other sources of variation are unconstrained by a clear and potent system of instructional guidance.

Classrooms around the world are traditional in form, often much more so than in the US. But classrooms here exhibit a distinctive sort of diffuse, academically relaxed traditionalism. The forms of instruction are conventional and often dull and the work is not demanding. Yet the content lacks consistency (Goodlad, 1984). Teachers' work is guided by inherited practices and individual decisions, not by any common, overarching sense of what is to be covered, or how it is to be covered, or why. In this sense, American schools have the worst of both worlds.

My argument is not that instructional guidance makes no difference in US schools. Rather it ordinarily makes a difference only when someone chooses to notice it, and to do something about it. In a sense this is true in any system: Even teachers in Singapore or France must notice guidance and choose to do something about it, before the guidance can make an instructional difference. But the consistency, prescriptiveness, authority and power of instructional guidance in such places increases the chances that teachers will notice the same advice, and that they will choose to pursue similar courses of action in light of it. In contrast, teachers' autonomy in the US is enhanced because they subsist in such a diffuse system of instructional guidance. The classroom doors behind which teachers work are no thicker here than elsewhere. But fewer strong and coherent messages about instructional content are broadcast here than in many other nations. Hence teachers and students have more flexibility in that domain, once the door is closed.

What does this account imply for decentralization and choice?

First, these reforms would occur in an unusual education system, in which school governance is largely decoupled from instructional guidance. In this system, even large and powerful state agencies cannot easily influence the content of materials that text or test publishers purvey. Decentralized local jurisdictions or schools of choice would do no better. They would have no more leverage than existing jurisdictions, in efforts to increase the strength and consistency of instructional guidance. In fact, they might well have less, since these reforms would increase political and market fragmentation.

Second, these reforms would occur in an education system that lacks a consistent, potent, and detailed framework for instruction. That leaves teachers and students plenty of autonomy. The result is a diffuse, academically relaxed, dreary and undemanding instructional regime. Autonomy and initiative are essential to any system of instruction; without them, teaching would be deadly and learning difficult. But autonomy only exists within some broader frame that defines and supports, and therefore limits it. And in American education that broader frame is sadly inadequate. It offers students and teachers little support in efforts to do good work, and leaves them unusually vulnerable to social and political pressures.

Decentralization and choice would not alter this situation. Indeed, they would compound it, for these reforms assume that school improvement works best in a school-by-school fashion. Yet in a fragmented system like our own, the tasks of school improvement are extraordinary.

They include setting academic goals, devising or adopting assessment systems, settling on curriculum, organizing instruction, and deciding on a discipline system. Any one of these would be a formidable undertaking for any educational organization, for each task would increase the uncertainty and political conflict with which schools must cope.[18] But US schools that wish to seriously improve must take on these tasks in combination, which is an awesome agenda.[19] Few schools have the time, money, experience, and knowledge to take such work seriously.

And even if they did take it on, the resources required for success are in short supply, and quite unequally distributed. Teachers and administrators in most schools, have terrifically busy schedules quite apart from school reform, even in rather privileged communities. Educators may have the knowledge, skill, and energy to successfully reform their schools, but their time is very limited. In contrast, these resources are in especially short supply in schools in disadvantaged areas. Capable educators often avoid such schools, and the capable teachers who are already there often have been worn down. Additionally, even if capability and commitment were equal across schools, there would still be a problem, for the demands on teachers are greater in such schools because the social and educational problems are greater. School improvement also requires resources in the school community: Social and political support for improvement, facilities for recreation or tutoring, and opportunities for decent part-time employment for students. Many persons and institutions in disadvantaged areas support school improvement, but poverty and discrimination exact a price in hope, time, and knowledge, as well as in money. Those schools and communities that need school improvement the most generally have the least resourcs to promote it; and those that need improvement the least generally have the most resources to promote it.

Moreover, choice and decentralization are unlikely substantially change the allocation of school and community resources required for improvement. A few reform proposals thoughtfully attend to resource issues, but these reforms are more likely to be taken as a cheap alternative to increasing or redistributing resources.

There is no technical reason that Americans could not devise a consistent and intelligent guidance system for instruction. But there are many reasons to doubt that most individual schools could solve that problem on their own. The assignment seems entirely out of scale. The currently common view that schools can solve such problems individually suggests that reformers either hold an heroic view of teachers and administrators — something like those mythic cowboys and Indians who populate grade-B westerns — or that they have a sadly diminished vision of instructional reform. It is quite unlikely that most students, teachers, parents and school boards would be able to heroically devise much improved instruction on their own. Some unusual schools would doubtless prosper. But the best that might be expected in most cases would be some version of Effective Schools. To expect major instructional improvement from decentralization and choice, as many reformers do, only reveals how far Americans are from understanding what it might take to seriously improve teaching and learning.[20]

Conclusion

Proposals for decentralization and choice have many appealing features. They hold out the promise of better education for students, more influence and independence for parents, simpler and more responsive governance for citizens, and better places for teachers to work. Moreover, some of the plans discussed in these volumes have been carefully designed to deal with important practical problems of parent information, transportation, and other matters. Though some versions of these governance reforms are crude and even regressive in design, others are quite thoughtful.

But I have not focused on design issues. For the greatest problems with decentralization and choice would arise from the political and social circumstances of US education — or rather from the reforms' interaction with those circumstances. Decentralization and choice have some great strengths. But in US education today, these strengths would be great weakness. I have explored this point in three ways.

First, part of the appeal of choice and decentralization is their promise to improve schooling by opening it to greater influence from parents. But both reforms would thus only be effective to the extent that parents mobilized to take advantage of the opportunities that new market or political organization offered. Some parents would make good use of these opportunities, but many others would not. And those parents with the greatest need for improved education would have the greatest difficulty taking advantage of the reforms. These problems might be less troubling if US society had less vast social and economic inequalities, or if schools had more capacity to repair the educational consequences of such unequalities.

Second, both reforms are appealing because they propose to simplify government, and make it more responsive to popular pressures. But these hopeful proposals are premised on the view that government has gone wrong because it has become a great monolith. Education government in the US is undeniably clumsy, but this is due more to fragmentation than centralization. Decentralization and choice would be more likely to exacerbate fragmentation than to reduce it. Hence these reforms would be likely to make government more clogged, more clumsy, more difficult, and even less responsive in some respects. Choice and decentralization would make much more sense if US school governance were much more coherent and simple.

Third, both reforms are attractive partly because they seek to harness governance change to instructional improvement. But that is a weak approach in the US, because the guidance for instruction is both fragmented in its own right, and decoupled from school and government. The resulting instructional guidance is both chaotic and weak. Decentralization and choice would make much more sense within a much more coherent system of instructional guidance. One reason is that consistency and quality would not be so vulnerable to local conditions. Another is that such a system would offer teachers, parents, and students much more help in figuring out what good instruction was, and how to mobilize to create it.

Decentralization and choice could be quite appealing in some circumstances. But in the current political and social circumstances of US education, these reforms would have perverse and probably damaging effects. American schools would require a different set of changes before these governance reforms could help to make instruction more demanding and intelligent. One such change would be a stronger, more thoughtful, and more consistent instructional guidance system. Another would be less inequality in the allocation of resources within and across jurisdictions. Still another would be more, and more sophisticated assistance in improving instruction. If such improvements were well under way, the reforms discussed in this chapter could be well worth the effort. But the improvements that I just mentioned would be immense changes. To realize them would require extraordinary investments of intelligence, money, time, and political will. Indeed, we can envision the changes only dimly, partly because our educational imaginations have been crippled by the very schools that we seek to repair. It is exciting to live in an age that speaks of fundamental improvement in education. But it is daunting to notice Americans' persistent fascination with easy solutions, and their modest appreciation of the work to be done.

Notes

1 These conclusions are based partly on interviews with public and non-public school officials in New South Wales [Australia] and Singapore, conducted in 1986 and 1987. On private education in France, see Teese, 1986 and 1989.

2 Americans often see things differently. Many advocates of private education, for example, see the sort of regulation described here as heavy handed and onerous. There are terrific political battles and many lawsuits over such issues

as whether private schools should have to file reports on the number of teachers they employ, and their formal qualifications.

3 There is much less cross-national research on such matters than one would prefer. On system differences generally, see Meyer (1983). My interviews in Singapore and New South Wales, with school officials and teacher educators, support this analysis.

4 A classic account of the fragmented character of American government is presented in Kaufman (1969).

5 Gary Sykes (personal communication) argues that this is changing, at least at the margin. He argues that his current research in South Carolina reveals a potent state system of surveillance and inspection.

6 On fragmentation in other social policy sectors than education, see Rogers and Whetten (1982).

7 The New York City experiment with school decentralization certainly supports this view (Zimet, 1973).

8 Few analysts have deeply considered the organization of local school districts, and the problems that afflict them. One exception can be found in Jason Epstein's essay, 'The politics of decentralization', *New York Review of Books*, 6, June 1968, pp. 26–31. After reviewing the political events that eventuated in proposals for decentralization, Epstein concludes that there was 'a collapse of central authority'. He writes ' . . . the problem in New York is not that there is too much central authority, as the various decentralization plans seem to imply, but that there is not enough, and that, what central authority there is, is ineffective'.

David Rogers' *110 Livingston Street* is interesting in this light. Rogers argued for decentralization in New York City, based on an extended account of the schools' failure to desegregate. One of his key themes was the central office's unresponsiveness to pressures for desegregation, and one key explanation was the overgrown size and centralization of school headquarters. But when he came to document the lack of responsiveness, Rogers referred to quite a different explanation: Pressure from white community organizations. On this view, the problem was not central power, but the collapse of central power in the face of contrary political pressure. Jason Epstein's analysis fits Rogers' evidence at least as well as Rogers' own analysis does.

Melvin Zimet's careful study of one sub-district in New York City exhibits a similar tension (Zimet, 1973). Zimet views the organization of New York schools as follows: ' . . . the Central Board was characterized by a pattern of multiple authority, which violated the principle of unity of command . . . ' (p. 5). He also approvingly quotes a New York Civil Liberties Union report: 'Integration failed at least partly because . . . the system was already administratively decentralized to the point where recalcitrant principals were not forced to comply with board policy . . . ' (p. 11). Zimet also presents a useful summary of some of the organizational incoherence within New York schools (pp. 64–7). He nonetheless argued that the key problem of New York's schools was over-centralization.

9 It is unclear whether the new decentralization scheme in Chicago will develop

in this direction. On the one hand, some planners have tried to minimize the possibilities of political expansion and maximize parent participation. On the other, the city has many powerful neighborhood political organizations, and a potent tradition of ward-based, patronage politics.

10 James Comer's descriptions of his careful work with schools and parents in New Haven offers helpful insights into the extraordinary requirements such development (Comer, 1988; Comer, 1980).

11 These ideas are particularly clear in the literature on effective schools, and school-based management. For a review, see Purkey and Smith (1983).

12 William Firestone has commented helpfully on the fragmented relations between governance and instruction, in his recent analysis of education policy as an 'ecology of games' (Firestone, 1989).

13 Instructional guidance is a term of my own devising. But the idea is familiar in discussions of curriculum and instruction, though often buried in discussions of centralization or decentralization in curriculum policy — e.g., Robitaille and Garden (1989).

14 Such prescription has been common in France (Resnick and Resnick, 1985), as well as in many former British colonies. My studies in Singapore and New South Wales (Australia) revealed quite prescriptive curriculum guidance, at least by US standards.

15 Such monitoring has been standard in Singapore and New South Wales, among other systems.

16 There have been a few US counterparts for external examinations in the past, but the Advanced Placement exams seem to be the chief example currently extant. The notion of integration between examinations and curriculum has been discussed in the US under such headings as Criterion Referenced Instruction, and instructional alignment. See Carroll (1963), and Cohen (1987).

17 Some of these incentives are cultural and social — i.e., Japanese mothers encourage their children's primary grade performance by working closely with them on assignments (Stevenson, Lee and Stigler, 1986). Schools can capitalize on such incentives, though they often are unable to manipulate them directly.

18 Deciding educational goals and assessing their attainment is unsettled and unsettling work, much more than some accounts of school improvement suggest. For instance, Americans have been teaching reading in public schools for nearly two centuries. Social scientists have been investigating the nature of reading, and how best to learn and teach it, for nearly a century. Yet despite these long traditions of practice and research, there is still much uncertainty about the nature of reading. There is similar uncertainty about how it should be taught. And there is considerable uncertainty about the effectiveness of various means to teach any given version of reading. One expert recently said of this field that 'Reading is more a religion than a science' (Rothman, 1989). It sounds crisp and efficient to assert the need for clear educational goals. But efforts to specify goals regularly end in deep puzzles about what they should be, or how any one of them might be specified for instruction. And efforts to assess progress toward goals often stumble on puzzles about how such

progress might reliably be measured. When schools embark on instructional improvement efforts, they run the risk of increasing such problems rather than reducing them.

Hence they open themselves to political conflict. Some disputes about reading instruction arise in academic scholarship or professional practice, and often remain muted. But many educational disputes have popular roots, and can stir powerful passions. Some parents are deeply committed to traditional and didactic instruction, while others are equally passionate about the virtues of 'discovery learning', or 'process' writing. Some parents care deeply that reading be taught in English, while others want it taught in children's first languages. These differences and others regularly boil over onto schools, quite apart from school improvement. But efforts to set precise goals or introduce new curriculum can provoke or exacerbate such concerns. Instructional improvement often is a political minefield. The disputes that are now swirling around the California State Education Department's effort to upgrade science teaching are only one of many current examples. Protestant fundamentalists there have attacked the Department's new curriculum framework on the grounds that it ignores biblical accounts, in favor of evolution. And the Department has been forced to modify its new curriculum guide, which is widely expected to have an effect in new science texts.

19 The Coalition of Essential Schools offers an example of the demands of serious school improvement. The coalition aims at expansive goals, such as students' capacity to demonstrate understanding of academic subjects. Few US teachers and students have pursued such goals, so instructional know-how in this department is modest at best. Nor do we have well developed means to observe and assess progress toward such goals. Efforts to figure out whether students, teachers, and schools are succeeding thus will be technically difficult and politically bumpy. In addition, the Coalition seeks to engage teachers, administrators, and students in a fundamental re-thinking of education, and an equally fundamental reconstruction of the curriculum. For example, the Coalition proposes to reduce students' and teachers' choice in academic matters, by focusing studies on a few key subjects. And, as these comments suggest, Coalition schools also must re-think evaluative standards, instructional methods, and school schedules. The Coalition's work is admirable, and often exhilarating for those involved. But its seriousness also is extraordinarily demanding and exhausting, and can provoke terrific conflict. It would take enormous organizational and personal resources for the schools to carry on long enough to make the desired changes.

20 Historically, American schools have coped with the problems of instructional improvement by avoiding conflict over educational ends and means. One common avoidance mechanism has been to set only very abstract goals, like citizenship education, or educating each child to the limit of his potential. With a few exceptions, educators have eschewed efforts to set more precise common goals for entire school systems, as might be represented by a system of common examinations. More precise goals have largely been confined to schools of choice, most of them non-public. Additionally, Americans have

tacitly delegated many difficult decisions about educational ends and means to the relative obscurity of teachers' and students' decisions, by permitting considerable individual choice in academic matters. And more recently, as pressure for instructional improvement has mounted, Americans have focused on lowest common denominator goals. State-mandated tests of minumum competency are one example, and the 'Effective Schools' movement is another. See Purkey and Smith (1983), and Rosenholtz (1985). These approaches are relatively undemanding: A focus on test scores, 'leadership', and a bit of teacher training can be organized quickly, with only modest resources. On instructional improvement more generally, see Rowan (1988), and Rowan, (in press).

References

BANKSTON, M. (1982) *Organizational Reporting in a School District: State and Federal Programs*, (Stanford: Institute For Finance and Governance, School of Education.

BANFIELD, E. and WILSON, J. (1965) *City Politics*, Cambridge: Harvard.

BISHOP, J. (1987) 'Information externalities and the social payoff to academic achievement', Ithaca, NY, Cornell University, Center For Advanced Human Resource Studies.

BISHOP, J. (1989) 'Why the apathy in American high schools?' *Educational Researcher*, Jan–Feb, pp. 6–10.

BOYD, W. (1973) *Community Status, Citizen Participation, and Conflict in Suburban School Politics*, Unpublished PhD thesis, University of Chicago.

BOYD, W. and SMART, D. (1987) *Educational Policy in Australia and America: Comparative Perspectives*, Philadelphia: Falmer Press.

CARROLL, J. (1963) 'A model of school learning', *Teachers College Record*, **64**, pp. 723–33.

CENTER FOR EDUCATION STATISTICS (1987) *Digest of Education Statistics*, Washington: Government Printing Office.

CENTER FOR THE STUDY OF PUBLIC POLICY (1970) *Education Vouchers*, Cambridge: Author.

CLARK B. (1965) 'Interorganizational patterns in education', *Administrative Science Quarterly*, **10**, pp. 224–37.

CLARK, B. (1985a) 'The high school and the university: What went wrong in America, part I', *Phi Delta Kappan*, Feb, pp. 391–7.

CLARK, B. (1985b) 'The high school and the university: What went wrong in America, part II', *Phi Delta Kappan*, March, pp. 472–5.

COHEN, D.K. (1978) 'Reforming school politics', *Harvard Educational Review*, **48**, 4.

COHEN, D.K. (1982) 'Policy and organization: The impact of state and federal educational policy on school governance', *Harvard Educational Review*, **52**, 4.

COHEN, D.K. and FARRAR, E. (1977) 'Power to the parents?' *The Public Interest*, **48**, Summer, pp. 72–97.

COHEN, S.A. (1987) 'Instructional alignment: Searching for a magic bullet, *Educational Researcher*, Nov. pp. 16–20.

COLEMAN, J., HOFFER., T. and KILGORE, S. (1982) *High School Achievement*, New York: Basic Books.

COMER, J. (1980) *School Power: Implications of an Intervention Project*, New York: Free Press.

COMER, J. (1988) 'Educating poor minority children', *Scientific American*, **259**, 5, Nov., pp. 42–8.

COONS. J. and SUGARMAN, S. (1978) *Education By Choice*, Berkeley: University of California.

DARLING-HAMMOND, L. and BERRY, B. (1988) *The Evolution of Teacher Policy*, Santa Monica: RAND.

EPSTERN, J. (1968) 'The politics of school decentral-iszation', *New York Review of Boots*, 6 June, pp. 26–31.

FANTINI, M. (1970) 'Community control and quality education in urban school systems', in LEVIN, H. (Ed.) *Community Control of Schools*, Washington: Brookings.

FIRESTONE, W. (1989) 'Educational policy as an ecology of games', *Educational Researcher*, **18**, 7, Oct. pp. 18–24.

FREEMAN, D., KUHS, T., PORTER, A., FLODEN, R., SCHMIDT, W. and SCHWILLE, J. (1983) 'Do textbooks and tests define a national curriculum in elementary school mathematics?' *The Elementary School Journal*, **83**, 5., pp. 501–14.

FREEMAN, J., HANNAN, M. and HANNAWAY, J. (1978) *The Dynamics of School District Administrative Intensity*, Unpublished research report, Stanford.

FRIEDMAN, M. (1962) *Capitalism and Freedom*, Chicago: University of Chicago.

FUHRMAN, S., CLUNE, W. and ELMORE, R. (1988) 'Research on educational reform: Lessons on the implementation of policy'. *Teachers College Record*, **90**, 2, Winter, pp. 237–57.

GITTEL, M. (1970) 'The balance of power and the community school', in LEVIN, H. (Ed.) *Community Control of Schools*, Washington: Brookings.

GOODLAD, J. (1984) *A Place Called School*, New York: McGraw-Hill.

HIRSCHMAN, A. (1970) *Exit, Voice, and Loyalty*, Cambridge: Harvard.

JENNERGREN, L.P. (1981) 'Decentralization in organizations', in NYSTROM, P. and STARBUCK, W. *Handbook of Organizational Design, Vol 2*, New York: Oxford University Press, pp. 40–59.

KAUFMAN, H. (1969) 'Administrative decentralization and political power', *Public Administration Review*, Jan–Feb, pp. 3–15.

LAWTON, D. and GORDON, P. (1987) *HMI*, London: Routledge.

MALEN, B., OGAWA, R. and KRANZ, J. (1990) 'What do we know about school based management? A case study in the literature (Volume 2 of this collection).

MASOTTI, L. (1967) *Education and Politics in Suburbia*, Cleveland: Western Reserve University.

MCLAUGHLIN, M. (1987) 'Learning from experience: Lessons from policy implementation', *Educational Evaluation and Policy Analysis*, Summer, **9**, pp. 171–8.

MEYER, J. (1983) 'Centralization of funding and control in educational governance', in MEYER, J.W. and SCOTT, W.R. *Organizational Environments: Ritual and*

Rationality, Sage, Beverly Hills.

Orfield, G. (1969) *The Reconstruction of Southern Education*, New York: Wiley.

Peterson, P. (1974) 'The politics of education', in Kerlinger, F. and Carroll, J. *The Review of Research in Education*, Itasca, Ill: Peacock.

Peterson, P. (1981) *City Limits*, Chicago: University of Chicago.

Peterson, P. (1983) 'Background paper', in Twentieth Century Fund, *Making the Grade*, New York: Author.

Peterson, P. and Rabe, B. (1983) 'The role of interest groups in the formation of educational policy: Past practice and future trends', *Teachers College Record*, **81**, 3, Spring, pp. 708–29.

Peterson, P. Rabe, B. and Wong, K. (1986) *When Federalism Works*, Washington: Brookings.

Powell, A., Farrar, E. and Cohen, D.K. (1985) *The Shopping Mall High School*, Boston: Houghton Mifflin.

Purkey, S. and Smith, M. (1983) 'Effective schools: A review', *Elementary School Journal*, **83**, 4, pp. 428–52.

RAND (1981) *A Study of Alternatives in American Education, Vol VII: Conclusions and Policy Implications*, Santa Monica: Author.

Ravitch, D. (1983) *The Troubled Crusade*, New York: Basic.

Ramirez, F. and Rubison, R. (1979) 'Creating members: The political incorporation and expansion of public education', in Meyer, J.W. and Hannan, M. (Eds.) *National Development and The World System*, Chicago: University of Chicago.

Resnick, D.P. and Resnick, L.B. (1985, April) 'Standards, curriculum, and performance: A historical and comparative perspective', *Educational Researcher*, **14**, pp. 5–20.

Robitaille, D. and Garden, R. (1989) *The IEA Study of Mathematics II: Contexts and Outcomes of School Mathematics*, New York: Pergamon.

Rogers, D. (1968) *110 Livingston Street*, New York: Random House.

Rogers, D. and Whetten, D. (1982) *Interorganizational Coordination*, Ames, Iowa: Iowa State University.

Rosenbaum, J. and Kariya, T. (1989) 'From high school to work: Market and institutional mechanisms in Japan', *American Journal of Sociology*, **94**, 6, May, pp. 1334–65.

Rosenholtz, S. (1985) 'Effective schools: Interpreting the evidence', *American Journal of Education*, May, pp. 352–87.

Rothman, R. (1989) 'NAEP board is seeking a consensus on reading', *Education Week*, 27 Sept. 1989, p. 7.

Rowan, B. (1982a) 'Organization structure and the institutional environment', *Administrative Science Quarterly*, **27**, pp. 259–79.

Rowan, B. (1982b) 'Instructional management in historical perspective: Evidence on differentiation in school districts', *Educational Administration Quarterly*, **18**, pp. 43–59.

Rowan, B. (1988) 'The technology of teaching and school reform', Unpublished mss, College of Education, Michigan State University.

Rowan, B. (in press) 'Commitment and control: Alternative strategies for the organizational design of schools', in Cazden, C. (Ed.) *Review of Research in*

Education.

SCHWILLE, J., PORTER, A., ALFORD, L., FLODEN, R., FREEMAN, D., IRWIN, S., and SCHMIDT, W. (1986) 'State policy and the control of curriculum decision', *Institute For Research in Teaching*, Michigan State University.

SCOTT, R., and MEYER, J. (1983) 'The organization of societal sectors', in MEYER, J.W. and SCOTT, W.R. *Organizational Environments: Ritual and Rationality*, Sage, Beverly Hills.

SPROULL, L. and KIESLER, S. (1982) 'Managerial response to changing environments: Perspectives on problem sensing from social cognition', *Administrative Science Quarterly*, **27**, pp. 548–70.

STACKHOUSE, E. (1982) *The Effects of State Centralization on Administrative Structure*, Stanford: Author [Ph.D. diss].

STEVENSON, H., LEE, SHIN-YING, and STIGLER, J. (1986) 'Mathematics achievement of Chinese, Japanese, and American children', *Science*, **231**, 14 Feb., pp. 693–9.

TEESE, R. (1986) 'Private schools in France: Evolution of a system', *Comparative Education Review*, **30**, 2, May.

TEESE, R. (1989) 'The political functions of the central administration of Catholic education in France', *Journal of Education Policy*, **4**, 2, pp. 103–14.

THOMAS, N. (1975) *Education in National Politics*, New York: McKay.

TROW, M. (1961) 'The second transformation of American secondary education', *International Journal of Comparative Sociology*, September.

TYACK, D. (1974) *The One Best System*, Cambridge: Harvard.

TYACK, D. and HANSOT, E. (1982) *Managers of Virtue*, New York: Basic Books.

US BUREAU OF THE CENSUS (1989) *Statistical Abstract of the United States, 1988*, Washington, DC: Department of Commerce.

WEST, E.G. (Ed.) (1976) *Nonpublic School Aid*, Lexington, Mass: D.C. Heath.

WEISS, J. and GRUBER, J. (1987) 'The managed irrelevance of federal education statistics', in ALONSO, W. and STARR, P. *The Politics of Numbers*, New York: Russell Sage.

WIRT, F. and KIRST, M. (1982) *The Politics of Education: Schools in Conflict*, Berkeley: McCutcheon.

ZIMMER, B. and HAWLEY, A. (1968) *Metropolitan Area Schools*, Beverly Hills: Sage.

ZIMET, M. (1973) *Decentralization and School Effectiveness*, New York: Teachers College.

Commentary

Choice Requires More Than the Absence of Control

Andrew C. Porter

In announcing their conference on choice and control in American education, Professors Clune and Witte proposed to elucidate 'the theoretical and empirical case for choice and decentralization in education', noting that the contribution of scholarly analysis thus far has been limited. With the conference now behind us and the set of papers in hand, we see clearly that some progress toward that goal was made. Nevertheless, what we heard and what has now found its way into print is far from conclusive.

A part of the problem may lie with the concept of choice itself. It resists objective analysis, at least in our society. It would be un-American to argue against choice. This was most evident when Jack Coons challenged the conference to provide a rationale for trusting affluent parents to make educational choices with their children while not trusting low-income parents to make the 'right' decisions. It is easy (acceptable) to argue against control in contrast to choice. We pride ourselves as a nation of individualists. The affective valence of choice and control make analysis difficult and communication virtually impossible.

There is another aspect of choice that, at least in the short run, may help to explain both its current popularity and the difficulties it presents for scholarly analysis. Decentralization and choice, as solutions to today's education problems, have the appearance of requiring no knowledge or constructive action from those currently in charge. All they need to do is stay out of the way of knowledgeable and well-intended teachers and parents. This appearance is almost certainly wrong; choice requires much more than the absence of control. The argument here is parallel to the argument made by Floden *et al.*, (1988, p. 100) when pointing out that 'teacher autonomy requires more than an absence of central directives'.

Requiring parents to make choices without adequate knowledge and sharply defined alternatives is being arbitrary, not exercising power.

Paradoxically, the few spectacular examples where choice has apparently led to positive results also contribute to the difficulty of scholarly analysis; several of these examples were chronicled in the conference papers. But are these anecdotes really data points in favor of the benefits of choice, or are they more correctly attributed to heroic efforts of charismatic leaders? In David Cohen's words, 'reformers either hold an heroic view of teachers and administrators . . . or they have a sadly diminished vision of instructional reform' (p. 378, in this volume). We Americans love heroes and heroines but they are likely to remain in short supply; the widespread problems of public schools will not be solved if heroism is required. In education, spectacular examples tend to be at least as distracting as they are illuminating.

At the conference I had the impossible task of offering a final word. As should now be clear, a final word on choice and control is not in order. What follows is my attempt to put in perspective and add direction to the conference proceedings. I start with commentary on David Cohen's analysis of connections between policy and school practice. Tying that to the rest of the conference, I consider why there is so much interest in choice and control in education. Then, commenting separately on what is known about control in education and what is known about choice in education, I conclude that connections between the two concepts are more problematic than the title of the conference would suggest.

Theoretical Frameworks for Understanding Control in American Education

David Cohen considers in the title of his chapter, 'The promise of decentralization and choice' for realizing the desperately needed improvements in education. From his analysis, he concludes that improving public education is more complicated than simply decentralization and offering choice. He reminds us that much of what happens in schools is not related in any predictable way to policies emanating from the formal school hierarchy. Why, therefore, should removal of policies have dramatic positive effects on practice? He describes US education as a nonsystem of policy, not rational in design, with each new layer of policy piled on top of the last, and with no wiping the slate clean in between.[1] In addition, he portrays the guidance that schools receive from agencies outside the formal school hierarchy as serving to further weaken the connections between policy and school practice in the United States. With all this disorganized advice, a great deal of discretion is left to schools and teachers.[2] For those who wish to take the initiative, and apparently few do, sufficient freedom already exists. Reform efforts aimed at decentralization and choice are no more likely to have the intended effects on practice than have control oriented reforms.

Cohen does an impressive job of drawing from the literature and experience to speculate about the likely consequences of reform efforts aimed in the directions of decentralization and the stimulation of choice. But his analyses are necessarily limited to what we have learned about the effects of various strategies to control the nature and functions of schools. Borrowing from our formulations of curriculum control in elementary school mathematics (Porter *et al.*, 1988), he argues convincingly that current levels of control in the US are weak and fragmented in comparison to what they could be, at least in theory. These weak and fragmented efforts at control do influence practice, but they do so in unpredictable ways and without the standardizing effects envisioned for efforts to control. These findings appear to hold true whether standards are set on educational outputs or on educational processes and whether standards hold students accountable or standards hold teachers accountable (Porter *et al.*, 1988). But analyses of efforts to control schools are not, in any direct sense, analyses of decentralization and choice. Until recently, most policy reform initiatives have been in the direction of control of one type or another and, understandably, control is what we know most about. Cohen's extrapolation to effects of decentralization and choice may or may not be correct.

What Do We Hope to Accomplish Through Choice or Control?

Despite what many believe is a disappointing history of education reform in the United States (at least over the last twenty years), educators and policymakers are as intent on changing education today as they have ever been. Results from assessments of student achievement are disappointingly low in comparison to what we want our schools to accomplish and embarrassingly low in comparison to other countries. High school completion rates, especially among the urban poor, are frighteningly low. Apparently too many students get very little that is worthwhile from school participation. Even the goals that our schools strive to achieve are being questioned. The basic skills agenda of ten years ago is no longer seen as adequate. To maintain our quality of life, schools must prepare students to solve novel problems and reason about complex issues (e.g., Carnegie

Forum on Education and the Economy, 1986). The new agenda is for *all* students to learn *hard* content. In comparison, the post-Sputnik reforms, which attempted to upgrade the curriculum for only our most academically able students, and the compensatory education reforms, which attempted to guarantee the learning of only basic content by all students, look easy. Today's goals for education require massive changes;. fine-tuning solutions will not do.

Cohen is not optimistic about choice as a solution, and neither am I. First, choice assumes that all parents and students see school as important and their successful participation in school as relevant to their future life chances. We know this is not true (e.g., Ogbu, 1983). For many students and parents, schools are seen as irrelevant. Families of second- and third-generation poverty see little hope in what schools have to offer, and they may be right. Connections between school quality and success as an adult are tenuous (e.g., Jencks *et al.*, 1972, 1979). Second, choice assumes that today's educators know how to do what needs to be done to make schools more successful. What stands in their way are either bureaucratic regulations, which decentralization would undo, or lack of motivation, which a choice-oriented market economy would turn around. This assumption also seems false. Much has been learned about effective teaching and learning (e.g., Porter and Brophy, 1988), but a great deal of confusion remains.

What was said over and over in the conference papers, but perhaps less directly, is that choice and decentralization alone, without further definition, are inadequate to address the serious problems that schools confront today. Perhaps choice is the focus of attention today because most of us who have studied control-oriented solutions have already concluded that control is not a solution.

Control

Whatever the connections between choice and control may be, these two concepts are not simply opposite ends of a single continuum. Even control and decentralization can coexist. For example, desired outputs of schooling, what students are to accomplish, could be centrally controlled, while mechanisms for achieving those outcomes could be left to the discretion of the school or teacher. Both choice and control seek to increase the probability of good teaching of worthwhile content to all students. In addition, choice attempts to increase the probability that students perceive their school and what it is trying to do as relevant to them. But control is not at odds with this; it is simply silent.

Since we have a great deal more experience with efforts to improve education through controlling mechanisms, we know much more about control than choice. In listening to presentations at the conference and in reading the papers, I was reminded of two findings from my own studies of control as potentially informative in attempting to understand connections between choice and control. First, policies and practices designed to control the content of elementary school mathematics instruction have not led to standardization. Instead, these efforts at control have had the surprising effect of increasing the variance in classroom content practices. Second, when seeking to understand the factors that influence teachers' decisions about what content to include in their elementary school mathematics instruction, we considered the potential influence of parents. Our finding was troublesome. Low-income parents have little authority with schools and teachers, while schools serving predominantly affluent families pay close attention to the wishes and demands of parents. But it is especially students from low-income families that choice must benefit; it is the poor who are least well served and most in need.

The Nonstandardizing Effects of Control

A little over ten years ago, I began studies of content determinants. The early work focused on content in elementary school mathematics. More recent work has shifted the research agenda to high schools and expanded the content focus to include social studies and science as well as mathematics. The early studies were designed to identify any and all influences on what teachers decide to teach in elementary school mathematics. Education policies were found to be among the important influences, and subsequent work was designed especially to clarify the characteristics of education policies that make them influential on what is taught and to clarify ways in which policy influence takes place.

We were surprised to find that policies designed to standardize the content of instruction (e.g., curriculum frameworks, assessment devices, professional development activities) often have the opposite effect. In part, content 'standardizing policies' increase the variance in content practices because of their ambiguity; the policies are often vague and incomplete about their intended effects on practice. Simply put, they are subject to differences in interpretation. Another part of the explanation is that new policies typically call for changes in practice. The result is varying degrees of implementation according to differences in effort expended and capability to respond. A third part of the explanation for the nonstandardizing effect is that education practice within United States schools is surprisingly homogeneous, even in the absence of control policies. Initiation of a new control policy, then, is similar in effect (if not explanation) to starting a race. Runners, bunched together on the starting line, become spread out as they race toward the finish line. Two examples help to illustrate the nonstandardizing effects of control policies.

Seven teachers in six schools located in three school districts participated in one of our first studies of elementary school mathematics (Porter, 1982). Data collection was open ended and intense: pre- and post-year interviews with teachers and principals, daily teacher logs of the content of mathematics instruction for each student that were collected on a weekly basis, accompanying weekly teacher interviews designed to identify all sources of advice received regarding the content of mathematics instruction, ethnographic accounts of school meetings, school board meetings, and teachers' participation in professional development activities. Our goal was to identify the nature and strength of as many influences of the seven teachers' content decisions in elementary school mathematics as possible.

The district with three teachers participating had a management-by-objective system for mathematics with 130 objectives in a single strand. At the beginning of the year, teachers were to use a locator test to place students within the single strand of objectives. Students were to progress through the objectives as they mastered posttests. For each objective, there were assignment sheets keyed to each of several textbooks.

Andy, a fourth-grade teacher, followed the MBO system faithfully. The result was an individualized mathematics program responding to differences among students, both in their starting points in the single strand objectives and the speed with which they worked through the objectives. Only when Andy was satisfied that a student had met district expectations did instruction deviate from his interpretation of what policy required. Once a student had reached a point in the objectives Andy considered 'well beyond grade level', the student was taken out of the objectives and expected to work, individually, through 'the rest of the textbook'. Teri, another fourth-grade teacher in the district, responded to the MBO system by teaching mathematics twice each day, once along the lines described for Andy and a second time using a different textbook. With this text, Teri continued her previous teaching technique of working systematically from page one through the book, going as far as time and student aptitude would allow. Lucy, teaching fifth-grade for the first time during the year of our study, showed less commitment to covering a grade-level text. Her instruction was characterized by whole-group instruction and a commitment to drawing on teaching materials from a large number of sources. The result of Lucy's attempts to cover district objectives was confusion and relatively little coverage of content for any students. Clearly, initiation of the MBO system by the school district had substantially different effects on the content decisions of these three teachers.

A more recent example of the nonstandardizing influences of control policies comes from an ongoing study of high school social studies and mathematics (Porter, 1989). In that study, teaching practices are being contrasted between a high and a low SES school in each of a high- and a low-control district. The plan is to replicate this design in three states, but data are only available for California. For our two California districts, the contrast in degree of control is more sharply defined in mathematics than social studies; the high-control district is vigorously pursuing greater emphasis on problem solving and higher order thinking. Initial results show that mathematics teachers in the high-control district are putting greater emphasis on problem solving and higher order thinking. At the same time, however, their emphasis on problem solving and higher order thinking is more variable than emphasis among teachers in the low control district. Not directly relevant to the point here, but interesting nevertheless, is that teachers in the high-control district also reported holding their students to lower standards of achievement, accepting less responsibility for student achievement, and having lower school spirit than did teachers in the low-control district. Thus, the control policies had the intended influence of increased focus on problem solving and higher order thinking, the predicted effect of increasing the variance among teachers in content practices, and some unanticipated negative effects on standards, acceptance of responsibility, and school spirit. Apparently, at least in the short run, when asked to teach content they judge difficult, teachers expect less of themselves and of their students.

From these two findings, I conclude that curriculum control might work well in combination with choice. Control policies would stimulate the variation in school practices necessary to make real choice possible. Over time, choice would provide a mechanism for eliminating the weak alternatives and enhancing the strong alternatives.

Authority and Status

In several of our studies of elementary school mathematics, teachers were interviewed about what they perceived as legitimate sources of advice for the content of their mathematics instruction. In schools serving high concentrations of children from poor families, teacher after teacher doubted the legitimacy of content advice from parents. Some even questioned the ability of parents to provide quality help on student homework. In sharp contrast, teachers in a district selected because of its unusually high affluence described parents as one of the most powerful influences on content decisions. Parental influence on content was received from individuals but was especially powerful at the aggregate level.

This finding raises the question of whether, in systems of choice, poor parents will have the kind of clout they need to have positive influences on the productivity of schools serving their children. If teachers do not see low-income parents as legitimate sources of advice, and if the children of these parents are the kinds of students teachers would just as soon be without, the overall effect of choice may be negative for the students most in need.

The black box of choice

One of the difficulties for the conference, especially for the academics participating, has been our impoverished vocabulary for talking about choice. The concept of choice has been discussed in the most general of ways, leaving great ambiguities in exactly what the speaker/author might have in mind. As the concept gains popularity in education practice, and as scholarly analysis follows, the term will become differentiated and gain precision of meaning. Proposals for choice and analyses of their effects will carefully describe and distinguish the nature of choice alternatives envisioned and the nature of effects sought. Hopefully, these elaborations will answer many of the basic questions that plagued this conference.

- What, if any, constraints will be placed on alternatives, or will alternatives be identified *a priori* and carefully developed?
- Who is to be given choice?
- Will it be possible to provide choice that is independent of the consumers' income?
- Will quotas be necessary?
- Will choice be extended to providers as well as consumers? For example, will schools be free to decide which students they will accept and which they will not, as Coleman suggested? (in this volume)
- Will the private sector become merged with the public sector through mechanisms such as performance contracting?
- What obligations will there be to guarantee informed choice, and how will that be monitored?

Just as experience and scholarly analysis have taught us that policies of control can take on many different features, which in turn determine their acceptability and effects, the same must surely be true for choice.

As clarity about a definition of choice emerges through answers to the above questions, research will need to systematically document effects (a matter on which this conference has provided little information). For example:

- What are the costs of choice (e.g., the cost of making sure that consumers are equally well informed; the cost of making choice independent from income)? Are the benefits from choice reasonable in terms of the costs?
- In order for choice to work, must interesting educational alternatives already exist, or will offering choice create an economy that generates interesting alternatives?
- What are the connections between parent choice and teacher empowerment? These ill-defined concepts seem potentially at odds.
- Are the effects of choice on a limited scale the same as the effects of choice when it is offered to all schools and all students on a large scale, for example, statewide (e.g., will choice strengthen the entire system or merely redistribute good students and effective schools)?

A final thought

From the conference presentations and papers, one thing is very clear. It is easier to be *inspirational* about choice and its benefits than it is to be *informative*. The stakes are high and the concept is emotionally charged. At present, we are not sure what choice means, and we surely do not know its effects. This lack of knowledge should not be taken as a reason to stop experimenting with choice; just the opposite is true. We should be experimenting with choice and carefully documenting the nature of the experimentation and the effects. It is essential that we observe the effects of choice on teaching and learning, since teaching and learning are at the heart of the educational process. In this conference on choice and control, hardly anyone said anything about teaching and learning; in fact, teaching and learning were only mentioned by five of the thirty-five presenters, and all five of these were reactors. When the heat of the current reform cools and when politicians and policymakers have become intrigued with some other educational innovation, only what has *proven* useful from our experimentation with choice will remain. Scattered anecdotes of success, ungrounded in theory and untied to successful teaching and learning, will leave no trace.

Notes

1 Cohen's conclusion that the US is a nonsystem is in part based on his comparison to this theoretical framework and in part based on his comparison of the US to other countries. When comparing US education policy and practice to education policy and practice in other countries, however, there is a serious confounding with a bias in favor of making the US look complicated and irrational. Not only are US education policy and practice more frequently studied and written about than are policy and practice in most if not all other countries, but US scholars' knowledge of education literature in other countries is quite limited. Sometimes US scholars appear to weigh heavily their own casual knowledge of another country's education system in their comparative analysis of the US. Generally, the more something is studied and experienced, the more complicated it appears. This bias may explain a portion of the claim of highly rational education systems in other countries and a nonsystem in the United States.

2 This point has been made in other analyses of education policy and practice in the United States (see, for example, Schwille *et al.*, 1983).

References

CARNEGIE FORUM ON EDUCATION AND THE ECONOMY (1986) *A Nation Prepared: Teachers for the 21st Century*, New York: Author.

COHEN, D. K. (1989, May) Can Decentralization or Choice Improve Public Education? Paper presented at the Conference on Choice and Control in American Education, Madison, Wisconsin.

FLODEN R.E., PORTER, A.C., ALFORD, L.E., FREEMAN, D.J., IRWIN, S., SCHMIDT, W.H. and SCHWILLE, J.R. (1988) 'Institutional leadership at the district level: A closer look at autonomy and control', *Educational Administration Quarterly*, **24** (2), pp. 96–124.

JENCKS, C., BARTLETT, S., CORCORAN, M., CROUSE, J., EAGLESFIELD, D., JACKSON, G., MCCLELLAND, K., MUESER, P., OLNECK, P., SCHWARTZ, J., WARD, S. and WILLIAMS, J. (1979) *Who Gets Ahead: The Determinants of Economic Success in America*, New York: Basic Books.

JENCKS, C., SMITH, M., ACLAND, H., BANE, M.J., COHEN, D., GINTIS, H., HEYNS, B. and MICHELSON, S. (1972) *Inequality: A Reassessment of the Effect of Family and Schooling in America*, New York: Basic Books.

OGBU, J.U. (1983) 'Minority status and schooling in plural societies', *Comparative Education Review*, **27**, pp. 168–90.

PORTER, A.C. (1989, March) Impact of the New Curriculum Policies on Course Content, Teachers' Sense of Teaching Effectiveness, and Teacher Morale. Paper presented at the 1989 annual meeting of the American Educational Research Association, San Francisco, California.

PORTER, A.C. (1988) *External Standards and Good Teaching: The Pros and Cons of*

Telling Teachers What to Do (Occasional Paper No. 126), East Lansing, MI: Institute for Research on Teaching.

PORTER, A.C. (1982, March) A District Management by Objectives System, Its Messages and Effects. Paper presented at the 1982 annual meeting of the American Educational Research Association, New York, New York.

PORTER, A.C. and BROPHY, J. (1988) 'Synthesis of research on good teaching: Insights from the work of the Institute for Research on Teaching', *Educational Leadership*, **45** (8), pp. 74–83.

PORTER, A., FLODEN, R., FREEMAN, D., SCHMIDT, W. and SCHWILLE, J. (1988) 'Content determinants in elementary school mathematics', in GROUWS, D.A. and COONEY, T.J. (Eds) *Perspectives on Research on Effective Mathematics Teaching* (pp. 96–113), Reston, VA: National Council of Teachers of Mathematics.

SCHWILLE, J., PORTER, A., BELLI, G., FLODEN, R., FREEMAN, D., KNAPPEN, L., KUHS, T. and SCHMIDT, W. (1983) 'Teachers as policy brokers in the content of elementary school mathematics', in SHULMAN, L.S. and SYKES, G. (Eds) *Handbook of Teaching and Policy* (pp. 370–91), New York: Longman.

The Authors

Michael J. Alves is educational planner for the city of Boston and several other school districts outside of Massachusetts. His primary interest has been in initiating and implementing 'Controlled Choice' pupil assignment plans.

David A. Bennett is Superintendent of Schools in St. Paul, Minnesota. He has also served as Deputy Superintendent of the Milwaukee Public Schools from 1976 to 1984.

Rolf K. Blank is Project Director with the State Education Assessment Center of the Council of Chief State School Officers in Washington, D.C. He is directing an effort to build a 50-state system of indicators of the status of science and mathematics education in elementary and secondary schools.

Anthony S. Bryk is Associate Professor of Education at the University of Chicago. His research activities include development of hierarchical linear models in educational research and investigations of high school organization and its effects. He is currently collaborating with staff from the Chicago Public Schools and others in a planning effort to create a Center for School Improvement which will support selected reform activities in Chicago Public Schools.

John E. Chubb is Senior Fellow at the Brookings Institution. He is the author and editor of several books and is best known for his support of parental choice in public schools.

William H. Clune is Voss-Bascom Professor of Law at the University of Wisconsin Law School, Director of the Wisconsin branch of the Center for Policy Research in Education (CPRE), and a member of the executive Committee of the La Follette Institute of Public Affairs at the University of Wisconsin–Madison.

David Cohen is John A. Hannah Distinguished Professor of Education and Social Policy at Michigan State University.

Michael Cohen is Director of Educational Programs at the National Governor's Association. His most recent publication is entitled, 'Restructuring the Education system: Agenda for the 1990s' (National Governor's Association 1989).

James S. Coleman is Professor of Sociology and Education at the University of Chicago. His publications include *Individual Interests and Collective Action* (1986) and *Public and Private High Schools: The Impact of Communities* (1987).

John E. Coons is Professor of Law at the University of California-Berkeley. He is a long-time scholar and advocate of family choice in education and is co-sponsor of the California Initiative for Family Choice in Education.

Richard F. Elmore is Professor of Education and Political Science at Michigan State University, and Senior Research Fellow with the Center for Policy Research in Education.

Joseph A. Fernandez a former teacher and principal, has served as the Superintendent of Dade County Public Schools since 1986; he has recently been appointed Superintendent of Schools in New York City.

Seymour Fliegel a former teacher, principal and Deputy Superintendent of District 4 in New York City, is an educational consultant and an Adjunct Professor of Education at Hunter College.

Patti L. Fry, a graduate student at Rutgers University with a special interest in educational public policy.

Susan H. Fuhrman is Research Professor at the Eagleton Institute of Politics at Rutgers University, and Director of the Center for Policy Research in Education.

Charles L. Glenn has been responsible for equity and urban education programs for the Massachusetts Department of Education since 1970. His latest book is *Myth of the Common School* (1988).

Susan Moore Johnson is Associate Professor of Administration, Planning, and Social Policy at the Harvard Graduate School of Education. An experienced teacher and administrator, she studies the policies and practices of schools.

Valerie E. Lee is Assistant Professor of Education at the University of Michigan. She teaches courses in quantitative research methods and the sociology of education.

Henry M. Levin is Professor of Education and Affiliated Professor of Economics at Stanford University. He is also Director of the Center for Educational Research at Stanford (CERAS).

Dan A. Lewis is Associate Director of the Center for Urban Affairs and Policy Research at Northwestern University and Chairman of the Graduate Program in Human Development and Social Policy in the School of Education and Social Policy at Northwestern University.

Karen S. Louis is Associate Professor of Educational Policy Administration at the University of Minnesota. Her major areas of specialization are organizational behavior, knowledge utilization, sociology of education, and research methods and evaluation research.

Betty Malen is Assistant Professor in the Department of Educational Administration of the University of Utah. Her central interest is education policy and politics.

Cora B. Marrett is Professor of Sociology and Afro-American Studies at the University of Wisconsin-Madison. She is also a member of the Advisory Committee for the Washington Office of the College Board.

Richard M. Merelman is Professor of Political Science at the University of Wisconsin-Madison and is the author of several books and articles, many of them on education.

Mary H. Metz is Professor of Educational Policy Studies at the University of Wisconsin-Madison. Her latest book, *Different By Design: The Context and Character of Three Magnet Schools* (1986), is based on an ethnographic study of three magnet schools.

Donald R. Moore is Executive Director of Designs for Change, a children's research and advocacy group based in Chicago that he founded in 1977.

Richard J. Murnane is Professor at the Graduate School of Education, Harvard University. He has written extensively about the determinants of effective schools, the effects of family choice on American schooling, and the meaning of public school-private school achievement comparisons.

Fred M. Newmann is Director of the National Center on Effective Secondary Schools and Professor of Curriculum and Instruction at the University of Wisconsin-Madison.

Rodney T. Ogawa is Associate Professor in the Department of Educational Administration at the University of Utah. His main interests are the application of organizational theory and the study of administrative leadership in educational settings.

Gary A. Orfield is Professor of Education and Political Science at the University of Chicago. He has written extensively on school desegregation.

Paul Peterson is Professor of Government and Director of the Center for American Political Studies at Harvard University.

Andrew C. Porter is Professor of Educational Psychology and Director of the Wisconsin Center for Education Research at the University of Wisconsin-Madison.

Stewart C. Purkey is Assistant Professor of Education at Lawrence University, a private liberal arts institution in Appleton, Wisconsin. He has published in the areas of school effectiveness, education reform, and educational policy.

Julia L. Smith is a doctoral student in the School of Education at the University of Michigan. Her primary interest is in school equity issues, particularly in mathematics education.

David B. Tyack is Professor of Education and History at Standford University. In his research, writing, and teaching, he has explored the social and intellectual history of American education.

Janet A. Weiss is Associate Professor of Organizational Behavior and Public Policy at the School of Business Administration and the Institute of Public Policy Studies, University of Michigan. Her published work bridges many policy areas, including education, social services for children, statistical policy, civil rights, environmental protection, and mental health.

Charles V. Willie is Professor of Education and Urban Studies at the Graduate School of Education, Harvard University. His research interests are education, race relations, and the urban community.

John F. Witte is Professor of Political Science at the University of Wisconsin–Madison. His recent research has included work on federal and state income tax policy and urban education.

Contents: Volume 2 The Practice of Choice, Decentralization and School Restructuring

Index